The Cruft of Fiction

Frontiers of Narrative

SERIES EDITOR
Jesse E. Matz, *Kenyon College*

The Cruft of Fiction

Mega-Novels and the Science of Paying Attention

DAVID LETZLER

University of Nebraska Press | Lincoln and London

∞

Library of Congress Cataloging-in-Publication Data

Names: Letzler, David, author.
Title: The cruft of fiction: mega-novels and the science of paying attention / David Letzler.
Description: Lincoln: University of Nebraska Press, 2017. | Series: Frontiers of narrative | Includes bibliographical references and index.
Identifiers: LCCN 2016044209
ISBN 9780803299627 (cloth: alk. paper)
ISBN 9781496201645 (epub)
ISBN 9781496201652 (mobi)
ISBN 9781496201669 (pdf)
Subjects: LCSH: Fiction—Psychological aspects. | Reading, Psychology of.
Classification: LCC PN3352.P7 L48 2017 | DDC 808.3—dc23
LC record available at https://lccn.loc.gov/2016044209

Set in Minion Pro by John Klopping.

Contents

Acknowledgments

Many thanks to the following individuals—

To Jesse Matz, Gerhard Joseph, Nico Israel, Frank L. Cioffi, and Mario DiGangi for advising me on this project,

To the staffs of *Studies in the Novel* and *Contemporary Literature*, who published excerpts of this material in their pages and have permitted me to reprint them here.

To Jay Barksdale, Carolyn Broomhead, Melanie Locay, and the New York Public Library for granting me access to the Wertheim Study while I researched,

To James Phelan, Peter Rabinowitz, Marc Dolan, Edmund L. Epstein, Reagan Lothes, Nikolina Nedeljkov, Josh Schneiderman, Judd Staley, and Alaya Swann for reading and providing feedback on earlier drafts,

To Russell Backman, Ben Barber, Martin Brick, George Derk, Abram Foley, Laura Hensch, Stephen Hock, Teffany Hunley, David B. Olson, Gavin Pate, and Kyle Smith for copresenting with me on various conference panels where I introduced much of this material,

To H. Porter Abbott, Stephen Burn, William K. Wootters, and Jason Tougaw for graciously responding to my emails with important suggestions and references,

To Robert Bell, Rachel Blau DuPlessis, Stephen Fix, and David Greetham, in whose classes many of the ideas expressed in this book took root,

To Gloria Fisk and Carrie Hintz for their mentorship over the past several years,

To Jim Shepard and Chip Delany for shaping my prose style,

To everyone I've cited, for being just right enough to prevent me from making some silly mistakes and just wrong enough to allow this book to come into being,

And to Katie, for everything else.

The Cruft of Fiction

Introduction

Information and Attention in the Mega-Novel

The Agony and Ecstasy of Big Books

Why do we respond so strangely to big books?

I mean a certain type of big book: the extremely literate, erudite tomes around which one must plan one's life for a month; the books one hesitates to approach without the assistance of a university course, a reading circle, or at least a reader's guide; the books whose spines stare down from bookshelves, holding dominion over entire rooms; the books that inspire fanatical devotion and revulsion in equal parts, even though both seem exaggerated well beyond even the books' own elephantine materiality. I mean the books Frederick R. Karl calls "mega-novels," most notably including ambitious work by postwar American writers like William Gaddis, John Barth, Thomas Pynchon, Don DeLillo, and David Foster Wallace, but also, if we take a more catholic view, earlier behemoths like Gertrude Stein's *The Making of Americans* and James Joyce's *Finnegans Wake*, as well as contemporary global novels ranging from Haruki Murakami's *The Wind-Up Bird Chronicle* to Roberto Bolaño's *2666*.[1]

I ask this question because it seems that mega-novels' most distinctive quality, outpacing even their inimitable heft and learnedness, is the way they prompt otherwise sensible readers into hyperbolic responses. In some readers mega-novels inspire love and reverence, exemplified by Tom LeClair's declaration that "our big books are our big books," because they "gather, represent, and reform the time's excesses into fictions that exceed the time's literary conventions and thereby master the time, the methods of fiction, and the reader."[2] For other readers, though, the words most often used to describe mega-novels (and their devotees) include "disgust," "illegitimate," and "frauds"—though such readers will also admit to feeling "deeply ashamed" at their own inability to appreciate these books.[3] It is not uncommon, in fact, for these contradictory responses to be produced in the same readers: Jonathan Franzen, for instance, credited the inspiration for his bestseller *The Corrections* to his devotional reading of Gaddis's *The Recognitions* but subsequently railed that most mega-novels, including Gaddis's, merely "punis[h] the reader," with their excess and difficulty just a "smoke screen for an author who has nothing interesting, wise, or entertaining to say."[4] We might understand, then, why Mark O'Connell's widely read essay about mega-novels claims that the experience of reading them resembles Stockholm Syndrome and that the discourse surrounding them "has at least as much to do with our own sense of achievement in having read the thing as it does with a sense of the author's achievement in having written it."[5] Similarly Raymond Federman seems on point in observing that, whereas once upon a time one needed to have read the latest ambitious novel to appear cultured, a reader now need merely declare on which page of a mega-novel he decided to give up.[6]

What causes this array of responses? Their length goes only so far in explaining it. Most long novels do not provoke the kind of reactions described above—consider V. S. Naipaul's *A House for Mr. Biswas* or Tom Wolfe's *The Bonfire of the Vanities*, to say nothing of *Harry Potter* or *Twilight*. The books' difficulty and its relationship to pleasure seem important, too, but explaining exactly what we mean by these terms is not easy, especially since many mega-novel admirers deny that mega-novels are either particularly difficult or unpleasurable.[7] Our inability to clearly lay out exactly why mega-novels provoke these reactions, I suspect, is why existing conversations around them get so wound up in circular logic and polemic regarding the conflicts between realistic and experimental fiction, the competition of commercial and artistic interests, the place of entertainment in the reading process and contemporary capitalism, the indisputability of taste, and so on.

Something else is going on. Consider, for instance, this excerpt from Gaddis's dialogue-loaded *J R*, about a sixth-grader who wheels and deals his way into a Wall Street empire from a cafeteria phone booth:

> —Tell them he's been wait give it to me can't tell what he's been, hello . . . ? Not here right now no he's been . . . Davidoff yes Davi . . . Cohen oh calling on Nepenthe yes ran it up to sixteen today think

> the Boss is sitting tight on about nineteen percent of the issue just wants control so he can . . . wait no wants to work the nursing homes into this Health Package made to order outlets for Nobili got Hopper here now with his cemetery Brisboy bringing in his funer . . . what? General who? One thing we need right now anoth . . . Oh why didn't you say so without the h yes why didn't you say so, thought you were on your way up brought in one of our own legal boys waiting here now to go over your figures had Piscator run down your Dun and Bradstreet told the Boss you looked a little overextended mentioned controlling interest in another company sounds dead on its . . .[8]

How, exactly, can we characterize this whirling array of verbal static and interchangeable financial jargon, which begins one of the book's typical page-long stretches of one-sided telephone dialogue? I will offer a counterintuitive thesis, one that I believe identifies the characteristic feature of all mega-novels: this passage stands out because it contains a lot of text that is, basically, pointless.

The Significance of Insignificance: The Cruft of Fiction

There will be immediate objections. What do I mean by "pointless"? According to what standards? Why need literature have a "point" at all? To begin answering these questions, let's examine two foundational essays in narrative theory by Roland Barthes. In 1966 Barthes's "Introduction to the Structural Analysis of Narrative" argued that literary text could never be without purpose, writing, "Art does not acknowledge the existence of noise (in the informational sense of the word). It is a pure system [. . .]. Though a particular notation may seem expendable, it retains a discursive function: it precipitates, delays, or quickens the pace of discourse, sums up, anticipates, and sometimes even confuses the reader."[9] Even in its blandest moments, in other words, literary text cannot help but have *some* purpose. However, several years later, Barthes substantially revised this position in his famous essay about "reality effects," those "concrete details" in realist fiction (e.g., the wall barometer in Flaubert's "A Simple Heart") that seem to have no purpose at all.[10] Asking, "if there exist insignificant stretches, what is, so to speak, the ultimate significance of this insignificance?," Barthes eventually concluded that such *effets de réel* negotiated the aporia in bourgeois realism's conflicting drives toward narrative meaning and realistic mimesis, suggesting "it is the category of the 'real,' and not its various contents, which is being signified."[11]

Yet such text exists in abundance beyond the realm of the well-made realist narrative, too. Decades earlier Henry James had perceived stretches of such writing not within his own quintessentially realist novels, but in more fanciful, longer novels:

> A picture without composition slights its most precious chance for beauty, and is, moreover, not composed at all unless the painter knows *how* that principle of health and safety, working as an absolutely premeditated art, has prevailed. There may in its absence be life, incontestably, as "The Newcomes" has life, as "Les Trois Mousquetaires," as Tolstoi's "Peace and War," have it; but what do such large loose baggy monsters, with their queer elements of the accidental and the arbitrary, artistically *mean*? We have heard it maintained, we will remember, that such things are "superior to art"; but we understand least of all what *that* may mean, and we look in vain for the artist, the divine explanatory genius, who will come to our aid and tell us. There is life and life, and as waste is only life sacrificed and thereby prevented from "counting," I delight in a deep-breathing economy and an organic form.[12]

Tolstoy's philosophical fantasies, Dumas's pseudoromances, Thackeray's metafiction: these cannot be construed as attempting to convey unmediated reality in the manner Barthes describes. Their volume and variety might be interpreted as mimicking the richness of life's connectedness, but as James points out elsewhere, "Really, universally, relations stop nowhere, and the exquisite problem of the artist is eternally but to draw, by a geometry of his own, the circle within which they shall happily *appear* to do so."[13] In other words one can always, arbitrarily, add more interconnections to a novel, and at a certain point, that additional material generates not a greater sense of life, but gratuitousness.

James would surely ask similar questions of contemporary mega-novels, all looser and baggier in construction than any Tolstoy or Dumas envisioned. As Karl writes, the mega-novel "*is* long, but lacks any sense of completion; while it has no boundaries for an ending, of course it does end; it seems to defy clear organization—it seems decentered, unbalanced—yet has an intense order; it is located outside traditional forms of narrative, but still employs some conventional modes."[14] This unwieldy balance is why, as Mark Greif puts it, mega-novels "feel stuffed, overfull, or total; they feel longer than their straightforward story would require, and bigger than other books of similar length or complexity of plot."[15] But to say that a mega-novel is "overfull" implies not vitality, but decadence. Certainly that is the argument James Wood makes when suggesting that while "all the many thousands of pages of the big, ambitious, contemporary books" do not "lack for powers of invention [. . .] there is too much of it," which "almost succeeds in hiding the fact that they are without life."[16] Even Franco Moretti's generally positive analysis of mega-novel prehistory in *Modern Epic* acknowledges that large swaths of them "do not really work all that well."[17] It would be one thing were this charge of excessiveness purely pejorative, but, oddly, it is assented to by mega-novel supporters. LeClair's book in praise of mega-novels (which he calls "systems novels") is, after all, named *The Art of Excess*. Ironically the mega-novel's gratuitous text appears essential to its nature.

To my knowledge no one has identified and explored this specific case of the mega-novel's excessive text. That is what I propose, in this book, to do. To undertake such a study, we should start by naming the phenomenon. I will suggest "cruft," a half-slang / half-technical term from programming circles that has expanded into general Internet culture. Defined by *The New Hacker's Dictionary* as "Excess; superfluous junk; used esp. of redundant or superseded code," cruft is generally characterized as code that is "[p]oorly built, possibly over-complex."[18] Cruft is not technically wrong, but it is unnecessary, inelegant, or too complicated for its own good. The term has widened to cover several digital phenomena, especially within wikiculture, where it is often applied to encyclopedic text that editors find trivial, overwritten, redundant, or unreadable.[19] Although the term is almost always intended negatively, it is also associated with a certain obsessive attraction, most obviously in the case of "fancruft," those excessively detailed wiki entries about extremely minor elements of some niche subculture.[20]

What does cruft look like in a mega-novel? Let's glance back at the passage from *J R*. Chapter 1 will examine this book in more depth, but

Hagia Sophia, Ravenna's interior of the Mausoleum of Galla Placidia, Rome's S. Stefano Rotondo or S. Maria Maggiore or S. Clemente, or Milan's S. Lorenzo, or even the plan of Old St Peter's, nor the slightest trace of classical foundations whether Greek, Hellenistic, or Roman, as might be exemplified by the Temple of Jupiter, Diocletian's palace at Spalato, the gateway to the market at Miletus, Algeria's Timgad with its Arch of Trajan, apartment housing in Ostia, Trajan's Market in Rome, also in Rome, the Baths of Diocletian, the Basilica of Maxentius, Baths of Caracalla, the Temple of Venus, near the Golden House of Nero, Hadrian's Mausoleum, the Mausoleum of Caecilia Metella on the Via Appia, the Canopus of Hadrian's villa, the interior of the Pantheon, Hadrian's villa at Tivoli, or the Piazza d'Oro with peristyle court and pavilions, or the Flavian Palace, the Villa of the Mysteries in Pompeii, plan of the Villa Jovis at Capri, Arch of Tiberius at Orange, France, Trajan's column in Rome, the Imperial Forum, Temple of Mars Ultor, Forum Augustum, Forum of Nerva, the Forum Romanum with the arch of Septimius Severus, the Arch of Titus and the Temple of Castor and Pollux, or in Spain the aqueduct at Segovia, or back in Rome the theatre of Marcellus, the Colosseum, the sanctuary of Fortuna Primigenia, Praeneste with its axonometric reconstruction, the Temple of Vesta at Tivoli, the Forum Boarium in Rome, the Maison Carrée at Nîmes, or the House of the Vettii in Pompeii, the walls of Herculaneum, the terrace of Naxian Lions on Delos, the Tower of the Winds in Athens, the Stoa of Attalus in the agora of Athens, the plan for the city of Pergamum or city center of Miletus or the Bouleuterion in Miletus, or the Temple of Apollo at Didyma, Temple of Athena Polias at Priene, Mausoleum at Halicarnassus, the theatre at Epidaurus, the Choragic Monument of Lysicrates in Athens as well as the Temple of Olympian Zeus, or the tholos at Delphi, or the Temple of Apollo at Bassae, or the Erechtheion on the Acropolis, the Porpylaea on the Acropolis, the Parthenon with its Panathenaic frieze, Athen's acropolis, the temple of Aphaia at Aegina, the Temple of Olympian Zeus at Acragas, the Temple of Hera or Poseidon or Neptune at Paestum, the Temple of Apollo at Corinth, the shrine of Anubis at the Temple of Hatshepsut, Deir el Bahari, or the Lion Gate at Mycenae, or the palace at Mycenae, the palace of Tiryns, the Palace of Minos, Knossos, Crete—which seems like a good place to end though it cannot end there, especially when there is still the Great Zimbabwe Enclosure, the Giza pyramids of Mykerinos, Cheops and Chefren, to say nothing of Ireland's New Grange passage grave, France's Essé gallery grave, Malta's Ggantija temple complex, Scotland's Skara Brae's settlement, the Lascaux cave, the Laussel pre-historic rock-cut Venus, or the notion of the Terra Armata hut which is also a good place to end though of course it cannot end there either—[147]

bricks, whether split paver or red bullnose, or wall studs, firestopping, or braces, nor evidence of floor joists, end joists, or ledgers, bridgings, girders, double plate, gable studs, ceiling joists, rafters, king posts, struts, side posts, ridge beams, collar ties, gussets, furring strips, or bed molding (at least the stairs offer some detail: risers, treads, two large newel posts, one at the top and one at the bottom, capped and connected with a single, curved banister supported by countless balusters) though among other things no wallpaper, veneer plaster, Baldwin locks, any sign of glass,

Perhaps[165]

here

is as good a place as any to consider some of the ghosts haunting *The Navidson Record.* And since more than a handful of people have pointed out similarities between Navidson's film and various commercial productions, it seems worthwhile to at least briefly examine what distinguishes documentaries from Hollywood releases.[166]

In his essay "Critical Condition" published in *Simple Themes* (University of Washington Press, 1995) Brendan Beinhorn declared that Navidson house, when the explorers were within it, was in a state of severe shock. "However *without* them, it is completely dead. Humanity serves as its life blood. Humanity's end would mark the house's end." A statement which provoked sociologist Sondra Staff to claim "Critical Condition" was "just another sheaf of Beinhorn bullshit." (A lecture delivered at Our Lady of the Lake University of San Antonio on June 26, 1996.)

[165]Mr. Truant refused to reveal whether the following bizarre textual layout is Zampanò's or his own. — Ed.

[166]In his essay "It Makes No Difference" *Film Quarterly* v.8, July, 1995, p. 68, Daniel Rosenblum wrote: "In response to the suggestion that the names of the ghosts haunting Navidson's house are none other than *The Shining*, *Vertigo*, *2001*, *Brazil*, *Lawrence of Arabia*, *Poltergeist*, *Amityville Horror*, *Night of the Living Dead*,

134

Fig. 1. Excerpt from *House of Leaves: The Remastered, Full-Color Edition* by Mark Z. Danielewski, copyright © 2000 by Mark Z. Danielewski. Used by permission of Pantheon Books, an imprint of the Knopf Doubleday

[168]Aside from cinematic, literary, architectural, or even philosophical ghosts, history also offers a few of its own. Consider two famous expeditions where those involved confronted the unknown under circumstances of deprivation and fear only to soon find themselves caught in a squall of terrible violence.

I.

On September 20th, 1519 Ferdinand Magellan embarked from Sanlúcar de Barrameda to sail around the globe. The voyage would once and for all prove the world was round and revolutionize people's thoughts on navigation and trade, but the journey would also be dangerous, replete with enough horror and hardship that in the end it would cost Magellan his life.

In March of 1520 when Magellan's five vessels reached Patagonia and sailed into the Bay of St. Julian, things were far from harmonious. Fierce winter weather, a shortage of stores, not to mention the anxiety brought on by the uncertainty of the future, had caused tensions among the sailors to increase, until on or around April Fools Day, which also happened to be Easter Day, Captain Gaspar Quesada of the *Concepcion* and his servant Luiz de Molino planned and executed a mutiny, resulting in the death of at least one officer and the wounding of many more.[169] Unfortunately for Quesada, he never stopped to consider that a man who could marshal an expedition to circle the globe could probably marshal men to retaliate with great ferocity. This gross underestimation of his opponent cost Quesada his life.

Like a general, Magellan rallied those men still loyal to him to retake the commandeered ships. The combination of his will and his tactical acumen made his success, especially in retrospect, seem inevitable. The mutineer Mendoza of the *Victoria* was stabbed in the throat. The *Santo Antonia* was stormed, and by morning the *Concepcion* had surrendered. Forty-eight hours after the mutiny had begun, Magellan was again in control. He sentenced all the mutineers to death and then in an act of calculated good-will suspended the sentence, choosing instead to concentrate maritime law and his own ire on the three directly responsible for the uprising: Mendoza's corpse was drawn and quartered, Juan de Cartagena was marooned on a barren shore and Quesada was executed.

Quesada, however, was not hung, shot or even forced to walk the plank. Magellan had a better idea. Molino, Quesada's trusty servant, was granted clemency if he agreed to execute his master. Molino accepted the duty and

whether clear, reflective, insulated, heat-resistant, switchable, tinted, bad-guy, antique; or even tin-plated steel, factory-painted steel, brass; or even a single nail or screw, whether sheet-metal, particleboard, drywall, concrete, drive, aluminum, silicon bronze, solid brass, mechanically galvanized, yellow-zinc plated, stainless steel, epoxy coated, black finish, Durocoat; to say nothing of the sheer absence of anything that might suggest a roof, whether pitched, gable, hip, lean-to, flat, sawtooth, monitor, ogee, bell, dome, helm, sloped, hip and valley, conical, pavilion, rotunda,

Cabinet of Wonder, Jim Kalin's *One Worm*, Sartre's *Huis Clos, or Les Mouches*, Jules Verne's *Journey to the Center of the Earth*, Lem's *Solaris*, Ayn Rand's *The Fountainhead*, "The Turn of the Screw" by Henry James, Nathaniel Hawthorne's "Young Goodman Brown" or *The House of Seven Gables*, or *The Lion, the Witch and the Wardrobe* by C. S. Lewis? To say nothing of *Brodsky & Utkin*, Frida Kahlo's "Blue House" in Coyoacán, Diego Rivera's "Nocturnal Landscape: Paisaje Nocturno" (1947), Rachel Whiteread's *House* or Charles Ray's *Ink Box*, Bill Viola's *Room for St. John of the Cross* or more words by Robert Venturi, Aldo van Eyck, James Joyce, Paolo Portoghesi, Herman Melville, Otto Friedrich Bollnow (*Mensch und Raum*, 1963), and Maurice Merleau-Ponty (*The Phenomenology of Perception*, 1962, in which he declares "depth is the most 'existential' of all dimensions")? To all of it, I have only one carefully devised response: Ptooey!"168

[147]*Of course, it is impossible to consider any sort of construction, whether of homes, factories, shops, stores, department stores, market halls, conservatories, exhibition buildings, railway stations, warehouses, and office buildings, exchanges, and banks, hotels, prisons, hospitals, museums, libraries, theatres, churches, bridges, airports, town halls, law courts, ministries, and public offices, Houses of parliament, monuments, parks, even towns, and cities, public works etc., etc., without paying heed to such names as Thomas Hall Beeby, Ricardo Bofill, John Simpson, Steven Holl, Léon Krier, Richard Neutra, Andres Duany, and Elizabeth Plater-Zyberk, Ramon Fortet, Daniel Libeskind, Quinlan Terry, Allan Greenberg, Jane B. Drew, Robin Seifert, Frank Gehry, Jean Willerval, Arat Isozaki, Kisho Kurokawa, Gisue and Mojgan Hariri, John Outram, Zaha Hadid, Peter Eisenmann, Richard Meier, John Hejduk, Aldo Rossi, Herman Hertzberger, Louis E. Fry Sr., Louis E. Fry Jr., Louis E. Fry III, Santiago Calatrava, I. M. Pei, Recardo Scofidio, Harry G. Robinson III, Terry Farrell, Bernard Tschumi, Charles F. McAfee, Eva Vecsei, the Coop Himmelblau, Cheryl L. McAfee, Charles Eames, Simon Rodia, Ray Eames, Ricardo Bofill, Donald L. Stull, M. David Lee, Michael Graves, Elizabeth Diller, Charles Moore, Bruno Taut, Robert Traynham Coles, Mies van*

for now it should suffice to say that while several of this passage's references have some larger relevance to the book (e.g., those involving General Haight and Nobili), most of its financial schemes are basically meaningless and interchangeable with a dozen others in the larger work. The noisy speech represented in this passage may seem "realistic," but there is a reason such starts and stutters are usually omitted in literary narrative: they take up space without communicating anything meaningful. We could probably elide this entire passage into a sentence of summary (e.g., "Davidoff rattled off the details of J R's plans before turning back to his secretary") with little narrative loss. If we wish an even more obvious example of cruft, consider the passage reproduced in figure 1 from Danielewski's *House of Leaves*, recounting an expedition through the physics-defying labyrinth that has emerged within its protagonist's house. Down the left margin we see a list, containing dozens of entries, of every architectural style that does *not* describe the labyrinth, while down the right is a similar, inverted list of every architect who would *not* have built it, and slightly off center on each page is an equally long catalog of furniture that is *not* to be found. It is hard to imagine any sane reader processing more than the first few entries of any of these lists. In fact it turns out that the labyrinth signified by these elaborate marginalia is nothing but an empty sequence of rooms, rendering the text almost literally insignificant.

What exactly are we supposed to do with such text? Literary studies has traveled a long way from the Jamesian organicism formalized by Percy Lubbock's claim in *The Craft of Fiction* that a novel must be built around "[a] subject, one and whole and irreducible," with anything deviating from that subject being "wasteful," but even allowing that we need not be so rigid, how would we explain why good novels would include text that seems merely to gum up and lengthen their already very long narratives?[21]

There are several possible arguments. One, exemplified by Steven Moore, suggests that this text is not actually excessive, but merely appears that way to insufficiently knowledgeable readers:

> I remain convinced that negative reactions to unconventional modern fiction can be blamed partly on ignorance of the novel's long, colorful, and decidedly unconventional history. No one familiar with

> Lyly's *Euphues* is likely to accuse a contemporary writer of being showy and pretentious; Lyly makes them all look as modest as nuns. Gaddis' alleged difficulty is a walk in the park compared with Subandhu's *Vasavadatta*. Those who balk at the length of some of today's literary mega-novels (*Gravity's Rainbow*, *Infinite Jest*, *2666*) might be chastened to learn that the best novels in China, Arabia, and France during the late medieval period are *thousands* of pages long.[22]

Another view, though, which might be aligned broadly with poststructuralism, takes precisely the opposite approach, as exhibited in John Johnston's claim that mega-novels' "value, therefore, would seem to lie in the fullness with which they bring to awareness and propagate the complexity of this cultural moment. They do this, as I try to show, by transforming the novel into various 'writing-down systems' that articulate and render visible a postmodern discourse network defined first by the formations of information theory and cybernetics, and only secondarily by textuality and simulacra. At the same time, inasmuch as they remain novels, they model and reflect new forms of postmodern subjectivity."[23] Johnston claims that mega-novels, rather than unearthing the narrative structures of the past, create an entirely new—and at least partially emancipatory—form of writing for the contemporary moment, in which the entire conventional concept of purpose is "short-circuited or exceeded such that the novel no longer makes sense."[24]

These two positions will define the dialectic by which the rest of this study proceeds. Individually both have serious weaknesses. Though as Moore suggests, many mega-novels draw on narrative forms predating the modern novel, in doing so they almost always distort or omit narrative elements crucial to those genres' goals. Conversely Johnston's argument fails to distinguish mega-novel excess from garden-variety incoherence: after all, text that "no longer make[s] sense" typically characterizes bad writing rather than good. We need a better way to articulate how cruft can provide value to a narrative, one that acknowledges cruft's insignificance without falling into the fallacious argument that the reproduction of chaos constitutes a meaningful response to a chaotic world. And I believe we can do so via a subject frequently invoked regarding mega-novels: attention.

Attention, Overload, and Boredom

That mega-novels pose substantial challenges to readers' attention has long been acknowledged. LeClair, for example, argues that "the dominant strategy in systems novels is, at least initially, overload. [. . .] In a systems novel, overload—or what I call excess—can stop the reading, cause scanning, or produce a reorientation to the novel's information."[25] As Joseph Tabbi points out, this feeling of being overwhelmed by excessive text is closely related to the classical sublime, wherein the mind's immediate perceptual capacities collapse and yield to alternate cognitive modes, "keep[ing] readers from understanding too quickly" what they perceive.[26] However, both critics subsequently suggest that these attentional challenges should be overcome quickly by a competent mega-novel reader. Mega-novel critics often, in fact, exhibit disdain for those who have any prolonged attention difficulties, as might be best exemplified through Moore's retort to a critic complaining of the demands *J R* made on its readers' attentions: "as though a better novelist would make allowances for daydreaming."[27]

This sentiment has its roots in an attitude, going back at least to Victorian England, that conceives the principal goal of literary education to be the development of sustained attention. Nicholas Dames has written about the "physiological" theory of novel reading popular among the Victorians, for whom (as he puts it) "the Victorian novel was a training ground for industrialized consciousness."[28] John Ruskin's lecture "Of Kings' Treasuries" codified the now-standard attitude that the classroom should inculcate attentionally intensive reading habits in students, and I. A. Richards's epochal emphasis on "close reading" derives from his fear that mass media were eroding students' abilities to maintain close attention by conditioning "stock responses."[29] Such concerns extend today to the worries expressed by humanists like N. Katherine Hayles that digital media have caused "[d]eep attention, the cognitive style traditionally associated with the humanities" to be displaced in younger students by "[h]yper attention [. . .] characterized by switching focus rapidly among different tasks, preferring multiple information streams, seeking a high level of stimulation, and having a low tolerance for boredom."[30] The corollary to this notion, that contemporary readers' attentions might become degraded to the point where they will not be able to read long books at all, is often invoked by mega-novel critics, who frequently cite

J R's Davidoff discussing "longer works of fiction now dismissed as classics and remaining largely unread due to the effort involved in reading and turning any more than two hundred pages."[31]

But what is attention? William James, in his *Principles of Psychology*, famously wrote, "Every one knows what attention is," and as is typically the case with such a statement, there is little actual agreement on the term's definition. Among cognitive theorists it is disputed whether attention is the basis of consciousness or a phenomenon created by consciousness.[32] Within neuroscience Donald Broadbent's so-called bottleneck model postulated the nervous system as a "single communication channel" in which attention works as a "selective operation" necessitated by limited channel capacity, while Alan Allport more recently argued that attention is decentralized throughout the brain, meaning "There is no *one* uniform computational function [. . . but] a rich diversity of neurophysical control mechanisms of many different kinds."[33] It is also still unclear how precisely "voluntary" and "involuntary" attention interact, though they seem to produce different readings in event-related potential experiments.[34] Attention's relationship to other difficult-to-define phenomenal constructs like awareness and working memory is similarly tricky.

What can be agreed on is that attention is necessarily selective. As George A. Miller classically demonstrated, our working memory is limited to about six or seven represented objects at a given time.[35] Whether limitations on attention are caused by a central processing region, as Broadbent would have it, or by local neuronal competition in highly stimulated areas, as Allport would, they clearly exist.[36] The major question in examining attention, consequently, becomes how the brain selects that which is to be attended. This is generally approached in terms of the tension between "bottom-up" forces (i.e., our natural neurosensory attraction to certain kinds of environmental stimuli) and "top-down" ones (i.e., the way our longer-term plans and decision making direct our relevance judgments).[37] Michael Posner's influential theory posits three attentional stages: alerting (in which bottom-down forces make us aware of new aspects in our environment), orienting (in which we integrate them into our conscious state), and executive (in which we resolve conflicts and make decisions about how to attend stimuli).[38] The executive level is particularly important for our purposes. According to Posner's model, the prefrontal cortex—the region associated, since the infamous case of Phineas Gage, with the highest-order elements of cognitive decision making and human personality—is unsurprisingly a key player, but so are several regions on the interface of the frontal lobe, such as the anterior cingulate cortex.[39] Other neuroscientists have identified the frontal eye-fields, also near that interface, as a key part of the executive system.[40] The remaining parts of the brain dealing with attention tend also to be located on interfaces. Intriguingly one of them, in the temporoparietal junction, happens to abut Wernicke's area, the key region of the brain for reading.[41] High-level reading skills, then, might well be linked to high-level capacity at attentional selection.

Though current cognitive research has confirmed that attentional control is vital to the development of reading abilities and that attention lapses can cause significant reading difficulties, the idea that all serious reading must be done in a cognitive mode of unbreakable attention, then, is misguided.[42] Given the length of any nontrivial piece of writing, reading always requires strategically allocating attention to text that seems more important at the expense of text seeming less important. As Gaddy, van den Broek, and Sung's cognitive study of reading cycles puts it, any analysis of the reading process must acknowledge its selectiveness, because "[w]hen attempting to comprehend text, readers must devise ways to condense the wealth of information that is presented to them. Limitations on working memory or attentional resources make this task particularly important, for without the ability to selectively attend to particular textual information, readers would be faced with the burden of trying to retain every piece of information that is presented in text throughout the reading process. Successful comprehension of text therefore involves a reader's ability to appropriately allocate his or her attention to the most important aspects of a text, and at the right times, during reading."[43] Experimental research shows that our default method for attending text is probably shallow processing.[44] This is especially so for long novels: as Barthes observed, "it is the very rhythm of what is read and what is not read that creates the pleasure of the great narratives: has anyone ever read Proust, Balzac, *War and Peace*, word for word? (Proust's good fortune: from one reading to the next, we never skip the same passages.)"[45]

To counteract this basic fact about the reading process, writers have long used certain devices to cue readers' attention toward important passages. We might find a taxonomy of such techniques—repetition, section breaks, segmentation, beginnings and endings, the use of titles, and so on—in any book on the craft of writing. Discussing such "Rules of Notice," Peter Rabinowitz points out that the very standards of our discipline require us to analyze text cued by these methods more thoroughly than text that is not.[46] After all, "[i]f one assumes that all features of a text are to receive close attention from an interpreter, then a text (even a lyric poem, certainly a novel) becomes an infinite and impenetrable web of relationships."[47] Higher-level thought, in other words, requires our attention to focus on certain things very closely and to ignore most everything else. What we need to develop, then, is not the ability to pay closer attention to everything, but a sophisticated *attentional modulation*. Indeed, as Natalie Phillips concludes from her recent fMRI study of what happens in the brain when we read at a relatively deep and shallow attention, "the best scenario for activating the most parts of our brain would be to sustain cognitive flexibility and read with both kinds of attention."[48]

This process becomes increasingly important, and more difficult, as we progress further and further into the information age, because an inability to focus on one important thing amid a large number of unimportant ones will lead to chronic boredom. Though classically characterized in cognitive psychology as occurring when we are "(a) prevented from doing what we want to do or (b) forced to do what we do not want to do"—in other words when we experience stimuli deprivation—recent research points out that boredom can also be "a condition of apparent freedom in which the individual is nonetheless *unable to maintain attention* on, or interest in, any object."[49] Boredom, after all, unlike subjective deficits such as apathy and anhedonia, is at least partly dependent on environment: someone who is bored has the capacity and desire to pay attention but cannot figure out what to pay it to.[50] As Otto Fenichel noted in his classic analysis of the subject, a bored person "is searching for an object, not in order to act upon it with his instinctual impulses, but rather to be helped by it to find an instinctual aim which he lacks."[51]

What does this tell us about reading the mega-novel? As a glance at the passages from *J R* and *House of Leaves* will suggest, mega-novels often flagrantly violate any Rules of Notice, barely distinguishing between relatively important and unimportant text. Moreover, unlike the terse, oblique social dioramas of late-realist / early-modernist fiction, mega-novels multiply the unimportant text beyond its usual proportion and render it even more purposeless. The resulting overload is almost certain to create attentional confusion, leading to lapses in focus, difficulties in consolidating short-term into long-term memory, and boredom. Against the critical tendency to assert that all mega-novel text is equally and fabulously interesting, then, we need to examine how, as Samuli Hägg puts it, mega-novel "overwriting" induces boredom and how "part of the 'interest' [. . .] is witnessing everything becoming a blur and attempting to figure out ways of enjoying the event—and conjuring out its interpretive significance."[52]

I do want to be careful about the extent to which I generalize this point. Boredom is, after all, as dependent on its subject as its object, and something that one reader might find boring another might not find boring at all. As Patrick Colm Hogan notes in his discussion of the relationship between cortical stimulation and aesthetic appreciation, we experience art as "boring" when we find it "too easy" or repetitive, since it does not provide us with any "novel stimuli"—but we also become bored when it is "too hard," because we experience it "as random, thus as noise," making it "an experience, not of novelty, but of sameness."[53] Furthermore Hogan adds that "judgments of both excessive difficulty and excessive simplicity vary from person to person, and for different ages."[54] Lionel Trilling's witticism about the modernist canon is instructive on this point: "these books at first rejected me; I bored them. But as I grew older and they knew me better, they came to have more sympathy with me and to understand my hidden meanings."[55] Usually when someone (e.g., a student) tells us that a great book is boring, we should indeed attribute the problem to the reader rather than to the text. That said, one cannot claim that cruft is merely the subjective illusion of readers with insufficient attention for great writing, because it often is both "too easy" and "too hard" *at the same time*. For instance, in the passage above from *House of Leaves*, a reader with a low threshold for textual stimulation will surely be overloaded by its wild typography into boredom almost immediately, but a reader looking for higher degrees of stimulation will soon realize that all this text is so mechanical as to say virtually nothing and will become equally bored with it. Here we can say the text is objectively pointless and objectively boring. We can categorize this passage as cruft, because—as if to invert *Annie Hall*'s joke about resort food—it doesn't mean enough, and there's far too much of it.

Why should cruft be valuable in a mega-novel, though? There are, after all, clear negative cognitive and emotional impacts to attention lapses, since an inability to sustain attention tends to generate prolonged negative affect and can literally cause the regions of the brain involved in higher-order thought to disconnect from each other.[56] While there is an argument that boredom inspires creativity and provides relief from overstimulation, this perspective frames boredom merely as a temporary condition, useful either as a repellent to or an inoculation from worse mental states, not as something one ought to actively seek out.[57] Certainly boredom is almost never construed as a positive element of the reading experience by literary critics: as Sianne Ngai notes, it "tend[s] to be written off as unsophisticated: from this point of view, only a philistine would be bored by the later Beckett."[58] Even Patricia Meyer Spacks, author of a literary history of boredom, insists that writing itself (and thus implicitly reading, I would add) "resists boredom": about fiction writers for whom boredom is itself an "aspect of discourse," she writes, "I know readers who declared they are bored by [them . . .]. Such readers do not include me."[59] Ngai attempts, like Tabbi, to recover this experience as a variation on the sublime (the "stuplime," in her terms), believing the ineluctable materiality of excessive text "perform[s] a doubling-over of language that actively interferes with the temporal organization dictated by conventional syntax" and drives us toward "new strategies of affective engagement and to extend the circumstances under which engagement becomes possible."[60] However, again, she does not describe how this is different from reading merely *stupid* text: most text that constantly reminds us of its own materiality does so because it is badly written. To address what is going on in the mega-novel, then, we must look elsewhere.

Reading in the Information Age

As I noted earlier, it has become common to speak of our age as characterized by information overload. Ironically, despite several decades of humanist hand-wringing about the coming dominance of the image over the word, most of this information is textual.[61] Of course, as James Gleick writes in his history of information, anxiety about information overload has been expressed practically since the invention of the printing press, but the current moment poses particularly acute societal problems regarding how to collectively manage information.[62] As the narrator of Wallace's final novel, *The Pale King*—a fanciful take on the lives of IRS tax examiners in mid-1980s Peoria, Illinois—puts it, "Fact: The birth agonies of the New IRS led to one of the great and terrible PR discoveries in modern democracy, which is that if sensitive issues of governance can be made sufficiently dull and arcane, there will be no need for officials to hide or dissemble, because no one not directly involved will pay enough attention to cause trouble. No one will pay attention because no one will be interested, because, more or less *a priori*, of these issues' monumental dullness."[63] There is simply so much information to process in the digital age—and so many alternative, entertaining sources of it to distract our attention when we become bored—that any sufficiently boring material will be ignored, even if there might be important information buried within it. This is probably why the result of increased information tends not to be greater engagement with other perspectives but more reliance on preconceived ideas, since the mind must resort to confirmation bias to filter the information with which it is faced.[64] As Gleick puts it, "The old ways of organizing knowledge no longer work. Who will search; who will filter? [. . .] Which is worse, too many mouths or too many ears?"[65]

It would be tempting to argue that depicting this contemporary situation requires mega-novelists to write in a commensurately excessive and boring style.[66] However, this view would lead us toward the mimetic fallacy, which, in fact, Terry Eagleton's *How to Read a Poem* exemplifies as "the belief that, say, a poem about boredom should itself be boring."[67] After all, if information overload is a serious societal problem, a mimetic treatment of it threatens to exacerbate that problem rather than alleviate it, which Lev Grossman suggests in his objection that the mega-novel "treats the world as an infinite network, but we already have an infinite network, the Internet, and our nose is rubbed in it on an hourly basis. We don't need more of that—more hysteria."[68] It is quite possible, moreover, to be brief about complex subjects, just as it is to be lengthy about simpler ones: as Thomas Pavel points out, the scope of a single Borges story can exceed that of *À la recherche du temps perdu*.[69]

I will argue, instead, that cruft's value comes in how it helps us develop our abilities to modulate attention when processing information.

Though we still do not understand many things about what causes differences in our capacity to control attention, there is evidence suggesting that it can be trained and improved with practice.[70] Furthermore, since much attentional control is done unconsciously, attentional control can probably be improved through complex cognitive tasks that involve substantial automatic components, like critical reading.[71] This might be well exemplified by *The Pale King*'s tax examiners, who are placed in as pure a battle of attention against information overload as can be imagined. They must cull endless pages of data, bureau jargon, and coded cross-references, seeking the hidden needles of tax evasion within haystacks of paperwork. However, the task's dullness makes any breakthroughs from dulling trivia to hidden discovery ever more valuable, because they are so unlikely to be found. This causes one of the examiners to conclude that the only essential skill in the modern world is "the ability, whether innate or conditioned, to find the other side of the rote, the picayune, the meaningless, the repetitive, the pointlessly complex. To be in a word, unborable. [. . .] It is the key to modern life. If you are immune to boredom, there is literally nothing you cannot accomplish."[72]

However, though some critics suggest that the novel urges us to learn to "transcend" boredom, such an ability is not so positive as it seems.[73] Consider the one character in the book who has achieved this state, Frederick Blumquist:

> Supervisors at the IRS's regional complex in Lake James township are trying to determine why no one noticed that one of their employees had been sitting dead at his desk for four days before anyone asked if he was feeling all right.
>
> Frederick Blumquist, 53, who had been employed as a tax return examiner with the agency for over thirty years, suffered a heart attack in the open-plan office he shared with twenty-five coworkers at the agency's Regional Examination Center on Self-Storage Parkway. He quietly passed away last Tuesday at his desk, but nobody noticed until late Saturday evening when an office cleaner asked how the examiner could still be working in an office with all the lights off.
>
> Mr. Blumquist's supervisor, Scott Thomas, said, "Frederick was always the first guy in each morning and the last to leave at night.

> He was very focused and diligent, so no one found it unusual that he was in the same position all that time and didn't say anything. He was always absorbed in his work, and kept to himself."[74]

This passage's significance is not that the tedium of Blumquist's work gave him a coronary—it's that his state of unbreakable attention is indistinguishable from death. To have perfect focus on something, after all, means that one is totally shut out from the rest of life. One must not be unborable, then—one must instead have a high resistance to boredom *as well as* the ability to become bored by totally useless data, allowing one to break attention and move on in search of more important information. Though I will critique Kenneth Goldsmith's argument that linear reading has become obsolete in the information age in chapter 1, there is something to his claim that our task as contemporary readers involves "parsing" (i.e., skimming, browsing, filtering) text as much as analyzing it word by word.[75] Our attentional modulation must function, essentially, like Maxwell's Demon, sorting relevant from useless information as it enters the consciousness. To develop this ability, though, we must seek out text whose important material is sometimes contained within large amounts of pointlessness.

This ability will be most pressured when there is minimal apparent difference between important and unimportant text. That, I argue, is the function of cruft in the mega-novel: it takes up a great deal of space to no apparent purpose, but in doing so, it masks similar-looking text that does have purpose, challenging readers to refine the way they modulate their attention in processing it. That is why these books tend to be suffused with tropes like waste, immensity, and perceptual failure: being so draws attention to the importance of the distinctions we must make in processing their enormous and often wasteful text. I believe, also, that the extremity to which mega-novels push this process is responsible for the characteristic affective responses noted at the introduction's outset. These do not merely result from differences in taste: they arise from more serious disputes over the adequacy of readers' information-processing abilities. Readers' attempts to rapidly modulate through the different cognitive modes required by mega-novels will already cause an initial vacillation in affective states, but this affective complex will be further complicated by readers' more or less frequent self-perceptions of having either failed in adequately attending the text (e.g., having passed over a plot point that becomes important two hundred pages later) or in having achieved a particularly hard-won success. Furthermore, interacting with others' self-reports of the reading experience will complicate that affect even more by either confirming one's self-evaluation of success and failure or by implying that one's method for evaluating cognitive successes and failures is faulty.

Cruft and Genre in Poststructuralism and Cognitive Theory

We still have yet to establish, though, exactly how to determine the "purpose" of fictional text. Recent narratology, after all, has established that there is no foolproof way to determine what is or is not inherently "interesting" about a particular text.[76] I believe we can address the issue of purpose, though, through genre. One need not go so far as E. D. Hirsch's claim that "an interpreter's preliminary generic conception of a text is constitutive of everything that he subsequently understands" to acknowledge the importance genre plays in how we ascribe purpose to narrative.[77] Genre establishes relevant knowledge bases and intertextual schemas for a text, as well as specifying to which elements we should and should not pay attention.[78] Rolf A. Zwaan famously demonstrated that readers who are told that a given narrative is a news article will read it quickly and with more attention to real-world situational implications than language, whereas those told it is a work of fiction will read slowly and with more attention to language than situational implications.[79] In this way genre allows us to combine the objective elements of narrative with the subjective aspects of reader-based models of literary study.

Genre is especially important for discussing mega-novels because they frequently violate readers' standard schemas for narrative, prompting them to grasp for alternate models. That is likely why, as Michael Sinding notes, early criticism on mega-novels often invokes genre, because "such large-scale framing" is vital for initial comprehension, subsequently "clearing the way for finer-grained interpretation."[80] For instance one tradition of criticism, most often associated with Edward Mendelson, has dubbed mega-novels "encyclopedic narratives," explaining their non-novelistic proliferation of technical data (e.g., mathematical equations, documentary materials) as an effort to organize and understand their cultures.[81] Another identifies them with the classical Menippean satire, understanding their outlandish and often grotesque representations as large-scale critiques of society.[82] Similarly mega-novels' fabulating tendencies have been described by many critics via the picaresque and frame-tale genres, just as their enigmatic figural structures have been explained using the epic and allegory. Genres like these will provide the organizational structure for this book.[83] However, though these schematic purposes may initially appear to be fulfilled by mega-novels' excessive text, each chapter will demonstrate how they often omit or distort key elements necessary to those genres' goals, on the basis of which I categorize their excessive text as cruft. It is not enough to say that such moments might be justified simply because they "violate expectations": again, unless accompanied by some alternate positive effect, which would cause us to recategorize the text and lead us back toward genre, the failure to fulfill expectations is much more characteristic of bad writing than good.

This emphasis on genre may suggest how my argument contrasts with the standard poststructuralist approach to mega-novels. Poststructuralism has tended to be deeply suspicious of genre, as best exemplified in Jacques Derrida's warning that, "[a]s soon as the word 'genre' is sounded [. . .] a limit is drawn. And when a limit is established, norms and interdictions are not far behind."[84] When poststructuralists find it necessary to describe an overall structure, they generally prefer Deleuze and Guattari's pliable model of the rhizome to any conception of genre.[85] Yet this attitude—which amounts to a principled rejection of categorization—is simply not cognitively tenable. As Sinding notes, "I am unashamed to say I like categories: I use them every day, all the time; they enable me to make sense of things; they keep me sane [. . .]. I do not know what I would do without them."[86] Without categories we are like Borges's eidetic Ireneo Funes, who lives in "the teeming world of [. . .] nothing but particulars," consequently rendering him "not very good at thinking," because his endless memory prevents him from developing the ability to group and hierarchize sensory data.[87] Though the Derridean view makes a valid criticism of exegetes' overconfidence in neat analysis—exemplified by Moore's insistence that if we "keep reading [. . .] even the most difficult novel will eventually make some sense"—it leaves us unable to distinguish wildly heterogeneous structures from sheer structurelessness.[88]

A more cognitively coherent approach might be seen in Northrop Frye's method of categorizing prose fiction not through separate classes but via generic strands (e.g., the novel, the romance, the anatomy) that are capable of combination and blending.[89] Such an approach will equally demonstrate, though, that many parts of mega-novels *don't* fulfill any apparent generic purpose. We need to be ready to recognize these when they occur, because otherwise a procedure designed to organize and make navigable our world will instead render it even more unreadable by forcing pieces that don't fit. We need, in other words, to be able to separate generic innovation from cruft.

Of course one might justly ask in what sense cruft really *is* pointless if, as I argue, it contributes positively to the text. We might explain this paradox by inverting Kant's famous formula that objects of aesthetic interest have "purposiveness [. . .] without any purpose": cruft, conversely, is text that has purposive*less*ness *with* purpose.[90] Cruft, in other words, provides little benefit to deep processing, but that very resistance to attention might have a valuable attentional impact within a given context. A good comparison might be the purer forms of the mystery device known as the red herring. For instance, in one early chapter of Arthur Conan Doyle's *The Hound of the Baskervilles*, Sherlock Holmes identifies three leads he believes might direct him to the killer of Charles Baskerville: a threatening note to Henry Baskerville whose text is cut from a recent issue of the *Times*, a black-bearded spy who resembles the Baskervilles' caretaker Barrymore, and a cabdriver whom that black-bearded spy had used to tail Holmes. However, all three end up being dead ends: the original newspaper is never found, a telegram confirms that Barrymore has an alibi, and the cabdriver tells Holmes that the black-bearded spy had identified himself only as "Mr. Sherlock Holmes."[91] Not only do none of these clues lead to the killer, but they provide minimal information about anything else—especially the threatening message, whose true author is revealed only as an afterthought after the mystery is solved. Why, then, does Doyle delay Holmes's thrilling trip to the moors with these three broken threads in London?

I believe the answer is that they provide misdirection, because these three red herrings obscure the one clue in the chapter that does help solve the mystery, namely Henry's new brown boot, which is stolen from his hotel only to be returned and switched with his old black one. Were this incident treated by itself, readers might be able to deduce its significance—that is, that the old boot bears Henry's scent—but when placed amid the other pointless clues, the puzzling affair of the missing boots seems as if it might be every bit as opaque to plotting as the three broken threads. As with many mysteries, then, the goal of *The Hound of the Baskervilles*' readers is not to try to make all the clues fit together equally, but to distinguish the useful clues from the red herrings and solve the mystery using only the former.[92] Though mega-novels do not have "solutions" in quite the same way that mysteries do, their readers similarly must sift through a large quantity of opaque text to understand the narrative.

To sum up let me lay out the key principles regarding cruft. As cruft is a multifaceted concept, it will be used in several senses, but all will cluster around the same basic ideas:

1. Cruft is text that does not reward—and in its purer forms flatly refuses—focused attention.
2. Cruft refuses deep attention because it is mostly—and in its purer forms, entirely—pointless or incoherent.
3. Consequently cruft generally takes up much more space than a conventionally well-crafted approach to its content would, causing the novel containing it to expand and appear excessive.
4. Since it is impossible to empirically prove negative propositions, there is no rigorous way to show that a given sequence of text has *no* conceivable purpose. To demonstrate that a given passage is cruft, then, one can only prove that it does not serve the generic function(s) that other critics have claimed for it—with "generic" referring both to the vernacular notion of literary genre as well as, more broadly, any general literary or narrative function, such as plot, humor, poetry, and so on.
5. One reasonably reliable test for cruft is to ask whether the given passage might be arbitrarily replaced with something else—or, in purer cases, condensed or skipped over entirely—with minimal significant effect.
6. Though the term "mega-novel" may and has been used in many ways, I define it here as a novel of well-above-average and (according to popular sentiment) excessive length, caused at least in part by its abundance of cruft.[93] A very long novel without cruft (e.g., *Vanity Fair*) is not, according to this definition, a mega-novel.

7. There is a special category of books similar to mega-novels that I will call limit mega-novels. These are very long novels that address the problem of overabundance and may even give the general impression of excessiveness. However, they do not contain very much text that, on its own merits, is quite pointless enough to be termed cruft. Examples range from *Middlemarch* to *The Man without Qualities* to *Foucault's Pendulum*. These will be mentioned in passing, but they are not meant to be grouped with the other key texts.
8. When used well, mega-novel cruft often occurs in proximity to text that *appears* to also be cruft, but is actually quite important.
9. The most important cognitive benefit of well-used cruft is in how it helps its readers train their abilities to modulate attention.
10. Since there is no clear top-down algorithm to determine whether a passage is or is not cruft, the cognitive training I describe depends, instead, on developing readers' flexibility in responding attentionally a variety of textual environments.

Some Caveats on Cruft

Before commencing my argument in earnest, I wish to clarify a few points about the scope of this book's aims and its limitations. Most important is to acknowledge that this book deals with only one kind of attentional interaction, as it applies to one specific kind of text. There is a much wider variety of possible critical applications of attention, boredom, and distraction to the reading process. However, their possible implications spread much more widely than this study's focus, so I will have to largely omit them.

The relationship of difficulty to my argument is also complicated. Difficulty, of course, implies some struggles with attention similar to those caused by cruft, as it creates a situation in which one cannot figure out exactly how to orient one's focus. Certainly learning to modulate one's attention so as to better manage these difficulties is one of the important processes addressed by this book. However, as the typology presented in George Steiner's famous essay "On Difficulty" might remind us, not all difficult text is cruft. Some difficulties in mega-novels are heavily reader dependent. A reader unfamiliar with, say, the probabilistic equations in *Gravity's Rainbow* may find them opaque in a way that a more numerate reader would not. This difficulty is not quite the same as the more universal challenges posed by the more purposeless encyclopedic information that chapter 2 discusses. Such difficulties probably exacerbate the problems posed by cruft to attention for many readers, but they are not themselves cruft. Similarly some ambiguous or experimental text may be difficult to parse initially yet yield an eventual poetic value that, say, the extremely entropic text analyzed in chapter 1 does not have.

We should also distinguish the challenges posed by cruft from the related but distinct difficulty in maintaining focus on mega-novels' many hundreds of pages of text over the indeterminate amount of time it takes to read them, as well as the congruent challenge in reading the mega-novel's often inordinately intricate sentences and paragraphs. As all human brains regularly experience lapses in attention and working memory, the cumulative strain on concentration and memory caused by reading a novel requiring dozens of hours of attention is enormous, especially if the narrator does not periodically remind us (à la Fielding or Dickens) about text from earlier in the novel that may have been understandably forgotten in the interim.[94] I am not quite sure that Moore is joking when he suggests that *J R* (which lacks any explicit section divisions) should be read in one sitting, but for many obvious practical and cognitive reasons, that approach is not feasible.[95] There is much that might be explored regarding these issues—for instance, why eighteenth-century readers rarely reported boredom in reading Samuel Richardson's million-word *Clarissa* even though many contemporary ones (who have no trouble with the similarly long *Harry Potter* saga) find it unbearably tedious—but, again, they are highly dependent on individuals' capacities and thus unfeasible to analyze here.

All this is to acknowledge that I will discuss only certain types of excessively long books, and certain types of boredom. Other types of books evoking other types of boredom may well be worth pursuing elsewhere, but they are different enough from what I am discussing that to treat them here would be more confusing than helpful. Moreover, while I suspect that it is possible to apply some of my arguments to a number of other long, quirky books frequently cited as mega-novel predecessors (e.g., *Gargantua and Pantagruel*, *Don Quixote*, and especially *Tristram Shandy*), I think that those books are sufficiently different that I will only mention them in passing. Lastly, contemporary books written in the tradition of the nonnovel genres I invoke that do not make use of cruft—for example, contemporary picaresque "road novels" or recent epic poems—will not be addressed either.

This brings us to periodization. The book primarily addresses a number of major works of American postmodern fiction, and I have already suggested that the way they treat the relationship of information to attention may tell us something about the contemporary moment. On the other hand, it also deals with books outside this period. In particular the early chapters reach back into the early twentieth and late nineteenth centuries, while the last two address contemporary works from around the globe. There are several ways to explain this incongruity. One is that I am primarily interested in the mega-novel less as a representation of the contemporary era than as a cognitive tool for contemporary readers, and therefore I am less intent on creating a cogent historical narrative than in selecting several texts that provide the most illuminating examples of how cruft functions. Another is that there actually is a loose historical narrative compatible with my organization. Because the first two chapters, addressing the dictionary and encyclopedia, deal with purely textual overload, which has been an obtrusive phenomenon for serious scholars over some centuries, it makes sense that we might use relatively older novels to examine that subject. On the other hand, the later chapters' emphasis on the overload of textual representations of persons, actions, and concepts are more characteristic of the contemporary, globalized world, and so it is useful to compare books written in the United States or Europe during this time with those produced in Asia or South America.

But perhaps most important, I approach periodization the way I do because, as Thomas Pavel has written, "ontological systems [. . .] rarely command an unqualified loyalty": in other words people inhabiting the same temporal, material world often do not inhabit precisely the same imagined one, while those living in different material realities can have overlapping imagined ones.[96] Especially since we no longer inhabit a planet in which, say, a composer like Beethoven would have little access to the music written by his countryman Bach less than a century earlier, but one where books from many eras and traditions are available to many people worldwide, lines of literary influence and affinity are rarely chronologically or geographically constrained. As Wai Chee Dimock has suggested, viewing periodization this way usefully "mudd[ies] temporal, spatial, and generic lines."[97] Consider, for example, how we would periodize Gertrude Stein's *The Making of Americans*, a book set in the rural nineteenth-century American Midwest, but written in Paris during the first decade of the twentieth century, published only two decades after that, and at its peak in critical prominence only when adopted by the twenty-first-century American avant-garde. To which of these periods does it "really" belong? To all.

Along these lines readers might notice that there are relatively few mentions of "modernism" or "postmodernism" in this book. I spent some time attempting to make the mega-novel function as a subcategory of one or the other, but while there are meaningful distinctions to be made between the two, I think it is best, along Frye's lines, to consider them as generic strands that may or may not be combined with the mega-novel rather than overarching categories that subsume it. Adopting this perspective will also prevent my argument from suggesting that the interaction between cruft and attention is the only interesting thing happening in mega-novels. For example Salman Rushdie's film adaptation of *Midnight's Children* jettisons nearly all the material I address in chapter 6 but is otherwise faithful to the original and retains many of its other valuable elements.

As was LeClair in composing his own guide to mega-novels, I have been asked several times about how gender relates to this genre, as all but three of the examples I will discuss here were written by men.[98] There are certain implications this question raises: Are there great female mega-novelists who have been suppressed? Are, perhaps, mega-novels inherently sexist? I wish I had something rigorous and interesting to say on this subject, but outside of some observations in chapter 3, I don't. One of the most dangerous temptations in literary criticism is for critics to make generalizations about purported cultural attitudes held by millions of people based on their interpretations of a handful of novels. I can think of no plausible systematic method for drawing a conclusion about the former group from the latter, so I won't, except to say that the literary world would probably benefit from a few more excellent mega-novels by female authors.

Some readers have also objected to my method. Do I really think mega-novel authors, actual or implied, intended to write pointless text? If not, why shouldn't we just interpret the textual meaning, as intended, rather than overlaying my cognitive framework? To the first question, my answer is "sometimes": certainly essays by Wallace, Dorothy Richardson, and Georges Perec show some cognizance of their writing's tendencies toward pointlessness and the implications for readers' attentions. But this does not apply to every mega-novelist, some of whom really seemed to think every word they wrote was brilliant. The reason I am less interested in what these authors thought about their own work is related to my theoretical perspective on literature. I do not have space here to rehash debates in reader-based versus author-based methods of literary analysis, nor to make a thorough argument for cognitive-based literary analysis, nor offer a complete articulation of my theoretical positions on literary study. I will say only that, as writers of fiction, novelists do not accept accountability for their work's reference to the actual world, so any defense of the value of fiction must consequently emphasize what happens (or can happen) to readers during the reading process, which may or may not be what the author intended. (The most interesting things that happen when I read are, frequently, not what the author intended.) Our most important object of study, then, is the critical and cognitive faculties on which a novel acts.

Finally I want to make a few more remarks on the nature of cruft. Since the term is pejorative in its original context, some early readers have been taken aback by my argument regarding its pervasiveness in acclaimed mega-novels. Certainly to call a book pointless or excessive is usually not a compliment: if one notes, for instance, that Ayn Rand's *Atlas Shrugged* is overlong and has lots of drab text, it is generally understood that one is making a criticism. Furthermore some mega-novels are genuinely overwritten, without the excessive text doing anything terribly interesting (e.g., Gilbert Sorrentino's *Mulligan Stew*). I am not interested, here, in analyzing text that is merely bad. The instances of cruft that I want to discuss are those in which the text's very purposelessness has some positive value. I acknowledge, though, that the line between the two is exceedingly thin. It is illustrative that even Pynchonist Luc Herman admits he had a hard time deciding whether his boredom with Pynchon's *Against the Day* was a valuable part of the book's aesthetic or simply a sign that it wasn't that well written.[99]

For that matter other readers might still claim that my entire notion of cruft is merely masking personal impressionism with pseudonarratological terminology. Who am I, after all, to judge a passage to be cruft, when some other reader might easily ascribe it some great purpose or weighty interpretation? If this charge asks whether cruft is a matter of personal judgment, I freely admit it is. However, I do not think that this is a flaw in the concept. It has become oddly taboo to admit within the academy, but all literary reading demands judgment. If a novel is to be valued, it must be because its text presses us toward new thought, and precisely because that thought is new, it cannot be easily schematized, but only be articulated through specific local judgments of its value. I may be wrong about some of the individual judgments in this book, but I can be proved wrong only by arguments against those judgments rather than by a categorical complaint that I have employed judgment at all.

A few more minor notes. First, since I have chosen to use several in-depth examples from mega-novels rather than create a historical survey, this book is not meant to be exclusive: that I have not addressed certain authors or certain mega-novels is not meant to suggest that they do not contain cruft or achieve the effects I describe. My most notable omission is probably Joyce's *Ulysses*, about which I will take Frye's escape route and simply assert that it combines all the phenomena I discuss.[100] Furthermore that I analyze a book in one chapter does not mean that it does not also engage the issues discussed by the other chapters: a different organization, for instance, might easily have swapped *Infinite Jest* into chapter 4 and *The Recognitions* into chapter 2. There may also be other possible varieties of cruft that I have not addressed.

Here is what I hope to accomplish in this book. As I have suggested, there has long been an attitude expressed by mega-novel admirers that, while one might initially face some minor attention lapses during the reading process, these difficulties should soon be cast aside. Boredom, this view assumes, is a condition suffered only by weak minds and need not be given any serious thought by the committed mega-novel reader. I argue instead that it is not only acceptable but crucial to be occasionally bored by mega-novels. Understanding their text requires not only learning to read their crucial passages well, but learning to avoid getting hung up on the cruft. To paraphrase the old skin cream ads, the feeling of boredom is how you know the process is working. Consequently the way we establish the reading "rhythm" about which Barthes wrote—that is, the balance between what we pay close attention to and what we attend more shallowly—becomes of paramount importance to describing their peculiar value. That many readers establish this rhythm only upon rereading a mega-novel is likely not only because they have, upon the second attempt, committed to reading more closely, but because their first reading has cued them toward specific ways to better modulate attention to the book's needs. For instance readers on their second tour through *Ulysses* often learn to note the man in the mackintosh mentioned in passing at Dignam's funeral, who recurs later on—but they can do this only because they know they needn't devote much attention to the tailor George Mesias, also mentioned in passing, who does not appear again.[101]

As a result this book will give the spotlight to passages that most critics have learned to ignore. In fact, given that such habits are so ingrained in most academic critics, I will often engage with contemporary reviews and other initial responses to mega-novels, because whatever these analyses lack in the sophistication that accretes over time in scholarship, they make up for it in their honest consideration of the possibility that stretches of a book might not have much of a point. Their consideration for the strategic decisions by which our brains choose how to evaluate and process text is, in many respects, what I wish this book to recover. I do not dispute in the least that many passages of mega-novels are brilliant and worthy of substantial close attention: I will examine a few of these, also. At the same time, though, many passages are not, and any reading of these books must acknowledge that. I cannot articulate as a general principle how the mind does or should determine which is which, or when to modulate back and forth between modes best suited to these different kinds of text, but given the mind's extreme plasticity and adaptability, I am confident it can train itself (consciously or not) to better perform that task as we read, and that as it does so, it can learn to apply these methods to the information overload we face in our everyday lives. Instead of feigning thralldom, then, to every nonstandard usage, gratuitous datum, fleeting impression, broad parody, wandering subplot, and enigmatic symbol that a mega-novel contains, we ought to investigate how our minds manage an overwhelming amount of text with ambiguous function, how they work through material that is often pointless and boring, and how they adjudicate the intelligent use of stupid text.

1 The Dictionary

The Unreadable Dictionary

Unique among the generic categories structuring this book, the term *dictionary novel* has not, to my knowledge, been generally used to describe mega-novels.[1] This, I believe, is an oversight, because at least one strain of mega-novel shares with the dictionary its most distinctive characteristic: the desire to expand the boundaries of language. Dictionaries, after all, especially those in English, have long been used to increase their users' linguistic aptitudes. The original English dictionaries were bilingual translating references, and the first ones written entirely in English were designed mainly to enlarge readers' vocabularies with "hard" words, a function that can still be seen in the dictionary-browsing habits of poets, crossword aficionados, and spelling-bee contestants.[2] The modern English dictionary's attempt to formalize this impulse by seeking out and compiling all the language's words into one place is, as Simon Winchester notes, an endeavor peculiarly appropriate to the capaciousness of English.[3] *Merriam-Webster*, for instance, makes an annual ritual of revealing what new coinages from throughout the Anglophone world it has incorporated into its latest edition. Consequently the resulting volumes sometimes appear overwhelming, filled as they are with alien combinations of letters and obscure definitions. In this sense they are comparable to mega-novels like James Joyce's *Finnegans Wake*, with its dozens of polyglot neologisms per page, ranging from "aardappel" to "zyngarrettes."[4]

However, both the dictionary and the mega-novel's all-embracing expansiveness swiftly encounters a potential problem: the principle of linguistic accretion tends quickly to generate useless text. As Winchester notes, for instance, among early English dictionaries, the competition to produce ever-higher word counts caused lexicographers to stuff them full of ephemeral slang and jargon with little practical value.[5] Similarly mega-novels' impulse to experiment can quickly lead to incomprehensibility: a reader of the *Wake*, for instance, who wishes to explicate "Fleppety! Flippety! Fleapow!" will find no elucidation among even the book's most thorough commentaries.[6]

This is the basic conundrum on which Dr. Samuel Johnson stumbled when composing his *Dictionary of the English Language*: the competing tendencies in language toward an expansive descriptivism and a compressing prescriptivism. As Johnson realized, "Those who have much leisure to think, will always be enlarging the stock of ideas, and every increase of knowledge, whether real or fancied, will produce new words, or combinations or words," but at the same time, "[c]hange [. . .] is not made without inconvenience, even from worse to better. There is in constancy and stability a general and lasting advantage, which will always overbalance the slow improvements of gradual correction."[7] While linguistic innovation always offers new possibilities, if it is not restrained by some stable conventions, it quickly becomes bloated gibberish. Writing on this problem several centuries later, David Foster Wallace observed, "The most obvious problem with [descriptivist grammar] is that not everything can go in The Dictionary. Why not? Well, because you can't observe every last bit of every last native speaker's 'language behavior,' and even if you could, the resultant dictionary would weigh four million pounds and have to be updated hourly."[8] Even in an era when many dictionaries have moved online and the logistical problem of size no longer looms, the potential for entries of lasting value to get crowded out by local ephemera and idiotic junk (as appears to have occurred to the *Urban Dictionary*) remains quite real.

This chapter, then, will examine the frequent charge that mega-novels are overwritten with pointless experimentation to the point of being unreadable. Is it possible to process such writing, and if so is there any benefit to it? For instance consider William Gaddis's *J R*, which even George Steiner, who praised modern poetry's "ontologically difficult" text in "On Difficulty," excoriated for its unreadable incomprehensibility, writing, "what, then, of the truly unreadable book? This surely must be in every man's reach. Yet again the answer is no. To produce an unreadable text, to sustain this foxy purpose over seven hundred and twenty-six pages, demands rare powers. Mr. Gaddis has them."[9] Steiner goes on to characterize the novel's rarely broken blocks of mimetic dialogue, filled with the phonetic/syntactic errors of everyday speech and numerous other irregularities, as a clutter of "interminable screeds of direct address, [. . .] patches of narrative and an auxiliary stream of P.A. interjections," so chaotically unstructured that the book could be "dipped in nearly at random and skimmed."[10]

On the other hand, though, too much pattern can cause an equally unreadable excess. Several decades prior to Steiner, Edmund Wilson, while valorizing the modernist canon in *Axel's Castle*, charged Gertrude Stein's self-proclaimed masterpiece *The Making of Americans* with unbearable repetitiveness. Of the way in which its grammatical structures seem to rigidly and endlessly replicate the same phrases, Wilson wrote that Stein's "patient and brooding repetitiousness [. . .] is here carried to such immoderate lengths as finally to suggest some technique of mesmerism. With sentences so regularly rhythmical, so needlessly prolix, so many times repeated and ending so often in present participles, the reader is all too soon in a state."[11] Much as Steiner critiques chaos, Wilson critiques repetitiveness, suggesting that when a book so severely limits its novelty, it will evacuate readers' abilities to process text. As a result, Wilson writes, "I have not read this book all through, and I do not know whether it is possible to do so."[12]

How do we establish the point at which experimental writing collapses into nonsense? And if a mega-novel's text really does become unreadable, is there any positive function that the resulting cruft might serve? To answer these questions will require a more rigorous examination of what constitutes "unreadable" text. We will need to briefly examine how we process text and determine what depth of attention to devote to it.

Text Processing, Literary Convention, and Information Theory

As far as at least one strain of literary theory is concerned, to argue that innovative text might be unreadable is not necessarily a criticism. One of the central principles of the last hundred years of poetics has been the idea that literary text is supposed to impede, rather than facilitate, our ordinary reading processes. A century ago Viktor Shklovsky claimed that when perceptions becomes habitualized, "life fades into nothingness," and that consequently the purpose of literature is to "mak[e] perception long and 'laborious.'"[13] Some decades later Roland Barthes distinguished between "readerly" text, which emphasizes simple and unimpeded decoding, and "writerly" text, which enables its readers to pursue the "infinite play of the world," a division he adapted later to one between texts that generate "pleasure" and those that generate "bliss."[14] As Reuven Tsur has since pointed out, such arguments are essentially about cognition, since they prioritize text that commits "organized violence against cognitive processes."[15] Under this reasoning a text that appears unreadable may be all the more valuable for being so. Postmodernist Raymond Federman has made this argument explicitly, quipping that reviewers level the charge of "unreadability" at long novels only because they don't get around to reading them and otherwise inverting the usual readable-unreadable distinction:

> If **readability** is the pleasure of recognition (easy pleasurable referential recognition), then **unreadability** must be the agony of unrecognition.
>
> **Unreadability**: what disorients us in a text (especially in an experimental novel) in relation to ourselves (and I do not mean here the bulk, the thickness, the degree of difficulty, the self-reflexiveness, the tediousness of the text—these are weak excuses for not reading a book). **Unreadability**: what prevents us from recognizing that something is happening, but also prevents us from looking up and away from the text to relocate ourselves in the world. **Unreadability**: what locks us into the language of the text.[16]

Federman might agree with Steiner and Wilson's respective descriptions of *J R* and *The Making of Americans* as unreadable but would suggest that that is their most valuable attribute.

However, his thesis needs to be qualified. As Anthony J. Sanford and Catherine Emmott's experimental work shows, creative deviations in language often do disrupt our text-processing apparatus and consequently increase neural activity, causing a spike in negative electrical readings in event-related potential tests after four hundred milliseconds.[17] However, precisely the same neural effect occurs when we read unintentionally bad writing, because we must waste mental effort to figure out what the inarticulate writer is trying to say.[18] In both cases this momentary increase can subsequently lead to deeper processing, but it can also reduce processing when the mind becomes too confused.[19] After all how would one process the sequence ooeqpcqpovfnxffipsbxpezlqgkxmqtptwubplhfixluipuctqjjchegrqqrwhjjbqtplvsorevdbrhrnspuwjqilscvdfqlptsk? Even the most ardent Joycean, I suspect, would pass quickly over this randomly generated string of one hundred characters (as you probably did just now), because outside of a few brief sequences, there is no pattern to be recognized by Anglophone readers. Contra Federman, such text is *more* likely to prompt "looking up and away from the text," because its random letters so obviously refuse significance.

This is not a trivial point. Randomness, after all, is text's normal state, as is demonstrated by Jorge Luis Borges's story "The Library of Babel," which figures the textual world as an enormous library of identical hexagonal rooms whose bookshelves contain "all possible combinations of the twenty-two orthographic symbols (a number which, though unimaginably vast, is not infinite)—that is, all that is able to be expressed, in every language."[20] However, this abundance does not lead the librarians toward a greater richness of understanding, because "[f]or every rational line or forthright statement there are leagues of senseless cacophony, verbal nonsense, and incoherency," like the string produced above.[21] Certainly this situation forces the librarians to be active readers, constantly constructing ciphers to create meaning out of senseless material, but instead of providing them with rich reading experiences, the librarians are plagued by madness owing to the futility of their work.[22] Pure pattern without variation equally frustrates their reading efforts, as the Babel librarians realize upon finding a volume that simply reads "M C V" for 410 pages, which they cannot imagine even "belong[s] to any language, however dialectical or primitive."[23] The Library, that is, ought to remind us how valuable and rare is the conventionally readable text so often excoriated by experimentally minded critics, and how much less impressive linguistic transgression appears when viewed in the context of the Library's vexing books.

If unconventional text only sometimes affects cognition positively, how can we analyze the benefits or drawbacks of linguistic innovation? We might begin by following N. Katherine Hayles's advice to replace the poststructuralist dialectic of presence/absence, which dominates the above perspectives, with information theory's dialectic of pattern/randomness.[24] Formalizing our textual analysis via information theory will allow us to more rigorously evaluate the extent to which a given passage conforms to or deviates from normal textual structure in discussing how readers process it. This will require a few key terms. In information theory the text a sender intends to send is called the *signal*, while anything added to the signal in transmission is called *noise*. A message's *information*, meanwhile, is a measurement of its statistical unpredictability with respect to its receiver's expectations: for instance a string of one hundred digits that strictly alternates 1s and 0s has less information than a string of forty random digits, even though it is longer, because while each digit of the second string provides a new, unpredictable bit of information, the first one is largely predictable.[25] (Throughout this chapter I will use the word "information" only in the technical sense; in other chapters I use it in the vernacular sense of "data.") Alternately one might refer to information as roughly measuring a text's *complexity*. In Andrei Kolmogorov's definition, complexity is a measure of the minimum text naming a string, which will almost always decrease as the text becomes more predictable: in our previous example, all the second string's forty digits are needed to describe it, while for the first we may use the compressed phrase "10 50x."[26] Information's complement is *redundancy*, a measure of its predictability: for instance, after its first few digits, the hundred-digit string above is almost totally redundant, since we can easily predict what will come next. Some redundant text often can, if necessary, be eliminated from the message, allowing compression. Translation between any given message and a concept with which the receiver's dictionary associates it we call *coding*, while any message that does not decode with respect to the dictionary must have one or more *errors*. Errors are frequently caused by noise, and they tend to increase the text's total information by eroding predictable structures. If we can confidently change an errant message to a decodable one, we call this a *correction*, which is made easier by higher redundancy, because redundancy will allow reconstruction of text the error obfuscates elsewhere.

An important aside to these definitions is that, in the formulation of information theory founder Claude Shannon, information is calculated using an equation formally identical to that for physical *entropy* (i.e., the energy unable to do work in a thermodynamic system), and so the magnitude of a text's information is often referred to as its entropy.[27] Independently and contemporaneously, MIT mathematician Norbert Wiener also invoked the equation for entropy to calculate information but defined the two as each other's negative, a distinction that will shortly become important.[28] Either way we need to be careful when discussing entropy, because substantial confusion has been caused by humanists muddling its technical uses and popular overtones over the past six decades, conflating the physical and informational definitions with the Second Law of Thermodynamics, which declares that entropy in a closed system increases over time.[29] While informational and physical entropy are similar—both measure disorder, and since information is sometimes transmitted in a physical channel that adds noise, both tend to increase—their distinctions are significant enough that jumbling them may lead us toward misconceptions.

Additionally we should recognize an important corollary to Shannon's equation: since any ordering principle imposes a pattern on a text, it will consequently make the text more predictable, causing the text's information to decrease. This leads to the counterintuitive results that (a) the text with the most order (i.e., the most predictable text) has the least information, and (b) the text with the least order (i.e., the most random text) has the most information. For literary critics, who tend to associate complexity and information with order, this may be confusing. Even Hayles gets turned around on this point, claiming "in some instances, an infusion of noise into a system can cause it to reorganize at a higher level of complexity."[30] If we are addressing text, though, the definition of complexity we ought to use is Kolmogorov's, in which case Hayles is exactly wrong: while noise typically does make a text more complex, it does so because it *disorganizes*; if it reorganizes the text, it *lowers* complexity. As librarian Jan O'Deigh observes in Richard Powers's 1991 *The Gold-Bug Variations* while researching the work of pioneering geneticist Stuart Ressler:

> [M]utations are almost never beneficial. A message, carefully crafted over time, is altered at random. The text will almost certainly suffer, if it remains intelligible at all. The introduction of noise into a signal is much more likely to garble than improve. Failure is lots more probable than anything else going.
>
> Typing too late at night, I begin to insert letters that distort my words diseasterously [*sic*]. Rereading, I piece some alterations back into partial sense. Only an infinitesimally few typos—the lucky comma that leaves a sentence more comprehensible—will produce clean, let alone enhanced final copy.[31]

Deliberately increasing a text's information, entropy, or complexity, then, is typically destructive.

This property complicates the relationship between information and literary value. Some critics have attempted to equate the two, such as Umberto Eco, whose *The Open Work* argued that literary text could be distinguished from ordinary language by its high information density, since "*certain unorthodox uses* of language can often result in poetry, whereas this seldom, if ever, happens with more conventional, probable uses of the linguistic system," but it had to qualify this point by noting that an artist who opposed conventionality too rigorously put himself "constantly in danger of losing the thread and of becoming a mere photographer of the unrelated and the uniform."[32] It is difficult, in other words, to make categorical judgment about texts' quality from their abstract level of order. However, we may assert three points generally: (a) all worthwhile literary texts must be, at least in part, patterned and decodable; (b) all readable texts are characterized by a balance of textual information and redundancy that, in its absolute value, remains constricted to a conservative band, no matter how "radical" it may claim to be; and (c) there exists no readable text that enacts anything near an absolute principle of order or disorder.

If *J R* and *The Making of Americans* are great novels, then, the former's apparent randomness must be counterbalanced somehow by pattern, and the latter's maddening redundancy offset by some entropy. How they achieve these mixtures, as I will demonstrate, comes via the unusual manner in which their pattern and randomness are mixed. Where standard English more or less efficiently alternates its unpredictable elements with more strictly patterned ones (e.g., consonants with vowels, nouns and verbs with connectives), the patterns and randomness in *J R* and *The Making of Americans* are frequently disentwined, allowing each to proliferate to the point where many passages contain locally unreadable cruft. Often this causes the text to expand, as additional text is required to render at least parts of the excessively random or patterned text readable, causing unusual effects to readers' text processing and attention. In this chapter, then, by examining some characteristic passages, we will examine how nonreadable text is used in the dictionary novel by seeing how *J R*'s purported entropic errors are undercut by regular redundancy and how *The Making of Americans*' repetitions are broken up by underlying variety, before concluding with how error and redundancy work together to allow correction in *Finnegans Wake*.

Error: Is *J R* Readable?

Certainly *J R*'s text frequently appears disordered. The book's main narrative—in which a mathematically gifted but academically unengaged sixth-grader named J R Vansant becomes inspired by a school trip to Wall Street to play the stock market's esoteric system of regulations, tax credits, and loopholes against each other until he has built his class's single share of corporate stock into a financial empire—features frequent communication breakdowns: information is not received as intended, is sent with errors already embedded, and is decoded improperly. Consider this exchange, where two teachers at J R's school, aspiring composer Edward Bast and frustrated writer Jack Gibbs, run into each other after the aforementioned Wall Street trip, during which they had both been pressed into service as chaperones by J R's ailing teacher, Amy Joubert:

> —Yes but, Mrs Joubert is she all right?
>
> —Momentary recovery Bast, got inhaled each momentary recovery thought I had a newspaper.
>
> —It's under your arm yes but was she, what happened . . .
>
> —Got lost in the dark caverns of her throat Bast, bruised by the ripple of unseen muscles ought to be ashamed of myself, told me I should apologize to you how's that.
>
> —Well no but that's not what I . . .
>
> —Told me you're talented sensitive purpose Bast sense of purpose need help and encouragement lock yourself in write nothing music, take defeat from any brazen throat get to be like Bizet only not Bizet where the God damned doors . . . he hunched as though with cold, hands buried in pockets—dum dum dedum . . .
>
> —Over here yes, but . . .
>
> —Don't spit upon the, garden path lead the whole God damned wait, Bast? Something I'm supposed to give you these right here she forgot to give me wait, forgot to give them to you here.[33]

We may observe that, at least *as written*, several passages here are unreadable. Gibbs, drunk as usual, slurs his phrases into an incomprehensible mess ("Don't spit upon the, garden path lead the whole"), produces phrases that do not parse (e.g., "sensitive purpose"), and can't even keep track of all the text on his person, such as the newspaper he can't find and the student train tickets he belatedly remembers to give Bast at the passage's end (which, moreover, he has accidentally mixed with racing stubs). For his part Bast speaks at cross-purposes with his interlocutor, failing to pick up on the latter's encouragement of his musical endeavors and never finding out about the health of Joubert. Adding to the confusion, no narrative voice steps in to clarify either man's garbled speech, explain his thoughts, or identify who is present in the scene. In fact the narrator's only appearance—"he hunched as though with cold, hands buried in pockets"—is so unmarked as to initially appear another nonsensical remark by Gibbs. Given all the chaos in this passage, it's no wonder many readers charge *J R* with wasteful incoherence.

Many critics celebrate this strategy, though. According to John Johnston, it enacts "the destabilizing and entropic effects of capitalism," which create a world "catastrophically disorganized, as if it had fallen under the baleful spell of some disruptive and noisy machine that operates by inefficiency, producing only accidents, spillage, waste, breakdown, and misunderstanding."[34] Gaddis appears to have felt similarly, citing in relation to the book a quote from Wiener about the deleterious impact of entropy on language and civilization: "We are always fighting nature's tendency to degrade the organized, and to destroy the meaningful. The more probable a message, the less information it gives. Clichés, for example, are less illuminating than great poems."[35] Many critics write that, in *J R*, that cultural battle seems to have been lost, with Gaddis serving only as a mute "collector and transmitter" of voices, each "thoroughly transmuted [, . . .] dispossessed" and "decontextualized" into pure "transaction."[36]

There is a problem with this view, however. Despite Wiener's many valuable insights about the relationship between information theory and the structure of society, in moving from his pure math to the literary application, he appears to have conflated two types of opposition that are clearly distinguished in the former but not in the latter: additive inverses and polar opposites. Wiener's equation for entropy and information sets them as additive inverses, related as –1 is to 1, but his comment about clichés treats them as polar opposites, related as 0 is to 1. While it is true that clichés, which are eminently predictable, have less information than great poems—think of the book of *M C V*s from the Library of Babel as a reductio ad absurdum of the cliché's repetitiveness—it would follow that the gibberish books that characterize most of the Library would have *more* information than a great poem. Since gibberish is clearly not more "organized" or "illuminating" than great poetry, Wiener's argument collapses, as do the cultural critiques for which it provides theoretical groundwork.

This problem reveals something of a contradiction within criticism on the book. Though many critics argue that *J R*'s language represents the collapse of human communication, they often also paradoxically characterize it as a highly refined achievement of literary writing. As LeClair points out, the passage's unpredictable twists and turns actually "increase the technical information value of any one word," so those holding that literary text is unpredictable and information-dense should identify this as a sign of aesthetic value.[37] Certainly that appears to be Steven Moore's position in arguing that the book's prose is "lean and economical."[38] Gaddis himself seemed to think that way, too, construing *J R* as an important aesthetic counterweight to conventional novels "requiring [of readers] no effort whatsoever except some degree of literacy."[39] If *J R*'s entropic text is the corrupted refuse of a decadent society, how can it also be the pinnacle of literary prose? How we answer that question has enormous implications for how we process the text: if the former is the case, we should reduce our attention to avoid getting sucked into meaningless chaos, but if the latter, we must focus even harder to better understand the text's intricacies.

We may begin to answer that question by observing that *J R* does not actually increase entropy everywhere, but adds redundancy in subtle ways to balance out its more obviously unpredictable textual elements. Consider the passage below, set at J R's Long Island school, in which Principal Whiteback discusses another school trip with Joubert and maintains a phone conversation:

> —Yes well thank you for ahm, for coming in Mrs Joubert excuse me, hello . . . ? Yes excuse me I have someone on the other phone here, hello Leroy . . . ? But what happened to them that many, even that many picnic forks can't just disap . . . yes but where transshipped where, who auth . . . I know it said six J yes she just left I meant to

> ask her what . . . no well then do they know where the rest of the shipment went that never got here in the first pla . . . No I know it, I know we never found them in the budget that's why they must have something to do with the cafeteria lunch program, if it looks like we're turning down a federal subsidy they might withhold funds like they're threatening on the milk if this Coke machine's installed in the . . . What . . . ? No now wait a minute just tell him to wait a minute Leroy, we . . . no there's nothing in the curriculum that calls for brake linings unless Vogel of course ahm, how many . . . How many? No well even Vogel couldn't use that many bra . . . No I'm not coming down to the freight office no, you . . . no well that can't . . . no now wait a minute, what caliber . . . ? No well that's no, no we don't even have a rifle club unless of course the government is ahm, yes well just tell them to . . . no no I don't want to talk to Agent Teets no just tell him to . . . no I have someone waiting on the other phone here just tell him to, to hold everything there I have somebody at the door, yes . . . ?[40]

There are many obvious errors in this passage, which render it less predictable and more entropic. Some "words" are pure noise, like Whiteback's *ahms*, while others err from standard English, like *transshipped*, probably the result of Whiteback's initial intention to say *transported* and subsequent midword shift to *shipped*. Similarly *auth*, *disap*, and *pla* appear to be the beginnings of English words but do not re-create the words' full structures. Syntactically many clauses don't parse because key elements are left out: verbs are missing ("wait a minute Leroy, we . . . no there's nothing"), articles never find nouns ("if this Coke machine's installed in the . . . What?"), and punctuation is skipped over ("what happened to them that many, even that many picnic forks can't just disap . . .").

Yet many instances of communication breakdown work against that entropic tendency by being highly predictable. After all much of the rest of Whiteback's dialogue comprises repetitions, multiword filler, and clichés. For instance he repeats consecutively or in parallel the phrases *that many*, *how many*, *wait a minute*, and *just tell them to*; he also uses *of course* twice and *that is to [say]* twice, while beginning four clauses with *no well* and two with *yes well*. Some of these phrases might impede Whiteback's *meaning* by drowning out more important text with empty language, but they actually *lower* his dialogue's average entropy.

It's important to observe this technical difference. Since critics usually associate entropy with general decay, they tend to see the book's "heterogeneous discourse made up of incongruent diction, specialized jargon, mixed metaphors, and tortuous syntax" as interchangeable forms of corrupt language.[41] Yet while they all impede meaning in some way, their differences with respect to information are extremely important, because they work to stabilize each other and render text processing possible. For instance, in the absence of speech tags and narrative depiction of consciousness, Whiteback's characteristic clichés provide the closest thing to an identity he possesses. J R's "I mean" and "holy shit," as well as Gibbs's "God damned," function much the same way. In other cases the dialogue's high level of redundancy emphasizes important material not foregrounded otherwise, as with how Gibbs's otherwise incoherent reference to the "garden path" in the passage with which we began this section echoes a comment he'd made in a previous scene about Wagner's fear of the outside world.[42] Elsewhere syntactic context renders errors legible. For example, when Whiteback says *auth* he clearly intends to say *authorized*, because the only other standard past-tense English verbs beginning with those four letters are *authored* and *authenticated*, neither of which decodes in context.

This oscillation explains how, overall, the text avoids unreadable levels of mathematical entropy. However, it does not so easily justify the sometimes deleterious impact on meaning produced by this style of writing. Gaddis's strategy can often cause character strings to verge on meaninglessness, whether because they produce empty mimetic phrases that conventional writing wisely elides ("yes well just tell them to . . .") or are so ungrammatical that it is difficult to construct a coherent message from them ("got inhaled each momentary recovery"). Undoubtedly this excess is what Jonathan Franzen meant when he scoffed at Moore's claims about the book's concision, arguing instead that it "suffers from the madness it attempts to resist."[43] It is not enough to say that Gaddis is simply reproducing, and thereby critiquing, the speech of real life: as Steiner notes, "A governed irony crystallizes; it does not reiterate the object of its anger."[44] The resulting cruft can cause readers to lose focus on important text, especially when that text's importance is clear only later, as with how Whiteback's hemming and hawing throughout the passage nearly overshadows the fork shipment that will become the basis of J R's junk empire. In such places it is not always clear what separates the book's text from sheer incoherence.

If *J R*'s cruft is to be defended, it must be done, I think, on a cognitive basis. The best gesture toward explaining this effect might be Moore's point that the book's real art is in how "*this* particular idiotic comment is chosen from many others and placed next to *that* one, so that together they echo a remark made in a dissimilar context elsewhere, and in turn anticipate a line from Tennyson, and so on."[45] The argument needs to be specified further. Within the book a great deal of text appears to be disordered to the point of incomprehensibility, clichéd to the point of pure repetition, or simply of little relevance. However, within that apparent cruft are patches of text that are quite important for understanding the larger machinations of the novel's structure. In an environment filled with so much junk text, though, it can become easy to gloss over such passages. Just as *J R*'s characters struggle to retain personal coherence without falling into mere sequences of clichés, *J R*'s readers must struggle with discovering and keeping track of, over the course of seven hundred pages, which of the text's entropic and redundant passages might be important to attend to and which should be ignored.

These challenges to our attentional abilities are pushed furthest by the novel's use of jargon, a textual category that muddies the relation between information and meaning more than any other. Famously George Orwell lambasts jargon in his essay "Politics and the English Language," which, like *J R*, addresses the "political and economic causes" of the "decline of a language."[46] As far as I know, though, Gaddis critics have not highlighted affinities between the two, likely because, despite their shared aims, Orwell's essay ends by prescribing a prose style at odds not only with *J R*'s but with that of Gaddis's academic defenders: clear, concise, jargon-free.[47] While many have criticized Orwell for what seems to them an endorsement of anti-intellectual simplification, though, Orwell does not attack jargon because it is too difficult to read—instead he attacks it because it is too *easy*. Though apparently complex to outsiders, jargon is meant to be quickly breezed over by insiders, for whom it functions essentially as cliché. Consequently, Orwell notes, it allows those who use it to believe their thoughts are more sophisticated than they are, while "sav[ing] much mental effort," because jargon "will construct your sentences for you—even think your thoughts for you."[48] Jargon deceives by presenting redundancy as information, allowing it to become "an instrument for [. . .] concealing or preventing thought"; when one uses such language, one may "defen[d] the indefensible" without even having to think about what one is saying.[49] If one avoids jargon, at least, "when you make a stupid remark its stupidity will be obvious, even to yourself."[50] How we allocate attention to jargon in a given situation, then—whether we simply eliminate it to focus on the rest of a text, as is the wont of, say, the symbolic logicians in Isaac Asimov's Foundation, or to examine it all the more for underlying political motives, as Orwell does with totalitarian rhetoric—profoundly tests our abilities to process language.[51]

This property of jargon may be exemplified best by *J R*'s climax, a twenty-five-page scene set in the hospital room of J R's aging, ill corporate rival Governor Jack Cates (Joubert's father), in which Cates barks into the telephone while simultaneously firing off orders to his assistant Beaton. Many pages read like this:

> —Planned to miss three dividends in the first place didn't we? No damn voting rights on it unless we miss the fourth one, pay that everything's under control got Beaton here keeping an eye on the . . . who Freddie? Any word on Freddie Beaton?
>
> —You mean the actual reconstituting hasn't even excuse me, no sir Mrs Cutler is placing ads in the pap . . .
>
> —Still out loose Monty no Wiles thought he saw him in Tripler's elevator while back with Emily must have been wrong, Beaton says she's got ads in the pap . . . must have got it from the doorman when she moved that drunk into their old place up on Seventy . . . Joubert no don't know she . . . don't know must have paid him off, damn lulu need it for lawyers job in a Swiss bank there dipped in the cash drawer bought back into Nobili when this outfit ran it up to nineteen turned right around wiped it out with their own Far East market nothing left but what . . . ?
>
> —Lost in transmission but that's prepos . . .
>
> —Same damn fool yes got the bit in his teeth there tried to give them away too, launched a big drug donation dates running out thought they'd deduct at retail, IRS disallows it lets them write off

> at cost under eighty thousand wholesale value damn near two million, drugs show up in every black market in the Pacific dates expire damn druggists returning them hand over fist get the wholesale price back nothing left of the company but this happy pill Zona's on lose that patent suit all they've got's this damn green aspirin FDA's got them up on not worth . . .[52]

As Johnston notes, "this is not a human being talking, but money itself."[53] The conventionalized language of cash drawers, deductions, and write-offs comes so automatically to Cates that he breezes from one deal to the next without even thinking about them. And why should he? Individually they mean nothing to him except in terms of their interchangeable cash value. For many readers, on the other hand, this barrage of technical and otherwise irrelevant financial jargon may seem extremely complicated, but we will also probably barely think about it, because we lack the larger structure of Cates's accrued financial acumen to contextualize these points within his larger empire. In other words each deal's individual fungibility to Cates is matched by its blurred incomprehensibility to us, seeming to require that we pass over most of it as meaningless.

Yet if we skim these deals so as to focus on events that appear more important to the main plot—say, those involving Cates's daughter, Joubert—we will miss the train of action leading to the novel's climactic moment, where the heretofore milquetoast Beaton suddenly uses this dialogue's most wonkish element, the delayed fourth-quarter dividend, in combination with Zona's dangerous "happy pills" to wrest away the dying Cates's holdings and transfer them to Joubert. As Moore notes, it is easy to overlook this sequence of events, likely because their setup occurs within such otherwise apparently interminable cruft.[54] Only by an extremely subtle filtering can the important details be emphasized—and, just as important, the unimportant ones skipped.

The real problem with language in *J R*, then, is not necessarily that capitalism has corrupted it into an entropic chaos: in fact, in many cases, the text is insufficiently entropic, since the predictability of Wall Street language causes its movers and shakers not to think closely about the consequences of what is happening. Instead the problem with language is that the financial world's frequent extremes of both entropy and redundancy make it extremely difficult to isolate regions of meaningful text, subsequently rendering the workings of the financial system difficult to process adequately. That is, I think, precisely the source of the novel's aesthetic value. Because it so subtly dissolves text of genuine importance within an avalanche of cruft, *J R* provides one of the most rigorous tests in contemporary literature of readers' high-level attention modulation. Given that we live in a world in which an international economic collapse occurred (at least in part) because the rate at which the financial system produces data so thoroughly outpaces any individual human's capacity to interpret and understand it, high-level attention modulation is an absolutely vital skill for us to hone. If we cannot cut through the enormous amount of junk information produced by our culture to the truly vital material, we will be absolutely at the mercy of anyone who can, or else fall victim to the cacophony of our own excessive production of data.

Redundancy: Is *The Making of Americans* Worth Reading?

Substantially different challenges to processing are presented by Stein's multigenerational family epic *The Making of Americans*, which narrates the lives of two wealthy families from the eastern city of Bridgepoint—the Herslands and the Dehnings—who have moved to the midwestern town of Gossols. Where *J R* makes use of an expanded vocabulary and fractured syntax, *The Making of Americans* deploys instead a limited arsenal of short words and repetitive sentences. These, however, can prove no less difficult to read. Yet how do we discuss, for instance, the difficulty of a passage like this one from the beginning of the "Martha Hersland" chapter?

> To begin then again with a few of them who slowly come to be each one of them a whole one to me.
>
> Each one slowly comes to be a whole one to me. Each one slowly comes to be a whole one in me. Every one always is repeating. As I was saying sometimes it is very irritating hearing, feeling, seeing repeating in some one, in every one. More and more then when such a one is a whole one to me, more and more then as loving repeating is all my being, more and more then I am happy in my loving repeating being. Now then.

> Each one slowly comes to be a whole one to me. Each one slowly comes to be a whole one in me. This is now a description of learning one.[55]

Unlike so many passages in *J R*, no words in this excerpt are errant or even unusual, and while it possesses a few syntactic irregularities, most of its sentences are short, single claused, and correctly constructed. The Gunning-Fog measure of reading difficulty grades it just under 7, but there is near-universal agreement that one should not expect a seventh-grader to read *The Making of Americans.*

The difficulty's main cause is the one cited by Wilson, both exemplified in and described by this passage: the book is always repeating itself, to the point where its extreme redundancy over the course of nine hundred pages is likely to wear down its readers' interest. This redundancy is most apparent in those phrases—and even those whole sentences—that recur verbatim throughout the text, like "Each one slowly comes to be a whole one in me," but can also be seen in the meaningless filler expressions like "More and more" and "Now then." On first analysis the text appears information poor and resistant to deep attention.

Even some Stein scholars seem receptive to the notion that the book is not really readable. Even Marianne DeKoven, author of a monograph celebrating Stein's experimental language, claims that reading the whole book is "an arduous and unrewarding task."[56] This perspective is widespread enough that Tanya Clement claims in her digital corpus study of the book that close reading has "yielded limited material for scholarly work."[57] Perhaps poet Kenneth Goldsmith articulates the nonreading approach to *The Making of Americans* most boldly, arguing that "[t]rying to read Gertrude Stein's *The Making of Americans* linearly is like trying to read the Web linearly. It's mostly possible in small doses, dipped in and out of."[58] As far as Goldsmith is concerned, Stein's book is prophetic of the contemporary world, in which we are so overloaded with text that we should abandon close reading entirely, replacing it with a practice of "parsing" and skimming.[59] Certainly Goldsmith's own books—like *Day*, which copies one day's *New York Times* into an eight-hundred-page plaintext monograph—are meant to be browsed rather than read cover to cover.

But this notion that close reading is obsolete in a text-overloaded world has already been confronted and rejected by John Barth, whose 1967 "The

Literature of Exhaustion"—despite its reputation as a manifesto of postmodernism—is largely a defense of traditional literature against conceptual writing. Barth points out that since conceptual work is intended to provide an occasion for aesthetic discussion rather than to be read, then "for intellectual purposes [one] needn't even write it ": that is, a book like *Day* is little more compelling as a physical object than as a mere idea.[60] True literature, he argues, is actually "worth doing" rather than simply "worth remarking."[61] To illustrate that, even at a point of apparent exhaustion, there still exists literature "worth doing"—that is, for which close attention is valuable—Barth invokes Borges's story "Pierre Menard, Author of the *Quixote*," which centers on a fragmentary *Don Quixote* by a French writer seeking to independently reproduce Cervantes's work. Such a book itself might be interesting to contemplate as an illustration of the problems of interpretation, but as Barth points out, Borges's story is not that book. Instead of creating nine hundred pages of redundant text—that is, *Don Quixote*'s textual double—Borges creates his own brief narrative about an artist's struggles with originality, and paradoxically he achieves originality in doing so.[62] In this way Borges and Barth demonstrate that, despite our age's rapidly mounting archive of extant textual patterns, a reserve of uncompressible unpredictability still remains available to writers.[63]

The Making of Americans, similarly, is not merely an object to idly pontificate on but is worth reading on its own merits. If we do read it linearly, in fact, we can see that it incorporates substantial unpredictability within its more apparent large-scale patterns. As Randa Dubnick has pointed out, Stein's difficulty does not derive merely from repetition, but from a manipulated balance between vocabulary and syntax. In *The Making of Americans*, Stein severely limits her vocabulary, causing some repetition, but in turn makes her syntax nonstandard, as might be seen in the above passage's brief but unexpected prepositional phrases and irregular participle-gerund sequences (e.g., "seeing repeating in some one").[64] These sorts of moves distinguish *The Making of Americans* from the Library of Babel's "M C V" volume: its syntax is too strange to be skimmed, even when many individual word sequences repeat.

We may take this point even further by noting that the book's vocabulary and syntax each also feature an internal dialectic of pattern and randomness. On the one hand, William Gass demonstrates in his introduction to *The Making of Americans* that the book's odd syntaxes are often paralleled in adjacent sentences, as might be seen in the passage above.[65] On the other, the book's repetitive words also often shift in meaning, altering the way we process identical text, as may be seen in this passage's use of the word *repeating* itself, which shifts the meaning of later uses of *whole one*.

The concept of repetition, in fact, long fascinated Stein, and we might conceive *The Making of Americans* as exploring the boundaries of what can be expressed by it, how variation can be introduced into it, and how it can be read. Stein actually claimed to be "inclined to believe there is no such thing as repetition," believing that words, upon their reuse, acquire an "insistence" that differentiated them in emphasis, remarking on "how everybody said the same thing over and over again with infinite variations but over and over again until finally if you listened with great intensity you could hear it rise and fall and tell all that that there was inside them."[66] How recurring words may acquire "insistence" in a prose volume like *The Making of Americans*, though, is unclear, since written text lacks the vocal emphases to which Stein alludes.

Many critics have tried to account for this repetitiveness in Stein's work, but none have been quite satisfactory. When Sianne Ngai argues that Stein's "hyperbolic uses of repetition, reflexivity, citation, and cliché [. . .] tend to draw us *down* into the sensual and material domain of language and its dulling and irritating iterability," it is unclear why this result should be positive, especially since she argues the same result occurs in relatively unreadable books like Goldsmith's.[67] Other critics emphasize repetition's ability to parody that which it repeats, but while chapter 4 will discuss how repetition is vital to satire, a glance at the not-especially-funny passage above should demonstrate that this argument is neither sufficient to explain many of the book's individual repetitions nor the sheer lengths to which they go in the work as a whole.[68]

Those pursuing Stein's own investment in cognitive studies have gotten closer to the main issue. Many invoke the concept of the "continuous present" Stein derived from her psychological studies with William James, especially as relates to his notion of the stream of consciousness. Stephen Meyer claims that the book's style is "the story of Stein freeing herself from James's [. . .] descriptive psychology," using the rhythms of her writing to break James's distinction between consciousness and content.[69] On similar lines Lisa Ruddick claims that Stein's sentences "bring back all the 'slack and wandering and superfluity'" of consciousness that James insisted must be streamlined out by attention.[70] According to Paul Stephens, with such overloaded language, "Stein aspired to overcome the complete organization of society [by promoting] states of distraction in her readers."[71] We will discuss cruft and the depiction of consciousness more in chapter 3. But if the most important job of the brain's attentional systems, as the neuroscientists discussed in the introduction argued, is to select the most important thoughts and subordinate or eliminate the enormous remaining amount of repetitive and irrelevant mental activity, it is not clear why a representation of immediate consciousness or a valorization of distraction and wandering for its own sake would be valuable.

To see how Stein creates "insistence" out of apparent redundancy, let's examine the passage from the book's penultimate chapter that describes the final days of the youngest and most philosophical of the central characters, David Hersland:

> He was not really needing anything. He was not needing being certain that being living is existing. He was not needing being one going on being living. He was needing understanding that he was being living. He was almost completely needing being one completely clearly thinking. He was almost completely wanting to be feeling needing that any woman he was seeing was completely beautifully something. He was almost wanting to be giving advice strongly enough to some. He was almost being one coming to be beginning succeeding in living. He was completely clearly expressing something. He was completely understanding any one's understanding anything of that thing.
>
> He was not really needing anything. He was not needing being one going on being living. He was almost completely needing being one completely clearly thinking. He was not needing being one remembering that any one can come to be a dead one. He was not needing being certain that being living is something that is existing. He was not needing to be remembering anything. He was not needing to be forgetting something. He was understanding that he was being living. He was almost needing to be one almost only eating one thing. He was being living. He was understanding that

> thing. He was clearly expressing something. He was not forgetting anything. He was not forgetting everything. He was not needing to be one remembering anything. He was not needing to be one remembering everything.[72]

The passage's limited vocabulary causes certain words to recur frequently. *Need* and *needing* alone appear sixteen times (nearly 7 percent of the total word count), which leads to both repeating phrases like "He was not really needing anything" and otherwise redundant ones like, "He was not needing to be one remembering anything. He was not needing to be one remembering everything."

Yet "He was not really needing anything" is not quite the same phrase in its two appearances. When beginning the first paragraph, it may decode into an expression of independence (i.e., "David lacks nothing, because he is self-reliant"), rendering the next two sentences, which merely provide examples of "anything," apparently redundant. A few sentences later, though, the narrator describes some things David *does* need: "understanding that he was being living" and "being one completely clearly thinking." To avoid complete contradiction, we might want to revise how we decoded the earlier sentence: perhaps we should've placed greater emphasis on the qualifier *really* in decoding, or considered *anything* as referring merely to physical things, or emphasized the past-tense implication of *was*. Similarly we could consider how different decodings of *understanding, being, living,* and *thinking* (especially in their gerund forms) might alter our take on David's *needing*. Regardless, when we come across the second "He was not really needing anything," we cannot repeat our original decoding. Under the force of the syntax, the words' meanings and their attendant probabilities have changed—as, for that matter, they have been changing all throughout the nine hundred pages of the novel leading up to this point. In this manner *The Making of Americans* redefines the words of our language even as we read them.

However, just as *J R*'s redundancy does not fully balance its error, not all of *The Making of Americans*' recurring phrases have this kind of dynamism. The most egregious example appears on pages 443–44, recurring almost exactly on page 480. I overlay the two here—the single bracketed letter is the only text from the first occurrence not to appear in the recurrence, and the underlined words are the only text that the recurrence introduces:

> Some as I am saying have sure feeling in them, have honor in them and religion from the nature of them when this is strong enough in them to make it their own inside them. Some can make their own honor, some their own l[i]oving, some their own religion, some are weak and can do one thing, make one thing their own, some are strong enough and all of it, loving, honor, certainty and religion in them, all of it is some one else's, of some one else's making, some can just resist and not make their own anything, there are many of them. Some out of their own virtue make a god who sometimes later is a terror to them. Out of their own virtue they make a god who sometimes later is a terror to them. Some make some things like laws out of the nature of them, out of the nature of some other one. Some are controlled by other people's virtue, and then it scares them. Listen to each one telling about their own virtue and that grows to make a god for them, grows to be a law for them and often afterwards scares them, some afterwards like it, some forget it, some are it. Some honor what is right to them for them to be doing. Some separate honor from the doing of the thing, have it as a feeling.[73]

This is not all that repeats: the next paragraph does as well, differing only by one added comma in its recurrence. Since some of the passage's sentences are already redundant (e.g., "Some out of their own virtue make a god who sometimes later is a terror to them. Out of their own virtue they make a god who sometimes later is a terror to them"), their second iteration seems even more so. Though the two versions of this passage do appear in different contexts—the first comes as part of a description of Martha's husband Phillip Redfern, while the second more generally describes the narrator's plan to make a "history of every one"—the potential for an insistent difference between the two is defused by the vague *some* and *sometimes*: since *some*'s relation to *loving*, *honor*, and *religion* is decodable in so many ways, it dissipates any syntactic pressure. The minimal altered text does little to generate insistence, either, especially as the *living-loving* distinction deployed in the first version is erased in the second. That it took Clement's corpus study to highlight these passages should demonstrate how so much of the book is flatly repetitive: not even such a lengthy repetition stands out.

We might understand why such repetition can have value in the larger scheme of the book, though, by returning to the passage about David's death, especially the statement that he is "almost completely needing being one completely clearly thinking." If we read this sentence as not only describing, but representing, David's own thought process, we should ask: is he actually "completely clearly thinking" here? It is difficult to say. On the one hand, this passage is engaged in constant, intricate variations on its key ideas, as in phrases like, "He had not been one needing that thing really needing being a dead one. He had not been one needing that thing really at all needing that thing needing being a dead one. He was then understanding something and understanding any one else who was understanding something of that thing," which suggest David is engaged in sophisticated attempts to understand basic existential issues about self-knowledge and the value of human life.[74] Yet it also frequently self-contradicts, as when the narrator claims "he was one who did not remember everything," then several sentences later that "[h]e remembered everything."[75] While elsewhere contradiction can insist that we produce nuanced shifts in the meanings of words, in this case the contradiction is so absolute that it does not seem to allow any such subtle processing, moving the passage toward an incantatory nonsense rather than profound reflection. Consequently we cannot really tell whether the dying intellectual has established a profound peace with himself or simply collapsed into a confused rambling.

And that is probably the point. Finding the line between profundity and rambling is, it turns out, a tricky process. In describing David's inability to consistently maintain insistence within the patterns of his thought without falling into contradiction on the one side or repetition on the other—a problem shared by many of the book's characters—*The Making of Americans* shows us the hidden richness possessed by the mundane words that govern our higher consciousness, but also what muddled use we often make of them, and how maddeningly hard it is to distinguish between our most insightful and most nonsensical thoughts. The tightrope our minds walk in attempting to establish the necessary patterns that make consciousness possible, without simply becoming calcified, is treacherous. Trying to make sense of Stein's writing, hopefully, can make us more attentive to how we process the disparate elements of our world, our language, and our own thoughts, requiring that we find a way of reading that is adequate to their complexity without descending into gibberish.

Correction: How Does One Read *Finnegans Wake*?

No mega-novel, though, presses our ability to rapidly modulate modes of attention more relentlessly than *Finnegans Wake*, a book without which any discussion of unreadable text would be incomplete. Where *J R* may tweak several clauses per paragraph, very few sentences pass in *Finnegans Wake* without several words being warped into near unrecognizability; while *The Making of Americans* may repeat many phrases, the *Wake* constantly repeats the entire Viconian life cycle over its six hundred pages, via the trope of the Liffey's daily flow inward and out. Regarding this circularly plotted, neologism-loaded tome, even Joyce's friend Ezra Pound—certainly no stranger to long, impenetrable literary works—found himself forced to admit bafflement: "I will have another go at it, but up to present I make nothing of it whatever. Nothing so far as I make out, nothing short of divine vision or a new cure for the clapp [*sic*] can possibly be worth all the circumambient peripherization."[76]

It is hard to criticize Pound for this attitude. After all what would it mean to "read" the following passage?

> In the name of Anem this carl on the kopje in pelted thongs a parth a lone who the joebiggar be he? Forshapen his pigmaid hoagshead, shroonk his plodsfoot. He hath locktoes, this shortshins, and, Obeold that's pectoral, his mammamuscles most mouseterious. It is slaking nuncheon out of some thing's brain pan. Me seemeth a dragon man He is almonthst on the kiep fief by here, is Comestipple Sacksoun, be it junipery or febrewery, marracks or alebrill or the ramping riots of pouriose and froriose. What a quhare soort of a mahan. It is evident the michindaddy. Lets we overstep his fire defences and these kraals of slitsucked marrogbones. (Cave!)[77]

Of this passage's 110 words, thirty-one do not belong to the dictionaries of any known language, so how can they be read? *Finnegans Wake*, more than any other book, makes critics ask what it means to "read" a book at all, as it is rarely clear what successfully processing its text would entail.

As impenetrable as it may appear, however, the *Wake*, like *J R* and the *The Making of Americans*, is characterized by an unusual mixture of information and redundancy, though each is allowed to proliferate to an extreme degree within its own domain. The relationship between the two may be explicated via the tension Margot Norris long ago articulated in *Wake* criticism between "radical" and "conservative" approaches to interpretation.[78] The radical strand emphasizes the text's entropic randomness, describing its language with terms like "chaos and complexity."[79] The conservative strand, conversely, points out how incredibly repetitive are the book's motifs, observing, in Edmund L. Epstein's words, that the book "repeats its stories and symbols dozens or hundreds of times," often seeming simply to replay one "basic story."[80] Even the confusing passage above manages to allude to the Viconian cycle and to one of Joyce's favorite narrative references, the rise and fall of Charles Parnell.[81] As I have already suggested, I believe that any adequate method of reading the book requires us to balance the two: the radical and conservative approaches are not enemies but depend on each other for coherence. To see how, we must look to the textual feature on which both camps establish their arguments, the book's errors, described by Vicki Mahaffey as the *Wake*'s "most far-reaching [. . .] innovation"[82] Addressing them will require an informational technique that places the pattern and randomness of error in dialectic: correction.[83]

Some Joyceans might balk at the idea of correction, though, because while *Wake* studies have long engaged with errors, they generally do not believe readers should correct them. Conservative critics generally leave error correction to textual scholars, who attempt to correct any transmission or editorial errors that might have muddied the text Joyce truly intended, as might be observed by the kerfuffle over the 2011 Rose and O'Hanlon edition of the *Wake*. For radicals, on the other hand, any clear division between correct and incorrect language is anathema to the *Wake*, as may be seen in Derek Attridge's claim that the book "insists that the strict boundaries and discrete elements in a linguist's 'grammar of competence' are a neoplatonic illusion."[84] The former's perspective, though, is complicated by Joyce's having intentionally welcomed errors into the book's composition.[85] Regarding the latter's persepective, we should observe that if anyone could have deconstructed the notion of correctness for the *Wake*, it would have been Jacques Derrida, and tellingly his essay on the *Wake*'s phrase "he war" begins by correcting the text into several grammatically valid variations ("he wars," "he was," etc.).[86] One cannot process text at all, after all, unless one has some sort of internalized dictionary with which to at least partly decode it, and any dictionary requires distinctions between correct and incorrect uses of the language.

As we already saw with *J R*, correction can be undertaken with ordinary English because, as Shannon demonstrated, our language has a high level of built-in redundancy. Using letter frequency tables alone, in fact, Shannon calculated a baseline redundancy in English text of at least 54 percent and experimentally demonstrated that, in practice, ordinary English text could be guessed correctly by literate readers about 70 percent of the time.[87] This inherent redundancy is not merely waste but helps protect communications from being corrupted. Codes without redundancy are vulnerable to noise, because while, for instance, a simple binary code in which 1 denotes *yes* and 0 denotes *no* may be maximally efficient, a single error will cause the receiver to decode the message incorrectly (e.g., 1 is altered to 0). To detect and correct even one error requires substantially more redundant text (e.g., 111 to signify *yes* and 000 for *no*).[88] For a book like the *Wake*, though, which introduces many errors, there is often not sufficient redundancy left in the language's structure to allow unambiguous correction. As an experiment I conducted on Joyce's prose demonstrated, while educated readers are generally able to predict the letters in a sentence from *Portrait of the Artist* at a rate consistent with Shannon's findings, a representative *Wake* sentence lowered their accuracy to 24 percent.[89] Twenty-four percent redundancy is not total randomness, but it reduces our correction abilities to the point where the text becomes frequently difficult to process.

However, the *Wake*'s entropic errors are partly counteracted by several other sources. Most prominently the redundancy the *Wake* loses in its vocabulary is partly replaced by its underlying structure of motifs. The mathematician Charles Bennett, unsatisfied with the low value information theory placed on intricate information deriving from simple equations (e.g., astral orbits), developed a measure called "logical depth," referring to the degree of effort needed to produce a set of textual values from a relatively simple basis, and we might apply that idea to the *Wake*.[90] The "buried redundancy" to which Bennett credits such depth would include, for the *Wake*, repetitions like the character sequences

HCE and ALP—the closest thing the book has to protagonists—as well as references to Tristan and Isolde, Huckleberry Finn, and the drinking song from which the book takes its name. Furthermore the redundancy provided by English syntax remains largely intact, giving us a stable structure into which to place our corrected words.[91] Last, since, as neuroscientist Stanislas Dehaene writes, our brains simultaneously process text visually and phonetically, the *Wake*'s implied phonetics assist the correction process via its famous puns: for example, the tipsy "Comestipple" arriving in "febrewery" mentioned above are easily corrected to the heteronymic, but nearly homophonic, "Constable" and "February."[92]

Still, correction in the *Wake* is rarely straightforward. Consider this relatively uncomplicated (by *Wake* standards) clause in which Jarl van Hoother gallops out of his castle: "And he clopped his rude hand to his eacy hitch."[93] Prior to the *Wake*, *eacy* belonged to no known language, so unless we wish to discard it as unreadable, we must try to correct it. The syntax requires an adjective, and there are several common English ones with a "Hamming distance" (the number of digits differing between two strings of text) of 1 to *eacy*, such as *easy*, *lacy*, *racy*, or *each*. Though written English gives us no mandate as to which we ought to choose, most *Wake* readers will likely correct to *easy* upon analyzing the candidate words' lexical Hamming distances (the difference in letters, henceforth d_l) and their phonetic Hamming distances (the difference in phones, henceforth d_p). Phonetically, changing *e* to the consonants *l* or *r* would not only add another phone but also change the vowel from a long *e* ([i]) to a long *a* ([eI]), while correcting to *each* would remove a whole syllable; meanwhile, changing the *c* to *s* to make *easy* would merely swap two similar consonant sounds.[94] Furthermore this error in *eacy* suggests that other words in the clause may also have at least one error within them, even those that decode in English, which should cause us to mentally scroll through the words or phrases that might be created by changing one letter or sound in the passage. The most interesting result comes when we change the initial vowel sound in *hitch* from a short *i* ([I]) to a long *a* ([eI]), which turns "eacy hitch" into ECH. In any book other than the *Wake*, this would be unremarkable—we might as well note that those words are an anagram of "Hey, I catch!"—but the HCE sequence and its permutations are repeated so frequently throughout the book that we ought to anticipate it any time a sequence of letters or sounds within a small Hamming distance appears.

In inducing this complicated correction process, the *Wake*'s errors and redundancies often produce greater linguistic richness. In this case they link Jarl van Hoother with the larger male principle embodied throughout the book by equestrian figures like Napoleon and Washington. Similar phenomena occur with the book's many portmanteaus, such as the "violet indigonation" that Jarl feels elsewhere in this passage.[95] This phrase's second word may be corrected, with one additional space, to "indigo nation," but if we delete the middle *o* it becomes "indignation" ($d_l = d_p = 1$). Merging the two corrections together, we may conjure a vision of the powerful Jarl growing so angry that his face becomes not just red but indigo and violet, an event that, given his position, might have great national (and possibly violent) implications. These conceptual blends are the backbone of the *Wake*'s literary value.

However, the plasticity of this process, even in simple phrases such as this one, can provide so many options as to send the text toward incoherence. After all many other words in the "eacy hitch" passage also have $d_l = d_p = 1$ alternatives: we could change *hand* to *band*, *clopped* to *clipped*, or *rude* to *prude*. We would create further semantic links in doing so, but these new semes would multiply out the sentence's possibilities so far that it would become nearly impossible to process it at all. And what do we do with those words possessing more than one error, or that correct to words from non-English languages? For instance the same passage describes Hoother's legwear as "panuncular," which *Wake* annotator Roland McHugh corrects to "peninsular."[96] This seems reasonable, given that Napoleon's Peninsular War is a minor motif in the *Wake*, but *peninsular* requires not a single correction from *panuncular*, but three. This implies a much noisier channel: if we had to consider all alternate words with differences of three letters or more to each other word of this section, we would have to cycle through so many different possible permutations as to be utterly baffled. The Latin *panuncula*, or bobbin-thread, is closer, at $d_l = d_p = 1$, but that only seems incidentally relevant to the passage, and reaching into another language adds further distance between these words. What about *avuncular*, which has $d_l = d_p = 2$ to *panuncular* but seems a bit alien from the military context; or a drawling American South *nucular*, which is relevant to that context but has a larger Hamming distance and is slightly anachronistic; or some conceptual blend of *pan* and *uncle*? Which of these are appropriate corrections? If all which is to be emphasized most? If all are to be treated equally, at what Hamming distance do we finally refuse to add more possible corrections, so as to keep from rewriting the book entirely?

The belief that adding semantic layers automatically improves the text—that is, that more meaning is better meaning—has not been questioned in *Wake* criticism for some time. Even otherwise opposed views on the *Wake*'s language, such as Eco's structuralist valorization of its "cunningly organized network of mutual relationships" and Attridge's deconstructive claim that "the portmanteau problematizes even the most stable signifier by showing how its relations to other signifiers can be productive," agree on that point.[97] Yet why should it be so unambiguously good that the *Wake*'s language is productive of relationships when what it produces is not necessarily of any value? Certainly that two words happen to be connected by a few shared letters or sounds doesn't mean that they provoke any real insight. Consider the ambivalence about such wordplay expressed by the Anglophone literary critic most responsible for expanding our attunement to semantic richness, William Empson:

> It is in the third type of ambiguity, when the two notions of the ambiguity are most sharply and consciously detached from one another, that one finds oneself forced to question its value. [. . .] When there is no connection between the two halves of an ornamental comparison, the two meanings of a pun, except that they are both relevant to the matter in hand, one would think that the comparison can only give trivial pleasure and the pun not be particularly funny. [. . . To think otherwise,] one must assume that $n + 1$ is more valuable than n for any but the most evasively mystical theory of value. Those who adopt this view are taking refuge in the mysterious idea of an organism, of all things working together for the good[.][98]

Like the other linguistic innovations we have considered in this chapter, the *Wake*'s portmanteaus will mostly tend to produce junk, and given the enormous amount of error in the book, that volume of that junk can drown our abilities to see any more meaningful connections if we are not careful. How we determine which combinations are beneficial and which must be ignored, though, is a difficult matter. Inasmuch as the

Wake's fascinating use of error, however, gives us the opportunity to examine that question in greater depth than any other book, we can use it as a starting point to examine the processes by which we make those decisions.

Perhaps the way in which the *Wake*'s disruption of normal English communication with puns, errors, and polyglot incursions sometimes impairs dialogue, yet sometimes aids the emergence of something more profound, may be best seen in the early dialogue between the inebriated Irishman Mutt and the approaching Danish explorer Jute, which in its representation of communication difficulty displays the impact of noisy, errant messages:

> Jute.—Are you jeff?
> Mutt.—Somehards.
> Jute.—But you are not jeffmute?
> Mutt.—Noho. Only an utterer.
> Jute.—Whoa? Whoat is the mutter with you?
> Mutt.—I became a stun a stummer.
> Jute.—What a hauhauhauhaudibble thing, to be cause! How, Mutt?
> Mutt.—Aput the buttle, surd.
> Jute.—Whose poddle? Wherein?
> Mutt.—The Inns of Dungtarf where Used awe to be he.
> Jute.—You that side your voise are almost inedible to me. Become a bitskin more wiseable, as if I were you.
> Mutt.—Has? Has af? Hasatency? Urp, Boohooru! Booru Usurp! I trumple from rath in mine mines when I rimmimirim![99]

This passage might recall Franco Moretti's counterintuitive contrast of Mikhail Bakhtin's otherwise closely related notions of dialogism and heteroglossia by noting that "if people don't speak the same language, after all, how is dialogue ever going to be possible?"[100] There is much that is linguistically innovative about the encounter of these two, but because Mutt and Jute have no common language, they cannot communicate with each other extremely well. Further impeding communication, Mutt admits to being a little deaf and soft-spoken: *jeff* corrects to *deaf* ($d_l = 2$, $d_p = 1$, aided by the proceeding *jeffmute*), and *stun a stummer* not only sounds like a stutter but includes the German word for muteness.

As a result the messages they produce end up having many errors. For instance Mutt's "Aput the buttle" is errant as soon as he speaks it: *Aput* is not an English word, and *buttle* is a verb rather than the noun the syntax requires, causing most commentators correct to *bottle* or to *battle* or to both. Moreover *buttle* acquires even more noise when Jute mistakes it for *poddle* in his follow-up question, making it doubly errant. Interestingly, however, Mutt's response, "The Inns of Dungtarf where Used awe to be he," despite its own errors, is mostly adequate for responding to each of the questions, "Whose bottle?" "Whose battle?" and "Whose poddle?" One might acquire a bottle at an inn, and one might have a battle at "Dungtarf," which commentators associate with the Battle of Clontarf, a bloody conflict between the Vikings and Irish that saw the death of the latter's chief Brian Boru and the precipitation of territorial wars, including some battles over the Poddle River. As Mutt's "Boohooru!" suggests, this was historically disastrous for the Irish. Thus by combining these three words in the exchange, the *Wake* suggests how the Irish drown themselves in the bottle in grief over their battles for the Poddle. This three-way confluence occurs by chance, the result of a noisy channel, yet the correction generates a complex metaphor about Ireland's aimlessness that could not be so well expressed otherwise.

On the other hand, the word Mutt actually says, *buttle*, does not appear to contribute to this confluence at all, nor do many other words within smaller Hamming distances to *buttle* than *poddle*, like *bustle*, *huddle*, and *cuddle*. Words elsewhere in the passage are nearly unreadable, like *Somehards*, and even words that correct easily seem to acquire little additional meaning in the correction process, such as *inedible* (presumably correcting to *inaudible*). That these errors are not entirely beneficial should not be especially surprising: the *felix culpa*, after all—or *foenix culprit*, as the *Wake* has it—is the rarest of *culpas*.[101] We should revise Stephen Dedalus's comment on Shakespeare that "A man of genius makes no mistakes. His errors are volitional and are the portals of discovery": his errors are *sometimes* the portals of discovery, but often they are portals to nowhere.[102] The substantial cruft produced in the process can swiftly overload readers attempting to make sense of the text, especially if they are convinced it can be corrected to produce some deeper meaning. Even the most ardent Joyceans, staring at a *Wake* sentence for the hundredth time, will find themselves anxiously wondering whether they have missed an important joke, or whether the real joke is that a long-dead Irishman has gotten them to spend hours of their time trying to locate a joke where none exists.

But even in failing to be portals to discovery, the *Wake*'s errors are important to the book's project. To read the *Wake* requires a mindset constantly warping and deforming words to see how they might be corrected, which each error encourages even when it leads nowhere. It is a draining process, one that needs a lifetime's effort to attend adequately. I have not yet devoted the requisite thousand hours that Thornton Wilder recommended for any critic wishing to speak to the book as a whole, so I have limited myself here to the *Wake*'s first chapter. Yet this should not be too problematic, even in an essay directed toward the girth of the mega-novel, because the cruft in Joyce's book does not only, or even primarily, derive from the actual text's many errors and constantly repeating motifs. The book's 628 pages are only the beginning of its real text, because for each word we must also process *the entirety of language*, searching out possible corrections and connections that might enrich it. Almost all of what we come up with will fail to add to what we read, with only the rare breakthrough. All the attempted connections that don't quite work are the book's real cruft, as our effort to read it inevitably, in Ruben Borg's words, "produces a hesitation [. . .] between work and waste."[103] Like the other dictionary novels, the *Wake* places us on the edge between all that should be said but has not yet been formulated and all that has not been formulated because it should not be said, challenging us to stay as close to the line as we can without, like HCE's avatar Humpty Dumpty, falling off it.

2 The Encyclopedia

The Paradox of Encyclopedic Fiction

Having in the last chapter treated "information" in its technical sense, this chapter will treat the more colloquial use of the word by examining a mega-novel subgenre drawing on a different type of reference work, the encyclopedic novel. That term has been frequently used over the past six decades to refer to mega-novels that incorporate substantial specialized information from the sciences, the arts, and history.[1] Most famously Edward Mendelson defined encyclopedic narratives as those that "attempt to render the full range of knowledge and beliefs of a national culture," echoing Northrop Frye's earlier claim that encyclopedic fiction presents "a total body of vision that poets as a whole class are entrusted with."[2] Even more postmodern takes on the genre, like that of Tom LeClair, still argue that only such "extraordinarily knowledgeable" works are able to "give readers an intellectual mastery [of their culture]."[3] In gathering and organizing so much data, Hugh Kenner notes that such books exploit not only the encyclopedia's educative intent but its print format, inviting annotation and cross-reference and thereby creating the conditions under which books like Joyce's *Ulysses* can "contain, as Homer's work was reputed to contain, a systematic compendium of arts, sciences and moral teachings; symbols, rituals and practical counsels."[4] Given these objectives, an encyclopedic novel obviously must be extremely long, and if readers complain that this makes it excessive or too difficult to process, this may merely be a sign that they have yet to adequately comprehend the enormous complexity of contemporary culture.

However, other critics have inverted such claims by framing the genre as a critique, rather than a celebration, of the encyclopedic project. Countering Mendelson, Stephen Burn argues, "the encyclopedic urge emerges from a culture's awareness of its own fragility rather than from a sense of national coherence," occurring when the "mass of data exceed[s] the synthesizing powers of even [the encyclopedic novelist's] encyclopedic grasp."[5] Other critics, taking up a more overtly poststructuralist attitude, lambast those encyclopedically minded authors "who bombard us with the certainty of their knowledge," asserting that the encyclopedic novel can present only "the illusion of a totalizing system."[6] They usually conclude that encyclopedic novelists should not try to use their fictions to encyclopedize in a conventional way, but instead seek more "open" approaches to knowledge, often invoking Deleuze and Guattari's notion of the rhizome.[7]

Though these approaches to encyclopedic fiction obviously conflict with each other, what may be more interesting is the underlying paradox to which they both ascribe, namely that of asserting the qualities of a reference book to a work of fiction, which is (in Dorrit Cohn's formulation) a "literary nonreferential narrative."[8] In other words, if an encyclopedia's value requires that it accountably and more or less accurately describe referents within the real world, how can its goals be either achieved or criticized by fictional text, which has no real-world referent? This is not a trivial point, to be resolved through an appeal to commonsense distinctions of facts from fiction, or even to theoretical analysis and cognitive research that has demonstrated readers must constantly integrate their real-world knowledge to read fiction.[9] In fact empirical data shows that this necessarily blurred boundary between the factual and the counterfactual makes it all the more important to be wary of treating a novel as an encyclopedia. For instance experiments have shown that even when readers know they are reading fiction, they will often accept the inaccurate information it presents as true, and furthermore will sometimes believe that they had "known" this information beforehand.[10] As Lisa Zunshine notes, constantly "source tagging" data in stories as only relevant to a fictional world can be cognitively taxing, so our minds often skip this step.[11] Combined with the fact that a narrative's ability to shape its readers' beliefs has been empirically demonstrated to depend more on whether it immersively "transports" them than whether it is factual or not, we need to be extremely wary of learning about the external world through fiction.[12] We cannot believe what we read without performing additional research, and if we go that far, we have rendered the novel-as-encyclopedia redundant anyway.

Fiction's rejection of any standard of truth, however, also prevents it from really critiquing encyclopedism. It can burlesque it, as might be demonstrated by Jorge Luis Borges's *First Encyclopedia of Tlön* in "Tlön, Uqbar, Orbis Tertius," a reference guide to a loopy alternate world ruled by the extreme subjective idealism of George Berkeley, but this says nothing about either the real world we inhabit or our systems for organizing knowledge about it. Michel Foucault, commenting on a similarly idiosyncratic Borges encyclopedia (which divides the animal kingdom into categories like those "belonging to the Emperor," that are "fabulous," and "that from a long way off look like flies"), praised such parodic structures for "breaking up all the ordered surfaces and all the planes with which we are accustomed to tame the wild profusion of existing things," but as neuroscientist Rodrigo Quian Quiroga points out, what is really important about Borges's example is how it is so "bizarre and clearly useless."[13] To dismantle all forms of order does not free our minds, as implied by Foucault, but instead handicaps our cognition. As Quian Quiroga exemplifies with Borges's Funes the Memorious, coherent categorization of data is prerequisite to identifying similarities between our countless disparate perceptions so that we may gradually learn how to respond to future ones and hence is "the key to thought."[14] As an analogy consider the labyrinthine drawings by Giovanni Piranesi and M. C. Escher. By taking advantage of the surreal possibilities of their medium, these can play with space to marvelous effect, but for precisely that reason, they cannot critique the law of universal gravitation to which we are beholden in the actual world.

Fictional encyclopedias, consequently, say very little about the capabilities of real encyclopedias, and while they can use their data for amusement or to develop plot, that data is empty as information. This makes it all the more puzzling, then, that many encyclopedic mega-novels contain lengthy accounts of obscure subjects that do not seem to serve any diegetic purpose. One early example is Herman Melville's *Moby-Dick*, especially in chapter 32, "Cetology." Mendelson, who claims that each encyclopedic novel must "include a full account of at least one technology or science," believes that this chapter qualifies *Moby-Dick* as encyclopedic, echoing midcentury claims like that of Howard Vincent that "[i]n *Moby-Dick* we have the best popular introduction ever written on the subject of the American sperm-whale fishery."[15] Yet one cannot construe Ishmael's account of cetology as an accurate account of a science. Early in "Cetology," Ishmael writes:

> First: The uncertain, unsettled condition of this science of Cetology is in the very vestibule attested by the fact, that in some quarters it still remains a moot point whether a whale be a fish. In his System of Nature, A. D. 1766, Linnaeus declares, "I hereby separate the whales from the fish." But of my own knowledge, I know that down to the year 1850, sharks and shad, alewives and herring, against Linnaeus's express edict, were still found dividing the possession of the same seas with the Leviathan.
>
> The grounds upon which Linnaeus would fain have banished the whales from the waters, he states as follows: "On account of their warm bilocular heart, their lungs, their movable eyelids, their hollow ears, penem intrantem ferminam mammis lactantem," and finally, "ex lege naturae jure meritoque." I submitted all this to my friends Simeon Macey and Charley Coffin, of Nantucket, both messmates of mine on a certain voyage, and they united in the opinion that the reasons set forth were altogether insufficient. Charley profanely hinted they were humbug.
>
> Be it known that, waiving all argument, I take the good old fashioned ground that the whale is a fish, and call upon holy Jonah to back me.[16]

It should be clear that dismissing the founder of modern biology in favor of one's minimally educated lunchmates is not how one should begin an account of a science. For that matter Ishmael's only argument for his position, the whale's habitat, is so easily dispatched (are plankton, sponges, and ducks also fish?) that it is hard to think that he means this seriously, and nearly impossible to think Melville does. This is not the only glaring error, either, even from the perspective of 1851: Ishmael also insists, for instance, that the sperm whale is the world's largest, instead of the actual titleholder, the blue or "sulphur bottom."[17]

The poststructuralist approach to this chapter, however, fares no better. Critics often claim that the book's cetological sections present a "farcical mass of pseudo-erudition and specialization" revealing that "cetological insight [. . .] can never be acquired in the gesture of mastery" but only "through the renunciation of logic, syllogism, and traditional study."[18] However, Ishmael's failure to achieve a coherent cetology is less due to the inherent limitations of science than to his own lack of scientific ability. Had he followed Linnaeus instead of Simeon Macey and Charley Coffin, there is every reason to think his cetology would stand much stronger scrutiny. Ishmael does not achieve scientific mastery, in other words, because he does not adequately attempt it. It is Ishmael's pseudoscientific pronouncements that are farcical, not cetology itself.

Still more puzzlingly, though, this farcicality is not consistently developed in Ishmael's encyclopedia. Consider this representative entry in Ishmael's taxonomy of whales:

> BOOK I. (*Folio*), CHAPTER IV. (*Hump-Back*).—This whale is often seen on the northern American coast. He has been frequently captured there, and towed into harbour. He has a great pack on him like a pedlar; or you might call him the Elephant and Castle whale. At any rate, the popular name for him does not sufficiently distinguish him, since the sperm whale also has a hump, though a smaller one. His oil is not very valuable. He has baleen. He is the most gamesome and light-hearted of all the whales, making more gay foam and white water generally than any other of them.[19]

Though there is some whimsy to the taxonomy's figurative formulations, especially the folio-octavo-duodecimo system, for the most part this entry relays information in a straightforwardly encyclopedic manner, even though Ishmael has already discredited himself as an accurate source of such information. Since "Cetology" halts *Moby-Dick*'s central plot, we would be justified in wondering what purpose there could be to such apparently useless blocks of information, which Jennifer Doyle frankly calls the book's "boring parts."[20] No wonder that the greatest challenge reported by those teaching the novel is handling students who are "impatient with these long desert stretches of information."[21] So what is this encyclopedic cruft doing?

The Three Casaubons and *Moby-Dick*

To answer this question, we will need a more specific account of how information is organized by encyclopedias, processed by readers, and incorporated into fiction. Though many approaches to encyclopedism have emphasized the impulse toward total knowledge as its defining characteristic, Hilary A. Clark more subtly argues that encyclopedism is better characterized by the discrete processes of "discover[ing]," "ordering," and "retriev[ing]" knowledge: for our purposes we will say that information is discovered by a researcher, ordered by an encyclopedist, and retrieved for practical use by a librarian.[22] This division emphasizes knowledge's collaborative and practical elements. After all, while information cannot be used if it is never discovered, it is equally worthless if it is never placed into context with other information or if it is not readily retrievable.

Furthermore this division shows the centrality of critical selection and compression, rather than exhaustive accumulation, to a coherent encyclopedic approach. Though the medieval encyclopedists may have believed they could compile all that had been discovered into one coherently structured work, by the Renaissance they realized that one had to select only the most important information to encyclopedize or else the encyclopedia would grow unfathomably large.[23] For that matter the Enlightenment *Encyclopédie* acknowledged that, because its entries were generating so many unruly webs of cross-references, the encyclopedia could no longer be adequately ordered into discrete subject headings, necessitating an alphabetical arrangement.[24] This requires the librarian to be as selective as the encyclopedist, because retrieval now can be conducted only by carefully selecting which of a subject's many avenues of cross-reference to proceed down. Though the recent history of encyclopedias has made retrieval somewhat easier through the tagging system first envisioned by Paul Otlet and now implemented in the contemporary electronic database, in other ways the librarian's task has become even more complicated, because the many links to any given tag might lead to so much data from so many various sources as to be overwhelming.[25] Navigating this abundance, then, becomes the chief problem of knowledge. Perhaps the most prominent example of this is the great encyclopedic project of our time, Wikipedia, whose highly cross-referenced and constantly accruing data on almost every conceivable subject frequently causes its entries to become disorganized and confusing to read.[26]

The goals and challenges involved in these three processes might be illustrated by well examining three literary Casaubons. The first is Isaac Casaubon, the sixteenth-century philologist and literary researcher widely regarded as the most learned man of his time, who made pathbreaking translations of many classical texts into modern languages and whose knowledge of Greco-Roman culture was unparalleled in Europe.[27] Though the Genevan's work relied on ordering and retrieval, his original linguistic discoveries were perhaps his most important contribution to knowledge, which introduced substantial and otherwise unknown data about classical languages to his contemporaries, including the historical derivation of the word *satire* (see chapter 4).

Ordering, on the other hand, is better exemplified by the encyclopedically minded Reverend Edward Casaubon from George Eliot's weighty *Middlemarch*, who works to compose a "Key to All Mythologies":

> [H]e had undertaken to show (what indeed had been attempted before, but not with that thoroughness, justice of comparison, and effectiveness of arrangement at which Mr Casaubon aimed) that all the mythical systems or erratic mythical fragments in the world were corruptions of a tradition originally revealed. Having once mastered the true position and taken a firm footing there, the vast field of mythical constructions became intelligible, nay, luminous with the reflected light of correspondences. But to gather in this great harvest of truth was no light or speedy work. His notes already made a formidable range of volumes, but the crowning task would be to condense these voluminous still-accumulating results and bring them, like the earlier vintage of Hippocratic books, to fit a little shelf.[28]

Casaubon has not discovered original facts but surveys and collects the facts that have already been discovered. He does not do so to express the totality of all that is known, but instead to judge how these facts may be combined and condensed into a cogent encyclopedia. However, he is unable to achieve this goal, because in the quarter-century he spends gathering his citations and deciding how they should be arranged, his methods are rendered obsolete: even if the project were not ultimately scuttled by his death, Casaubon realizes toward the end of his life that the publication would likely have drawn only ridicule.[29]

Our third Casaubon, the narrator of Umberto Eco's *Foucault's Pendulum*, exemplifies the work of the librarian. In the novel's middle, the underemployed scholar-protagonist decides to create a bibliographic detective agency catering to befuddled researchers. His clients lack neither information nor the ability to order it when available but often cannot retrieve a given datum's context when encountering it amid their daily mass of heterogeneous facts. For instance a confused economist comes to Dr. Casaubon to identify a Lord Chandos whom he cannot locate in any historical record, while an Italian publisher is puzzled as to where to fact-check information from an English author about a similarly evasive St. Anselm of Canterbury; Casaubon retrieves out of his elaborate index-card system that Chandos is a fictional Hugo von Hofmannsthal character and that Anselm is known as Anselmo d'Aosta outside the Anglophone world.[30] These are not themselves arcane facts, but knowing how to look for them when encountered out of their usual specialized context is not always easy.

The real problems of encyclopedism, then, are at least as much of practical use as they are of theoretical totality. The futility of projects like the Reverend Casaubon's are caused not by the Gödel Incompleteness Theorem, as Thomas Pynchon implies regarding a similar omnibus on European politics assayed by *Gravity's Rainbow*'s Brigadier General Pudding, but by limited resources, such as the reverend's mortal lifespan and his necessarily slow pace of work.[31] In many cases these are historically contingent: were Reverend Casaubon to labor with modern academic institutional support, his speed would be multiplied to the point where the project might become feasible. Similarly, as Eco's Dr. Casaubon already intuits in the 1980s, computer databases and search engines would soon decrease the difficulty in searching for out-of-context information.[32] Yet these advances always create new difficulties. Making material more easily accessible leads to more material overall, and while one might have better tools with which to manage that material, the demands on one's ability to filter become increasingly large. Since everything is preserved in the archive and has equal intrinsic value, it becomes increasingly hard to separate junk from useful material, and increasingly hard to read it at all. In Robert Musil's *The Man without Qualities*, General Stumm, attempting to find the best idea to ground the Year of Austria, goes to the library to read through its contents, only to realize that the three million volumes would take him ten thousand years to read. Exasperated, he asks the head librarian, "How do you find your way in this madhouse of books?" The librarian replies, "Because I never read any of them."[33]

Encyclopedism is not, then, primarily about epistemology or mastery, but about organizing, searching, and filtering an unmanageably vast amount of data into a form wherein it can be used. Given the ever-increasing amount of information to which we now have access, how we process that information, and especially how we separate out important data from junk, is a vital element of contemporary life. Consequently, while encyclopedic fiction cannot contribute to our discovery of knowledge, because we cannot reliably learn about any subject from reading it, it can engage and test our abilities to order and retrieve material. Since the cognitive acts involved in reading fiction and nonfiction are, as we saw earlier, closely related, an encyclopedic novel can engage readers' information-processing apparatus by challenging us to comprehend its vast amount of fictional data, modulating our attention so as to prioritize and group important pieces of information while deemphasizing less important information.

This is where cruft comes in. Cruft is an inevitable by-product of encyclopedism, as even the best encyclopedic processes will not be able to ignore or excise every piece of minimally relevant material. Though *Middlemarch* and *Foucault's Pendulum* discuss encyclopedic cruft, they do not produce examples of it, as Eliot spares us from having to read Reverend Casaubon's notebooks and Eco does us the same favor for Dr. Casaubon's index cards. Other encyclopedic novels, though, do present us with such text directly. How we manage such text speaks to how we will manage the overwhelming data of the real world.

Let's return to *Moby-Dick*'s "Cetology" chapter. What should we do when faced with this pointless encyclopedia? I think that Jed Rasula's claim that this chapter does not derive from an abstract drive to knowledge but instead from "indigence [. . .] delay, meander, filibuster" is a good place to start.[34] After all, Ishmael has gone to sea to escape the "honorable respectable toils" of Manhattan, whose rat race of prudent Protestants has been simultaneously so overwhelming and so predictable as to leave him with "nothing particular to interest me on shore."[35] When he finally reaches the water, his desire to purge himself of the draining cognitive practices of clerical life requires a drastic reordering of his relationship to information, which he achieves by creating an encyclopedia that is useless, leisurely, and idiosyncratic. Outside of its occasional amusing sentence, I am not sure that it contains any text worth deeply processing. It does, however, provoke a kind of boredom antithetical to that of the boring productivity required on land, one that consequently reorients Ishmael's and the readers' modes of attention. Only by establishing this opposed pole of cruft can the novel slow down and alter its readers' perceptions so that they are prepared for the ruminating, philosophical essays that make up much of the novel's middle. Quasi-scholarly chapters like "The Whiteness of the Whale" and "Fast-Fish and Loose-Fish" have too much poetry and economy to be true cruft in the manner of "Cetology," but without that chapter's assault on novelistic reading, we would not be able to process these essays in a manner commensurate to the mystical questions they raise.

This is a relatively limited use of encyclopedic cruft, reflecting a society whose abilities to generate and transmit text were beginning to accelerate but were nowhere near as vast as they are today. For the rest of this chapter, we will examine in some more detail several more recent and complex cases of cruft created by authors concerned with later periods' astounding powers to proliferate information.

The Unhappy Retirement of *Bouvard and Pécuchet*

Described in his notes as "two rather lucid, mediocre, and simple souls," the protagonists of Gustave Flaubert's final, unfinished novel, *Bouvard and Pécuchet* (initially projected at two substantial volumes, with only the first left mostly complete before his death), meet one evening on the Boulevard Bourdon after finishing their respective days' clerical work, become friends, then unexpectedly inherit money and merrily retire to the countryside, only to end up spending their final decades caught in cyclical, ill-fated investigations through various fields of knowledge.[36] Each time they decide to investigate a subject, they inevitably become so overwhelmed and confused by their reading that they make disastrous decisions leading to financial ruin and personal misery. As a result the novel's summaries of their attempts to synthesize the age's encyclopedic information often turn into incoherent, self-contradictory messes. For instance, in a characteristic passage, Pécuchet has these thoughts while arguing with the Abbé Jeufroy over the source of the Catholic Church's authority:

> But who granted it this infallibility?
>
> The councils of Basel and Constantine attribute it to the councils. But the councils often differ: witness what happened to Athanasius and Arius. The councils of Florence and Lateran confer it on

> the pope; but Adrian VI asserts that the pope can be as mistaken as anyone else.
>
> Mere pettifoggery! All this has no bearing on the permanence of dogma.
>
> Louis Hervieu's book lists the divergences: Once, baptism was for adults only. Extreme unction became a sacrament only in the ninth century. Real Presence was decreed in the eighth, Purgatory recognized in the fifteenth, and the Immaculate Conception dates from practically yesterday.
>
> And Pécuchet got to the point of not knowing what to think of Jesus. Three of the Gospels call him a man. In a passage from John, he seems to be the equal of God, but in another passage by the same author he recognizes himself as God's inferior.[37]

Even though Flaubert's free indirect discourse minimizes some of the text's tendencies toward nonsense (see chapter 4), many critics have still concluded that such catalogs of disordered pseudofacts are near-unreadable junk. Franco Moretti asserts that any honest reader will acknowledge that such text is "boring" and goes so far as to say it "abolish[es] the difference between a book on stupidity, and a stupid book."[38] Similarly Leo Bersani claims the style of Flaubert's encyclopedism makes the narrator's summarized information self-negating and meaningless, since "[h]uman knowledge is cut off from both its sources and its reception."[39]

Is there any value to such text? The best way to answer that question is to discover why Bouvard and Pécuchet's efforts are always doomed to failure. At the beginning of the twentieth century, René Dumesnil famously asked whether Bouvard and Pécuchet were imbeciles. More recently critics have supposed that the problem is not stupidity, but a hubristic encyclopedism emblematic of post-Enlightenment western culture, one abstractly seeking "truth for its own sake." Bouvard and Pécuchet's "Odyssean zest" to "master their age's knowledge," such critics believe, leads them to a "naive reliance on expertise and erudition" that is bound to failure.[40]

However, though Bouvard and Pécuchet are in fact described as seeking "truth for its own sake" once in the novel, Flaubert's use of that phrase implies something slightly different from what the critics suggest. During the fourth chapter, when the pair discovers that historians disagree profoundly on the French Revolution's relevant causes, events, and results:

> They no longer had a single fixed idea about the individuals and events of that time. To form an impartial judgment, they would have to read every history, every memoir, every newspaper and manuscript, for the slightest omission could foster an error that would lead to others, and on unto infinity. They gave up.
>
> But they had acquired a taste for history, a need for truth for its own sake.
>
> Perhaps the truth was more easily uncovered in earlier periods?[41]

This passage describes Bouvard and Pécuchet's pursuit of ancient history as motivated by an abstract desire for knowledge, yet this motivation arises only after a chapter and a half of futile and disillusioning research in other fields, ranging from chemistry to anatomy to architecture. If they are pursuing "truth for its own sake" only now, what have they been doing for the past fifty pages?

They have been trying to achieve very mundane goals, in fact. The great irony in evaluating Bouvard and Pécuchet's project as one of overweening ambition is that Bouvard and Pécuchet are tremendously *un*ambitious characters. When they meet, the copyists express no desire more profound than to escape the urban bourgeois boredom caused by loneliness, noise, and the grind of work.[42] They may wish to gain some culture but lack real intellectual goals.[43] When Bouvard's "uncle" (really his biological father) dies and leaves him a considerable fortune, Bouvard's first thoughts are not of the great life he might now live, but to exclaim, "We are going to retire to the country!"[44] Upon settling in a new home in chapter 2, their main concern is merely to tend some crops and a garden—a task that, a century earlier, another encyclopedically minded French novelist had presented as the exemplarily humble and self-contained activity for avoiding the snares of western philosophical, political, and scientific optimism.[45] Questing for total knowledge is the *last* thing Bouvard and Pécuchet seem interested in doing at this point. How do such characters, then, move from this blissful desire for leisure to spending their retirement agonizing over books?

They do it because, as it turns out, even Voltaire was too much the optimist. Tending one's own garden is not as simple as it sounds. Bouvard and Pécuchet misuse manure, sow too densely, and light their flowers badly.[46] They follow their neighbors' planting advice, purchase recommended tools, and follow practical farming wisdom, but nothing works—at least not consistently, as their occasional successes only prompt overconfidence and new failures.[47] Finally, when their homemade liqueur still explodes at the second chapter's conclusion, Pécuchet makes the fateful exclamation: "Maybe we just don't know enough about chemistry!"[48] Their fruitless learning, then, is prompted not by some abstract drive for total knowledge, but because the motley bricolage that is common sense fails them in everyday life. As the book's chapters proceed, Flaubert not only recounts the clerks' encyclopedic reading but alternates it with episodes describing the practical endeavors making those studies necessary: they study beauty and literature in chapter 5 with an eye toward courting the women with whom they are infatuated in chapter 7; they study political science in chapter 6 when their town is wracked by the 1848 revolution; they study religion and spirituality in chapter 9 because it had led them away from a suicide attempt at the end of chapter 8. That their self-education is no abstract exercise is clearest in chapter 10, when they try to use all they have learned to raise and educate the orphans Victor and Victorine. These encyclopedic efforts all fail, but only after *not* encyclopedizing has also failed: their love lives had also been unsuccessful before their readings in belles lettres, the revolution fizzled elsewhere without their help, and Victor and Victorine terrorized their previous foster household before Bouvard and Pécuchet's.

Still, why does their encyclopedic research meet with so little success? Some assert that it is the fault of "bourgeois values, beliefs, and life styles," which has alienated the clerks from everyday life, while others refer deconstructively to "the contradictions in scientific systems," but these charges do not stand up.[49] As Trilling writes:

> We therefore naturally suppose that the savageness which the book was intended to express [. . .] will constitute the fierce indictment of the bourgeois democracy.
>
> But again our supposition is disappointed. The horrors of the culture of the bourgeois democracy play a considerably smaller part that we anticipate. [. . .] If their tenant farmer cheats them, if their handyman diddles them, we cannot conclude that rural cupidity and the unreliability of rural labor have been brought about by the

> ascendancy of the bourgeoisie. If Bouvard, in two wonderful scenes, witnesses the terrible power of sexuality, in human beings and in peacocks, and cannot himself go much further in the direction of passion than a warm flush of inclination, or if Pécuchet contracts gonorrhea from his first sexual experience, we are not exactly being given examples of the effect of the bourgeois swinishness. When the hailstorm destroys the fruit which the two beginners have been almost successful in bringing to maturity, the phenomenon is not cultural but meteorological and, in its context, cosmological.[50]

And regarding Flaubert's supposed indictment of science:

> This is the mode of comedy, which perceives that if any abstruse discipline is confronted with an actual human being, no matter how stupid—and, indeed, the stupider the better—it is the person who is justified against the discipline. [. . .] In any vaudeville dialectic the intellectual advantage always rests with the obtuse or primitive person; the straight man, the patient teacher who believes in the subject, is always discredited. No discipline which is confronted with the simplicity, the intellectual *innocence*, of Bouvard and Pécuchet can long maintain its pretense to value.
>
> Then we must have in mind the large part that is played in the book by intellectual and quasi-intellectual absurdities which are as ridiculous as we want to call them, but about which it is impossible for a sensible man to be seriously troubled.[51]

The last point is slightly overstated, but basically sound.

No, their real problem is the obvious one, the one we least like to admit: that the world itself, and not merely its political, epistemological, or linguistic framing, is too complicated for any individual to understand. It is not that the world doesn't make sense—what tortures Bouvard and Pécuchet most is that from time to time they *do* understand something—but that it is beyond any person's (or pair of persons') capacity to systematically order it. Bouvard and Pécuchet's troubles are perhaps best addressed by Italo Calvino, who concludes, "However much effort they put into [their studies], the two scriveners are lacking in the kind of subjective gift that enables one to adapt ideas to the use one wishes to put them to, or to the gratuitous pleasure that one wishes to derive from them, a gift that cannot be learned from books."[52] "Gift" is the right word, because it emphasizes the arbitrariness of Bouvard and Pécuchet's struggles. That they fail to understand their chosen subjects either by logic or intuition seems no fault of their own: as Dumesnil concluded, Bouvard and Pécuchet are not actually imbeciles, and as Ronald T. Swigger further points out, they "have a knack [. . .] for penetrating to the very conceptual center of whatever field they are studying, for finding the paradox, the circular argument, or fatal antinomy."[53] They simply cannot order together their information well enough to have consistent success. Yet they have no alternative but to continue. Encyclopedism might not reliably produce understanding adequate to the real world, but without it, as we noted earlier, everyday functioning becomes impossible. Encyclopedizing is not an abstract activity divorced from the world, then: it is simply life by another name.

If Bouvard and Pécuchet's encyclopedizing is fated only to produce gibberish, though, is there any use in our reading it? Trilling is right to an extent when he claims that there are few points in the novel that present real philosophical conundrums: professional historians can navigate around conflicting perspectives on historical eras without losing faith in their discipline, for instance, while theologians might argue plausibly why one might have faith despite scriptural contradictions. However, Trilling's "sensible" reader is not likely a theologian, and even if so, he is not likely also a political scientist. Understanding any given subject requires specialized study that precludes time spent at other subjects, and one's ignorance of those subjects may at some point prove debilitating. Bouvard and Pécuchet may be "mediocre" individuals, but all of us are necessarily mediocre at most things, and yet somehow we have to muddle through life anyway. As we lack expertise, our confusion will likely bring us to a great deal of information that we will be unable to order into context, and as such will be rendered nonsense. And even when we do stumble into an insightful thought, as Bouvard and Pécuchet occasionally do, how would we know that it is not merely more nonsense? That is the great problem the novel presents, the one that prompted Flaubert himself to accidentally recapitulate the activities of the characters he set out to satirize by reading a reported fifteen hundred books over his final six years to try to understand the subjects the clerks could not. We need to read Bouvard and Pécuchet's confused thoughts, then, to distinguish the confusion caused by their lack of knowledge from the profound realizations that they are not quite able to recognize.

Let's return to the passage from the Pécuchet-Jeufroy exchange quoted at the beginning of this section. The passage might be considered pure cruft by two types of readers, one believing Pécuchet too stupid to understand the clarity of Christian doctrine and another finding Christianity as a whole to be such nonsense that Pécuchet wastes his time trying to make it coherent. Though I am more partial to the second view than the first, neither is quite right. Consider the final paragraph, in which Pécuchet—who, let us remember, has been dissuaded in the previous chapter from suicide by hearing a hymn to Christ—begins to question the Gospels. What does their apparent contradiction mean? Does it mean that Jesus was not God, or does it simply point to human writers' confusion in the face of the divine? Either way, does it imply that Pécuchet's decision against suicide was illegitimate, or might the hymn have revealed to him some greater spiritual truth independent of Christ? These are not stupid questions—Pécuchet has a vital interest in figuring out the second—but unfortunately the illogical contradictions of Catholic doctrine swamp this thought so thoroughly that he is unable to focus on it, causing his reasoning to become a disordered blob. As readers we need to attempt to manage the contradictions of the different sources more adeptly, lest we fall prey to the same conundrums.

Bouvard and Pécuchet, however, are finally unable to distinguish anymore between sense and nonsense. They revert to the simple copying of their working days, jotting down everything they see and collating into alphabetical order, no matter how stupid or trivial, the entries that were to constitute the novel's unfinished second volume.[54] Doubtless this would have been even more boring and cruft-laden than the first. While Trilling believes that at the book's end, "Bouvard and Pécuchet, sitting at their double copying desk, having a work and each other, but stripped of every idea, every theory, every shred of culture beyond what is necessary to keep men alive and still human, are [. . .] intended by Flaubert to be among the company of his saints," I do not know that it is wise to praise such uncritical mindlessness.[55] Much of what Flaubert did produce, after all, appears a dull collation of his time's readymade popular wisdom, as with entries like "DARWIN: The fellow who said we descended from apes," most of which deserve skimming.[56] In some cases it does seem as if Bouvard and Pécuchet are almost able to reassert critical judgment and even irony, but it's not actually clear whether this is intentional. Is "CORN (foot): Predicts changes in weather better than a barometer. Removing one carelessly can be very dangerous: cite examples of horrible accidents" Bouvard and Pécuchet's parody of folk wisdom or an unselfconscious perpetuation of it?[57] It's difficult to say, and that indeterminacy is perhaps what characterizes the book's encyclopedic difficulties more than anything else.

This is Bouvard and Pécuchet's tragedy: they realize the importance of information to their lives but never develop the ability to order and filter it. Instead of mocking the pair's stupidity and wondering whom to blame for it, then, we should try to find ways to manage the information, both valuable and useless, that they cannot. Their failed enyclopedizing may be arcane and obscure at times, but it is far more relevant to practical life than we may wish to acknowledge.

The Deadly Endnote: *House of Leaves* and *Europe Central*

Such are the struggles with knowledge faced by the late nineteenth century. While many of these problems still remain a century and a quarter after Flaubert's death, some have been alleviated by the increased accessibility of the expertise necessary to order data. This has come, however, at the cost of exponentially increasing the amount of data through which we must wade to retrieve any information, furthered by the expansion of print culture at the end of the nineteenth century through the growth of the World Wide Web at the start of the twenty-first. Consequently the ability to retrieve information from amid the cruft becomes all the more important. Though it might seem that the print novel would have increasingly little to say to the cognitive problems presented by this state of affairs, it remains resourceful by virtue of being more capacious than film and television and more manageable than the Internet. We will conclude this chapter, then, by looking at a device distinctive to the printed book that nonetheless has interesting applications to digital culture, and which has become the contemporary mega-novel's exemplary method of incorporating encyclopedic cruft: the note.

The use of notes in literary fiction is a strange development. After all, the note has typically been a scholarly tool for confirming that one has represented factual information accurately and for facilitating its retrieval, with the traditional view being, as Anthony Grafton puts it, that "the text persuades, the notes prove."[58] As Grafton points out, notes are rarely processed with much depth and are likely to go unread entirely by anyone but the most invested scholar, meaning that "[i]n the end, the production of footnotes sometimes resembles less the skilled work of a professional carrying out a precise function to a higher end than the offhand production and disposal of waste products."[59] After all, notes break one's attention, moving it to a different part of the page or even to the back of the volume, and if there is not likely to be much of interest, one is best served cognitively by ignoring them. This would seem to render the note especially unsuited for fiction, where the text's nonreferentiality inhibits even their reference function.

Yet the note's history is not wholly drab. As Hugh Kenner notes, the development of the footnote allows one "a way of speaking in two voices at once," which, as Shari Benstock argues, can create a complex, self-reflexive tonal texture not unlike the kind found in literary narrative.[60] Such uses have inspired a minor tradition of notes in literature. While Edward Maloney and Gérard Genette describe a wide variety of possible types, for our purposes they may be divided into two chief, diametrically opposed categories.[61] The first mimics the traditional scholarly use, best exemplified by T. S. Eliot's *The Waste Land*, in which an author, though writing fiction, seeks to establish a factual basis for his text by referring back to scholarly sources and documents, thus bolstering the authority of his voice. The second type, though, takes advantage of the note's bivocal possibilities by letting playful narrators insert undermining asides or allowing additional narrative voices to chime in. The erudite eighteenth-century writers who employed it (Swift, Pope, Fielding, Sterne) found this type of note useful for parodying the scholarly voice, a use taken up in the twentieth century by the nutty annotators in Borges's stories and in Vladimir Nabokov's *Pale Fire*. This use is opposed to the first, as the note's creation of multiple narrative planes and potentially conflicting voices is typically construed as "subverting the unity of the text and destabilizing, rather than affirming, the central narrative."[62]

Over the past several decades, notes' similarity to hypertext has made them appealing to experimental writers with an eye toward the digital, allowing them to simulate the way readers retrieve hyperlinked online data.[63] What is different about the recent use of notes in encyclopedic fiction, however, is that they combine elements of the two incompatible types described, both piling on mounds of apparently genuine information while also producing inaccuracies, nonsense, and narrative inconsistency. Because the resulting third type of note can be neither processed as accurate information nor read for a consistently duplicitous literary effect, it creates a texture of cruft that gums up the novel, rendering retrieval of information extremely difficult.

We may observe this in the ninth chapter of Mark Z. Danielewski's *House of Leaves*, a novel framed as a commentary by twenty-something ne'er-do-well Johnny Truant on a manuscript he's discovered (one already loaded with notes, fragments, and comments) by a blind old man named Zampanó, which purports to describe a documentary film by photographer Will Navidson (fictional, even within the world of the novel) about a labyrinthine haunted house. (If this were not enough narrative layering, there is an additional editor commenting on Truant's work.) Many of these notes can be grouped in the second category described above, but as the passage reproduced in the introduction might show, those in chapter 9, in which Navidson's acquaintances explore the labyrinth's physics-defying space, work somewhat differently.[64] Of the chapter's first twelve pages, fewer than four are part of the main narrative, with the rest taken up by marginal notes, and while half of these pages are occupied by Truant's digressive comments and another two present a blotted footnote about the Minotaur, the rest of Zampanó's marginal text identifies quotations and suggests books for further reading, many of which are invented. What are we to make of this reading list: "for further insight into mazes, consider Paolo Santacangeli's *Livre des labyrinthes*; Russ Craim's "The Surviving Web" in *Daedalus*, summer 1995; Hermann Kern's *Labirinti*; W. H. Matthews' *Mazes and Labyrinths*; Stella Pinicker's *Double-Axe*; Rodney Castleden's *The Knossos Labyrinth*; Harold Sieber's *Inadequate Thread*; W. W. R. Ball's "Mathematical Recreations and Essays"; Robinson Ferrel Smith's *Complex Knots—No Simple Solutions*; O. B. Hardison Jr.'s *Entering the Maze*; and Patricia Flynn's *Jejunum and Ileum*"?[65] Five entries really do exist (Kern's, Matthews's, Castleden's, Ball's, and Hardison's), but the other six are unique to the novel. These aren't particularly funny—as are, say, the fake entries in Michael Martone's comic tourist manual *The Blue Guide to*

Indiana, which lists locations like the Trans-Indiana Mayonnaise Pipeline—nor do they really toy with narrative unreliability in the manner of Nabokov's demented Charles Kinbote, since their annotating voice is so devoid of personality.[66]

The reason for this cruft grows clearer as chapter 9 progresses. As alluded to in the introduction, its margins quickly become overloaded with notes listing dozens of architectural terms, but while these are initially overwhelming, the notes turn out to be almost all cruft, mechanically cataloguing only objects and styles *not* contained by the labyrinth. A quick scan demonstrates in each case that there will not be any surprises, insights, or even moderately useful information as they proceed from one page to the next. The insignificance is further underlined by our gradual realization that, while the labyrinth's rooms continue near endlessly, each is completely empty, enabling later chapters to represent them by simply replacing this ornate marginalia with large swathes of white space. The notes' apparent function, then, is not to be deeply processed in their entirety, which even the novel's partisans acknowledge is not really feasible, but to disorient, giving readers the sensation of being overcome by an impossibly labyrinthine void.[67] After realizing that there is little worth retrieving from this glut of data, we can adjust our attention accordingly, skip much of the marginalia, and follow the main text onward.

This is an interesting and playful use of cruft, if not an especially taxing one. Once one has oriented to the space and realized that its long lists are simply blocks of junk information, there is no need to undergo any complex attention modulation in retrieving data from them. Scholarly notes in fiction, though, become more problematic in other encyclopedic novels. For instance William T. Vollmann's *Europe Central*, which depicts in impressive depth German-Soviet relations from 1914 to 1975, ends with over one hundred pages of endnotes and bibliography documenting his extensive research for the novel. From these and his author's note, which insists he has "researched [. . .] carefully" and tried to be as "accurate [. . .] as possible," it may appear that Vollmann intends to seriously use the endnotes to verify his authority and educate readers.[68] However, *Europe Central*'s endnotes often have an ambiguous relationship to the factuality of the data they supposedly aid readers in retrieving. For instance the author's note admits that though the endnotes document some of the novel's central moments, they are unable for practical reasons to rigorously cite every historical element of which the novel makes use.[69] Consequently it often becomes unclear, even on important matters, which incidents from the novel are based on the historical sources and which Vollmann has made up. Some scholars of Dmitri Shostakovich, for instance, have complained that nearly everything in the novel about the composer's romantic life has been fabricated, even though Vollmann's frequent reference to real biographical resources gives the impression of historical accuracy.[70] Similarly, while the crucial chapter on the Russian general Andrey Vlasov's defection to the Nazis is substantially endnoted, these notes are littered with disclaimers that Vollmann "loosely" adapted his sources and sometimes even changed them altogether.[71] How loose was this adaptation? It would take substantial independent research to find out, and this would render the book's encyclopedism redundant. What is the function, then, of an endnote that admits its source does *not* verify the main text?

This problem might be circumvented if the notes more self-consciously undermined the narrative voice, but as Michael Hemmingson has observed, Vollmann's notes, in stark contrast to those of *House of Leaves* or *Pale Fire*, are usually devoid of polyvocal play or metafictional layering, with far more *Waste Land*–esque erudition to their bland (and usually accurate) citations than there is postmodern gamesmanship. Granted, Vollmann's frequent allusions to the standard German and Soviet encyclopedias of the time, *Meyers Lexikon* and the *Great Soviet Encyclopedia*, do nothing if not demonstrate how reference works may be corrupted when designed by perverse power systems: as one character ominously pronounces, "encyclopedias are subject to revision."[72] Yet our rejection of the German and Russian encyclopedias likely derives not from disapproving of their overweening grasps to systematize knowledge, but, conversely, from our own systematic knowledge that they are factually wrong about Hitler and Stalin.

It might still be argued that Vollmann's endnotes assure of us of his deep study of the historical period, yet justice regarding this darkest of subjects can and has been achieved with much less pretense to historical veracity. Roberto Bolaño's brief fictional encyclopedia *Nazi Literature in the Americas*, which presents thirty short narratives in the form of encyclopedia entries describing American Nazi writers, is every bit as profound as Vollmann's, even though each of Bolaño's tales is fiction. While Bolaño's book also concludes with an extensive bibliography, the hundreds of secondary resources it lists in its "Epilogue for Monsters" differ from Vollmann's endnotes in one key respect: none of them actually exists.[73] Looking at Bolaño's scholarly references beside Vollmann's, though, should highlight that the latter *might as well* be made up, given how freely he has adapted them, how rarely readers will consult the works he has listed (or even read the endnote text at all), and how little they are capable of communicating within their fictional context.

The primary function of the notes in both *Europe Central* and *Nazi Literature in the Americas*, then, seems not to be facilitating the transmission of any particular information, but implying via their vast catalogs of supplementary titles the overwhelming amount of information available on an overwhelming topic. There are so many different cross-references emanating from their bibliographies, and so little context to provide a sense of which may be significant, that they ought to impress on us some humility in trying to understand it all. Their cruft is a reminder that while books remain our most potent tool to communicate information, so many are published at a given time, and on so many subjects, that retrieving sufficient information on even the most important issues might be unfeasible.

"Handling Information in a Competent, Grown-Up Way": Navigating *Infinite Jest*

Even Vollmann and Bolaño's elaborate bibliographic cruft, though, have limited impact on how we process their novel's information on a word-by-word basis. This is not the case for the notes in David Foster Wallace's *Infinite Jest*, which centers on the obscenely gifted Incandenza family of the Enfield Tennis Academy, the recovering addicts at nearby Ennet House, and geopolitical intrigue involving legless Québécois terrorists' search for a film cartridge so pleasurable it permanently overrides its viewers' desires for anything else. Many critics have described how the book's unusual and encyclopedic structure, comprising not only 981 pages of multithreaded narrative but a further 388 endnotes covering subjects as diverse as pharmaceutical chemistry, calculus, political history, and tennis has a disorienting effect on the reading process. Frank L. Cioffi writes, "it is at once an easy, pleasurable novel to read—full of narrative action, excitement, local delights—and at the same time a trying, annoying, difficult novel that is constantly interrupting itself." He admits, "I did not abandon it, though I confess I was tempted to."[74]

These difficulties are posed most potently by the endnotes. As with the other fictional encyclopedic notes we have discussed, they do not fill a traditional literary-note function, as on the one hand they undermine the authority of the narrative voice too seriously to be used for regular data retrieval (as when the nutty Dr. Dolores Rusk's reference to something she calls the "Coatlicue Complex" keys to a note reading "No clue"), but on the other present too much straightforward, minimally relevant information (like that "B.P.D." stands for "Boston Police Department") to really parody encyclopedism.[75] In many cases the data is barely even readable. Early in the novel, for instance, when the narrator introduces us to Enfield, he provides a categorization of its students' recreational drug preferences keyed to five rapid-fire endnotes.[76] Note 8 is a representative example:

> [8] I.e., psylocibin; Happy Patchesa; MDMA/Xstasy (bad news, though, X); various low-tech manipulations of the benzene-ring in methoxy-class psychedelics, usually home-makable; synthetic dickies like MMDA, DMA, DMMM, 2CB, para-DOT I-VI, etc.—though note this class doesn't and shouldn't include CNS-rattlers like STP, DOM, the long-infamous West-U.S.-Coast "Grievous Bodily Harm" (gamma hydroxybutyric acid), LSD-25 or -32, or DMZ/M.P. Enthusiasm for this stuff seems independent of neurologic type.
>
> Homemade transdermals, usually MDMA or Muscimole, with DDMS or the over-counter-available DMSO as the transdermal carrier.[77]

How does one read this note? If one does not have a background in pharmaceutical chemistry or practical knowledge of synthetic street drugs, one simply can't. Since the narrator declines to explain the distinctions between, or qualities common to, the drugs he lists, the note's sequence of acronyms and Greek prefixes will be illegible to uninformed readers. At the same time, those with the knowledge to successfully differentiate these terms have nothing to learn: for them the passage's catalog of various drugs is entirely redundant. In either case the note adds nothing of practical use to our understanding of the narrative.

One might decide, then, that the notes are simply unreadable, like those we examined from *House of Leaves*. However, one should not merely skip through the notes, because as it turns out there actually *is* quite a lot of important data in Wallace's endnotes. As Marshall Boswell writes, "Readers of the book quickly learn that the notes can provide useless information, essential information, extra but nonessential narrative, or even, at times, narrative that is more important to the ongoing novel than the passage to which the note is attached. Readers can, and even must, devise some way to read through the book that allows them to keep their focus on the story while also mining the notes for all their information, comedy, and readerly pleasure."[78] Though he mentions this merely in passing, I think Boswell may have identified the novel's most profound narrative element. How we "devise some way to read through the book" is not just an interesting side-effect of the novel's structure: it is central to the way our minds interact with *Infinite Jest*'s data. Some of the most important information for understanding the book's overall narrative is contained in the notes, yet to identify it one has to wade through lots of cruft, which threatens to terminate any attention one might try to spend on it. Consequently the notes' alternating pointlessness and importance require a constant modulation in the rhythm of one's reading between focused attention and different levels of skimming in seeking out vital information.

Note 24, the filmography of the alcoholic and self-destructive auteur James O. Incandenza, provides a good case study. Taking up eight and a half pages, it comprises the production details and plot summaries of all Incandenza's seventy-eight films. The note is loaded with cruft, the extent of which has not been fully appreciated.[79] The five that merely read "*Untitled.* Unfinished. UNRELEASED" are pure cruft: their inclusion cannot further or enrich the novel's plot or characters, because Wallace tells us nothing about them, nor are they are necessary for factual completeness, because these unfinished films exist only inasmuch as they are invented by Wallace in the note.[80] Other entries are barely less insignificant, like the eight undescribed and "conceptually unfilmable" works called "found dramas," in which a randomly selected person's life, unseen and unrecorded by Incandenza, is arbitrarily decided to be a work of art.[81]

Even some substantial entries are clearly cruft, because as Wallace's narrator acknowledges, "a lot of [Incandenza's oeuvre . . .] was admittedly just plain pretentious and unengaging and bad."[82] Consider this one: "*Fun With Teeth.* B.S. Latrodectus Mactans Productions. Herbert G. Birch, Billy Tolan, Pam Heath; 35 mm.; 73 minutes; black and white; silent w/ non-human screams and howls. Kosinski/Updike/Peckinpah parody, a dentist (Birch) performs sixteen unanesthetized root-canal procedures on an academic (Tolan) he suspects of involvement with his wife (Heath). MAGNETIC VIDEO, PRIVATELY RELEASED BY LATRODECTUS MACTANS PROD."[83] Like most of the entries, almost half of this entry comprises boilerplate technical specs, which will be given almost no attention. But the film summary is not much more significant itself, since *Fun With Teeth* merely reproduces its targets' stupid clichés rather than exaggerating them into a reductio ad absurdum, precisely the sort of pointless postmodern irony against which Wallace railed in his essays and that chapter 4 will analyze in more depth.[84] Such passages dull cognition while diverting reading from a main narrative—which, incidentally, has been interrupted while in the midst of its vital overview of Incandenza family history—to which they seem largely irrelevant. It becomes very tempting to skip the note and return to the main text. That seems to be what Burn implies should happen when he writes that the encyclopedic tendency in the novel can become "a potentially dangerous addiction," suggesting it would be better instead to "take data pretty much as it comes," because those characters who do "may seem to know less, but they are in many ways more alive."[85]

Yet amid the cruft, many entries are important to examine. For instance, if one abandons note 24 at *Fun With Teeth*, deciding that the next six pages will likely be no more readable than the earlier notes' pharmaceutical catalogs, one will not read the summary of *It Was a Great Marvel That He Was in the Father without Knowing Him*, a filmed version of a scene described earlier in the book wherein Incandenza posed as a therapist as a pretext for having a conversation with his eleven-year-old son Hal.[86] This entry is not merely redundant, as it adds information about Incandenza inaccessible in the earlier passage. In the first version of the scene, Incandenza comes off not only as bewilderingly overbearing but as both so poor at responding to his son (whose speech he seems at times unable to hear) and so bafflingly inept at disguising his appearance that readers would be justified in questioning his sanity. The film summary, however, acknowledges that the father-therapist character is "suffering from the delusion that his etymologically precocious son [. . .] is pretending to be mute," demonstrating both that Incandenza (as director) is aware of how unhinged his own behavior appears and that he understands that the discussion's failure rests largely with him and not Hal.[87] This insight into Incandenza's recognition of his inability to communicate is necessarily incommunicable elsewhere in the novel.

Other entries similarly reflect on events in Incandenza's life. *As of Yore* appears to be a filmed version of a rambling monologue delivered by Incandenza's father during the former's childhood, while the passage in which Incandenza describes his inspiration in developing annular fusion becomes fodder for the film *Valuable Coupon Has Been Removed*.[88] In particular a perusal of the films starring an actor named Cosgrove Watt—a man alluded to only a handful of times otherwise—creates a sequence of meditations on Incandenza's anxieties about the difficulties of fatherhood articulated nowhere else in the novel so well, not even when Incandenza tries (in wraith form) to discuss the issue directly with Don Gately.[89] Retrieving this portrait of an artist unable to express his emotional intelligence anywhere except in his films, however, requires readers to dig through lots of junk data that does not contribute to it. "Taking data as it comes" is insufficient to achieve this result: one needs to be both disciplined enough to keep moving through the endnotes' cruft without resorting to skimming and flexible enough to avoid getting stuck trying to analyze the whole "pretentious and unengaging and bad" filmography at constant focused attention.

It is not an easy task. This difficulty in modulating between levels of attention is itself represented in the novel, during the scene in which we see how the teenaged Hal is able to watch his father's touching film *Wave Bye-Bye to the Bureaucrat* only as part of a wallowing "weird self-punishment" marathon of the latter's work, also involving *Fun with Teeth* and the putrid *Blood Sister: One Tough Nun*, whose amalgam of endless genre clichés proceeds at such excruciating length as to render the movie's intent to satirize religion totally invisible to Hal and his fellow glazed-over, sarcastic spectators.[90] That Hal's own mode of self-insulating irony is not sufficiently flexible to allow modulation is among the chief reasons he suffers a nervous collapse near the book's climax.

How these films test readers' cognitive processes shows in microcosm how the notes work in the novel as a whole, especially regarding the book's political background. For instance the larger motives of "Les Assassins des Fauteuils Rollents" are revealed only at the end of an otherwise tedious seventeen-page note mixing unrelated (and at times extraneous) documents and dialogue about the Incandenza family.[91] Note 304's description of why the A.F.R. are legless in the first place is even more cumbersome to retrieve, as the note is keyed only at page 732 despite being q.v.'d in no fewer than four earlier endnotes, 39, 45, 173, and 302, the middle two of which do nothing but q.v. the later note.[92] This offers readers the dilemma of either losing focus on the main narrative to skip ahead or maintaining attention on the main narrative while remaining ignorant of a key fact. That the novel's baroque politics are visible only to those who have found some way to modulate their attention to effectively retrieve data is perhaps best exemplified by note 114, keyed from an otherwise innocuous description of Incandenza's father's career as the Man from Glad, reading "© B.S. MCMLXII, The Glad Flaccid Receptacle Corporation, Zanesville OH, sponsor of the very last year of O.N.A.N.ite Subsidized Time (q.v. Note 78). All Rights Reserved."[93] In the midst of two lines of cruft corporatese, we are suddenly and unceremoniously told that the last year recounted chronologically by the book is also the final year of the novel's dystopic North American state's calendar. It is not clear as to whether this proclamation portends the restoration of political sanity or the end of civilization as we know it, yet in a book whose plot is left largely unresolved, this is one of few clues we have toward the fate of the novel's characters and imagined world.

The problem of filtering out pointlessness resonates outside the endnotes, too. Cruft's distinctive combination of expansiveness and emptiness also characterizes the recursive, paralyzed thoughts of the novel's many addicts. One character describes (in a footnote to endnote 269) the cycle of "Marijuana Thinking," in which many of the novel's characters are caught, as a tendency to "involuted abstraction" wherein addicts are hypermotivated to the point of being functionally unmotivated, stuck fighting through "labyrinths of reflexive abstraction that seem to cast doubt on the very possibility of practical functioning."[94] Not only are the self-negating thoughts this attitude produces essentially cruft, but in attempting to escape this state (which is experienced in analogous forms by the novels' overachieving student-athletes, crazed politicians, and manic depressives), addicts often veer into a different type of cruft, exemplified by the clichéd mantras of the novel's twelve-step programs. As one disgruntled AA member points out—again, in an endnote, number 90—"If you have some sort of Substance-problem, then you belong in AA. But if you say you do *not* have a Substance-problem, [. . .] why then you're by definition in *Denial*, and thus you apparently need the Denial-busting Fellowship of AA even more than someone who can admit his problem."[95] Such formulations pointedly circumvent all critical or independent thought.

Interestingly, though critics have recognized how dangerous the addicts' encyclopedic overthinking can be, they have tended to champion how twelve-step programs' "routines seem magically to have the power to release [them] from [their] addiction."[96] This enthusiasm among admirers of a novel as wildly inventive as *Infinite Jest* for a philosophy that one addict, Geoffrey Day, approvingly describes as turning one's "will and life over to the care of clichés" would be extremely puzzling were it not for the way those clichés provide relief from the manic textual overload that the addicted characters produce in the novel's other sections.[97] It's probably not an accident that, in the Ennet House scenes, the endnotes are cut back significantly, nor that they do not begin until two hundred pages have passed and we have had time to absorb how overwhelming *Infinite Jest* will be. Only after having endured the inescapable involutions of Kate Gompert's depression, the coked-up violence and semidecipherable English in yrstruly's monologue, and the painfully detailed analysis of how Americans' endlessly reflecting physical anxieties destroyed the videophone can the mantras that Day recites seem even remotely appealing.[98]

Fundamentally, though, Ennet's clichés are nearly as meaningless as the addicts' overthinking, tranquilizing attention to the point of making it wholly docile. Their cruft should be tolerated only as a temporary cure for the greater destructiveness of addiction. Perhaps this is best seen in how Day himself, not a week after praising AA's focus on clichés, goes on the rant quoted above from note 90. While the endnotes always bring with them the possibility of endlessly proliferating junk, they also allow the possibility for independent critical reflection, because to read them at all requires the development of a subtler attentional modulation. If readers seek to escape not just the hyperactive mindlessness exemplified by the addicts but mindlessness entirely, they cannot be totally repelled by the endnotes' frequent overload but must keep returning to them, hopefully better able to filter out the cruft. James Incandenza himself realized this principle late in life, understanding how AA forced its members to simply exchange one "slavish dependence" for another, characterized by intolerable "vacant grins and empty platitudes."[99] He sought to overcome both forms by addressing them in his films—as we are told most directly in an endnote, number 289—but attempting to create meaning from waste is an unstable and dangerous process, something surely known by the designer of the annular fusion program employed to generate power from garbage in the novel's Great Concavity. That Incandenza finally sticks his head in a microwave, however, is as much caused by submitting to recovery-program clichés as by resisting them, because they have rendered his mind incapable of sustaining a meaningful life.

In reading *Infinite Jest*, we can only hope to develop our attention modulation to the point where we can avoid Incandenza's fate. Whether we can reliably do so is unclear. In the years prior to his own suicide, Wallace expressed increasing anxiety about the mounting obstacles to adequate information ordering and retrieval posed by the information age. In his forward to the 2007 volume of *Best American Essays*, Wallace chastises Americans that "[t]here is just no way that 2004's re-election [of President George W. Bush] could have taken place [. . .] if we had been paying attention and handling information in a competent, grown-up way."[100] Yet as soon as he makes this criticism, Wallace acknowledges that this grown-up information handling is all but impossible. For each of the major world issues that a twenty-first-century American would need to consider when making such informed decisions, he notes, "the relevant questions are too numerous and complicated" to adequately investigate: if one really wants to understand any of the important political issues of our time, one would have to pore over so much specialized economic, historical, and sociological research in search of the core problems that "[y]ou'd simply drown. We all would. It's amazing to me that no one much talks about this—about the fact that whatever our founders and framers thought of as a literate, informed citizenry can no longer exist."[101] That's probably true, unfortunately. The difficulties that rendered Bouvard and Pécuchet incapable of managing their lives' information in the nineteenth century have so dramatically escalated that it's not clear how anyone can confidently avoid the sorts of catastrophes that befell them.

This insight is one that Wallace critics, trained professionally to reject the kind of independent subjecthood to which the quote above aspires, have appeared reluctant to embrace. In his essay on encyclopedism in *Infinite Jest*, for instance, Matt Tresco suggests that the inconsistent importance of the endnotes' information reveals "the absence of an ordering or categorizing principle," favorably comparing the novel to Wikipedia in that both are "are always threatening to overspill, to negate the purpose of their organizing principles" and thus challenge hierarchization.[102] Though the similarities between *Infinite Jest* and Wikipedia are interesting, more important is their markedly divergent incorporation of cruft. Wikipedia articles' frequent inability to distinguish between important and trivial information, which often results in unchecked cruft, does little to help its users to keep from drowning in the "tsunami" of information of which Wallace writes: in fact it becomes part of that tsunami.[103] *Infinite Jest*'s much more carefully calibrated cruft could not be more different in this respect, because its directed impact on attention is better able to reveal the inadequacies of our cognitive processes and guide us toward developing better ones. Inasmuch as there is any hope of mitigating the worst effects of information overload, we must develop our abilities to order and retrieve information to their maximum capacities. Encyclopedic novels are a powerful tool for doing so, not because they include information that is valuable itself, but because they force us to learn how to navigate around their junk data to find text that is actually important.

3 Life-Writing

The Life of Monday, Tuesday, and Every Day Afterward

The first two chapters have dealt with cruft that mimics the excessive, born-textual data of reference guides. However, ever since Tristram Shandy set out to recount his life and opinions, only to find upon finishing the fourth volume that he was barely past his own birth and that "things have crowded in so thick upon me, that I have not been able to get into that part of my work, towards which, I have all the way, looked forwards," we have known that the details of a single life can sprawl out similarly.[1] While Tristram finds this situation stressful, though, many writers and critics see in it opportunity. Life-writing genres are often celebrated for their expansive capacity, incorporating as they do the fleeting thoughts and actions of everyday experience that are often left out of literature. For those who value ordinary life—"the life of Monday or Tuesday," as Virginia Woolf put it—a mega-novel recounting its minutiae might be the ideal aesthetic form.[2]

In contrast to mega-novel subgenres addressed in other chapters, large-scale life-writing seems especially appealing to female writers. Susan Gubar observes that this may be because female authors have often felt as if they had no proper aesthetic subject but themselves, and thus their novels "cannot be finished because they are as ongoing and open-ended as the lives of their authors."[3] As an example she cites Dorothy Richardson's *Pilgrimage*—the novel to which the term "stream of consciousness" was first applied—whose thirteen books follow the life of its protagonist, Richardson's thinly fictionalized alter-ego Miriam Henderson, from adolescence to middle age. For similar reasons Rachel Blau DuPlessis suggests that for women who possess "the thrilling ambition to write a great, encyclopedic, holistic work," the most attractive form "is a diary: her bag, her desk."[4] Her exemplar is Doris Lessing's *The Golden Notebook*, which intersperses excerpts of a relatively conventional, domestic fiction by its writer-protagonist Anna Wulf (a character, again, bearing many similarities to her author) with entries from a set of Anna's journals covering her life over the 1950s. Both *Pilgrimage* and *The Golden Notebook* are loaded with details of their protagonists' lives, addressing not only their major romances and political commitments but what they happened to notice as they crossed their apartments' thresholds and what they felt about how tonight's dinner tasted. Such mega-novels of saturated female experience seem to say, with Hélène Cixous, "I, too, overflow."[5]

For that reason, though, many readers find them self-indulgent and boring. John Rodker, one of the editors of the *Little Review*—the modernist journal in which excerpts of *Pilgrimage* were serialized alongside early passages from *Ulysses*, beneath a banner reading "Making No Compromise with the Public Taste"—lost patience with Richardson's novel after the first few books, writing, "In this welter of material the reader feels like a Kafir carefully searching for the diamond swallowed the day before. Much is irrelevant, sundry sparkles attract but they are not the indubitable article."[6] Lessing's novel provoked similar responses, such as Randall Swingler's comment in the *Times Literary Supplement* that Lessing's "material has gotten badly out of hand, and in desperation she has bundled the lot together and chucked it at the reader to make of it what he can."[7] We might put this rejection down to any number of causes, including sexism, but its core may be the sense that, as Charles Altieri put it, "we have plenty of ordinary life without asking our poetry to submit to it."[8] We all experience everyday life already, that is, and it tends to be quite boring—so why should our literature give us more? Recalling our discussion from chapter 1, we might say that the quotidian tends to be predictable, hence largely redundant, hence not necessarily worth reading.

To address whether life-writing intentions can justify mega-novel excess, we will need to survey thought on the aesthetic value of the everyday and on those life-writing methods that aim to capture it, particularly the stream of consciousness and the diary. In doing so, though, we will see that the mega-novels that are praised for achieving these goals, like *The Golden Notebook* and *Pilgrimage*, generally extend well beyond their theoretical frameworks. What they do instead, I will argue, is highlight the complicated dynamic—observed as early as William James's *Princi-*

ples of Psychology—between consciousness and attention. Life-writing mega-novels explore the problems in how we conceive and define consciousness, discovering that different methods of doing so will always suppress some aspects of experience in their efforts to encompass others. By seeing how even the most broad-minded novelistic approaches to the life of the mind fail to adequately achieve the conscious fulsomeness at which they aim, we may come to a better understanding of conscious variety and, as important, why attentional selection is necessary to control its contents.

Why It's Hard to Describe Conscious Experience

What is consciousness? For literary studies the most influential framework has been James's "stream of consciousness." "Consciousness," he wrote, "from our natal day, is of a teeming multiplicity of objects and relations [. . .]. Such words as 'chain' or 'train' do not describe it fitly as it presents itself in the first instance. It is nothing jointed; it flows."[9] In combination with Henri Bergson's similar notion of *durée*, James's emphasis on consciousness's rich, interwoven nature had a profound influence on modernist depictions of interiority. Reviewing the earliest installments of *Pilgrimage*, May Sinclair summarized the novel (approvingly) with the description, "Nothing happens. It is just life going on and on. It is Miriam Henderson's stream of consciousness going on and on."[10] Edmund Wilson similarly praised James Joyce's *Ulysses* for finding "the unique vocabulary and rhythm which will represent the thoughts of each" character.[11] In these accounts the stream of consciousness is praised for its elimination of narratorial mediation and for transmitting directly the entire contents of characters' minds, not just their inner speech. As Lawrence Bowling defined the technique, it is "that narrative method by which the author attempts to give *a direct quotation of the mind*—not merely of the language area but of the whole consciousness."[12] Stream of consciousness's contribution to literature, then, is to show that what characters rationally think is inextricable from all the other sensations, impressions, and thoughts underlying their conscious selves.

However, there are a number of potential problems with stream-of-consciousness prose. First, James's account actually argues that it is an unsuitable style for art. Insisting that the profusion of unimportant data in the stream's "undistinguishable, swarming *continuum*" would overwhelm any legitimate object of interest if left unchecked, he claims what "gives [. . .] works of art their superiority over works of nature, is wholly due to elimination."[13] Here James seems in alignment with his brother's aesthetic, insisting on literature's need to circumscribe the endlessly interwoven elements of mind so as to avoid generating "loose baggy monsters." And the tool of James's eliminative process is the "habits of attention."[14] For him the stream of consciousness and attention serve as opposed poles, the former serving to expand the mental life and the latter to constrict it. As James writes, "without selective interest, experience is an utter chaos."[15]

The ensuing century of research on consciousness, meanwhile, has questioned whether consciousness can be conceived as a linear stream at all. While many regard the question of whether we are conscious of something as a strictly binary question—that is, either we are or we are not, without intermediate grades—most conceptual schema regarding consciousness include multiple levels, rather than a single stream.[16] Even though Antonio Damasio's "movie-in-the-brain" metaphor for consciousness is relatively assimilable to a stream, he adheres to a distinction between core consciousness (i.e., integrated momentary awareness of time and place) and extended consciousness (i.e., a cross temporal sense of self and possibility).[17] Bernard Baars's global workspace theory, meanwhile, uses the metaphor of a theatrical spotlight that can illuminate anything on a large stage (but will emphasize only a small area at a given time) for consciousness rather than a stream, identifying the dimly lit areas surrounding the spotlight as "fringe consciousness."[18] Hardline materialists, like Daniel Dennett, reject the idea of a stream entirely, pointing to experiments in change blindness to suggest consciousness is "gappy" and possesses only the "*apparent* continuity" of a stream, generated largely from post hoc rationalizations that reconcile "multiple drafts" of experience.[19]

The basic problem is terminological. Since the mind is multilayered, and each layer functions in part by suppressing what occurs at other layers, what is contained by the term "consciousness" will often be less an empirical question than one of whether a given theorist wishes to include certain experiences within the concept. We can see this problem within James's own work, as his desire for an inclusive stream leads him to include elements of the mind that are clearly nonconscious: for instance he defines the stream as comprising the manifold of our "sensations" and "thoughts" but admits there are many sensations of which "common men never become aware," which would imply we are not conscious of them.[20] This inclusiveness threatens to negate the entire concept of "consciousness" by eroding its ability to discriminate between conscious and nonconscious mental contents. Similarly Dennett's insistence that our inability to register blind spots demonstrates that conscious continuity is illusory is countered by those like Gerald Edelman and Giulio Tononi, who insist that since consciousness has the ineluctable phenomenal appearance of continuity, that continuity (illusory or not) must be an aspect of consciousness.[21] There are several other tricky cases. For example we experience dreams both phenomenally and neurally as if they we were conscious, yet dream-states lack conscious elements like wakefulness and sensory response—so are we conscious when we dream? If we only notice the humming air conditioner when it turns off, or the squirrel across the street when it starts to run away, or the missing keys in front of our eyes after five seconds of staring blankly at them, where do they fit? It is difficult to say, but any act of exclusion will tend to move our definition closer to the abstracted rational thought that the stream of consciousness is designed to theoretically counterbalance, and any act of inclusion will gradually erode the special phenomenal status of consciousness as distinct from nonconscious brain activity.

In literary theory and practice, those interested in the stream of consciousness tend toward expansiveness. Literature, it is often suggested, ought to be "consciousness-raising," a view rooted (as we saw in chapter 1) in Viktor Shklovsky's defamiliarization, which rails against the human tendency for life to become automatic and nonconscious. "After being perceived several times," he writes, "objects acquire the status of 'recognition' [. . .]. We know it's there but we do not see it, and, for that reason, we can say nothing about it."[22] Shklovsky's goal is that conscious perception grow at the expense of nonconscious processing, a desire shared by the various aesthetes and ideological critics who have proselytized for defamiliarization. One prominent example is the recent vogue for a theory of the everyday, which, in Michel de Certeau's words, desires that "everyday practices, 'ways of operating' or doing things, [should] no longer appear as merely the obscure background of social activity."[23] Yet this attitude, it turns out, is problematic, because increased consciousness is not an unalloyed good. Consciousness is resource-intensive when compared to nonconscious activity, and actions associated with conscious mental states tend to be less skilled than nonconscious ones.[24] This may sound counterintuitive, but it should make sense to anyone who has worked steadily to improve at an instrument or game: you perform best when you perform without thinking. To make oneself as conscious as possible, then, is to hinder general skillfulness. If one really tried to be mindful of every dish one washed, every step one took, every key one pressed, life would become impractically cumbersome.

That is why most theories of the everyday tend toward contradiction: for something to be part of the everyday means for it to be habitual and hence nonconscious; to construct a theory of it, though, is to pay special attention to it and give it conscious meaning, removing it from the everyday. As you can practically make only so much conscious, attempts to formulate the everyday tend to crash into either the Scylla of Henri Lefebvre's overdetermined Marxist pomposity (e.g., "All we need to do is simply to open our eyes, to leave the dark world of metaphysics and the false depths of the 'inner life' behind, and we will discover the immense wealth that the humblest facts of everyday life contain") or the Charybdis of Certeau's disparate mumblings ("one can follow the swarming activity of these procedures that, far from being regulated or eliminated by panoptic administration, have reinforced themselves in a proliferating illegitimacy [. . .] combined in accord with unreadable but stable tactics to the point of constituting everyday regulations and surreptitious creativities").[25] If we are to pay attention to any previously everyday aspect of life, then, it had better be because there is a particular reason to devote conscious energy to it rather than because we want to increase consciousness indefinitely.

As literary theorists have argued for some decades, novelistic prose is the most refined method we possess for depicting consciousness, and as we saw in the introduction, all reading comprehension requires both conscious effort and selective attentional focus. Consequently consciousness's inherently messy terminological status will cause those attempting to depict it to produce divergent prose styles. That is likely why even the most canonical, consensus examples of stream-of-consciousness writing have few common formal characteristics. Here are excerpts from the three texts perhaps most associated with the technique. First, Proust's madeleine:

> Will it ultimately reach the clear surface of my consciousness, this memory, this old, dead moment which the magnetism of an identical moment has travelled so far to importune, to disturb, to raise up out of the very depths of my being? I cannot tell. Now I feel nothing; it has stopped, has perhaps sunk back into its darkness, from which who can say whether it will ever rise again? Ten times over I must essay the task, must lean down over the abyss. [. . .]
>
> And suddenly the memory revealed itself. The taste was that of the little piece of madeleine which on Saturday mornings at Combray (because on those mornings I did not go out before mass), when I went to say good morning to her in her bedroom, my aunt Léonie used to give me, dipping it first in her own cup of tea or tisane. [. . .] But when from a long-distant past nothing subsists, after the people are dead, after the things are broken and scattered, taste and smell alone, more fragile but more enduring, more immaterial, more persistent, more faithful, remain poised a long time, like souls, remembering, waiting, hoping, amid the ruins of all the rest; and bear unflinchingly, in the tiny and almost impalpable drop of their essence, the vast structure of recollection.[26]

Second, Leopold Bloom approaching Dignam's funeral in the "Hades" episode of *Ulysses*: "Gasworks. Whooping cough they say it cures. Good job Milly never got it. Poor children! Doubles them up black and blue in convulsions. Shame really. Got off lightly with illnesses compared. Only measles. Flaxseed tea. Scarlatina, influenza epidemics. Canvassing for death. Don't miss this chance. Dogs' home over there. Poor old Athos! Be good to Athos, Leopold, is my last wish. Thy will be done. We obey them in the grave. A dying scrawl. He took it to heart, pined away. Quiet brute. Old men's dogs usually are."[27] Third, Peter Walsh crossing Regent's Park in Virginia Woolf's *Mrs. Dalloway*:

> A sound interrupted him; a frail quivering sound, a voice bubbling up without direction, vigour, beginning or end, running weakly and shrilly and with an absence of all human meaning into
>
> *ee um fah um so*
> *foo swee too eem oo—*
>
> the voice of no age or sex, the voice of an ancient spring spouting from the earth; which issued, just opposite Regent's Park Tube sta-

> tion from a tall quivering shape, like a funnel, like a rusty pump [. . .].
>
> Through all ages—when the pavement was grass, when it was swamp, through the age of tusk and mammoth, through the age of silent sunrise, the battered woman—for she wore a skirt—with her right hand exposed, her left clutching at her side, stood singing of love—love which has lasted a million years, she sang, love which prevails, and millions of years ago, her lover, who had been dead these centuries, had walked, she crooned, with her in May [. . .].[28]

These are all closely focalized depictions of mind, but there are few similarities among them. Proust's passage registers the close relationship between sensory stimulation and memory, but Marcel's perfectly structured sentences evidence a highly refined, attentive reconstruction that suppresses the immediate conflicts and confusions that our raw sensations engender. We see the latter more vividly in *Ulysses*, where the sensory input of the gasworks sets off a series of clipped, associative sentences that carry Bloom fleetingly across thoughts about illness, advertising, and his father's dog—yet Joyce must conversely suppress those aspects of consciousness (emphasized by Proust) that can observe and articulate the more complicated aspects of its own processes.[29] Woolf's sentences, meanwhile, are as long as Proust's but as twisting as Joyce's, depicting consciousness less as a private matter than an intersubjective state that floats from Peter to the narrator to the demented old woman to (just beyond the end of this passage) Rezia Warren Smith, without obvious break. It would be a stretch to map any of these literary depictions of consciousness directly onto the models of consciousness described above, but much as there is no scientific consensus as to what constitutes consciousness, there is no literary consensus as to how to write it. As a result the stream of consciousness cannot justify textual excess merely on the grounds that it is attempting to record all the contents of thought, because there is no way to do that. Like every other kind of writing, it requires heavy authorial selection.

This principle also holds for novelistic experiments with the diary form, equally an attempt to linguistically capture present experience. The increased academic interest in diaries over the past forty years has often celebrated their incorporation of the undirected details of life, in contrast to more polished literary forms that treat these things as beneath notice. William Matthews, editor of Samuel Pepys's diaries, noted that diaries are the one place where we might find "the trifling details and reflections that happen to interest the diarist from day to day."[30] Felicity Nussbaum, in a more poststructuralist direction, generalizes this principle to the diary's ability "to imitate human chronology without overt rearrangement, evaluation, or closure" and narrate "events in their incoherence, lack of integrity, scantiness, and inconclusiveness."[31] Diaries, that is, are not submitted to the compression and streamlining that other narratives forms are. As Philippe Lejeune puts it, "The diary's value lies in its being the trace of a moment. If I begin fixing things the next day, I do not add value to my diary: I kill it."[32] In this manner we might imagine the diary as a whole record of an individual's thought.

Yet the diary cannot really achieve that end for much the same reason that stream-of-consciousness writing cannot. As the Japan scholar Edward Seidensticker noted upon writing his memoirs, even detail-oriented inclusionism turns out, in fact, to exclude things. Looking over his youthful diary, he writes, "there may be a certain tendency to leave the really important things for a later day, when they can be lingered over, dissected, commented upon [. . .]. I am astonished at things I did not mention."[33] By focusing on his most immediate impressions, that is, he ignored elements of his experience that required more distanced reflection. As Lawrence Rosenwald notes, this comes down to a conflict between diaristic modes of "honesty" (i.e., recording one's imprecise initial impressions) and "accuracy" (i.e., recording events thoughtfully and with precision).[34] We are likely to have several layers of thought about any given event, and these will tend to be incommensurate to each other. If we praise a diary for seeming authentic, we probably mean only that the author is "giving his first thoughts rather than his second—or rather, perhaps, his sixth rather than his seventh."[35] But it is not clear that we ought to privilege the former over the latter, and since including them all would devolve the entry into nonsense, the diary must exclude.

Even when we acknowledge that diaries are highly selective, the form remains ill suited for adaptation to the novel, since real diaries are nearly unreadable and often not meant to be read. As Rosenwald notes, many diarists regard their entries primarily as a product of writing rather than an object for reading, and would never find any interest in reading what they had once written.[36] Moreover, as Lejeune adds, dedicated diarists may produce dozens of volumes over the course of their lives, and no one but later editors are likely to read them exhaustively.[37] Of course there are plenty of novels that incorporate the diary form, but as Valerie Raoul notes, these generally involve the "subjugation of one set of conventions, those of the diary, to another set, those of the novel"—that is, diary-novels are fundamentally novels, not diaries.[38] As she writes with reference to diarists who also wrote diary-novels (e.g., André Gide), "One has only to compare the real and fictional journals of authors who have produced both [. . .] to be struck by the most obvious differences between the two, notably of length and time-span."[39] Novels, after all, have to end at some point, and as Lejeune writes, "A real diary is always written without the knowledge of where it will end."[40] Beside the logistical problem of endless expansion, the sense of a novel's ending controls and streamlines its narrative structure, while a diary can change direction every day.

What, then, can we make of mega-novels that engage in excessive life-writing? As we will see in the rest of the chapter, the protagonists of *The Golden Notebook* and *Pilgrimage* are entirely aware that much of what they record about their minds is pointless waste. They proceed with their efforts, though, because the conventional, nonconscious habits extant within their environments do not provide them with models of life that they find fulfilling. Attempting to map out lives as "free women," they must consciously build a way of life from the ground up, no matter how inefficient and boring that process might be. As they go about perceiving the world, they try to expand their consciousness as widely as they can to discover new possibilities, but in their doing so, much of what they register ends up not contributing to liberation. It takes them some time to gradually work out the relationship between attention and consciousness that allows them to become—in part—free women.

The Golden Notebook's Many Drafts

As Gayle Greene notes, the mixed initial reviews for *The Golden Notebook* frequently complained that its content was too "sociological," especially within the notebooks that Anna keeps to chronicle her writer's block: the black, reflecting on her past in colonial Africa and her subsequent first novel about the experience; the red, detailing her relationship to the Communist Party; the yellow, a fictionalized take on her doomed affair with the married ex-communist Michael; the blue, a diary of her domestic life; and the golden, which attempts to join them.[41] Greene interprets these reviews as combining New Critical antipolitical sentiment with sexism, but the "sociological" epithet probably has as much to do with the novel's narrative strategy as its perceived social stance. As if to test Raoul's principle that a diary-novel cannot help but really be a novel rather than a diary, the notebooks accrete so many quotidian details of Anna's life as to sometimes seem copied over from the day-to-day events of her author's. As Robert Taubman wrote in the *New Statesman*, "the book's striking quality is not that it is difficult in a profound or original way, but rather the reverse—the conviction it carries of being a close transcription of actual experience."[42] For the reasons we discussed above, this does not necessarily make for good fiction.

To overwhelm readers with that kind of naturalistic immediacy was part of Lessing's intention, but only part. In Lessing's retrospective preface to the book, she writes that it was designed to present the inner life "before experience has shaped itself into thought and pattern," which seems to align with the sentiments expressed above by diary partisans about the value of daily experience.[43] Yet at the same time, she expresses dissatisfaction at how postwar "novels, stories, art of every sort, became more and more personal," suggesting *The Golden Notebook* should be read instead as "novel of ideas."[44] These two arguments are in tension with each other: how can the novel get at the inchoate immediacy of experience while also constituting something as highly composed as "a novel of ideas"? The preface itself does not explicitly reconcile these approaches, but the novel's structure—alternating a domestic novella about (and, we later find, written by) Anna called *Free Women* with the notebooks mentioned above, with only brief, bracketed editorial comments to join them—seems to acknowledge a competition between different modes of perception. The fact that Anna is never really satisfied with any of her experiments—indeed frequently disparages and negates them in retrospect—should show us the difficulty that recording one's "true" experience entails.

Let's look at the most prominent case in which Anna declares a notebook passage to be waste. On September 15, 1954, she decides—in response to Michael's claim that she "make[s] up stories about our life together"—that she will "write down, as truthfully as I can, every stage of a day."[45] The resulting entry is dozens of pages long, accounting for each waking hour between five in the morning and midnight. It is, explicitly, an exercise not only in life-writing but in heightened consciousness, as Anna writes, "I chose to be very conscious of everything that happened yesterday."[46] Yet at the end of this entry, the bracketed voice tells us, "The whole of the above was scored through—cancelled out and scribbled underneath: No, it didn't come off. A failure as usual." The entry is followed by short paragraph summarizing the entirety of what has gone before in ten sentences.[47] Almost all of what she wrote, Anna implies, was a waste of space and, implicitly, conscious energy. Why?

Well, in some cases, there is a clear overelaboration of minutiae that is better left unconscious and automatic. For instance take this passage, in which Anna prepares her daughter Janet to go to school:

> While her room warms I go into the kitchen and prepare her breakfast—cereal, fried eggs and tea, on a tray. I take the tray back into her room, and she eats her breakfast sitting up in bed, and I drink tea and smoke. The house is dead still—Molly will be asleep for another two or three hours. Tommy came in late with a girl; they'll be asleep, too. [. . .] My firmness reassures her; and she goes on with her breakfast. Now the room is warm, and she gets out of bed in her white sleeping suit, looking fragile and vulnerable. She puts her arms around my neck and swings on it, back and forth, singing: Rockabye baby. I swing her and sing—babying her, she was become the baby next door, the baby I won't have. Then, abruptly, she lets me go, so that I feel myself spring up like a tree that has been bent over by a weight. She dresses herself, crooning, still half-drowsy, still peaceful.[48]

This whole passage—along with Anna's subsequent struggle with Janet to put on her raincoat and to later cook and serve her dinner—is boiled down in the second version to five words: "Janet as usual, no problems."[49] The implication is that, since these are largely common, habitual activities—ones that might be found on, say, any family television show of the period—depicting them in detail is mostly pointless. Later on Anna denigrates this passage, along with several similar ones describing her similarly habitual bodily functions, "because of its assumption that if I wrote 'at nine-thirty I went to the lavatory to shit and at two to pee and at four I sweated,' this would be more real than if I simply wrote what I thought."[50] The experience may be "real," but being "real" doesn't mean it deserves conscious thought, or that becoming more conscious of it for the sake of being more conscious—the philosophy she rejects when it is presented by her therapist, Mrs. Marks—will aid her in any way.[51] While critics like Deborah Martinson argue this passage shows how, "[c]aught between cultural taboos and literary tact, diary writers [like Anna] cannot record the sum of experience," it is the very notion that recording the "sum of experience" is either possible or desirable that causes Anna trouble.[52]

What Anna desires here is less fidelity to empirical correspondence than—as the film projector in Anna's dreams later jibes her—"the correct emphasis."[53] Though Anna sometimes claims the goal of the diaries is to be "truthful," she means this more in the manner of aesthetic truth than empirical truth, which is why she criticizes the entry for not "coming off" rather than for getting any particular datum incorrect.[54] This is why poststructuralist approaches to the novel (as well as some of Anna's own commentary) implying that Anna's failures are due to "the incapacity of language to mean" are offtrack: the problem is not hermeneutic signification, but aesthetic selection.[55] Anna insists several times that these are not "literary problems," yet that is not to limit the aesthetic but rather to expand it from the literary to the real world.[56] (*Aesthetic*, after all, derives from the Greek word for "perception.") She wants to find an aesthetic that will generate the right combination of the different elements of her conscious experience—the domestic, artistic, romantic, and political—in such a way as to help her understand what it would mean to be a liberated woman. However, the daylong diary experiment shows her that, even though she wishes to integrate all the disparate elements of her life so as to understand it fully, it also includes many elements that deserve less attention than she'd thought.

Yet the extent of Anna's reductive backlash against this passage overshoots the mark. We need only look to how the second entry begins by calling September 15 "A normal day," only to acknowledge later that two major life events occurred: her decision to leave the Communist Party and her realization that Michael was ending their affair.[57] Indeed, while the entry's compression seems to be a critique of overconsciousness, the fact that these two events occurred on the same day suggests the benefits of heightened consciousness. Anna observes that her experiment "changed the shape of the day. That just because I was conscious I made it a special day."[58] There is no major external event, that is, causing her break with either the communists or Michael. Instead she consciously notices all the microdynamics about these relationships—like her "housewife's disease" of permanent detail-oriented anxiety and her ritualistic function as the "captive critic" in the party—that doom them.[59] The second entry, though, eliminates most of this as ruthlessly as it does her morning routine. Why? It seems that Anna's displeasure with the cruft in her account is so intense that she is willing to shear away almost anything else just to get rid of it.

What should Anna have kept, and what was justly cut? In most cases the distinction is clear, but there is an interesting gray area. Among the unimportant bodily events Anna regrets recounting, alongside "going to the lavatory," is "changing a tampon."[60] A fair amount of space is, indeed, devoted to Anna's period.[61] In one respect tampon changing is as habitual and unimportant as any of the other everyday processes Anna describes, and she even claims it is "of no particular importance" to her.[62] But in another respect, it is revolutionary: as DuPlessis wrote, this is "[t]he first Tampax in world literature."[63] When critics praise the novel for registering "distinctively female experiences," the daily life of women otherwise unrecorded in literature, this is the kind of thing they mean.[64] Moreover consciously registering her tampon sends Anna into a meditation about how she dislikes the smell of menstruation and how she resents her period, which "would not have been in my head at all had I not set myself to be conscious."[65] Anna acknowledges the value of these observations later on when she notes that, though tampon changing is done "on an almost unconscious level, I can recall every detail of a day two years ago because I remember that Molly [Anna's flatmate] had blood on her skirt."[66] Yet her ambivalence about being conscious of it may still be somewhat justified. She *wants* her period to have the quality of the everyday—the less conscious, the less unpleasant—so using the word "blood" and speaking of its attendant discomforts "will be giving a wrong emphasis."[67] That she elevates this experience from the nonconscious to the conscious, she feels, "is changing the balance, destroying the truth"—with, again, "truth" here a matter of aesthetic emphasis.[68] In other words the tampon references introduce a new feminine subject to literature but also raise a complicated question about when and whether discussing such subjects has actual value.

This pattern of diligent recording, followed by vicious erasure, repeats itself later in the blue notebook. Following the September 15 entry, Anna spends eighteen months simply listing "short factual statements" accounting for her time on a given day without "emotionalism," such as "Janet is sick. Janet is well. Molly is offered a part she likes/doesn't like, etc." In some ways this seems like a diary without consciousness, the pure everyday. Yet we are told that it, too, like the first single-day entry, has been crossed out, with Anna writing, "So all that is a failure too."[69] What's more, not only does Anna cross it out, but the entries are not even directly presented. Although they must cover over a hundred pages of the blue notebook, they are summarized in a few sentences within the brackets. It is as if not only Anna, but the editorial voice, understands that the whole thing would be cruft and not worth asking anyone to read. Why do they both respond so harshly? Anna does not say, but the answer is probably the general absurdity in asking readers to consciously process text from which conscious experience has been almost wholly extracted.

Similar acts of erasure occur with her creative work. For instance, when asked (ridiculously, she feels) to send some journal entries to a small magazine in lieu of new fiction, she constructs a parody journal by a pretentious young writer. It is, essentially, a one-joke piece that stretches out for two pages. A characteristic entry reads, "April 18th. *Outside Buckingham Palace*. George Eliot is the rich man's Gissing. Must write to my father. Only ninety dollars left. Will we ever speak the same language?"[70] Here Anna evades her difficulty in finding an aesthetically satisfying integration of her own consciousness by writing an intentionally bad diary, as if her superiority to its impoverished sensibility will somehow validate her own. That the particulars of the text are worthless may be seen by how, after meeting an American writer named James Schafter, she tells us, "We concocted another thousand or so words," without needing to give examples.[71] What those words are, after all, is irrelevant, because we get the gist of the idea from the original's first few entries—which weren't all that funny, anyway. Anna soon understands, though, that these pastiches are not a solution to her problems. First, she and

James take no pleasure when his faux-African story, the pastiche "Blood on the Banana Leaves," gets accepted to a magazine as a serious piece, causing them to stop writing such work.[72] Second, at the end of the yellow notebook, she presents a series of story scenarios based on her contentious relationship with Saul Green, concluding with "The Romantic Tough School of Writing," a burlesque of his style.[73] After two pages of monotonous pseudo-Angry-Young-Man jabber, though, she writes, "If I've gone back to pastiche, then it's time to stop," promptly ending the notebook.[74] As we will see in more detail in chapter 4, merely copying an idiocy or cliché as Anna does in these cruft pastiches does not make a text into effective satire, but just propagates the thing it is supposed to be criticizing. It is not a path to a more developed consciousness.

Anna behaves similarly toward the news. Much of the notebooks is made up of news clippings. In *Free Women*, in fact, Anna becomes so obsessed that she starts pinning them to her walls.[75] The first group in the notebooks takes up a full dozen pages, covering three years in which Anna does not write any entries in the blue notebook. Anna tells Mrs. Marks that they are the "events that seemed important" to her at the time, and for a few pages they are edifying, as the headlines about nuclear proliferation and red hunting contextualize Anna's personal breakdown.[76] But they recount nothing that a reasonably knowledgeable reader wouldn't know, and, regardless, they get repetitive quickly enough that I suspect most readers skim them. As if to acknowledge the tedium of endless, monotonous news headlines, later groups of clippings in the black and red notebooks are summarized in brackets with only a few sentences.[77] As with the blue notebook's similar elisions, this implies the clippings were mostly cruft in the first place.

If Anna feels her notebooks repeatedly fail as satisfying depictions of consciousness, what would a successful style look like? Not *Free Women*—or at least not according to the novel's critics, who generally think it "fails in its very selective and 'objective' focus to convey the complexity of Anna's emotional life."[78] It would be something of a disappointment for an experimental novel, after all, if its best aesthetic mode turned out to be that of the relatively conventional, well-made novella.[79] The novel's title suggests that the ideal integration of consciousness might be found in the golden notebook, which Anna claims at the end of the blue notebook will contain "all of myself in one book."[80] Many critics seem to agree, believing that this volume, by "opening [it]self to chaos and emotion, achieves a mature vision" and shows why, as Lessing's preface puts it, we "must not compartmentalise."[81] Yet there is an unfortunate truth about the golden notebook that, so far as I have seen, no one is willing to acknowledge—not even Lessing, who claims to have intended it to be Anna's longed-for conscious integration.[82] The golden notebook cannot represent any breakthrough because it is stylistically indistinguishable from the final passages of the blue notebook. Both chronicle Anna's tumultuous affair with Saul Green; both proceed, diaristically, over a large number of undated but more or less continuous entries, interspersing reality, dream, and mental breakdown; both address the pair's strained relationships with communism; both refer to Anna's tendencies to fictionalize her romances; and, if anything, the blue deals more extensively with her ties to Africa in its references to the imprisoned dissident Tom Mathlong and the agitator Charlie Themba. I see no synthesis in style or content within the golden notebook that does not already exist in the blue. That synthesis is impressive on its own merits, but given that Anna is at her most mentally unwell during this period, we would be hard-pressed to cite it as the optimal model of conscious integration.

The only thing that marks the golden notebook as different is its ending, with Anna ceding the book to Saul, who proceeds to write (using a sentence provided by Anna) a moderately successful novella about the Algerian revolution. Yet because the novella is only summarized in brackets, we have no basis on which to determine whether it is any good or achieves "the correct emphasis." Certainly Saul has not appeared to develop intellectually since his arrival at Anna's flat, as he is no less of a preening, erratic boor than when we first met him. Conversely Anna receives the sentence from Saul that turns out to be the first sentence of *Free Women* (and consequently *The Golden Notebook*), breaking her writer's block. But again most of the novel's critics do not especially like *Free Women*, and given that the novella's conclusion sees Anna's fictional avatar abandon writing and take up a respectable job as a marriage counselor and join Labour, its composition does not seem to entail the kind of radical new consciousness Anna has searched for.[83] Even those who credit Anna with being the editor assembling *The Golden Notebook* cannot quite explain how the novel can be a literary success if she has simply collated together five individually failed notebooks and a novella that ends with the rejection of writing.

We might understand why if we realize that, while the golden notebook barely differs from the end of the blue, they are collectively quite different from the end of *Free Women*, which also treats the affair with Saul by fictionalizing him as "Milt." In the blue and golden notebooks, their relationship is depicted over nearly one hundred pages: in *Free Women* it covers merely ten. As with the two diary entries covering the single day in September 1954, this constitutes a long initial draft followed by a dramatically compressed revision. Written in a tranquilly recollective third person rather than a diaristic first, *Free Women*'s mental breakdown is less intense and more melancholy. The repartee between the lovers, too, is more polished, because Milt is simpler than the chameleon Saul: his needs are more self-aware, and his effect on Anna is more unequivocally cathartic. There is no happy ending—Anna and Molly drop their artistic ambitions, and Milt produces nothing on his own—but its closure is more pat. That closure has a clear cause: Milt clears up Anna's madness by stripping the news clippings from the walls. This is a blunter figurative event than anything that occurs in the golden notebook, where Anna's imagination is dominated by a gnomic tiger and a wily projectionist. It implies that Anna's acts of textual accumulation are not the solution to, but the cause of, her unease and must be excised. It is perhaps the most striking of the novel's consciousness-reducing moments. Yet in context it also seems like the right action for Anna's health. In the preface Lessing says the juxtaposition of the golden notebook and *Free Women* is meant to ask "how [. . .] this small neat thing [can] be true when what I experienced was so rough and apparently formless and unshaped," and most critics have taken this rhetorical question as a criticism of the novella.[84] The question is not unambiguous in being such a criticism. It may equally cast doubt on the value of the "formless and unshaped" experience, which, if left so amorphous, can lead to serious mental illness.

This juxtaposition is confusing only if we read the novel's climax as necessarily making some specific argument about what Anna's ideal consciousness should look like. But there are at least three Annas by the chronological end of the novel, each of whom takes a different approach to the representation of mind: Anna the *Free Women* character, who rejects writing entirely; Anna the *Free Women* author, who pursues a well-crafted realist aesthetic; and Anna the notebook writer, who indulges in a variety of experimental modes. *The Golden Notebook* does not reconcile them. In her efforts to truly portray female experience, Anna realizes that, frequently, many of its aspects are excluded from conventional writing not owing to oppression, but because conflicting elements of the mind always suppress each other's conscious expression. The different forms of life-writing Anna uses should not be ranked, then, as if one supersedes the others. They are, instead, complementary reminders that we must keep dipping back into the variety of our experiential modes, flexibly attending different things that may or may not turn out to be interesting. Separating Anna's mind into different notebooks does "compartmentalize" it, preventing its parts from interacting as well as they could—but it also gives them each space that they would not be allowed otherwise to discover interesting things that might be suppressed. (Imagine the radical Anna of the red notebook admitting, as she does in the blue, the pleasure she takes in cooking for a man.)[85] *Free Women*, far from being a parody of realism, represents the value of a reconstructed consciousness that shears away its incoherent parts, allowing the major themes to shine through. Critics who denigrate it generally ignore how much their sense of the book's gender politics relies on the opening dialogue among Anna, Molly, and the latter's ex-husband Richard, not to mention the clarity of Anna's novel-opening comment that "as far as I can see, everything's cracking up."[86] And as protagonist of *Free Women*, Anna shows us that there are benefits, sometimes, in simply reducing consciousness across the board. It may lead to conformity, but that's often preferable to the breakdown caused by trying to attend to everything. The golden notebook shows an attempt to integrate everything, but only one attempt—intense, beautiful at times, flawed, and necessarily temporary.

Finally, there is a fourth possible Anna, the bracketed editorial voice. This voice wants to show us the varieties of consciousness side by side and the value in their separate discoveries, even though the process leads to incompatibility and failure. This "multivocal, palimpsestic, personal, autobiographical, documentary, analytic, essayistic diary-novel," as DuPlessis calls it, aims for a solution that probably cannot be permanently found.[87] Yet Anna will, nevertheless, keep trying different ways of refining her consciousness, one day (and one page) at a time.

A *Pilgrimage* to Where?

Near the beginning of *Free Women*, Molly comments of her and Anna's situation as self-sufficient female roommates, "I've decided that we're a completely new type of woman," to which Anna responds, "There's nothing new under the sun."[88] Anna is, of course, correct. In Richardson's *Pilgrimage*, whose first book was published a half-century prior to *The Golden Notebook*, we have an account of another unmarried woman, Miriam Henderson, who also supports herself by whatever means are at hand, pursues artistic aspirations, and tries to learn what it means to be a free woman. *Pilgrimage* is, in fact, even more expansive in its presentation of the protagonist's conscious life than *The Golden Notebook*, with its thirteen books totaling three times the page count of Lessing's already-hefty novel. Jean Radford, at the start of her monograph on *Pilgrimage*, writes, "If Doris Lessing's *The Golden Notebook* can be compared to a capacious cupboard in which the reader rummages at will, *Pilgrimage* is more like an enormous room, crammed with portraits and memories, with light and dark places, scents and textures, dusty cretonne at the window—but with the window always open to the streets of London."[89] *The Golden Notebook* may often feel cluttered, but at least it is formally contained by its structural plan, whereas *Pilgrimage* often seems indefinitely open to anything that might enter Miriam's mind.

Its method for producing so much material is the stream of consciousness, but early analyses of *Pilgrimage*, while granting the innovative style, typically claimed it was used to excess.[90] In his book on the stream of consciousness, Shiv Kumar, despite praising the Bergsonian sophistication of Richardson's treatment of mind, brusquely concludes that, "[d]evoid of any dramatic interest, symbolic meaning, or skillful patterning, *Pilgrimage* remains at best only a literal and rather uninteresting record of Miriam's stream of consciousness."[91] Melvin Friedman similarly claimed that "even specialists find the need of skipping large sections which merely reiterate the same artistic convictions, with no appreciable change in treatment or technique."[92] We might put these criticisms down to sexism, except that Richardson's fellow female modernists often reached the same conclusions. A frustrated Katharine Mansfield wrote that Richardson, "leaves us feeling [. . .] that everything being of equal importance to her, it is impossible that everything should not be of equal unimportance," and Woolf even suggested that *Pilgrimage* left her pining for Victorian realism, writing, "The old method seems sometimes the more profound and economical of the two."[93]

What is it within *Pilgrimage*'s style that so frustrates its critics? Take, for example, this excerpt from *Pilgrimage*'s fourth volume, *The Tunnel*, describing a day of Miriam's work at Mr. Hancock's dental office:

> Drowsily and automatically Miriam went on rolling tin and gold—sliding a crisp thick foil of tin from the pink-tissue-paper-leaved book on to the serviette . . . a firm metallic crackle . . . then a silent layer of thin gold . . . then more tin . . . adjusting the three slippery leaves in perfect super-position without touching them with her hands, cutting the final square into three strips, with the long sharp straight-bladed scissors—the edges of the metal adhering to each other as the scissors went along—thinking again with vague distant dreamy amusement of the boy who cut the rubber tyre to mend it—rolling the flat strips with a fold of the serviette, deftly, until they turned into neat little twisted crinkled rolls—wondering how she had acquired the knack. She went on and on lazily, unable to stop, sitting back in her chair and working with outstretched arms, until a small fancy soap box was filled with the twists—enough to last the practice for a month or two.[94]

This is only one paragraph from an astonishing forty-three-page chapter that exhaustively details the daily work of a dental assistant. It is, surely, the longest description in our literature about the assembly of gold fillings, and still, somehow, not the most poetic. Frank Norris, the quintessential exemplar of flat naturalist description, gets his dentist McTeague through the filling-making process in a fraction of the time, while also managing to turn the fillings into a symbolic locus for Californian greed.[95] The fillings have no such resonance for Miriam. Indeed claiming this passage depicts a "stream of consciousness" is only half-true, since Miriam is explicitly undertaking this process in a largely nonconscious fashion. Like Anna's scratched-out, schematic entries from the blue notebook, this is a painstaking record of action mostly emptied of consciousness—but where *The Golden Notebook* compresses Anna's entries down to a brief summary, *Pilgrimage* spells Miriam's actions out at great length.

Why does she tell us so much about these rote matters? One possible argument is the logic of the everyday: mindless office work, some critics write, is part of a working woman's experience and hence should be part of a fictional text about a working woman. John Mepham, for instance, claims this passage is "among the very first attempts to bring the distinctive experience of the busyness and stress of a certain kind of white-collar work onto the page in fiction."[96] But since both consciousness and writing rely on our attending only a few of the countless details we perceive in the world, this take is not persuasive. As we know via the mimetic fallacy, one can depict "busyness and stress" without depicting every individual detail that causes them. Indeed Bryony Randall, in valorizing *Pilgrimage*'s treatment of the everyday, shows why that notion cannot account for this passage. To be perfectly in tune with Miriam's everyday life, she notes, the chapters at the dental office should properly take up half of the novel's middle volumes, because Miriam's time at work takes up roughly half of her waking life. That Richardson depicts only this one day in great detail is "to maintain the reader's interest, since if the narrative was divided between Miriam's working life and leisure time in their precise proportions, no doubt the reader would become as weary with the text as Miriam becomes with her work."[97] In other words the novel is *already* highly selective, because it acknowledges that tens of thousands of hours of Miriam's life are not worth reading about.[98] Yet to claim that Richardson is acceding to her readers' attentional needs by declining to write a thousand boring pages about dental work is still to assert that forty-three pages is a perfectly acceptable length over which to bore one's readers.

Sinclair's review provides the best clue for understanding the novel's strategy. At some points Sinclair does seem to think Richardson is presenting an unmediated simulation of raw experience, the "first-hand, intimate and intense reality of the happening."[99] However, at other points she acknowledges that Richardson's method entails lots of complex manipulation regarding what is depicted and for how long, writing, "On one page Miss Richardson seems to be accounting for every minute of Miriam's time. On another she passes over events that might be considered decisive with the merest slur of reference."[100] The latter category—as critics have confidently ascertained only through biographical cross-checking, so fleeting are the references—includes quite a lot of material to which one would think Miriam should devote significant conscious energy: the suicide of her mother, recounted only obliquely at the end of *Honeycomb*; a serious bicycle injury, only alluded to retroactively in *Deadlock*; her affair with the H. G. Wells stand-in Hypo Wilson and her subsequent miscarried pregnancy, dealt with in two blinks of an eye in *Dawn's Left Hand* and *Clear Horizon*. In other words we can tell Richardson's aesthetic is not just "Miriam Henderson's stream of consciousness going on and on" because *it leaves out all the interesting parts.*

Why is that? Let's turn to the first volume of *Pilgrimage*, *Pointed Roofs*. Here Miriam, finding her financially ruined father no longer able to support her indefinitely, has been sent to teach English at a boarding school in Germany. After her arrival there is little in the way of a traditional narrative arc: Miriam spends her time teaching and socializing with the other young women until, in the final chapter, she is dismissed by Fräulein Pfaff, purportedly for corrupting her French colleague Aline. Here is one midnovel passage, at tea:

> She wondered intensely what was in Elsa's mind behind her faint hard blue dress. She wanted to hear Mademoiselle's voice; Mademoiselle was almost invisible in her corner near the door, the new housekeeper was sitting at her side very upright and close to the table. Once or twice she felt Fräulein's look; she sustained it, and glowed happily under it without meeting it; she referred back contentedly to it after hearing herself laugh out once—just as she would do at home; once or twice she forgot for a moment where she was. The way the light shone on the housekeeper's hair, bright brown and plastered flatly down on either side of her bright white-and-crimson face, and the curves of her chocolate and white striped cotton bodice, reminded her sharply of something she had seen once, something that had charmed her . . . it was in the hair against the hard white of the forehead and in the flat broad cheeks with the hard, clear crimson colouring nearly covering them . . . something in the way she sat, standing out against the others . . . Judy on her left hand, with almost the same colouring, looked small and gentle and refined.[101]

What is interesting and characteristic about this passage is how Miriam allows her mind to wander about her environment in search of some greater understanding, but can never quite find it. She desires to know Elsa's mind from her blue dress but cannot; she thinks about sharing a gaze with Fräulein but can't bring herself to; and she tries to recall a particularly powerful memory from the housekeeper's visage, but the sight fails to have the desired effect. *Pilgrimage*, especially in its earlier volumes, often reads like what *À la recherche du temps perdu* might have looked like had Marcel decided not to tell us only about that single madeleine, but also few dozen other cookies he'd eaten that had not led to any vivid sequences of involuntary memory. Since all of us constantly have experiences in which we do *not* come to any particular realization, these passages are without obvious value to her or us.

Why does Miriam search so consciously, and yet so fruitlessly? Given the loss of her father's fortune and her disinclination for the marital route her sisters have chosen, she does not know what she is supposed to be looking for in the world. Since she does not have a sense of where she is going, she cannot rely on conventional or habitual patterns of behavior to guide her. Consequently she must expand her conscious efforts to discover new possible paths within the world, but as we noted before, highly conscious processes tend to be cumbersome and inefficient. Allison Pease writes that, "[i]n choosing an unconventional path, Miriam must remain constantly vigilant against boredom" because her rejection of convention is a rejection of the meanings to which society gives aspects of everyday life, and "[b]oredom is the frustration of meaning."[102] Yet where Pease believes readers can transcend meaninglessness by active "collaboration" with Richardson's text, it should be clear from the above passages that, frequently, there is no meaning for either Miriam or the reader to find.[103] Richardson did, in fact, explicitly aim to give readers attentional difficulties. In her essay on punctuation, she complains, "Most of our reading is a superficial swift gathering, as we loll on the borderland between inertia and attention, of the matter of a text."[104] Certainly her own writing disrupts readers' attention, largely because Miriam herself is often so unsure as to where it ought to be placed.

In heightening her consciousness, Miriam, like Anna, is trying to determine what it means to be a "free woman." As her similarly unmarried school friend Mag (who cohabits with another old acquaintance named Jan) says to her, "We may be slaves all day and guttersnipes all the rest of the time but, ach Gott, we are free."[105] Yet just as Richardson's flitting sentences have prevented many readers from being able to focus on the text, Miriam's freedom from convention often renders her consciousness so dispersed that she rarely feels the freedom to do anything positively. Indeed Miriam responds to Mag and Jan's merry carousing by reflecting that she was herself "somehow between two worlds, neither quite sheltered, nor quite free."[106] *Pilgrimage*, then, is a quest for Miriam to invent a mode of consciousness appropriate to the position of a free woman. If we want to know why Richardson passes quickly over most of the interesting moments in Miriam's life, then, it may be because those events are so obviously important that they cannot help her learn to filter her experiences more deftly. Subtler subjects are required for that process, like the fringe-conscious echoes—a recurring passage from a Chopin ballade, what her mother had said as she walked on a particular street—that Miriam discovers just beyond the center of her attention, which nevertheless seem to govern much of her emotional life.

The value of Richardson's technique, in other words, comes in the occasional surprise of the unexpected within material that might otherwise be quite boring. For instance Miriam achieves an intimation of freedom on a long bicycling trip, finding a rich appreciation of the darkness as she pedals through the countryside: "The dim road led on into the darkness of what appeared to be a private estate. [. . .] Her own darkness by right of riding through the day. Leaning upon the velvety blackness she pushed on, her eyes upon the little circle of light, steady on the centre of the pathway, wobbling on the feet of the trees emerging in slow procession of either side of the way."[107] But the feeling of conscious freedom is rarely simple. While in a steam-filled bathroom at her family's modest villa prior to her sisters' double wedding, "the row of objects ranged along the far side of the bath grew clear [. . .]—the upright hand-glass, the brush bag propped against it, the small bottle of Jockey Club, the little pink box of French face powder [. . .]. But as long as the powder-box were there it would be impossible to reach that state of peace and freedom Thomas à Kempis meant."[108] Immersing her consciousness within its sensuous present, that is, feels freeing only until she realizes it puts her at odds with a more austere, religious notion of freedom. Over the following pages, Miriam vacillates between the two views, unable to work through the contradictions between and within them—for example, her discomfort with many of the trappings of femininity as against the misogyny of Christian doctrine—well enough to understand which view of freedom she wishes to take.[109]

As with Anna, Miriam's struggles to find an optimal mode of consciousness eventually turn into a quest to discover how best to write. The major turning point comes in *Deadlock*, which features both the beginning of Miriam's relationship with—yet again, like Anna—an Eastern European intellectual named Michael and, perhaps more important, the beginning of her work as a translator, which sets into motion the *künstlerroman* plot culminating when she devotes herself to a *Pilgrimage*-like novel at the end of *March Moonlight*. As she works to edit the lecture of a Frenchman staying at her boardinghouse, with whose overheated style and rambling contents she has struggled to make any sense, she thinks:

> Avoid, she wrote, searching; some word was coming; it was in her mind, muffled, almost clear; avoid—it flashed through and away, just missed. She recalled sentences that had filled her with hopeless fury, examining them curiously, without anger. Avoid ornate alias. So *that* was it! Just those few minutes glancing through the pages, standing by the table while the patient talked about her jolly, noisy, healthy, thoroughly wicked little kid, and now remembering every point he had made . . . extraordinary. But this was life! These strange unconsciously noticed things, living on in one, coming together at the right moment, part of a *reality*.[110]

The stream of consciousness here is less like that of the earlier books, where present sensations flit rapidly across thoughts without ever really building or settling. It is more like Proust's madeleine, in which a fringe-conscious sensation comes into contact with nonconscious memory to form a deeper conscious understanding of one's environment. Observe that this requires suppressing, temporarily, Miriam's present surroundings: unlike the passages quoted earlier, there is no immediate sensory detail here, as the room at Mrs. Bailey's boardinghouse has become second nature to her by now. In combination with a similar epiphany about the relationship of one's consciousness to one's city (and of women to men) toward the book's end, Miriam begins to develop a more confident approach integrating the different parts of her mental life.[111]

Is she able to sustain this synthesis over the remaining seven books of *Pilgrimage*? Yes and no. Certainly the novel's style changes permanently.

The dashes vanish, and the ellipses are phased out, moving the prose into a more Jamesian style. Its refined hypotaxis gradually gives us a sense of Miriam less as a confused young woman and more of a mature intellectual. But as with Anna, perfectly achieved consciousness is an elusive target. Writing to Hypo, Miriam claims, "I have no waste paper basket. Yours, I know, is capacious"—that is, while Hypo's pen and mind both excise, moving toward a consistently chiseled edifice, Miriam constantly accumulates new methods.[112] Her integrations work, sometimes, until they don't, at which point she moves on to something else, letting the "worlds from which one after another she had retreated" steadily grow.[113] In politics she moves from socialists to suffragettes to Quakers; in male lovers, from Michael to Hypo to (at a distance) the Italian vacationer Guerini, then back again; in female intimates, from Amabel to Rachel Mary to Jean; in habitus, from Bloomsbury to Oberland to Dimple Hill to, finally, the apartment in St. John's Wood where she begins to write. Lest we are tempted to believe her final position on any of these fronts is the pilgrimage's destination, Lynette Felber reminds us that, as with many *romans-fleuves*, the endings in each of *Pilgrimage*'s books grow increasingly muddier and ambiguous—a tendency reinforced by how, for thirty years, *Dimple Hill* was presented as *Pilgrimage*'s last chapter, only yielding to the incomplete *March Moonlight* a decade after Richardson's death.[114] Moreover, when Miriam finally proclaims "Freedom" in the latter's final lines, it comes only as she holds Amabel and Michael's child, a bizarrely dissonant conclusion for a novel that has resisted the maternal path up to that point.[115] Stanley Fish famously wrote of John Bunyan's narrative of halting inner pilgrimage (one to which Richardson's novel alludes more than once), "There is, it would seem, no progress in *The Pilgrim's Progress*."[116] The same might be said of *Pilgrimage*.

If none of Miriam's resting places prove ultimately satisfying, what are we to make of her explorations in consciousness along the way? Take, for instance, this excerpt from *Dimple Hill*, in which Miriam walks with her host family, the Roscorlas, back from the Quaker meetinghouse and is unsure of what to discuss:

> If she could shake her mind free, topics would spontaneously arise. But effort brought only the realization, upon a tide of joy, that still it was only July. She decided for silence. Soon, the approaching

milestone would offer a topic and then, as slowly they climbed the last of the hill, the elms would come into sight and provide material that would branch and grow. They rounded the bend and there, just ahead, lay the milestone and the fork, the turning-point of her first excursion. A vehicle, rumbling along from behind, was almost upon them. An event. The old lady must gently be propelled a little nearer to the grass-fringed roadside. Already Miss Roscorla had dropped behind. Pressing the frail arm to her side, she turned and smiled, while making the necessary sideways movement, freely down into the bonneted face, making the most of the adventure of moving a few steps upon the surface of a shared earth in order to escape the impact of something moving more quickly along the same path.[117]

Like in the passage from *Pointed Roofs*, Miriam looks to her surroundings in hopes of achieving conscious freedom. As in that passage, there does not appear to be any epiphany: the milestone trees along the path to the church, about which Miriam had wondered earlier, do not end up yielding material for conversation, nor does the "event" of the coach's arrival.[118] Yet the tone is not so unsettled as the earlier passage. There is a benign patience in the absence of anything important occurring, neither mystically enlightening nor anxiety inducing. Much of *Dimple Hill* reads this way: conflict and narrative movement exists rarely, and then on only the most nuanced levels, as her attractions to both Rachel Mary and Richard first impel her toward, then repel her from, the community. These pages speak of maturity and contentment—yet 150 pages of that get boring quickly. Such passages have a plausible strategic purpose in the early volumes, since it is clear Miriam has not found a fulfilling structure for her consciousness yet, but here it is neither clear whether Miriam feels liberated by her explorations nor what Richardson wants us to make of her experience.

Yet the later books do produce some gorgeous prose, of a kind not available in the earlier ones. There is the "sleeping out" scene at the Wilsons' in *Revolving Lights*, where Miriam looks up and thinks "*This* is the real sky, in full power, stripping away sleep. Time, visible, pouring itself out. Day, not night, is forgetfulness of time."[119] There is the first view of the Swiss Alps in *Oberland*, where "the sunlit mountain corridors still seemed to be saying watch, see, if you can believe it, what we can do. And all the time it seemed that they must open out and leave her upon the hither side of enchantment, and still they turned and brought fresh vistas. [. . .] She still longed to glide forever onwards through this gladness of light."[120] If *Pilgrimage*'s early books see Miriam pass from one fleeting moment of consciousness to another in search of freedom, the later ones see her pass from one conscious integration to another in search of the same. It is not all fascinating, but the wheat is worth the chaff, and observing Miriam's process requires us to ask ourselves what would, in fact, constitute a free mind.

Can consciousness-raising set us free, then? Not if "consciousness-raising" simply means being more conscious of everything, in which case it will simply make us clumsy. Nor, either, if "freedom" is meant in terms of a specific material or political achievement: Miriam, after all, ends up toiling in yet another cheap apartment (as did her creator through her later years), and Anna's social ideals do not survive increased conscious scrutiny (much as her author's did not). But raised consciousness can reflect on and break routine, then send whatever positive results that have been created back to be habituated again. Similarly attention can compress the unmanageable world of sense into the manageable structure of mind, suppressing irrelevant aspects of consciousness that would distract us from more important ones. The work is frequently a tiresome process, and each success will work only for a while, after which we must rattle our habits up, expand our consciousness, then compress again. As Wallace Stevens wrote, "It can never be satisfied, the mind, never."[121] But it can make do.

4 The Menippean Satire

"Dull Difficult Dreary—&Disgusting"

Though the previous chapters have used mega-novels' relationships to several nonfictional genres to examine how their detailed accumulation of the facts of real life can overload readers' attention capacities and subsequently prompt them to modulate their methods of text processing, cruft is not limited to the small-scale cases of the incoherent word, the irrelevant datum, the passing moment of consciousness. The following three chapters will examine how mega-novels' incorporation of elements from other literary genres produces more extensive but equally pointless cruft, inducing the same characteristic frustration and boredom to provoke a similar reorientation of attention. We will begin by looking at cruft's place within a genre whose reputation for scale and heterogeneity has encouraged its application to several works in the mega-novel canon, the Menippean satire.[1]

Before we examine the genre's particulars, however, we must start by justifying our investigation into cruft's relationship with humor at all. To be sure, mega-novel humor is frequently described as excessive and overwhelming, but since we have defined cruft as objectively pointless text, to categorize mega-novel humor as cruft would imply it is somehow objectively not funny. Our basis for making such a judgment might seem questionable. The commonsense view of humor has long been that we should leave it to individuals' subjective impressions, as expressed by E. B. White's quip that "[h]umor can be dissected, as a frog can, but the thing dies in the process and the innards are discouraging to any but the pure scientific mind."[2] Since mega-novels have undeniably amused a large number of readers with their outrageous gags and set pieces, why should we doubt that they are funny?

We may do so because there is a type of gratuitous text in mega-novels that, though apparently comic, resists even this latitudinarian principle. Consider this excerpt from part 2, chapter 7 of William Gaddis's *The Recognitions*, depicting a Christmas party held for New York's artistic set by Esther Gwyon, estranged wife to protagonist Wyatt Gwyon:

> —Who's Esther?
>
> —Why, my dear, she's our hostess. There, talking with the tall fellow in the green necktie. She turned, as her husband approached with a martini.–What an *in*teresting group of people, she said.–And what *in*teresting music.
>
> —It's Handel, he said, handing her a glass.—*The Triumph of Truth and Justice.*
>
> She looked around her, and raised the glass to her lips.–Do you think *next* year we might get to the Narcissus Festival in Hawaii?
>
> Drinks were spilled, another brown line burnt on the mantel, people collided, excused themselves and greeted one another, and Ellery, tucking the green silk tie back in his jacket, said,–Just stop talking about it for a while. Who's that? he added, nodding at a blond girl.
>
> —I don't know. She came with somebody. She's going to Hollywood.
>
> —I want another drink, Ellery said, and went toward the blonde.
>
> —Ellery, please . . . But he was gone. She sat, holding her kitten.
>
> —What does it mean, said a heavy voice near her.—The garbage cans in the street, the kids on the East Side playing in the gutters, swimming in that filthy river, see? What does *that* mean?
>
> —Well *she* says Paris reminds *her* of a mouthful of decayed teeth, but *I* think Paris is just like going to the movies . . .
>
> —A lovely little hotel near Saint Germain, I don't think I crossed the river more than twice all the time I was there. I really *lived* on the left bank, it's so much nicer, the architecture, the cloud formations over there . . .
>
> —Of course if you like the Alps. I found them a fearfully pretentious bore myself . . . I mean, what can you *do* with an Alp . . .[3]

These inane, disconnected sputterings dominate the astonishing seventy-three additional pages of this scene. They might be of some interest if we had been following these characters throughout the novel, but they are as faceless in the larger work as they are in this excerpt, and their speech equally irrelevant to the novel's main events. Consequently the scene is usually explicated as social satire, ridiculing the "[c]liques of dishonest critics, backbiting literati, the entire rout of cocktail-party intellectuals and pen-pushers" that constitute the chattering classes.[4] But is this supposed mockery actually funny? Its only real joke, after all, appears to be the unnamed husband's Superman-influenced corruption of Handel's *The Triumph of Time and Truth* into *The Triumph of Truth and Justice*, which might provoke a chuckle from those readers with extensive enough knowledge of Handel's second-tier oratorios not to need Steven Moore's *Reader's Guide* to explain the reference. If most of what is said in this passage is simply banal rather than humorous, doesn't that propagate idiocy instead of satirizing it?

The few principles that have been established by systematic research in humor suggest that this may be the case. Though there is no generally accepted definition of humor, many believe that it can be broadly characterized as "nonserious social incongruity," often based in "bisociation": in other words we consider something funny when we are primed for certain cognitive processes by one social schema, but then suddenly see those expectations violated.[5] This causes us, according to Reuven Tsur, to become disorientated and undergo a rapid "shift in mental sets."[6] The most important subclass of this social incongruity is the one articulated a century ago by Henri Bergson, who claimed we laugh when we see human behavior lacking the flexibility commensurate to the flux of consciousness, instead displaying a "rigidity" that "*reminds us of a mere machine*."[7] The primary sign of this mechanism, Bergson continues, is repetition, since "a really living life should never repeat itself."[8] However, repetitive behavior itself is not funny but merely mechanical, requiring a comedian's inspired exaggeration or distortion to render the behavior obviously ridiculous.[9]

Looking back to Gaddis's dialogue, we may see that while it has plenty of mechanical behavior, the repetitions are not actually made incongruous by comic exaggeration or schema switching. Instead it simply continues its parade of shallowness unimpeded over dozens of pages. Indeed this scene is characterized not merely by clichés but *clichéd representations of clichés*: there is no more ham-handed a remark, after all, for Gaddis to have put into the mouth of an upper-class bore than the one about how "*in*teresting" she finds everything—except, perhaps, to have her call something else "such a pretentious bore" moments later. The text appears not merely about dullness or stupidity, then, but is dull and stupid itself. Given this point it is understandable that the novel's initial critics, to quote the alphabetic pastiche made by Gaddis's pseudonymous proselytizer Jack Green, considered *The Recognitions* "baffling, and a Bore [. . .] dull difficult dreary—&disgusting [. . .] repulsive or repelling."[10]

This kind of excess occurs throughout not only *The Recognitions* but a number of mega-novels. To understand what it is doing, we will need to more rigorously analyze the nature of humor, as well as the satire as a genre and the specific Menippean subcategory, to see what function cruft might serve when incorporated into them.

The Fallacies of Exposure and Subversion, and the Menippean Carnivalesque

Ever since Juvenal, satire has built its reputation on depicting the vicious, ugly, and stupid. Historically this has made it controversial among moralists, but it has consistently been defended on the grounds that its form censures the vices it depicts: as John Dryden wrote, "'Tis an Action of Virtue to make Examples of vicious Men."[11] Yet the constant tension between these two positions may suggest how tenuous is satire's rhetoric. Its duality may be best appreciated through Edward Rosenheim's famous definition of it as "*an attack by means of a manifest fiction upon discernible historic particulars*."[12] Satirists, in other words, always say two things at once: they must claim that their narratives are made up, but also that they depict the real social world; they must make their characters behave in deleterious ways, but only because they wish to criticize them. That is why comic incongruity is so crucial for establishing rhetorical distance. As suggested earlier satire's traditional method for signaling this duality is to prompt one social script but then to derail that script by exaggerating and distorting it. As Tsur notes, this strategy is aimed to disorient and alter its audience's cognitive patterns, because "[w]hen something suddenly seems to go wrong, one has to check the tuning of one's own schemata."[13] Laughter, in other words, is the body's way of discharging cognitive dissonance, which is why it is so useful in responding to social hypocrisy.

In producing this calibrated incongruity, however, satirists walk a fine line: should they make their material too incongruous, the satire might be dismissed as a perverse or even libelous fantasy, yet should they make it not incongruous enough, they might be charged with either heavy-handed dullness or, worse, insufficiently distinguishing themselves from that which they attack. The list of satires threatened with censorship resulting from overly fanciful exaggerations is considerable, including Robert Coover's mega-novel phantasmagoria on the Rosenberg execution, *The Public Burning*. Conversely, dangerous confusions have been caused by satires that were not sufficiently incongruous to cause cognitive dissonance. This famously occurred when Daniel Defoe's *The Shortest Way with the Dissenters* mimicked the voice of a blowhard Anglican zealot so closely that many contemporary readers took its argument for the mass execution and banishment of dissenting congregations seriously.[14] Kurt Vonnegut, introducing his *Mother Night*, about an American double agent working undercover as a Nazi radio propagandist, writes, "We are what we pretend to be, so we must be careful about what we pretend to be."[15] It is apt, then, that Fredric Bogel should observe that satire's closest aesthetic relative is the counterfeit, since the two genres share the ability to create "a space where distinctions are rendered problematic rather than reinforced," making crucial the ability recognize what is similar between the real and the fake while still distinguishing them.[16]

Given how essential fictional incongruity is to satire, then, we must reject as fallacies two common critical justifications for satire's drearier elements, both especially common when addressing mega-novel satire. The first is that a satire's greatest enormities may be justified on the grounds that they "expose" society's faults. That verb, echoing the muckraking "exposé," is obviously ill suited to the novel. After all, the novelist is deprived of the journalistic social critic's two most valuable tools, the ability to directly reference the real world and the authority to unequivocally present an argument in his own voice. As Bogel notes, a satirist does not "expose the satiric object in all its alien difference" but instead invents it as a fiction.[17] As we saw in chapter 2, reading fiction can and should affect our overall information-processing apparatus, but we must be vigilant against our natural tendency to accept the facts presented by fiction as if they were true.

Yet critics often appear vulnerable to this inclination. For instance *The Public Burning*'s admirers like to bash conservative intellectual Norman Podhoretz for calling it "a lie [. . .] because it hides behind the immunities of artistic freedom to protect itself from being held to the normal standards of truthful discourse," yet these critics, in trumpeting how the novel "exposes the American spirit that overlooks no opportunity to dominate, dehumanize, and humiliate the vulnerable" because it presents "a huge amount of verifiable historical information and multiple coiled patterns connecting the facts," make the same mistake Podhoretz does.[18] To debate the historical veracity of a book that sets the Rosenberg execution in Times Square—a Times Square connected by a magical swinging door to Sing Sing, no less, and one attended by a cavalcade of VIPs including the "Rat Pack" of Mickey, Minnie, and Goofy—is clearly ridiculous. The problem with Podhoretz's conclusion is not his politics but the belief, apparently shared by Coover's supporters, that a satire may be judged by how well it proves a "thesis."[19] Similarly, when Joseph Salemi claims that in *The Recognitions*' party scene, "the world of shallow art and intellectual falsity [. . .] is parodied and attacked, mostly through the devastating technique of quoting its representatives verbatim [. . .]—all are mercilessly exposed," he does not seem to realize that since these characters are Gaddis's inventions, Gaddis's dialogue does not "quot[e] verbatim" their stupidity from any preexisting reality but independently creates it.[20]

It is equally fallacious, however, to justify satire's ugliest elements on the mimetic grounds that, in an effort to accurately represent contemporary experience, they must dissolve all stable distinctions between truth and falsity or between the moral and immoral, as is frequently argued by postmodernists. In its most basic form, this position often argues that there is a "fading line between fantasy and reality," necessitating that fiction catch up in absurdity to an increasingly absurd world.[21] Steven Weisenburger, for example, argues that postmodern satires like those by Gaddis and Coover render obsolete the traditional view, in which satire rhetorically corrects social vices by reference to universal norms, by instead deconstructing all social norms and presenting only "degenerative, subversive fantasy."[22] If a satire actually did this, however, it would necessarily render itself incapable of any kind of critique, even of the mainstream culture that partisans of this view wish it to excoriate. This is likely why, when faced with specific works, such critics turn out to be more committed to universal norms and clear rhetorical argument than their theory otherwise suggests: Weisenburger, in fact, characterizes *The Public Burning* as "[a]n outraged catalogue of American self-deceits and lies masking themselves as genii of progress [. . .] the single most unrestrained condemnation of American civic identity to appear in the postwar decades."[23]

For all its limitations, however, the postmodern perspective does try to account for the excessiveness we find in mega-novel satires like *The Recognitions*. Historically satire has emphasized concision and targeted focus, as in Dryden's insistence that satire is "only to treat of one Subject; to be confin'd to one particular Theme."[24] However, mega-novels bearing a satiric impulse tend to increase their breadth in an almost grotesquely uncontrolled manner—indeed to the point that Alastair Fowler goes so far as to call them "generically inept, as well as too long."[25] Only one traditional satiric subgenre, in fact, has typically expanded to any real length, namely the Menippean satire. Though named for a Greek Cynic who wrote three centuries before Christ, this term became absorbed into mainstream literary-critical discourse only after mid-twentieth-century reclamations by Mikhail Bakhtin and Northrop Frye, both of whom stretched the term to cover a wide range of prose narrative satires of substantial size and variety. Frye, for instance, identifies the genre as an exemplar of the "extroverted intellectual" prose fiction strain that he dubs "anatomy," noting the genre's "tendency to expand" its "single intellectual pattern" so as to "overwhelm [its] pedantic targets with an avalanche of their own jargon."[26] Bakhtin, meanwhile, uses the term to group works that are "multi-styled and hetero-voiced," addressing "current and topical issues" while creating a hybrid of "philosophical universalism" and "experimental fantasticality."[27] More recently Howard Weinbrot asserts that a Menippean satire targets no less than the whole of "a dangerous, false, or specious and threatening orthodoxy."[28]

The lack of a consensus definition for the term, however, has created a certain ambiguity in how its satiric rhetoric is to be experienced. For Frye and Weinbrot, the Menippean is simply satire writ large, its subject not one vice but one society. For Bakhtin, though, Menippean satire derives less from classical satire than the medieval carnival:

> Let us say a few initial words about the complex nature of carnival laughter. It is, first of all, a festive laughter. Therefore it is not an in-

> dividual reaction to some isolated "comic" event. Carnival laughter is the laughter of all the people. Second, it is universal in scope; it is directed at all and everyone, including the carnival's participants. The entire world is seen in its droll aspect, in its gay relativity. Third, this laughter is ambivalent: it is gay, triumphant, and at the same time mocking, deriding. It asserts and denies, it buries and revives. Such is the laughter of carnival.
>
> Let us enlarge upon the second important trait of the people's festive laughter: that it is also directed at those who laugh. The people do not exclude themselves from the wholeness of the world. They, too, are incomplete, they also die and are revived and renewed. This is one of the essential differences of the people's festive laughter from the pure satire of modern times. The satirist whose laughter is negative places himself above the object of his mockery, he is opposed to it.[29]

In other words, unlike in classical satire, mocker and mocked are identical in the Menippean. No specific vice or ideology is attacked, but all humanity sprawls out into total ridiculousness. However, crucially for Bakhtin, carnivalesque laughter is as rejuvenating as it is degrading. Were the affirmative principle removed, he argues, the work would lose its effect, as a "grotesque world in which only the inappropriate is exaggerated is only quantitatively large, but qualitatively it is extremely poor, colorless, and far from gay."[30] Gargantua's drunkenness, for example, does not merely cause him to urinate all over Paris but inspires his characteristic merriment and love of companionship.

Yet this affirming principle often is absent from mega-novel satires, whose approach at times evinces both the carnivalesque's omnivorous maw and the satire's cool distance. For long stretches there is neither calibrated incongruity nor mirthful deprecation, only endless inanity and disgust. In this chapter, then, I will argue that the mega-novel Menippean satire, though it sometimes achieves conventional satiric or carnivalesque ends, often experiments with unbalancing the former's calibrated distortions and the latter's encompassing scope to create monstrosities either so fantastic as to be indecipherable or so dull as to be boring. In other words I will examine how they deploy cruft that challenges less society's ills than its reader's ability to attend a bloated representation of them. By creating a counterfeit world too expansive to process, what they satirize is the limits of their readers' own minds. Their cruft places us into a state in which, no matter how hard we try, we are likely to lose focus on what we are reading, causing our attention to fluctuate and our processing to lose its depth. The incongruity might provoke laughter, but mostly an unfocused, disoriented kind, deriving more from the termination of processing than its continuation. Consequently we can easily lose track of what exactly we are laughing at, how we ought to process it, or what is even going on at all.

Comic Overload: A Few Words on *The Sot-Weed Factor*

Some relatively straightforward examples might be seen in John Barth's *The Sot-Weed Factor*, a comic *künstlerroman* set in the 1690s about a naive and resolutely chaste poet named Ebenezer Cooke who is sent to manage his father's Maryland plantation. Based on a colonial satiric poem by a self-proclaimed laureate of the same name, *The Sot-Weed Factor* is frequently a conventionally funny book: opening to a random page, I come across the scene in which a rum peddler who has intoxicated a justice, cheated him at cards, urinated onto him, and had sex with his wife takes the couple to court so that he may sue for the price of the rum and the recovery of coins that fell from his pockets.[31] However, the book also presents some more unusual instances of humor, especially in the form of long lists. The list, of course, has an extensive history as a device within Menippean satire. Dustin Griffin notes how the genre often transforms the ugly into the pleasurable via a "great feast of words," especially through list-like devices such as the contest and the catalogue.[32] Though the list might tend toward repetition and thus encourage skimming, the lists of a great Menippean satirist, like Rabelais, are usually varied with invention to comic ends: for instance the list of surfaces with which Gargantua experiments wiping his ass has dozens of entries but is frequently broken by witty commentary (e.g., a cat's fur does well, but the cat will claw you) and is divided into several briefer sublists, the use of each element of which as an ass-wipe is ridiculous in its own way.[33]

Mega-novel lists, however, are often longer as a whole and more predictable item by item. Hugh Kenner has dubbed this technique "the comedy of the Inventory," which is a "comedy of exhaustion, comic precisely because exhaustive" in the way it aims to include the entirety of long, finite lists within the novel's text, as with the ninety-four figures of speech scattered through one chapter of *Ulysses*.[34] Kenner believes these are inherently funny, owing to their Bergsonian mechanism, but we must remember that while for Bergson the mechanical is worthy of mockery, it is not funny itself until it is exaggerated by a comedian. This raises the tricky question of when an extended list is funny and when it is simply boring—"the continuity," in Bergson's words, "having deadened [. . .] the comic quality."[35]

The Sot-Weed Factor's famous insult contest provides a good case study on this question, especially as it derives directly from a scene in the original poem, which will help us distinguish between the structures of traditional satire and those of mega-novel excess. In the original poem, the real Cook attempts to lambast the lawless colony of Maryland by stringing together several vignettes about a tobacco merchant's misadventures among the colonial populace, including this encounter with some women playing cards:

> I thought them first some Witches bent,
> On Black Designs in dire Convent.
> Till one who with affected air,
> Had nicely learn'd to Curse and Swear;
> Cry'd Dealing's lost is but a Flam,
> And vow'd by G——d she'd keep her *Pam*.
> [. . .] D——m you, says one, tho' now so brave,
> I knew you late a Four-Years Slave;
> What if for Planter's Wife you go,
> Nature designed you for the Hoe.
> Rot you replies the other streight,
> The Captain kiss'd you for his Freight;
> And if the Truth was known aright,
> And how you walk'd the Streets by night
> You'd blush (if one cou'd blush) for shame,
> Who from *Bridewell* or *New gate* came:
> From Words they fairly fell to Blows,
> And being loath to interpose,
> Or meddle in the Wars of Punk,
> Away to Bed in hast I slunk.[36]

This is a traditional, if not especially virtuosic, instance of satire, wherein the poor morals of a group of uneducated women is ridiculed and made incongruous by exploiting its similarities to both a brothel and witches' coven. Though the gags regarding the women's social class and sexual promiscuity have aged, their intended rhetorical goals should still remain clear.

Barth's revision of this scene, however, creates its comic effect differently. It begins similarly, with Ebenezer coming across the women at cards while seeking out Susan Warren (whom he will later discover to be his beloved, Joan Toast) inside his father's estate, Malden, which has been turned in his absence into an opium den and brothel. He proceeds to ask the women for assistance:

> "I beg your pardon," Ebenezer interrupted. "If you are servants of the house—"
>
> "*Non, certainement*, I am no servant!"
>
> "The truth is," said the dealer, "Grace here's a hooker."
>
> "A what?" asked the poet.
>
> "A hooker," the woman repeated with a wink. "A *quail*, don't ye know."
>
> "A quail!" the woman named Grace shrieked. "You call me a quail, you—*gaullefretière*!"
>
> "Whore!" shouted the first.
>
> "*Bas-cul!*" retorted the other.
>
> "Frisker!"
>
> "*Consoeur!*"
>
> "Trull!"
>
> "*Friquenelle!*"
>
> "Sow!"[37]

Though its comedy has more dirty-minded delight than the original's moralizing stance, Barth's version initially works similarly to Cook's, exaggerating bad behavior to satiric lengths. However, this changes when readers turn to the next page and see—

> "*Usagère!*"
>
> "Bawd!"
>
> "*Viagère!*"

"Strawgirl!"
"*Séraune!*"
"Tumbler!"
"*Poupinette!*"
"Mattressback!"
"*Brimballeuse!*"
"Nannygoat!"
"*Chouette!*"
"Windowgirl!"
"*Wauve!*"
"Lowgap!"
"*Peaultre!*"
"Galleywench!"
"*Baque!*"
"Drab!"
"*Villotière!*"
"Fastfanny!"[38]

—and another two hundred further insults, filling up the following six pages with an almost perfectly symmetrical, invective-laden layout.[39]

A half century of criticism confirms that many readers find this scene funny, but what are we actually laughing at? To an extent it is probably at the satire on a recognizable cultural obsession with generating insults based on female sexual promiscuity and appreciation of Barth's playful linguistic facility. Mostly, though, I think we laugh *at our own inability to read the text.* After all it is only upon perceiving the multiple facing-page complements of arcane pejoratives as a whole, and our ensuing decision to stop reading each word, that most readers really begin to guffaw. As Charles B. Harris asks, "how many of us read carefully every item in these catalogs? And need we? Is it not, rather the *idea* that Barth has matched 114 English synonyms for *whore* with an equal number of French synonyms that interests and delights us?"[40] Indeed that the passage's humor derives from overloading readers' processing abilities rather than simply exhausting the inventory of French and English epithets may be seen in the fact that one obvious synonym that not only would fit comfortably in this exchange, but is *in the original "Sot-Weed Factor" scene,* is notably absent, namely "punk." Even William Gass, as indefatigable a reader as any, claims that within this scene, "invention flags, the name calling becomes mechanical, vocal exhaustion ensues, and it's over."[41] What does it say about our cognitive abilities, though, that merely looking at these pages makes us chortle at our inability to read them? Laughing and skipping to the end might demonstrate healthy text processing, but it ought to remind us how easily our limited channel capacity can be overloaded.

In fact the ease with which the world's abundance can overpower our abilities to process it troubles Ebenezer throughout the novel, as he is constantly forced to determine whether his mind is too rigidly narrow to understand the world or whether the world itself simply possesses far more possibilities than it ought to. Though the contest above is *The Sot-Weed Factor*'s most excessive list, the book features several similar catalogs, such as Ebenezer and his chameleon tutor Henry Burlingame III's rhyming contest involving obscure words like "autoschediastic" and "catoptromancy"; Burlingame's catalog of twins worshipped by foreign cultures; and the page-long menu of the fish, fowl, rodent, fruit, and vegetables consumed at an Ahatchwhoop tribal feast.[42] They speak, more broadly, to the surfeit of options in the New World. If at his journey's outset Ebenezer had been so exasperated by the shopkeeper Bragg's elaboration of the sixteen types of notebook for sale that the poet attacked the wares with a sword, he is nearly driven mad in America by the much more various possibilities hidden within what appear to be simple matters.[43] Just as the would-be poet attempts twice during the whores' insult contest to cut them off and return to the question with which he had started, he often attempts to arrest others' extended stories from elaborating any more monstrously, like during Burlingame's account of Maryland's history while in the guise of Lord Baltimore, the valet Bertrand's story of the events that caused him to gamble away Malden, and Mary Mungummory's tales of her mother's sexual education.[44] However, just as the card players "possessed with mirth [. . .] paid him no heed," no one will stop for his sake, and his comic inability to keep up with the elaboration of possibilities proceeds unabated.[45]

We ought to sympathize with Ebenezer's situation. He seeks to limit the range of his world's possibilities not because he dislikes variety, but because he understands its implications all too well. During his student days, he writes to his sister, "*it were an easy Matter to choose a Calling, had one all Time to live in! I should be fifty years a Barrister, fifty a Phy-*

sician, fifty a Clergyman, fifty a Solider! Aye, and fifty a Thief, and fifty a Judge! All Roads are fine Roads, beloved Sister, none more than another [. . .]: to choose ten were no Trouble; to choose one, impossible!"[46] As he shuttles about Maryland, perpetually forced to change identity and allegiance, he finds the matter of how to manage life's overabundance no easier to negotiate. As Manfred Puetz has written, while some "human beings inevitably fall into despair when they lack possibility [. . .] Ebenezer Cooke has found out [. . .] that the reverse is valid too: human beings invariably fall into despair when confronted with too many possibilities."[47] His classical education encourages him to seek the Golden Mean, but to determine any mean would require him to comprehend the scale of his environment in the first place, and he finds it innumerable.[48]

Confronted with this same variety, many of the novel's critics similarly suggest the whole book might be too overcomplicated to bother with. Gerhard Joseph, for instance, has written that in Barth's "erudite catalogues of ideas, or in his name-calling contest between the prostitutes, Barth tries to convey the impression that sheer exhaustiveness for its own sake contributes to a meaningful comic order. The longer and more contrived the shaggy-dog fiction, the better. But [. . .] his characters frequently do not have much emotional depth."[49] Yet one can achieve sympathy with Ebenezer if one realizes that one can probably do no better in managing the cacophony of words that he must face. That the book is so wonderfully comic derives from how one cannot simply skip over all these expansive sections, since many passages that at first appear to be gratuitous larks end up being important. As David Morrell notes, when Barth's editors, assuming the book's episodic nature would make it easy to trim, suggested cutting out several chapters, they found none could be excised without damaging the narrative structure.[50] For instance Ebenezer's sensible impulse to ask Mary Mungummory to skip over the story she wishes to tell about her sister's conception serves him poorly when it later causes her to withhold the tale of Charley Mattasin's carnal secrets, which might've helped him learn sooner about the eggplant aphrodisiac required to avert Maryland's war with the Ahatchwoops.[51]

For similar reasons, though, we cannot simply embrace the book's profusion of language and ideas for their own sakes, either. While many critics describe the book as a satire enacting a "metaphysics of multiplicity" to criticize Ebenezer's "remaining obstinately constant in a changing world," this view ignores that, as with most satire, the book eventually does depend on establishing clear distinctions between the real and the counterfeit, the authentic identity and the mask, meaningful language and wasteful blabber.[52] Constancy's opposite, after all, is hypocrisy, and as much as critics valorize Burlingame's "cosmophilist" shapeshifting, were he as multiplicitous in his affections toward Ebenezer as toward his own personae, he would receive less critical approval.[53] The satire's apparent rhetorical attitude toward the value of constant identity is actually quite complex. Despite perceiving their likenesses, for instance, Ebenezer frequently fails to recognize the three people dearest him (Burlingame, Joan, and his sister Anna) when they are in disguise, yet in the end the coherence of their identities not only does not remain in perpetual doubt but is necessary to the book's affective resolution.[54] Similarly it may be endlessly amusing to see yet another character revealed to be Burlingame incognito, but his identity finally does possess some essential qualities: through all he does, he is generally on the side of peace, justice, and love.

Facing our own inability to reliably manage these multiplying possibilities, there may be nothing to do except laugh. Perhaps the novel's oddest feature is the way both its most mechanical and its most grotesque events—the violent deaths, the frauds and robberies, the countless attempted rapes—somehow all dissolve into the general comedy. The laughter is made possible, though, because the inability to manage life's fecundity is so general among the characters, as are the subsequent humiliations to which they are subjected, that power relations are leveled as in Bakhtin's carnivalesque, preventing anyone from laughing at others without laughing at themselves. The pirate Boabdil, for instance, may violently rape a prostitute, but he proceeds to contract her debilitating venereal disease and appears absurdly diminished whenever he later shows up; similarly Tom Tayloe, who makes his living swindling migrants into indentured servitude, gets hoodwinked into servitude by his own techniques.[55] In the novel's later stages, Ebenezer, having been taken captive by the Ahatchwoops and hearing his fellow captives admit the ways in which they have impersonated him in hopes of gain, remarks, "'Tis too late in the day for aught but general absolution."[56] The world's variety—much valuable, most pointless—is too much for us, but after a certain point that goes equally for us all: since none of our brains is any more than a clunky machine liable to break down at any moment, we might at least share a laugh over it.

The Public Burning and the Butts of Satire

Like *The Sot-Weed Factor*, Robert Coover's *The Public Burning* is an engagement with the nature and limits of comedy and satire. Not only do its two central characters—a fictionalized Richard Nixon and an embodied Uncle Sam—respectively derive from the traditions of classical clowning and American folk humor, but the novel's central event is surrounded by a sequence of routines Coover has imagined for midcentury American comedians like Jack Benny, Edgar Bergen, and the Marx Brothers.[57] Much of the book, granted, is conventional satire, targeted at the Eisenhower's administration's prosecution of the Rosenberg case. This is especially so in its early chapters, where, by setting historical documents to verse—for example, articles by the "national poet Laureate" *Time* magazine and the "Spirit of History" *New York Times*, as well as portions of Eisenhower's speeches and the Rosenbergs' letters—Coover makes incongruous the theatrical elements of public speech.[58] Even the famously grotesque scene in which a cinemagoer fails to take off his 3-D glasses after seeing the film *House of Wax* and perceives Times Square as an extension of the grisly film creates a satiric duality via its use of altered perception.[59]

However, as with Barth's book, *The Public Burning*'s catalogues and contests progressively spill beyond their traditional satiric use and generate cruft. Speaking for many initial reviewers, Robert Towers observed the ways in which the book seems to invoke satiric convention without really fulfilling it. On the one hand, the novel's many historical particulars are often not especially incongruous, meaning "the documentary effects of *The Public Burning* degenerate into mere cataloguing or recitation"; on the other hand, the more overtly fictional elements are often so incongruous as to be merely bizarre fantasy, such that "Coover, relying upon the strategy of excess, puts the reader in the position of a jaded sadist who must devise more and more exquisite elaborations of his tortures in an effort to catch up with a fast receding gratification."[60] Even Tom LeClair, in celebrating the book, agrees that the novel's panorama of American society at times presents "too much elaboration, too much information."[61] Collectively this excess engenders a grotesque stranger and more disturbing than that of the conventional satire, and as a result, in many passages toward the novel's end, one's cognition can become so disoriented that it becomes difficult to know where the book's satire is directed and how to process it.

From the book's beginning, its comic excessiveness is rooted in the voice of Uncle Sam. Towers compliments the "foulmouthed and amusing" pastiche of Americana that constitutes Uncle Sam's dialogue but subsequently adds, "how tiresome and unrelenting that voice becomes in the long haul!"[62] Take this characteristic monologue, uttered shortly after his introduction:

> Time is money! No pent-up Utica contracts our powers, but the whole boundless continent is ours, it's as much a law of nature as that the Mississippi should flow to the sea or that trade follers the flag! *Fear* is the fundament of most guvvamints, so let's get the boot in, boys, and listen to 'em scream, let us anny-mate and encourage each other—*whoo-PEE!*—and show the whole world that a Freeman, contendin' for Liberty on his own ground, can out-run, out-dance, out-jump, chaw more tobacky and spit less, out-drink, out-holler, out-finagle and out-lick any yaller, brown, red, black, or white thing in the shape of human that's ever set his onfortunate kickers on Yankee soil! It is our manifest dust-in-yer-eye to overspread the continent allotted by Providence for the free development of our yearly multiplyin' millions, so damn the torpedoes and full steam ahead, fellow ripstavers, we cannot escape history![63]

This amalgam of American quotation contains funny satire, drawing out the coarse exuberance latent within even the highest-minded American rhetoric (e.g., "manifest dust-in-yer-eye"). However, we should observe that not all are converted to "rich rhetoric." At times the passage's repetitiveness approaches cruft in its longer (hence harder-to-process) sequences, such as in "out-run, out-dance, out-jump, chaw more tobacky and spit less, out-drink, out-holler, out-finagle and out-lick." As with Barth's lists, one starts to laugh less because one has deeply processed its jokes than out of astonishment that it keeps going as long as it does.

What are we really laughing at in this passage? Do we mock Uncle Sam for how his official decorum descends into unsophisticated jingoism, or do we laugh with him for successfully fusing a wide swath of American culture and tradition into a single voice? Though many criticize Sam's catchphrase-laden dialogue as the blabbering "rants" of a mere "cartoon figure," John Ramage notes that "Sam also seems to contain some of the best of the American psyche—humor, spirit, resourcefulness."[64] There is something to be said for a sensibility that so effortlessly fuses a seamless national whole from many individual parts. That generates a problem for our understanding of the novel's satire. As Richard Walsh notes, "if satire is to remain functional as a critical tool, a distinction between laughing *at* and laughing *with* must be retained. Uncle Sam problematizes this distinction."[65] Put another way, the overwhelming barrage confuses our ability to recognize to what extent Sam represents either our ideal or real conceptions of American identity and, as a result, how we should understand ourselves with respect to him (see also chapter 6).

The novel's catalogues of historical data exacerbate this disorientation. Often invoking the "overabundant flow of events" in contemporary life, the narrator sometimes presents this flow directly, as shown by this account of the articles laid out around the *New York Times*' daily Rosenberg coverage:

> Circumscribing all these speculations: the picture of a man sweating behind bars in a B. Altman & Co. advertisement ("Are you facing a 90-day sentence?"), a movie review of *Devil's Plot*, and a floor-level peek up the skirt of a woman strapped into the seat of a Colonial Airlines plane to Canada. Father's Day ads for sizzling steaks. "The Mighty Atom" is dead. TONIGHT AT 8:30. "Something to fit every taste."
>
> [. . .] What compels the attention and taps the wellsprings of prophecy on these pilgrimages is not this announcement that little Arlene Riddett, 15, of Yonkers, won the girls' championship in the 28th annual marbles tournament in Asbury Park, New Jersey, nor that picture of two East Berlin demonstrators throwing stones at Russian tanks on Leipzigerplatz, but the fact that these things touch each other. [. . .] The government of Argentina orders the price of theater tickets cut by 25% and the President of the United States is given a large toy model of Smokey Bear. The execution of an unemployed housepainter in Berlin takes shape beside the report that a new collection of wall coverings and shower curtains offers a vari-

ety of choices to homemakers who wish to decorate the bathroom: BATH WALLPAPERS / ARE EASY TO CLEAN. "Panorama" is one of the wallpaper designs, made up of impressionistic scenes of the country against a background of abstract motifs reminiscent of ancient calligraphy. [. . .][66]

Even while acknowledging these stories' inapplicability to the rest of the novel, however, the narrator suggests we should consider these passages part of the general humor of the event, calling them an expression of "Arbitrariness as a principle, allowing us to laugh at the tragic."[67] Why laugh at the tragic and arbitrary, though? Presumably for reasons similar to those that make us laugh in *The Sot-Weed Factor*: sorting through all the irrelevant juxtaposed information in the news to recognize the tragic events amid the ephemera is often more than we are able to manage. As Elisabeth Viereck writes regarding the novel, we are faced with "Uncertainty no longer springing from the lack of information but stemming from information itself."[68] Similarly a Sing Sing guard tells Nixon later in the novel, "It's funny, isn't it, Mr. Nixon? [. . .] How billions and billions of words get spoken every day, like all these we've been speaking on the way down here, for example, and for some reason—or for maybe no reason at all—a few of them stick, and they're all we've got afterwards of everything that's happened."[69] The surplus of words makes us conscious of the likelihood we will focus on the wrong ones.

However, the equalizing force of *The Sot-Weed Factor*'s carnivalesque cannot fully take hold in *The Public Burning* because of the presence of Uncle Sam. Barth's characters, no matter their pretensions, are each at the mercy of plot strings beyond their control; Coover's Uncle Sam, though, appears legitimately marvelous and will not be so readily leveled. His authority over American identity forces other characters to constantly fear being made the butt of everyone else's mockery. In *The Sot-Weed Factor*, the ungovernable New World finally allows everyone some authenticity because no one can make a claim to total authenticity, but in the Cold War–era United States of *The Public Burning*, which fears the outside threat of communism—as Molly Hite reminds us, the Rosenbergs were often tarred as "inauthentic," impostor Americans—the characters are unable to reach that resolution.[70]

This becomes most obvious in the novel's final section, taking place at the ritual Times Square public execution, where the cruft produced by the excessive spectacle causes ceaseless laughing but confuses that laughter's focus. As the execution approaches, readers are overloaded by excessive lists. In the scenes recounting the preparations in Times Square, beginning in earnest around chapter 20, the heretofore controlled back-and-forth between cruft and satiric commentary soon becomes unbalanced in the former's direction. Chapter 20 names seventeen categories of VIPs in attendance, as well as fifteen human movie stars, several more cartoon ones, and dozens more popular singers, athletes, and other celebrities.[71] This, however, is nothing in comparison to chapter 24's list of the nicknames of thirty-four presidents reanimated to parade on the square, adjacent to a list of fifty-four American archetypes (e.g., "Roving Gamblers, Lumberjacks, Johnny Rebs and Damyankees, Sheepherders and Cattle Kings"), all marching while the crowd affirms an avalanche of the blandest Cold War slogans.[72] And even chapter 24's excesses appear concise next to chapter 26's account of dozens of generic functionaries from dozens of generic institutions on hand (e.g., "all the auxiliary personnel who serve the three federal branches, all the agencies, bureaus, departments, commissions, institutes, foundations, boards, councils, societies, administrations, appeal and claims courts, funds, organizations, banks"), or to Betty Crocker's roll call of forty-two congressional representatives and ninety-six senators.[73]

When this cruft is combined with a series of absurd, rapid-fire comic sketches, produced under the conceit of a contest among the nation's celebrities to make entertainment out of the Rosenbergs' letters, the scene becomes overwhelming to the point of being infectiously funny without it ever being clear what we are laughing at. Though many critics have claimed that these comedy routines suggest Hollywood's ideological complicity with the government, Coover's routines are too zany to either scapegoat the Rosenbergs or satirize American ideology. For the most part, the stars' characteristic physical and linguistic creativity—for example, the Astaire-Rogers dance number incorporating a mesh visitation screen, an Abbott and Costello number about "who goes first" to the execution, a Hope-Crosby-Lamour "Road to Radiance" sketch—generates not hostile mockery or exaggerated self-parody but the slapstick, punning comedy of vaudeville, creating grotesque incongruities from the execution materials.[74] This approach climaxes during the Marx Brothers routine, paced so quickly (in the brothers' characteristic style) that the audience laughs mostly at the pure speed of schematic switches. Here is Groucho as Julius Rosenberg and Chico as the jail keeper:

> GROUCHO: I'll name anybody! My mother, my agent, even my mistress!
>
> CHICO: Whatta you sayin'? You ain't got a misteriss! You ain' even got a cockyerbine!
>
> GROUCHO: I'll name her too!
>
> CHICO: Whatta you gonna name her?
>
> GROUCHO: (*singing and rolling his eyes*) I think I'll name her "Jasmine" . . .
>
> CHICO: Jas'yours?
>
> GROUCHO: (*continuing*) . . . Cuz she's mighty lak' a rose!
>
> CHICO: Oh, a Pinko, eh? We're getting to da bottomma dis!
>
> GROUCHO: You been there, too, hunh?
>
> CHICO: She'sa da one what's stole-a da bum' eh?
>
> GROUCHO: She didn't steal it, she was born with it!
>
> CHICO: And she gave it to da Russians?
>
> GROUCHO: She gave it to everybody![75]

These jokes less satirize the Rosenbergs than send up the usual targets of both the Marxes and the carnivalesque, the frailties of language and the human body.

Consequently citizens expecting to mock the Rosenbergs—and critics wishing to vindicate them—find laughter directed back from their intended targets toward human weakness generally. The former try to submerge themselves within the communal experience of laughter, but the conflicted aims of that laughter prevent them from realizing Bakhtinian rejuvenation: "Out front, a hundred million mouths open wide, a hundred million sets of teeth spring apart like dental exhibits, a hundred million bellies quake, and a hundred million throats constrict and spasm, gasp and wheeze, as America laughs. At much the same things everybody laughs at everywhere: sex, death, danger, the enemy, the inevitable, all the things that hurt about growing up, something that Americans especially, suddenly caught with the whole world in their hands, are loath to do. What makes them laugh hardest, though, are jokes about sexual inadequacy—a failure of power—and the cruder the better."[76] This is not really the "cold war public as a mindless, conformist mass," as Paul Maltby would have it.[77] The crowd does nothing stupid or immoral by laughing at dirty jokes: their laughter is explicitly universal rather than particular to a historical ideology. It is unclear, though, whether that universal impulse is to laugh at themselves communally or to target others and assert their own superiority. To do the former would require them to identify with the soon-to-be-executed Rosenbergs, which the political context forbids, even though some may recognize how closely their uncontrollable spasms resemble those shortly to be provoked by the Rosenbergs' electrocution. Given the stakes, they would likely prefer their laughter to be more clearly oriented—just as most critics would prefer Coover's scene make a clearer satire of the American establishment—but the question of who or what is being mocked here is not clearly resolved.

Likely for this reason, everyone is relieved when a bewildered Nixon stumbles onto stage—magically transported from his inept and messy seduction encounter with Ethel at Sing Sing—with his pants down, the words "I AM A SCAMP" written across his ass in Ethel's lipstick, allowing him to become the joke's new butt.[78] Ever the clown, Nixon is unable to get his pants back up but manages to convince the crowd that, since the Rosenberg affair has demonstrated national vulnerability, they ought to recommit America to openness together with a communal gesture, and with the rhetorical flourish "*I am asking everyone tonight to step forward—right now!—and drop his pants for America!*" he successfully redirects the laughter away from himself.[79] But where has the laughter now been turned? The crowd is uncertain: many appear enthusiastic about communal nudity, "staggering about in tight little circles to cheer the others on," but there are also "scattered screeches of protest from the timid."[80] Meanwhile Nixon's novel-long vacillation between identifying with the Rosenbergs as fellow Americans and demonizing them in hopes of political advancement makes his intentions similarly muddled.

Uncle Sam's arrival onstage to refocus the event on the Rosenbergs finally settles the confusion. When Nixon and the crowd insist that Sam drop his pants too, he objects they are "*going too far!*": Sam may be willing to let individual Americans degrade themselves by exposing their lower halves, but America itself will not do so.[81] Though the crowd does badger him into exposure, the revelation of his penis causes a blackout, at which point the fiction shoots so far into the marvelous that any satiric recognition becomes impossible. Flying through the darkness and casting fireballs like a mad genie, Sam regains control of the situation and brings the event back to its original purpose of executing the Rosenbergs—though only after the first attempt to electrocute Ethel fails and the event's VIPs rush to the stage to repull the switch, sending Ethel's body, in a final opaquely grotesque image, "held only at head, groin, and one leg, [. . .] whipped like a sail in a high wind, flapping out at the people like one of those trick images in a 3-D movie."[82]

What exactly are we to take from this bizarre conclusion, whose assault of comedy, cruft, and the fantastic prevents either crowd or readers from understanding their own laughter? Regarding this ambiguity Thomas Pughe notes that "there is nothing that is truly liberating, nothing that is 'other' about this episode [. . .]—it appears merely bizarre and ridiculous," adding that readers "will laugh a halting, painful and lonely laugh, provoked by the crisis of his or her reading experience."[83] I think this conclusion is basically correct, though actual readers will often dodge this crisis by simply asserting clearer satiric motives. I would only add that the ambiguity of the novel's comedy is propelled by its submergence within cruft. The general disorientation caused by the enormous lists and rapid-fire humor prevents readers from processing the scene as clearly as they otherwise might.

That may be why the final scene, in which Uncle Sam sodomizes Nixon so as to "incarnate" his spirit for a future presidency, feels more narratively pat, if more repulsive, than the rapes in *The Sot-Weed Factor*. Unlike Barth's rapists, Uncle Sam does not share his victim's weaknesses. When he concludes the book by quoting George M. Cohan's "Always Leave Them Laughing When You Say Goodbye"—a fast-paced patter song, incidentally, about a father who advises his son to keep people so amused with rapid-fire slapstick that he can avoid emotional ties with them—the laughter to which he refers appears less about communal acknowledgment of weakness than exercising power over others.[84] Yet it returns the book to conventional satire by rooting the source of our presidents' recognizably wearied mannerisms ("Hoover's glazed stare, Roosevelt's anguished tics, Ike's silly smile") in their penetration by the weight of American heritage.[85] If the climactic spectacle is too overwhelming for us to recognize what relationship we hold to our nation, we can at least recognize that its power is incomparably beyond that of our individual minds, and if we try to mock it, the joke will very likely be turned back at our expense.

The Fraudulent, the Satiric, and *The Recognitions*

Still, this discussion of cruft and laughter will not help us explain the passage with which we began the chapter, the party scene in *The Recognitions*. Even Moore admits that "the ferocity of Gaddis' satire, the contempt he heaps upon nearly everyone in the novel, betrays the stern moralist who doesn't so much invite the reader to laugh at the human foibles of his characters as to recoil in horror."[86] The novel's plot as a whole—nominally centered around a commercially unsuccessful mid-twentieth-century painter named Wyatt Gwyon, who is recruited to forge "newly discovered" pictures by fifteenth-century Flemish masters, but also featuring myriad subplots involving frauds and duplicities crafted by other aspiring criminals and artists—is simply too bleak and brutal to create much humor. It probably would have been impossible to sustain the leavening impulse of *The Sot-Weed Factor*'s carnivalesque, after all, through a thousand-page parade of (by my approximate count) four rapes, two castrations, eight characters institutionalized or otherwise gone insane, four attempted murders (three successful), four deaths by gruesome disease, five deaths by gruesome accident (including two in separate building collapses), and countless suicide attempts, not to mention many other fates so bizarre as to defy categorization.[87]

Given the caustic invective of the narrative voice, there might be an argument that the book's satire is of the harsher, Juvenalian variety. There seems to be general consensus that the book's goal is a caustic "exposure" of the fraudulence of a whole range of things, including contemporary mainstream society, New York's upper-class and bohemian subculture, religious and scientific epistemology, and modernist concepts of authenticity, tradition, and originality.[88] These views are perhaps best summed by John Johnston's claim that the book is "an extended contemporary Menippean satire directed against everything sham, fake, and imitative—artworks, ideas, identities, products, even languages—in the nascently consumerist, mass-media-directed American society of the 1950s."[89] In this view the book's rhetorical distance is generated primarily by Wyatt, praised for the "transformational power of [his] artistic imagination."[90]

However, valorizing Wyatt in this way is problematic if we are to consider *The Recognitions* a satire on fraudulence. Wyatt's most distinct characteristic, after all, is his ability to create forgeries indistinguishable from fifteenth-century paintings. According to Johnston, Wyatt's virtuosity "goes so far as to throw into question even the existence of some founding first or authentic version," erasing the distinction between original and reproduction via the poststructuralist notion of "simulacra."[91] As we noted earlier, however, that distinction between real and fake is necessary to any definition of fraudulence in the first place. In other words critics appear to justify Gaddis's swaths of banal text on the grounds that they expose fraudulence but then apotheosize the book's protagonist for deconstructing fraudulence as a coherent concept. Tony Tanner asks, "if the best artist is the best forger, what does 'originality' mean?," and we may extend his question by asking why, if the character most skilled in falsehood is the one critics most admire, they are so confident in attacking inauthenticity.[92]

This paradox extends more generally toward the novel's satiric status. To again invoke Bogel, the counterfeiter and satirist are analogous because they both possess the ability to make distinctions between false and true problematic. However, if that distinction vanishes, they cannot produce their desired effects: just as a forger's work depends on vendors' respect for authentic currency, a satirist needs readers to respect some kind of authentic values to find his or her targets worthy, on any grounds, of criticism. Postmodern critics may be wary of reifying a distinction between authentic and inauthentic, but if one deconstructs the distinction entirely, one does away with the difference between satire and satirized, too. Consequently one can no longer argue that the representation of doltish characters can critique superficiality, because the clear norm from which superficiality can be critiqued vanishes: banal text is simple banal text. One must consequently conclude, to recall Franco Moretti's comment on *Bouvard and Pécuchet*, that a book like *The Recognitions* "abolish[es] the difference between a book on stupidity, and a stupid book."[93] Yet outside the hostile early reviews, no one argues *The Recognitions* has done this. It is among the book's great achievements, in fact, that its readers can neither consistently rely on nor consistently reject its characters' authenticity: instead we must constantly struggle to consider how seriously to consider their attitudes on art, morality, finance, and religion.

What should we do, though, about the long stretches of purely stupid dialogue? Johan Thielemans's claim that the book's party scenes are designed "to deal with chaos, by being chaotic" in themselves will not suffice, because western literature has spent centuries developing literary techniques by which satire may treat the dull without being dull.[94] As I mentioned in chapter 2, for instance, Flaubert's last novel, despite Moretti's comment, is an example of how these tactics may be skillfully deployed. Consider the passage below, in which Bouvard and Pécuchet survey their new country estate:

> Bouvard, passing near the arbor, discovered the plaster statue of a woman beneath its branches. She was pulling up her skirt with two fingers, her knees bent, looking over her shoulder as if afraid of being discovered.
>
> "Oh, pardon me! Don't mind us!"
>
> And they found this joke so hilarious that, twenty times a day, for more than three weeks, they kept repeating it.[95]

The passage's satiric craft is especially apparent in its final sentence, which exaggerates the number of repetitions but compresses the text representing them to minimize the joke's dulling effect on readers. Similarly its free indirect style allows the passage to maintain enough proximity to the friends' mindset so that it becomes easier to recognize our own tendency toward mechanism, while still keeping its distance from the pair's attitudes. In Gaddis's party scene, by contrast, no remark is treated as so dull or stupid that it warrants elision into narration: they read the way Flaubert's vignette might have if he'd directly represented each of the four hundred utterances of Bouvard's joke over dozens of pages.

This style is particularly striking because *The Recognitions*' first chapter, a searing novella about Reverend Gwyon's confrontation with the shadows of older traditions on his journey to Spain, brilliantly employs such Flaubertian nuance and concision. This approach, though, all but vanishes after the first chapter—indeed from Gaddis's corpus entirely—with the remaining scenes featuring substantially more direct discourse. Here I must make an argument that will not be popular among *The Recognitions*' admirers, but which is necessary to articulate the book's weirdly brilliant innovations: as a result of this shift, much of the novel's middle suffers and, in particular, fails *as satire*. This is not to say that there are not some good satiric moments, but the narrative voice does not manage these effects as masterfully as it does in the opening. At its worst it devolves into heavy-handed diatribes that are little more than the warmed-over clichés that postwar highbrows spouted about the pernicious effects of mass culture.[96]

However, this strategy allows Gaddis to experiment with cruft in the resulting lengthy dialogues. These passages first occur early in the second chapter, where, after following Wyatt to Paris, the narrator scans the city's cafés and reports several patches of disconnected speech: "—Voici votre Perrier m'sieur.—Mais j'ai dit café au lait, pas d'eau Perrier . . . A small man in a sharkskin suit said,—Son putas, y nadas mas. Putas, putas, putas . . . Someone said,—Picasso . . . Someone else said,—Kafka . . . A girl said,—You deliberately misunderstand me. Of course I like art. Ask anybody."[97] Given that this chapter begins by proclaiming the city's "infinite vulgarity," it would seem this dialogue intends to satirize Parisian superficiality, yet upon inspection there is nothing blameworthy or even interesting about it: it reflects on no one poorly to have mentioned Picasso or Kafka, mistaken a drink order, or insisted on their own appreciation for art.[98] Perhaps the narrator has so little regard for the Parisian intellectual climate that he assumes the mere mention of Picasso ought to suggest vacuity to his audience, but this would be an extremely complacent satiric effort.

What the passage even more notably lacks, though, is Wyatt, whom the narrative has not yet rediscovered in Europe. Given that none of these voices appears to develop into anything more than a line of dull speech on its own, we likely assume that our protagonist must be among them: why bother describing such dull café conversation otherwise? Only after unsuccessfully seeking some attribute of Wyatt's voice in these bland exchanges over four and a half pages do we learn that, "With no idea of Paris when he arrived, [Wyatt] had been fortunate enough to find quarters in this neighborhood which maintained anonymity in the world of arts."[99] In other words, while prompting us to scan for a sign of recognition, the book has not only delayed providing one but has placed it somewhere unexpected, first heightening our attention but then discouraging it by making the text through which we comb so little worth attending. As Gregory Comnes notes, among *The Recognitions*' odder stylistic moves is how it does "not distingui[sh] between meaningful and irrelevant background detail, as most traditional novels do."[100] The textual space taken up by the novel's events is often far out of proportion to its importance, with unimportant passages given enormous space and important ones minimized.

As befits the novel's title, then, when we return to New York, Gaddis constantly uses imbalances like these to impede readers' ability to recognize the importance of what they read. That clutter's cognitive impact is the real source of the novel's famous difficulty. It is telling that while the majority of *Recognitions* criticism focuses on Wyatt, he appears in less than half of the book and his name goes unmentioned after the third chapter: the rest of the narrative both proliferates inconsequential exchanges among minor characters while consistently obscuring its most important plot thread, forcing us to look for telltale behavioral tics or speech patterns to register the protagonist's presence. Many similar tactics may be observed elsewhere in the book. For instance, in one midnovel subplot, the would-be playwright Otto seeks a reunion with his father, who turns out to be the otherwise undistinguished company man Mr. Pivner, the subject of several brief scenes otherwise unrelated to the rest of the book. Though most criticism treats this relationship as self-evident, Gaddis delays making it explicit for three hundred pages after Pivner's first appearance. In particular Otto's last name is never stated. There are several hints about their relationship: the narrator mentions, for instance, that Pivner wears rimless glasses, and later Otto is reported as hearing his father describe those glasses over the phone; similarly Otto hears that he should wear his green scarf to the meeting to match his father, and Pivner is described as wearing a green scarf.[101] These are very minor details, however, listed among the novel's many other unimportant data (e.g., Pivner's receding hairline, the color of his suit), and Gaddis deliberately obscures them by placing them in parenthetical asides and spacing them hundreds of pages apart. This seems designed so that readers will initially fail to recognize the connection, just as Otto misrecognizes counterfeiter Frank Sinisterra as his father when Pivner is delayed by a seizure just prior to their meeting.[102]

This tactic of disorientation via unimportant details is most evident in the extended party and bar scenes, featuring large casts of intermittently identified minor characters engaged in dull cross conversations over subjects of little importance, culminating in the one with whose opening exchanges we began this chapter. Again this scene's dialogue is characterized not by clichés but clichéd representations of clichés, combined with context-free non sequiturs that are neither insightful nor satiric (e.g., "—Mendelssohn Schmendelssohn, someone else said.—I'm talking about *music*").[103] As I pointed out, it cannot succeed as satire because it does not generate incongruity between different schemas for social behavior, but simply plays out one tedious script to great length. What it does do, however, is make itself *so* stupid as to render the characters and readers so dull-witted that they have trouble recognizing more important things going on around them.

For instance, after appearing and disappearing several times in the scene's first half, Esther's beloved kitten gets lost.[104] After going unmentioned for over thirty pages, the kitten finally reappears at the chapter's end, when a fight breaks out between Anselm and Don Bildow. The partygoers' response begins here with the Argentine trade commissioner, to whom Ed Feasley has been trying to sell a battleship:

> —Yes I was told to expect this sort of thing in New York.
>
> —Yes but I mean Chrast don't go away, or we'll both go, let's both go to your hotel, I'll stay there tonight.
>
> —But in another room.
>
> —Chrast yes.
>
> —I was warned about that sort of thing in New York, his companion commented, adjusting his perfectly adjusted tie.
>
> —Oh Rose, Esther said to where her sister sat on the floor in the dark with the records.—Aren't you tired?
>
> —Are you having a nice party?
>
> Esther put her face in her hands, and felt her sister's arm round her neck.—Oh Rose. Rose.

> The hand under her became rigid, the paralysis ran up her arm, through her shoulders and neck, her face yellowing as the blood drained from behind its bronzed canvas.—Stanley . . . Agnes Deigh whispered, staring at him bent over Anselm, an arm around Anselm.
>
> —You see, it's all right now, Stanley said, gripping his shoulder but unable to raise it from the floor. Anselm opened his eyes.
>
> In the hand she drew from under her, the white nails clutched a limp cinnamon-colored body.—I thought . . . it was something. Agnes Deigh said weakly to herself. Then she looked around quickly, opened her bag and pulled handfuls of things out which she stuffed in her coat pocket, to snap it closed a moment later upon the lifeless kitten. She summoned her voice in,—Stanley . . .
>
> —And now, you don't have to fight it any more, you . . . Anselm's arm was flung around him, and Anselm's unshaven face tore at Stanley's face with the kiss.[105]

As with most speech throughout the scene, the dialogue communicates nothing to anyone: Feasley and the Argentine simply repeat phrases they have thrown at each other for the past forty pages, Esther murmurs meaningless words to her impaired sister, and Stanley mutters clichés to Anselm. However, though no one is saying anything of importance, their propagation of the party's chatter prevents anyone from realizing what has happened to the cat, whom Agnes has sat on and killed. Even Agnes does not realize what she has done, apparently, given her worried reaction to her purse being stolen several pages later.[106]

Gaddis works hard to obscure this moment from his readers, too. The cat's death is recounted in a prepositional phrase concluding an aside between speech tags, and the previous paragraphs' anticipation of the event are misleadingly described: when Agnes reaches beneath her and suspects what she has done, the *her* ("The hand under her") is placed so that its antecedent appears to be Esther, not Agnes, making the sentence about the former's embarrassment rather than the latter's horror. Similarly most of Agnes's reaction to the kitten's death is reported before what she has done has been revealed, prompting us to misattribute it toward one of the other things that has been disturbing her through the novel, like her relationship with Stanley. Even the phrase "cinnamon-colored body" does not express exactly what has happened, since the cat's coloring has not been previously described. In other words the cat's death is clearly reported to readers by only two words dissolved in an entire scene's worth of cruft misdirection, to the extent that it becomes very easy to glaze over and miss the dead cat as entirely as the partygoers do.

This is not the only example in the chapter. None of the scene's three most consequential plot threads—Agnes's accidental crushing of the kitten, Maude Munk's abduction of the unexplained baby crawling around the apartment, and Charley Dickens's unsuccessful suicide attempts—take up more than a page of text, most of which is scattered several lines at a time across the scene's four-score pages of jabber. The latter does include some passages popular with critics—including Stanley's stuttering thoughts about fragmentation and tradition, Benny's blather about how the intellectual class doesn't understand "real life," and Otto's conveyance of Wyatt's half-baked criticism of America's youth-centered culture—but to take any of these passages as either serious philosophical statements or satires of their speakers' self-importance would reflect poorly on the book's craftsmanship.[107] Better we see them as blending into the rest of the stupidity. As with the Brueghel that Wyatt forges, the scene's suffering, in Auden's famous lines, "takes place / While someone else is eating or opening a window or just walking dully along," as unnoticed as Icarus's leg in the bottom right corner of his most famous landscape.[108]

The Recognitions' readers, then, must decide how to avoid getting bogged down in the constant hum of idiocy while also observing the important events that occur in that background. As the novel comes to its close, this process becomes exceedingly hard. On the one hand, some sections descend so purely into cruft that any concerted attempt to recognize anything within them would be wasted mental effort. Agnes's five-page letter of apology to Dr. Weisgall, whom she'd accused of child abuse, contains barely a coherent sentence.[109] Yet abandoning recalcitrant text is dangerous, too, as may be seen in two of the book's final scenes, in which Arny Munk and Stanley each decide to ignore a brief, incomprehensible message they assume is too unimportant to be worth bothering about, respectively a warning in French encountered while the former is trying to put out a hotel-room fire and one in Italian while the latter is practicing an organ composition. We all ignore stimuli like this every day, of course, since we are constantly faced with a million sources of ambient information, almost all of which are of no consequence. Arny and Stanley are not so fortunate, however, because ignoring these messages causes each to have a building collapse on and kill him.[110] This is illustrative of why *The Recognitions* is relatively humorless when compared to the other two novels we have discussed in this chapter. The penalties Gaddis administers on his characters for even the briefest slips in attention and memory are often sadistic and arbitrary. One hopes that Gaddis did not mistake the asymmetrical relation of author and audience for an exemption from human limitations: when the satirist returns to the real world, after all, his mind does not so easily encompass its unimaginable variety as it does that of his fictional one.

5 Episodic Narrative

Too Much Plot

Since the beginning of the twentieth century, one common complaint about western literary fiction has been that its overabsorption with artistry prevents it from "telling a good story." Summarizing this view in his "Reader's Manifesto," critic B. R. Myers groused that "any accessible, fast-moving story written in unaffected prose is deemed to be 'genre fiction' [. . .] never literature with a capital L."[1] Given that several touchstone twentieth-century theories of the novel significantly deemphasized story in favor of character or language—think of E. M. Forster's mournful, "Yes—oh dear, yes—the novel tells a story"—this criticism is understandable.[2] It is, however, markedly inapplicable to mega-novels. Instead of being devoid of story, they are often stuffed with kooky episodes, sometimes to the point of inducing critics who have argued for story's importance in other contexts to criticize them for having too much. James Wood has pejoratively termed extravagantly plotted mega-novels "hysterical realism," because, Wood claims, they "want to abolish stillness, as if ashamed of silence—as it were, a criminal running endless charity marathons. Stories and sub-stories sprout on every page, as these novels continually flourish their glamorous congestion."[3] For Wood, Thomas Pynchon's *Mason & Dixon* provides a case study, because its gratuitous profusion of isolated tales—including the adventures of "a talking dog, a mechanical duck, a giant octagonal cheese, and two clocks having a conversation"—end up diluting rather than increasing the narrative's richness.[4] "[H]owever dissimilar each new adventure is from its predecessor," he writes, "it resembles it in its mere adventurousness. The variety becomes homogeneous."[5] In other words, when story is added simply for the sake of adding story, it quickly loses any sense of novelty and instead comes off as repetitive and pointless. For critics like Wood, mega-novel episodes are simply cruft.

What does it mean to suggest part of a narrative is pointless, though? After all, if one takes the classic structuralist perspective, there can be no such thing as pointless narrative. Though any narrative might be reduced to a single sentence representing primary plot motion, as in Gérard Genette's boiling down of the two million words in *À la recherche du temps perdu* to "Marcel becomes a writer," structuralists generally believe that, in Roland Barthes's words, "there are no wasted units, and there can never be any, however long, loose, or tenuous the threads which link them to one of the levels of the story."[6] Obviously some plot functions are more important than others for achieving that overall expression—even in a conventional novel like *Pride and Prejudice*, Franco Moretti notes, a full 97 percent of scenes are low-importance "catalyses" rather than major "turning points"—but even the least important vignettes, in this theory, provide some small movement toward realizing the narrative structure.[7] Pointlessness is more possible in recent theories. For instance the "natural narratology" put forward by Monika Fludernik defines a story's "point" as the unusual or surprising segment of experience that motivates a speaker to recount a story: if narrators fail to establish a point, the resulting stories would consequently lose tellability and become pointless.[8] Brian McHale's notion of "weak narrativity," meanwhile, refers to avant-garde works in which a narrative skeleton merely provides an occasion for unconventional poetic effects.[9]

Mega-novel plots, though, are clearly focused on narrative for its own sake yet still frequently manage to tell irrelevant and indeterminate stories. Returning to the example of *Mason & Dixon*, for instance, while we might condense its overall narrative to "On a snowy winter evening in 1786, the Reverend Wicks Cherrycoke tells a family gathering about how Charles Mason and Jeremiah Dixon had surveyed their eponymous line," we would have difficulty construing all the book's narrative as positively contributing to that scheme. It is not merely that the novel subverts narrative logic by frame breaking, most prominently in the excursus from Cherrycoke's tale into a sensationalist magazine's captivity narrative that leads back into Cherrycoke's voice without any perspectival shift: moves such as these, after all, might be assimilable to current theories of "unnatural narrative."[10] Instead it is that some sections of the novel generate *so many* possible stories that each is rendered indeterminate and arbitrary. For example, in the middle of Mason and Dixon's journey across the Pennsylvania-Maryland border, the aforementioned captive, Eliza Fields, arrives at Mason and Dixon's camp, bringing with her the Chinese feng shui devotee Captain Zhang, who fears that he has been followed by his Jesuit nemesis, Father Zarpazo. Since the latter is purportedly a master of disguise, Zhang begins to suspect that any member of the company might be him and at one point disguises himself in Jesuit robes so as to better anticipate the Spaniard's motions:

> "He's [i.e., Zhang's] not a real Jesuit," Mason assures her.
>
> "Or, perhaps, all too real!" the Captain with a look of evil glee,— "for suppose I never was Zhang, but rather Zarpazo, all the Time! HA,—ha-ha!" His Laugh, tho' hideously fiendish enough, seems practis'd.
>
> "Or," replies Mr. Barnes, "that you are neither, but yet another damn'd Fabulator, such as ever haunt encampments, white or Indian, ev'ry night, somewhere in this Continent."
>
> "Too many possible Stories. You may not have time enough to find out which is the right one."[11]

At least four possible stories are suggested here: that "Zhang" is really Zhang, that "Zhang" is really Zarpazo, that "Zhang" is neither of them (both, perhaps, simply being characters from the aforementioned sensationalist rag) and has been deliberately playacting, or that "Zhang" is merely, as he is described a few pages later, "crazy."[12] All these indeterminate plots, however, are mutually exclusive, negating each other and providing no basis on which readers can even begin considering which is most accurate.[13] Since these hanging possibilities are never revisited as the novel progresses, what is the purpose of expanding them here?

Of course interpretive indeterminacy does not necessarily render narrative pointless. As Umberto Eco long ago noted, open narrative questions (e.g., those in Michel Antonioni's *L'avventura*) can drive a plot by constantly redirecting frustrated characters' and viewers' desires.[14] More recently H. Porter Abbott notes that the necessary incompleteness of any fictional world means there will always be gaps in which "multiple incompatible stories, together with their incompatible worlds, reside [. . .] but only as possibilities."[15] However, we cannot merely accept all these story possibilities as equally and positively enriching the narrative, because their ability to iteratively generate further possibilities quickly overrides our ability to process them. As Abbott points out, "It would, of course, require a mind of great and inhuman capability to entertain more than a fraction of all possible event sequences together with all the exponentially increasing numbers of possible event sequences nested within them."[16] Were we to capitulate entirely to the terms of Zhang's game, that is, we would have to pose further *perhaps*-es and *suppose*s ad infinitum: in addition to questioning Zhang's identity, for example, we would have to wonder whether Mason has really been Dixon the whole time, or Dixon Mason, or both of them other people entirely and not really in America but Mongolia, which the other characters have artificed to match the pair's expectations for the New World. Such possibilities, of course, spin themselves into dead ends so immediately that they can have no purpose to the plot, and since they may be thrown arbitrarily into any narrative at any time, they tend toward cruft.

How we process and compress such an excess of narrative possibilities has significant cognitive implications. As neuroscientist Antonio Damasio has suggested, consciousness itself may be the product of internal "wordless narrative [. . .] based on neural patterns," generating the self out of a record of observations of the organism's state and sensory perceptions.[17] This narrative is generated, of course, in a highly recursive manner, and its long-term records are subject to occasional revision, but the core narrative itself is quite linear: "It does have characters (the organism, the object). It unfolds in time. And it has a beginning, a middle, and an end."[18] Even Daniel Dennett's model of consciousness as founded on parallel-processed "multiple 'drafts' of narrative fragments" grants that experienced consciousness itself is a linear "Joycean machine."[19] When alternate realities multiply to the point that this main linear narrative dissolves, then, the basis of the conscious self might begin to erode. The stakes of this problem may be illustrated best by Jorge Luis Borges's Dr. Yu Tsun in "The Garden of Forking Paths," whose adoption of his ancestor Ts'ui Pen's view of space-time as a timeless, infinite array of coexisting possible worlds allows him to temporarily suspend any feelings of personal agency in murdering his friend Stephen Albert.[20]

Consequently if a fiction's sequence of events becomes too overloaded with alternate possibilities, both the storyworld and the consciousness processing it may face serious difficulty.

For many years "linearity" was a dirty word in studies of contemporary fiction, with the description "nonlinear" doubling as a positive aesthetic evaluation. That position needs to be reevaluated. We must realize that the nonlinear possibilities presented by novels are constantly in dialectic with the linear needs of consciousness. Subsequently we must ask how one distinguishes between storytelling that creatively exploits the alternate worlds of fiction from that which is simply nonsense. *Mason & Dixon*, in fact, is an excellent place for us for to do that, because while the book's disparate episodes sometimes appear about as linear as freehand doodles, the novel is very much about the establishment of linearity: its plot, after all, is guided by the perpendicular lines its title characters survey between Pennsylvania, Delaware, and Maryland.[21] To do that, however, we will first need to examine the two narrative genres that have historically included abundant nonlinear plots without being charged with pointlessness, the picaresque and the frame-tale, to determine the conditions under which proliferating stories can thrive.

Plotting Space and Time in the Picaresque and Frame-Tale, and Introducing the Circumfabulation

Both older forms than the novel, the picaresque and the frame-tale are perhaps the exemplary genres of episodic narrative. As a result they often appear less like coherent linear narratives than boundless structures for story, meandering in many directions and consequently increasing to an arbitrarily large size, as may be seen in the seven hundred pages of Mateo Aleman's picaresque *Guzman de Alfarache* or, to greater extremes, the thirty volumes of the Indian frame-tale *The Ocean of Story*. Despite the Aristotelian objection that "episodic [plots] are the worst" because "the sequence of episodes is neither necessary nor probable," both the picaresque and the frame-tale demonstrate how narrative may generate a wide variety of disparate stories while still maintaining coherent narrative purpose.[22]

The pair sustain their episodic plots by taking analogous but opposed approaches to what Bakhtin referred to as the "intrinsic connectedness of temporal and spatial relationships that are artistically expressed in literature," or "chronotope."[23] The picaresque, though often defined within the Anglophone world simply as any narrative about wandering adventures, initially grew its plot structure out of a specific need to narrate the lives of *pícaros*, peripatetic social outcasts roaming from town to town in search of work, food, and money, who often got involved in various illegal activities along the way.[24] The resulting "loosely episodic" plot—"strung together," in Claudio Guillén's words, "like a freight train and *apparently* with no other common link than the hero"—has frequently been critiqued as lacking structural cohesion, for instance in René Wellek and Austin Warren's objection that "[i]n the picaresque novel, the chronological sequence is all there is: this happened and then that."[25] However, in critiquing the genre, this objection articulates well how the pícaro's chronotope sustains its stories' point. The pícaro's spatial progress is so discontinuous and episodic because he is forced to experience only the most stable, linear progression of time: pressed by his moment-to-moment needs for survival, and lacking any education, he is incapable of contemplating pasts, futures, and other worlds. For this reason Peter Brooks sees in the picaresque structure not an exception to conventional plot but a quintessential example of its motivation by basic desire: the disparate adventures of a pícaro like Lazarillo des Tormes are held together because they are each "devised to overcome a specific form of the threat [i.e., starvation], and thus literally to enable life, and narrative, to go forward."[26]

The frame-tale's chronotope, on the other hand, is precisely reversed. As Robert Clements and Joseph Gibaldi have described, the "cornice"/"novella" structure of the frame-tale, where a skeletal outer frame recounts how one or more storytellers narrate several autonomous tales to an audience, guarantees that even tales whose temporality diverges wildly from chronological time must be mediated through a static ground state restraining the storyteller(s) to a single spatial location.[27] The tales of the *Thousand and One Nights*, for instance, no matter how far they reach into legendary time or how freely their adventures seem to proceed, are told only in Shahryar's bedchamber, and while the Florentine aristocrats of *The Decameron* might visit a different bucolic setting on some days during their plague-induced exile and Chaucer's pilgrims might advance gradually on the long journey toward Canterbury, for all intents and purposes they stay in the same space. Furthermore, as Clements and Gibaldi suggest, the individual novellas are often granted their points by the cornice's spatially restrictive situation, often a national disaster, which allows the storytelling either to help resolve that problem or to simply let its audience pass the time.[28] Like the pícaro, Brooks notes, frame-tale storytellers like Shahrazad provide an archetypal example of plotting because their temporality-manipulating storytelling is "life-giving in that it arouses and sustains desire, ensuring that the terminus it both delays and beckons toward will offer what we might call a lucid repose."[29]

However, there are two reasons why the picaresque and frame-tale's justification of multiplied story possibilities do not necessarily transfer to mega-novels like *Mason & Dixon*. First, despite the balances these genres strike between spatial and temporal freedom, each still bears the potential for cruft. As Ulrich Wicks notes, while picaresques' individual episodes usually have coherent plots, as a whole they can tend toward a "Sisphyus rhythm."[30] Similarly frame-tales, as Bonnie Irwin points out, can tend toward boring repetitiveness because they were not expected to be read from start to finish the way contemporary novels are: consequently it did not matter as much if the narrative as a whole tended to be "paratactic, open-ended, and unfinished."[31] To maintain their points in a contemporary context, though, each episode in a frame-tale or picaresque would need both to stand on its own as a distinct tale and to serve a purpose either in the rogue's progress or the cornice ground situation.

Second, moreover, many mega-novels, though often identified as picaresques or frame-tales, are better described as belonging to a third genre combining elements of the pair. *Mason & Dixon*, for instance, may seem at times like a picaresque, with its main section following the historical Mason's episodic logbook chronologically across the diffuse space of a lawless border territory, but on the other hand seems also to be a frame-tale, as the story is recounted to us only decades later by Cherrycoke, with his distillation of the duo's chronology frequently broken up both by his own parenthetical asides and by other characters' embedded tales.[32] To my knowledge this structure does not have a generally accepted name, though Walter Reed may have come closest when constructing a genre he called the "quixotic novel," which, in contrast with what he perceived as the picaresque's total anticonventionality, dialogically presses narrative conventions to their full potential.[33] Certainly he is right to name *Don Quixote* as belonging to this genre, given that book's alternation between temporally pedestrian but spatially expansive episodic adventures and spatially static but temporally complex interpolated narratives. It would be misleading, though, to imply it was invented by Cervantes, as Homer's *Odyssey* contains these features as well, as do many other works ranging across centuries and national borders.

Owing to these books' roundabout methods of storytelling, we might call them "circumfabulations." To adapt Cherrycoke's description of history, a circumfabulation's narrative might be conceived as a "great disorderly Tangle of Lines, long and short, weak and strong," given its episodes' freedom in both the temporal and spatial axes.[34] Distinguishing the circumfabulation from the picaresque and frame-tale is useful because its profuse narrative possibilities are designed not to prolong the hero's life, as in the picaresque and frame-tale, but to challenge the hero—or more typically heroes, as its dialectical structure usually benefits from having two central characters—to maintain a stable identity in the face of story conditions that shift constantly in both time and space. Consider, for instance, how Quixote must struggle with the cognitive dissonance caused by his vacillations between material and fantastic worlds, or how the obstacles Odysseus faces in various different lands question his status as a man, husband, and king. Individual episodes, no matter how outlandish, can sustain purposes if we view them as part of the heroes' progressive attempt to incorporate new, disorienting events into a linear, consistent self.

Obviously, however, such freedom on both the spatial and temporal axes can prompt the circumfabulation toward gratuitousness, just as with the picaresque and frame-tale. Tangles, after all, often contain superfluous individual threads that merely twist up the whole to no real benefit. This chapter will begin, then, by using *Mason & Dixon* to discuss how episodic narrative, especially when it involves a limited amount of cruft, pressures consciousness's abilities to move linearly forward. This will allow us to subsequently examine how mega-novel picaresques and frame-tales similarly present readers with greater cruft in the form of episodes lacking any apparent point, challenging them to plot out their mysterious overall structures without having their attention deadened by their narrative cruft.

The Line and the Tangle in *Mason & Dixon*

Let's return to Zhang's suggestions about his true identity in the middle of *Mason & Dixon*. The realm of possibilities Zhang opens up in this passage bear significant implications for how we read the whole book, because the problem of trying to plot "too many possible stories" figures the novel's entire central section. In surveying (i.e., plotting) the territory between Pennsylvania and Maryland, Mason and Dixon have wild, episodic encounters in the interior of the prenatal United States, which, though officially belonging to either the Calverts or Penns, is ruled ambiguously in practice. What occurs is bound to no particular rules of law and order, nor even, as Wood implies, to rationality. As is mentioned several times in the novel, the land exists in a "subjunctive" state of many possibilities. By structuring the novel's central section this way, Pynchon allows himself to incorporate limitless variety, ranging from a castle that functions on quantum principles, to an Indian golem supposedly created by one of the lost tribes of Israel, to a garden of enormous produce purportedly left by a race of ancient giants.[35] By the novel's end, though, the gradual extension of European settlements and scientific progress, both furthered by Mason and Dixon's survey, has necessarily erased many of these possibilities.

Most critics treat this erosion of possibility as a great loss, often citing Cherrycoke's suggestion that the survey's very linearity corrupts America, altering the land "from subjunctive to declarative, reducing Possibilities to Simplicities that serve the ends of Governments."[36] As Francis Collado Rodriguez argues, "in *Mason & Dixon* the term *line* is frequently used to suggest its pernicious and finally useless condition. Lines are continuously trespassed not only in the main story but, as we have seen, also between narratorial voices and different narrative levels."[37] Similarly many critics endorse Zhang's claim that the Mason-Dixon Line does violence on the authentic spiritual power expressed by the land's jagged natural boundaries: "Ev'rywhere else on earth, Boundaries follow Nature,—coast-lines, ridge-tops, river-banks,—so honoring the Dragon or *Shan* within, from which Land-Scape ever takes its form. To make a right Line upon the Earth is to inflict upon the Dragon's very Flesh, a sword-slash, a long, perfect scar, impossible for any who live out here the year 'round to see as other than hateful Assault."[38] Consequently, then, many believe that Pynchon's circumfabulating redeems the surveyors' work by retangling the border territory. "If surveying is conceived as a process of codifying the landscape," David Seed, for instance, writes, "Pynchon's novel subverts its apparently straightforward representational purpose by proliferating signs and signifying systems."[39]

At the same time, however, as Zofia Kolbuszewska notes, "the subjunctive offers not only utopian possibilities but also demonic ones," and we must observe that the more nonlinear plot possibilities the novel encompasses, the more it tends toward nonsense.[40] After all Zhang, the guru of subjunctivism, dissolves into a "dement[ed]" and "oblivious" loon by the book's conclusion.[41] Mason and Dixon are at times vulnerable to that fate as well. For instance midway through their commission, Dixon postulates that "something invisible's going on" and that the pair is "being us'd" to profit vested capitalist interests, to which Mason responds with these baroque speculations:

> If it were all true,—ev'ry unkind suspicion, ev'ry phantastickal rendering,—would we, knowing all, nonetheless go on? Do what's clearly our Duty? [. . .] Then as we've no choice, I may speak freely and share with you some of my darker Sentiments. Suppose Maskelyne's a French Spy. Suppose a secret force of Jesuits, receives each Day a summary of Observations made at Greenwich, and transcalculates it according to a system known to the Kabbalists of the Second Century as *Gematria*, whereby Messages may be extracted from lines of Text sacred and otherwise, a Knowledge preserv'd by various Custodians over the centuries, and since the Last, possess'd by Jesuit and Freemason alike. The Dispute over Bradley's Obs, then, as over Flamsteed's before him, would keep ever as their unspoken intention that the Numbers nocturnally obtain'd be set side by side, and arrang'd into Lines, like those of a Text, manipulated till a Message be reveal'd.[42]

Like Zhang's hypotheses, none of these paranoid allegations is ever corroborated elsewhere: they are, by Mason's admission, "Drivel, of course."[43] However, their sheer abundance has a paralyzing impact, as not only is the plot Mason puts forward too convoluted to respond to adequately, but its implicit suggestion of infinite other *ifs* evacuates each of meaning. We may classify them, consequently, as cruft. If plotting is integral to the maintenance of self, such tangles not only are incomprehensible themselves but erode Mason and Dixon's own identities, which is likely why the pair ask several times some version of the multivalent question, "What are we about?"[44]

If such moments demonstrate why perpetual subjunctivity is not tenable, they also suggest the benefits of linearity. As Samuel Cohen notes, "lines are not simply to be condemned," because they allow "[t]he possibility of connection across difference."[45] After all, for all that, the Mason-Dixon Line represents the destruction of natural potential or preexisting migratory cultures, it also creates connections between that which was previously incommensurable. While Sascha Pöhlmann, for example, criticizes the Mason-Dixon Line for the "obvious violence of such acts of demarcation" between North and South, he also notes how it joins East and West, as the "nation of Americans which Mason sees in the process of being created is actually *built*, not because those who share an essential group identity finally get to rule themselves, but because an imagined community is produced," bringing realms as diverse as Philadelphia's coffee houses, outlying colonial farms, and independent settlements into a sense of shared community.[46] When Mason and Dixon begin westward, the territory is defined by the lawless, violently anti-Indian Paxton gang that kills wantonly and without check; by the end of their survey, one can see the beginnings of something "already, unmistakably, American" emerging.[47] Just as measuring the parallax in the transit of Venus brings together scientists "all over the World all day long that fifth and sixth of June, in Latin, in Chinese, in Polish, in Silence,—upon Roof-tops and Mountain Peaks, out of Bed-chamber windows, close together in the naked sunlight," different communities are drawn together by the Mason-Dixon Line.[48] This requires, however, fidelity to the surveyors' calculations of what does and does not belong on the line. The multiplicities of "all that *may yet be true*" must be diminished when possibilities are converted to reality, but the ranks of the realized will remain forever empty if one does not eliminate nonsensical or incompatible possibilities. One cannot subjunctively have one's cake while indicatively eating it, too.

What to make, then, of all the quirky, digressive episodes and implied shadow stories encountered along the way? Are they beneficial for allowing us to imagine alternate worlds, or do they threaten the maintenance of consciousness? Interestingly, many of Wood's alleged examples in favor of the latter argument are somewhat ambiguous, because as the line progresses they become partly "disnarrated," Gerald Prince's term for when events "*do not* happen, but, nonetheless, are referred to."[49] For instance Mason implicitly begins to doubt the existence of the talking dog when a similar-looking Norwich terrier refuses to speak to him later, and the French chef Armand Allègre loses faith in his miraculously animated mechanical duck when it spends so much time invisibly flying into the western frontier as to fade into myth.[50] To plot one's experiences requires coherence between them, after all, and since the advance of the Age of Reason facilitated by the advance of the line is finally not compatible with talking dogs and flying robotic ducks, these stories must eventually be erased. The novel almost seems to grant Wood's point that these subplots are gratuitous and discardable.

However, these particular examples are not quite pointless (nor quite, consequently, cruft in the same manner of Zhang's shadow stories or Mason's conspiracy theory). Because the world's ideas about what may and may not be resolved into a scientific worldview are being massively revised during the period in which the novel is set, they are for a time held beside the novel's natural wonders in an unresolved fantastic state: after all, Professor Voam's electric eel Felipe, at first, appears every bit as improbable to Mason and Dixon as do the adventures of Allègre's duck.[51] Consequently their experience of such wonders is every bit as important as their scientific discoveries, because both equally motivate their wonder and their subsequent quests to understand the world around them. How to eventually decide what may be plotted cogently and what must be cast away as nonsense, however, vexes the surveyors to the ends of their lives, with Dixon maintaining a heterotopic but somewhat incoherent perspective in which scientific calculations can coexist with incompatible theories about hollow-earth underground civilizations and Mason dying while attempting to devise "a great single Engine, the size of a Continent" that will plot all the wonders of existence without contradiction.[52]

Similar decisions must be made by the audiences for Mason and Dixon's narrative. The stories may seem equally amusing and preposterous as they happen, but they accrete meaning differently: some become indispensable to characters within the narrative (and to readers outside it), while others are easily disposed. Which of the novel's many fanciful-sounding stories have real resonance for America's future, like Mr. Everybeet's search for the semimystical Oölite ore that will later be mined for munitions?[53] Which end up being nonsense but attract motivating emotional interest nonetheless, like Allègre's duck?[54] And which really are mostly cruft, like the Scandanavian ax-man Stig's yarn about a nation of albinos living north of Sweden?[55] The answers become clear only after we have progressed through the whole novel, by which time these possibilities must be whittled down from all those that may be imagined to all those that may be held together in a plot. Even the subjunctivist Cherrycoke realizes this principle upon reviewing for his audience his day-book speculations regarding the infamous Black Hole of Calcutta. Though he had imagined for himself in detail a variety of possible ways one might survive such an experience—"one might either transcend it spiritually, or eroticize it carnally"—his elaborations on how these narratives might proceed are interrupted by the narrator's parenthetical disnarration, "(Tho' he does not of course read any of this aloud,—choosing rather to skim ahead to the Moral.)"[56] Some possibilities, after all—whether too fanciful or too painful—simply cannot be maintained for long by a stable mind.

Yet imagining counterfactual possibilities is often all that propels consciousness onward, as may be best seen in the ambiguous coda to the novel's climax. Upon returning east, Mason and Dixon may have become convinced, quite understandably, that owing to the line's conduciveness to colonialism, it is a "conduit for Evil."[57] On the other hand, though, the narrator's recounting of a "more hopefu[l]," counterfactual version of their journey in chapter 73 is somewhat at odds with this view, because instead of destroying the line, it imagines its complete extension toward Ohio, the West Coast, and around the world.[58] The possibility of discovering new ways of being, after all, is what has always driven not only the scientific but the social and political mind to venture forward. That is why this passage, despite being little more than a postulation of arbitrary stories—an encounter with a half-breed sidekick named Vongolli, a visit with a tribe that worships the newly discovered planet Uranus, and so on—is so touching, and yet also so melancholy. Because it is propelled by Mason and Dixon's desire to keep discovering more of that which may exist, the line is also driven by the knowledge that it must eventually run out of space, all possibilities finally validated or excised. That is why Mason and Dixon, in the alternate ending, must retire as mid-Atlantic ferrymen. They are unable to settle on exactly where in such a various and yet fully mapped world they belong, but in both the real and alternate versions, they know that they have no choice but to try to determine the answer by navigating on their line.

Hopefully this illustrates plotting's stakes for the conscious self, especially regarding how it must deal with cruft. Granted, the amount of pure cruft in *Mason & Dixon* is limited, as it will tend to be in most circumfabulations: the necessarily strong protagonists will usually be able to redeem whatever they encounter into some degree of purposefulness. But it should show us that while we need to be able to imagine alternate narrative possibilities, we cannot allow them to become a complete tangle. They must eventually be straightened out, or we will never be able to proceed with anything, and consequently we need to be ready to discard narrative possibilities that will not aid us in doing so.

The Useless Room: The Frame-Tale and *Life a User's Manual*

We may now move our focus to the mega-novel picaresque and frame-tale, which can experiment with cruft to a significantly greater degree, as their respective chronological and cornice structures allow them to remove the dramatized central narrative voice. With the narrator obscured, the point of the narrative may frequently vanish, leading readers to encounter numerous mini- or pseudonarratives that invite plotting but are too bizarre or disjointed to allow it to be done cogently. Such episodes recall Brooks's famous claim that in all narrative, the reader plays the role of detective, deducing *fabula* from the clues within *sžujet*.[59] The mega-novel reader, similarly, must learn to sort out the plottable events from those that suggest either too few or too many possible plots to be understood.

The frame-tale mega-novel might be best exemplified by Georges Perec's *Life a User's Manual*. As with the frame-tales of Boccaccio and his imitators, which are not labeled as singular works but as groups of "novellas," Perec's book is subtitled *Romans* ("novels") rather than *Roman* ("a novel").[60] Also like the *Decameron*, *Life a User's Manual* is programmatically divided into a ten-by-ten structure, though where Boccaccio gave each of ten storytellers ten days in which to spin a fiction,

Perec creates a ten-story apartment building at 11 Rue Simon Crubellier with ten rooms on each floor, each of which is the focus of one's chapter's narrative. As if to further establish its debt to the tradition of Shahrazad, the book's voluminous index alphabetically labels the book's stories as if they were entries in *Thousand and One Nights* (e.g., "The Puzzle-Maker's Tale," "The Tale of the Actor who faked his own death"), and like that work, the actual number of chapters just misses a round decimal number: since Perec intentionally skips the left-most room of the cellar, only ninety-nine rooms are the subjects of stories.[61]

However, unlike in the classic frame-tales, *Life a User's Manual* has no explicit, dramatized storyteller whose personal situation gives the tales a point: the book's only cornice is the literal one atop the building. There is a narrator of a sort, but we learn little about him directly except through the preamble, a sly three-page essay on the relationship between the makers and solvers of jigsaw puzzles. The narrator hints at his purposes by noting that "despite appearances, puzzling is not a solitary game: every move the puzzler makes, the puzzle-maker has made before," and we might infer that if constructing a book like *Life a User's Manual* is like creating a jigsaw puzzle, the narrator's motivation may be his desire for this intimate relationship with his readers.[62] Yet at a given moment, the puzzle maker's intentions might be loving or hostile, cooperative or antagonistic, evident or ambiguous. In fact the preamble notes that the puzzle maker's guidance to the puzzler must be interspersed with "falsified elements, carrying false information," such as pieces that appear to fit in one part of the puzzle but belong somewhere else entirely.[63] When we add that the satisfying closure achieved by a puzzle's completion is far neater and more exact than the resolution of even the tidiest fiction, it should be clear how *Life a User's Manual*'s stories have the potential to generate cruft.

Chapter 4, describing the outer room of the fourth-floor-right apartment, is a good early example of this phenomenon. In later chapters we learn that this flat is inhabited by the record producers Caroline and Phillipe Marquiseaux, who have inherited it only after the death of the former's miserable mother and who are currently having sex in the inner room's shower while two musicians await them in the middle room.[64] Chapter 4 communicates nothing about any of this, though. Instead it merely tells us this about the room:

An empty drawing room on the fourth floor right.

On the floor there is a woven sisal mat, its strands entwined in such a way as to form star-shaped designs.

On the wall, an imitation of Jouy cretonne wallpaper depicts big sailing ships, Portuguese four-masters, armed with cannon and culverins, making ready to put into a harbour; the headsails and spankers billow in the wind; sailors have climbed up the rigging to clew up the others.

There are four paintings on the wall.

The chapter is completed by descriptions of the paintings (a still life, a cityscape, a mythic beast, and an English narrative painting), but as with many similar descriptions in the book, they have little apparent connection to the rest of the narrative.[65] Given the book's all but explicit self-identification as a frame-tale, not to mention the frequent critical valorization of Perec's power as a "visionary storyteller," this chapter is puzzlingly plotless.[66] It is not unusual in the book, either, as similar chapters occur throughout, notably including the scenes on the staircase, such as chapter 68's list of things dropped there over the years, which Myoung-Sook Kim has termed narrative "black holes."[67] As one initial reviewer complained, "by withdrawing himself from his creation, has the creator not left it empty?"[68]

The enigma posed by these useless rooms becomes especially important when we consider that uselessness is itself central to the novel's most prominent story line, about the building's British millionaire Percival Bartlebooth.[69] Even more than the narrator, Bartlebooth lacks clear motivation: unlike the heroes of most frame-tales, he is not under any spatial restriction, because he has inherited an enormous fortune from his great-uncle James Sherwood that not only satisfies all his material needs but allows him to travel anywhere he likes. Though for Bouvard and Pécuchet such a windfall meant an opportunity to retire to the country, Bartlebooth finds he needs something more substantial, and yet less purposeful, to motivate him. "[I]n the face of the inextricable incoherence of things," the narrator tells us, "Bartlebooth resolved one day that his whole life would be organised around a single project, an arbitrarily constrained programme with no purpose outside its own completion," one that would be "useless [. . .] a series of events which when concatenated would nullify each other."[70] This program develops into a fifty-year plan involving several of the building's other residents, in which Bartlebooth spends the first ten learning to paint watercolors with Serge Valène; the next twenty painting five hundred seascapes in locations around the world, which are sent to puzzle maker Gaspard Winckler to be converted into jigsaws; and the last twenty reassembling the puzzles in his apartment, after which they are chemically restored and sent back to their place of composition to be dissolved. Lacking intrinsic purpose, in other words, Bartlebooth decides to plot the rest of his life so that each of his actions is directly negated by another, rendering his entire existence useless.

Ironically the relationships Bartlebooth forms with those whom he has enlisted in his scheme, most obviously Winckler, end up motivating many of the book's tales and giving them purpose. As Paul Schwartz points out, "the gratuitous perfection envisioned by Bartlebooth" is not possible in "a universe obsessed with traces."[71] However, the questions about uselessness he raises become relevant when considered in light of the other chapters, like the one about the Marquiseaux' outer drawing room. How useless must a room be, after all, when it does not even relate to a plot about uselessness? Such chapters may be Perec's best attempt to pursue a thought experiment he posed in *Species of Spaces* about the possibility of a truly useless room—not a spare room or an all-purpose room, but one with absolutely no purpose at all. He imagines many rooms that asymptotically approach this condition, like "a room reserved to listening to Haydn's Symphony Number 8 in C [. . .] a room without either doors or windows" and so on, but finds that "[l]anguage itself, seemingly, proved unsuited to describing this nothing, this void, as if we could only speak of what is full, useful, and functional."[72]

Life a User's Manual attempts to achieve this goal more rigorously by generating its rooms out of an elaborate Oulipean constraint system. Perec prepared the book by developing forty-two themed lists of ten elements (e.g., fabrics, colors, nationalities, furniture, famous authors), from each of which one element would be incorporated into every chapter. Though Perec rarely managed to include of all his intended constraints, the strategy still gives much of the book's narrative a nearly arbitrary quality, which is likely what provokes the conflicting suggestions from the book's critics that the novel is devoted to purely mimetic descriptivism and that its self-conscious construction renders it "an emphatically anti-mimetic text."[73] For instance, if we return to the paintings in the Marquiseaux drawing room, we may see that the fourth is generated almost automatically out of a score of near-comically disjunctive constraint elements: the painting, a *reproduction* by the *British* painter Forbes, depicts a *nineteenth-century* scene in which a *white-leather-uniformed domestic* who is *climbing* a *Chinese-style chair* accidentally smashes an *alabaster* jeweled *egg* (one he had spent much time *repairing*) that is owned by his mistress, an *old lady*, with whom he had developed a late-life romance (à la *Philemon and Baucis*), believing it to be a *rat* hidden behind the *muslin curtain* (alluding to *Hamlet*).[74]

This capricious construction not only makes some chapters appear pointless but makes it difficult to plot larger narratives between chapters. While the individual flats of any urban apartment building might as well be on different planets for all that their inhabitants have to do with each other, in *Life a User's Manual*, even chapters set in different rooms of the *same* apartment sometimes have no apparent connection. This is furthered by the "Knight's Tour" structure Perec planned for the novel, in which the chapters are not sequenced by the flats' horizontal or vertical order in the building but by how a knight chess piece would visit each in turn, constantly breaking readers' attention regarding what is going on in each apartment and obscuring how its rooms might be related. For instance the apartment directly below the Marquiseaux'—justly labeled a "ghost flat," since no one has ever seen its purported owner, M. Foureau—is represented by three chapters, respectively the twenty-ninth, ninety-second, and third, which have no apparent relation to each other.[75] In the outermost room, two unidentified young girls recover from a party, with most of the chapter devoted to a list of uncleaned junk that tells no story and seems largely designed to satisfy constraints (e.g., "several odd shoes, a long white sock, a pair of tights, a top hat, a false nose, cardboard plates in piles," etc.); the middle room contains little besides twenty-one wall engravings filling a similar purpose; and the inner room features an unusual scene in which a Japanese pseudoguru initiates three victims into an elaborate pyramid scheme called "The Three Free Men," the potential interest of which is offset by its utter opacity.[76] How these men got into the apartment, whether either the girls or initiates are related to Foureau, or if any of these people are aware of the others' presence goes unmentioned. These chapters decidedly resist plotting.

However, despite such apparently pointless tales as these, it is not quite right to argue, as Gabriel Josipovici does, that in *Life a User's Manual* "time and chance [. . .] emerge with the force they have in life but which the traditional novel, committed as it is to a metaphysic of destiny and revelation, is never able to convey."[77] Though the constraint system does give much of the book the air of chance, many of its other stories are plotted with flourishes so sensational as to match the most melodramatic novel. Consider the tragedy of Elizabeth de Beaumont, who runs away from home, takes a job as an au pair, flees upon accidentally drowning the child she has been asked to watch (causing his mother to commit suicide), and is later tracked down and killed by the child's father, though not until after she has fallen in love with François Breidel and borne him two daughters—a sequence later reconstructed by the vengeful husband and then re-reconstructed by Madame de Beaumont's lawyer Léon Salini.[78] Can such a story really be construed as contributing to an antiteleological narrative? In fact one key element of the Bartlebooth plot, the swindle that two con men perform on his uncle Sherwood, succeeds only *because* Sherwood believes that the discovery of a valuable manuscript and the "lucky" sighting of the possessor of a legendary vase by an Massachusetts workman are related only by chance, when in fact they have been set up by the swindlers.[79] *Life a User's Manual* is a book, after all, that begins by telling us that Gaspard Winckler "is dead, but the long and meticulous, patiently laid plot of his revenge is not finished yet," and ends with that devious plot being realized when Bartlebooth dies holding a single W-shaped piece for an X-shaped hole in one of his final puzzles: its plot cannot be construed as lacking destiny and fate.[80] As Alison James argues, while "Perec's narratives manifest a degree of resistance to conventional narrative causality" they also "exploi[t] the causal tensions between different narrative levels."[81]

What does one make of this set of tales, then, in which some episodes are intricately plotted, some are autonomous but interesting on their own, and some seem simply useless? As with much cruft we have discussed, it turns out that many episodes that at first appear wasteful end up having some importance. For instance the painting of the coachman is revealed, sixty-two chapters later, to have been given to the Marquiseaux as a wedding present by the antique dealers Clara and Léon Marcia; furthermore it is suggested that its morbidly Gothic narrative sheds light on their attitude toward Caroline Marquiseaux, who had rejected their son David.[82] What had seemed a detail expressing life's randomness, then, turns out to be relevant to the rest of the narrative, appearing random only because Perec's chapter structure so starkly challenges his readers' ability to remember and plot it. This attention-straining strategy even impacts how we plot together scenes that do not appear individually pointless: for instance, when we first visit the Réol apartment in chapter 12, we see a merry middle-class family cleaning their dining-room furniture, which may easily be forgotten by the time we return in chapter 98 and learn of the years of financial strain their furniture caused them.[83]

Plotting such stories against the grain of the Knight's Tour structure is made even more difficult by how so much of the book's narrative does *not* have similar hidden significance. For instance none of the Marquiseaux' other three paintings from chapter 4 appears to have a meaningful story behind it the way that *A Rat Behind the Arras* does, nor do the score of pages of antique junk housed in the Marcias' private and shop rooms.[84] We can try to plot them, but doing so would either be totally fruitless or generate so many uncorroborated shadow stories that we would never continue on with the book. This problem is faced in exemplary form within the novel by Cinoc, the building's dictionary employee, who is responsible for pruning from the dictionary obsolete terms. While mourning the "hundreds and thousands of tools, techniques, customs, beliefs, sayings, dishes, games, nicknames, weights and measures" that he feels responsible for eliminating, Cinoc decides to restore eight thousand of them in a "dictionary of forgotten words" but soon realizes that, no matter how mysteriously alluring they are, these words—"ursuline," "loquis," "ruisson"—only "contain, obscurely, the trace of a story it has now become almost impossible to hand on."[85] Whatever tale might have been behind them can no longer be plotted, and so they must be abandoned.

Determining when these "traces" may be expanded into plots and when they cannot, of course, is not a simple process. As Bernard Magné notes, the most important tool in distinguishing the cruft from the plottable material is the index, which tags and cross-references the book's proper names and other key terms so that we may more easily make connections.[86] If we wonder during chapter 4, for instance, whether *A Rat Behind the Arras* will be mentioned again, or cannot recall in chapter 66 whether it had been previously mentioned, we need only look up "FORBES (Stanhope Alexander), English painter" in the index.[87] Just as important, the index can help us decide what stories cannot be plotted: for instance, of the twenty-seven items listed as having been left on the stairs in chapter 68, the index marks further cross-references for only one, the empty blueberry tart box from *Aux Délices de Louis XV*, which the index helps us discover was the longtime workplace of Madame Crespi and a favorite eatery of Winckler's.[88] Similarly the table of contents and floor plan facilitate connecting stories from the same apartment treated in separate parts of the book, while the chronology at the book's end helps us to create linear temporal narratives out of the chapters' constant prolepses and analepses.

The paratexts also help reveal that many parts of the narrative do not fall neatly into either the categories of pointless cruft or useful plot, prompting us to decide how much attention we ought to spend trying to plot them. On the one hand, cruft and plottable narrative frequently appear in close proximity, as in Madame de Beaumont's cellar, which looks like a mere collection of broken furniture and discarded papers until we discover the photos establishing the friendship between Véronique Altamont and Anne and Béatrice Breidel, which, when considered alongside their entries in the index and chronology, emphasizes the girls' shared interest in plotting their family's genealogies and histories, a key theme running through the book.[89] On the other hand, the paratexts sometimes suggest weak shadow stories that we may or may not want to develop. How much attention should we give, for instance, to the Breidel girls' speculations on their grandmother's dressing gown, which bears the image of a cat and a spade and keys to several cross-references in the index?[90] Should we, for example, spend any time plotting a connection between Madame de Beaumont's professorial lover Arnold Flexner, to whose thrillers about a cat burglar Anne thinks the robe alludes, and the other Ohio professor named within the index, the Nazi chemist Wehsal?[91] Probably not, but it is a tempting coincidence—one wants to do *something* with it.

That problem is emblematic of the one faced by all of *Life a User's Manual*'s many collectors and specialists: we do not lack material with which to work but are at a loss regarding how to manage it all. The jigsaw puzzle may be an apt metaphor for the book, but if one were to design a jigsaw correlate to *Life a User's Manual*, it would not look like those available at a store. Instead such a puzzle would contain a thousand pieces (or a thousand and one, perhaps), of which only two hundred would actually connect, and those pieces that did connect would form not a rectangle but a starfish, or a giant W, or something even more irregular. To correctly solve the puzzle would entail not only linking up the pieces that fit, but staying away from those intriguingly misleading little chards that appear as if they should slide in somewhere but don't.

Arguing against those who found *Life a User's Manual* overstuffed yet empty, Perec's fellow Oulipo member Italo Calvino claimed, "Someone might object that the more the work tends toward the multiplication of possibilities, the further it departs from that unicum which is the *self* of the writer, his inner sincerity and the discovery of his own truth. But I would answer: Who are we, who is each one of us, if not a combinatoria of experiences, information, books we have read, things imagined? Each life is an encyclopedia, a library, an inventory of objects, a series of styles, and everything can be constantly shuffled and reordered in every way conceivable."[92] Of course the "unicum of *self*" and the messy inventory of objects are always in dialectic with one another, related by the shuffling and reordering process we alternately call consciousness or plot. Putting more objects into the inventory might give it a greater range of possibilities, but it may also impede our ability to make a self out of them. This may best be seen in Bartlebooth's death, holding a final piece to a puzzle in which it does not quite fit. Winckler has tricked him, but whether he has done so by supplying Bartlebooth with a piece that cannot be placed or by getting him to put the puzzle together the wrong way is not clear.[93] The puzzle maker's revenge is not only that Bartlebooth can't fill the hole in his puzzle; it is, more cruelly, that he can never know *whether or not he has completed it correctly*. If the book's narrator is a puzzle maker and we are his puzzlers, this is an ominous place to be left: for all our reader-detective work, it may be impossible to know if our plotting is adequate.

On the Picaresque Road to *2666*

If a mega-novel's reader plays the role of detective, then the narrator must be his nemesis, the master criminal working to obscure the story hiding behind the narrative. The original literary narrator-criminal, of course, is the pícaro, but his narrative is minimally mysterious: since the pícaro tells us his actions and motives so straightforwardly, there is little for readers to puzzle out. Creating a picaresque mega-novel, then, would necessitate removing the pícaro's direct presentation of motive and plot, or perhaps removing his narrative voice entirely, and instead closely tracing his episodic actions at a remove without ever providing an explanation of the immediate purpose motivating each one. Such a structure might produce substantial cruft, as the actions' logic would remain constantly distanced and perhaps never brought to resolution.

This is the approach taken by Roberto Bolaño's two mega-novels, *The Savage Detectives* and *2666*. Both deal with the episodic activities of outlaws on society's margins, the former addressing the global journeys of "visceral realist" poets Arturo Belano and Ulises Lima (modeled on Bolaño himself and his friend Mario Santiago) as they flee the repercussions of a violent encounter in the Sonora Desert, and the latter centered on hundreds of separate, unsolved murders of women around a border city near Arizona. That both novels are set principally in late twentieth-century Mexico, where official institutions' practical jurisdiction dissolves quickly into a large periphery of extralegal economies, contributes to the picaresque atmosphere: as Frederick Monteser notes, the picaresque thrives in a state whose bureaucratic structure is so nonfunctioning that there is a "[s]urplus population, in the sense of human beings to be thrown away as useless."[94] Perhaps this is why Bolaño's two mega-novels also feature searches for lost literary figures, respectively Belano and Lima's quest for visceral realism's spiritual godmother Cesàrea Tinajero, and several European professors' attempt to track the mysterious German novelist Benno von Archimboldi: the contemporary world does not seem to have much of a use for writers, either.

That lack of purpose contributes to a proliferation of cruft in the novels. Though Javier Cercas is correct to distinguish Bolaño from some other great Latin American writers by noting that he "was never a hermetic or difficult author [. . .] busy with autophagic experimentalism," his subsequent claim that Bolaño was "a compulsively legible narrator, an immediately cordial, captivating, and endless storyteller" is mistaken.[95] As we have discussed, nonstandard prose is not the only kind of text that poses challenges to reading. In the central sections of Bolaño's mega-novels, we encounter dozens of distinct episodes, but they are narrated only by faceless investigators seeking something that they never quite find for purposes that they never quite explain, running into numerous dead ends along the way. In a given episode, it is often difficult to know precisely what the point is supposed to be, and even in retrospect, it can be either difficult or impossible to establish its larger function. Though Chris Andrews has argued that the "drifting" and "episodic" qualities in Bolaño's books are due to his rejection of a "diachronic" conception that narrative is central to human character, the individual desire that propels classical episodic narrative is often absent, and as we saw from Damasio, human consciousness does require a necessarily diachronic base.[96]

2666 is easily the more extreme of the two, employing episodes so disconnected as to appear entirely pointless. This is especially true of its middle third, "The Part about the Crimes," based on the notorious wave of "femicides" in Ciudad Juárez, Mexico. According to Daniel Zalewski, this section "may be the grimmest sequence in contemporary fiction," because it provides a "sickeningly comprehensive account of the killings, written in the frigid tone of a forensic report": 110 narratives, presented one by one, of female corpses discovered between 1993 and 1997 in the fictionalized border city of Santa Teresa.[97] Their grimness may come less from the detached tone or forensic detail, grisly though its litany of crushed hyoids and vaginal bruising may be, than by their sheer obtuseness to plotting. The description of the last murder, presented here in its entirety, might exemplify why:

> The last case of 1997 was fairly similar to the second to last, except that the bag containing the body wasn't found on the western edge of the city but on the eastern edge, by the dirt road that runs along the border and then forks and vanishes when it reaches the first mountains and steep passes. The victim, according to the medical examiners, had been dead for a long time. She was about eighteen, five foot two and a half or three. She was naked, but a pair of good-quality leather high heels were found in the bag, which led the police to think she might be a whore. Some white thong panties were also found. Both this case and the previous case were closed after three days of generally halfhearted investigations.[98]

As the final sentence implies, we discover nothing more about this body, just as we don't about dozens of other corpses described in almost identical fashion. Though some murders have a little more detail than this one—the victim's name, say—for the most part, their information is little more than differing permutations of physical attributes, crime scene locations, and causes of death, signifying nothing. In seventy-seven cases, there is not even a chief suspect. While some spin out into more capacious individual narratives, whether because the police manage to solve them or because they simply put in more effort, most of these accumulations of facts cannot be plotted.

The summaries cannot even be imbued with clear purpose by being grouped under the larger rubric of "the Santa Teresa murders." From the very first murder, the narrator admits that the list has no real criteria other than pure chronology. Regarding the "first" victim, Esperanza Gómez Saldaña, we are told, "Maybe for the sake of convenience, maybe because she was the first to be killed in 1993, she heads the list. Although surely there were other girls and women who died in 1992. Other girls and women who didn't make it onto the list or were never found."[99] In other words the section title "The Part about the Crimes" is misleading, because it implies the murders it lists are a coherently linked group of killings, when in fact the section simply records every violent female death discovered between 1993 and 1997. The start date could easily have been moved back a year, or for that matter forward to 1995, when the murder rate doubles (i.e., there are twenty-eight total deaths described in 1993–1994 and about twenty-eight per year in 1995–1997). It likely misses many bodies never discovered, as highlighted by the case of Kelly Rivera Parker discussed by reporter Sergio Gonzalez and congresswoman Azucena Esquivel Plata toward the section's end. Yet it also includes several that clearly have nothing to do with the others, as with the eccentric La Vaca, who starts a fistfight with her two best male friends when they interrupt her movie and is accidentally killed in the process.[100] This is not to mention the unresolved affair of the "Demon Penitent," a man who visits several churches to urinate on their sacred objects and occasionally attack their inhabitants, which is apparently unrelated to the killings but nonetheless recounted along with them.[101] As only thirteen cases are successfully brought to conclusion by the police, and as these have so little to do with each other that they provide little insight into the remaining ninety-seven, it can be almost impossible to see what purpose each new, repetitive murder bears.[102]

One might speculate that the episodes' disconnectedness is exacerbated by the fact that Bolaño was unable to finish the novel prior to his death, but the book's editor, Ignacio Echevarría, insists that the novel was essentially complete.[103] In other words there is no missing, unwritten resolution, à la Charles Dickens's *The Mystery of Edwin Drood*, that would have explained everything. One might also suggest that, owing to the historical Mexican authorities' lack of progress in solving the killings on which the section is based, the narrative could not have been made any easier to plot by providing a clearer solution. Indeed, as Andrews shows, the 110 murders hew closely to the actual 110 femicides in Juárez during 1993–1997.[104] However, the lack of a real solution to a historical mystery has rarely hampered authors from positing one in fiction: one of Bolaño's favorite American writers, Edgar Allan Poe, offered a solution to his era's unsolved Mary Rogers murder in "The Mystery of Marie Roget," and there seems to be an entire subgenre of popular fiction based on the Juárez killings that lacks the indeterminacy of *2666*. The individual murders' strung-out parataxis, in other words, appears to be a deliberate narrative choice.

Critics' preferred method for rendering these episodes legible has been to attribute them to large-scale societal factors rather than surreptitious individual actors. Sharae Deckard exemplifies this view by claiming, "Bolaño replaces the political violence of the dictator novel with the systemic violence of millennial capitalism, staging the femicides and narcoviolence attendant on structural adjustment in post-NAFTA Mexico in relation to the ascendancy of neoliberal capital."[105] That several of the victims are found in dumps or trash cans literalizes how their deaths might be viewed as industrial by-products. While the shifting global economy obviously plays some role in the murders, however, to refer to the crimes as "the maquiladora murders," as Grant Farred does, is misleading.[106] Not only are just twenty-seven of the victims current or former factory workers, and only nineteen others linked to the maquiladoras in any way, but in several of the cases about which we know most, neoliberalism is clearly not the problem. For instance fifty-year-old Felicidad Jiménez Jiménez does not seem to be a victim of global capitalism, even though she is a maquiladora worker, because her killer appears to have been her mentally disturbed son Ernesto, and his motivations seem no more complicated than the usual domestic ones behind killings we find in every culture.[107]

Similarly, while a misogynist "climate of impunity" regarding violence against women certainly contributes to the killings as well, as is argued by many of the novel's female characters, this is not an adequate explanation either.[108] Granted, as Yolanda Palacio, the only member of Santa Teresa's Department of Sex Crimes, notes, ten women are raped every day in the city, and her division receives little support from the rest of the department, whose male members seem to spend much of their time sharing uncreative misogynist jokes.[109] However, even Palacio admits that the murders have raised the male-female murder victim ratio only from 10:1 to 10:4: in other words, while the aforementioned 110 women listed in "The Part about the Crimes" are being killed, a further 275 men have also suffered violent deaths, yet receive little mention.[110] In fact the narrator comments that in early 1997 "the city got a break" because there were no violent deaths of women, only of men, which was "to be expected": "people who started off celebrating and ended up killing each other, uncinematic deaths, deaths from the real of folklore, not modernity: deaths that didn't scare anybody."[111] Though Jean Franco reads this line as unironically attributing Santa Teresa's killings to "a modernity that is the rogue version of civilization," it seems more accurately to underscore how the recent upturn makes only a modest contribution to the city's overall level of violence and how long its men have operated under the threat of death its women now do.[112]

These flaws in the large-scale societal explanations illustrate the challenges to plotting that this section poses. On the one hand, they overstate their own explanatory power, clearly attributing the wrong cause to a number of deaths. On the other hand, their emphasis on cultural and ideological factors ignores evidence pointing to a specific group of persons committing a significant percentage of the murders. One must not get carried away with this idea, as the police do when, infatuated with Hollywood serial killer films, they decide the key to all the murders is the "signature" breast mutilation that has occurred by then in only three cases.[113] To attribute the deaths to a single twisted psychopath might reassuringly absolve the city of larger social responsibility, but, as becomes clear every time the police awkwardly try to pin additional murders on the suspects they arrest, many separate actors are responsible for the killings. However, the similar methods of death and disposal among many of the killings, not to mention the frequent presence of mysterious black sedans, suggest that some subset might well be committed by one or several of the city's powerful criminal organizations, consciously taking advantage of elements within Santa Teresa's culture that allow them to get away with murder.

How could we actually plot out the causes of these crimes, though, when so many of the narratives tell us only meaningless details? As Poe's C. Auguste Dupin notes in analyzing the Roget case, "a vast, perhaps the larger, portion of truth arises from the seemingly irrelevant. [. . .] The history of human knowledge has so uninterruptedly shown that to collateral, or incidental, or accidental events we are indebted for the most numerous and valuable discoveries."[114] We must ignore this "collateral" material most of the time, of course, because it usually *is* irrelevant, and so vastly out-masses useful information as to make devoting any attention to it cognitively prohibitive. Trying to focus closely on such details will often lead us to arbitrarily emphasize the handful of attention-catching murders that settle most easily into our working memory, which may not be representative. What this situation may call for us to do instead is to abandon close reading and practice a more distant and shallow form of processing that mines the narratives for certain key points.[115] We are not guaranteed clear results from such an analysis, but given our minds' inability to simultaneously process dozens of distinct narratives at once, it is, I believe, a substantially better way to orient our attention for this part of the novel.

What does reading this way tell us? First, that all but three of the victims are girls or women past puberty and under the age of thirty-five, and twenty-five are sixteen or younger. Second, most of these inhabit a vulnerable societal position: of the seventy-three identified bodies, thirty-nine have low-wage hourly jobs and six more are sex workers. Third, except for the two murders committed in public, there are no independent witnesses to any of the murders, and except for ten found in their homes, the bodies are generally dumped in public but secluded areas, most often by the side of a road (twenty-nine) or in an industrial or waste area (sixteen). Fourth, at least forty-eight victims show signs of rape, and six victims' breasts are mutilated in a consistent pattern. Fifth, though the causes of death are sometimes ambiguous, thirty-nine have been strangled, thirty-three stabbed, fifteen shot, and seven beaten, with the strangling and stabbing victims several times more likely to have been raped than the others. Last, ten cases report sightings of expensive and otherwise mysterious black sedans near the last place the victims were seen.

These details are not much to go on. In many cases, in fact, they tell us almost nothing. Based on them, however, I believe we can make a few modest but specific conclusions. The deaths fall into roughly seven groups. Group 1 contains four deaths that are clearly not part of any larger pattern of deliberate violence toward women: La Vaca, Jiménez, Perla Beatriz Ochoterena (who hangs herself, albeit possibly in response to the killings), and Esther Perea Peña (who is shot accidentally). Group 2 contains five deaths that may be related to various underworld activities but diverge markedly from the others in key respects, including the method of death and the demographic of the victims: reporter Isabel Urrea (shot while getting into her car), Sofia Serrano (overdosed on cocaine in a hotel), nightclub owner Marisol Camarena (dropped in a vat of acid), and the drug-running Reynolds sisters (shot near Pueblo Azul). Group 3 includes twelve domestic disputes that, though they might be related to an atmosphere of misogynist violence, appear isolated otherwise. These three groups seem largely independent of the other murders, except in the broadest sense, and if we add to these twenty-one deaths some of the nine cases in which evidence is so sparse that even whether the body was murdered is not clear (we'll call this group 0), we end up with a figure approximating the twenty-seven violent female deaths that Palacio implies would have been typical in a five-year period for Santa Teresa prior to the crime wave.

Though the remaining eighty cases may be divided into three more groups, each is grounded in an overall set of shared characteristics. Generally they involve the corpse of a socially vulnerable young woman, found either strangled or stabbed to death, usually in a partly obscured public area, with her body bearing signs of sexual abuse. Group 4 contains thirteen cases, which share some characteristics of the larger wave of murder-rapes but go against them in others: for instance, the lab reports may be confident that the woman had not been sexually abused. Group 5 comprises twenty-six killings that, according the narrator's summary of the official reports, share most key characteristics of the larger pattern, but lack confirmation of some others. Finally, group 6 contains forty-one murders, each of which bears all the killings' common characteristics. Given the close match between the total number of these murders making up groups 4–6 and the increase in violent deaths during the period in question, it is primarily here that we probably ought to look for the influence of larger societal forces; tellingly, too, these groups also contain all ten sightings of the ominous black sedans. Furthermore it is particularly in groups 5 and 6 that we ought to look for the work of a specific organization of actors perpetrating a particular kind of murder-rape among at-risk young women, given the similarity of the crimes.

These conclusions are obviously not ironclad, especially as my categories are entirely dependent on information supplied by a dozen different investigators who, despite the narrator's uniform tone in summarizing their accounts, have wildly different approaches to and competence at police work. Unlike the unified vision provided by the classic picaresque, the differences in Santa Teresa's detectives has a significant impact on the way we can process the murders. Though this is never explicitly stated in the text, distant reading makes clear that the better the investigator assigned to the case, the more plottable the evidence produced by it. For instance Epifanio Galindo, among the police force's most effective and least corrupt members, manages to collect and put together enough evidence to successfully close several cases, though his zeal to plot connections out of his clues leads him to some unsound conclusions, as when he wrongly pins several unsolved murders on Klaus Haas. Other investigators range in ability from the talented Juan de Dios Martínez to the inept Ángel Fernández and José Marquez, the former of whose case reports often fail to recount vital evidence and the latter of whom rarely even manages to bring in a suspect. Consequently the cases investigated by the better detectives are more likely to fit into group 1 or 3 (most of which are solved), implying that some number of the group 4–6 murders (almost none of which are solved) might be classified elsewhere were their investigators more adept at their jobs. In other words we should not assume limited evidence implies a shadowy conspiracy especially skilled in covering its tracks: some of the group 6 deaths might easily be mundane killings that, owing to chance or incompetence, simply produced few traces.

However, even if this process takes us only so far, its insights do a better job plotting the otherwise impenetrable morass than most methods, including those pursued by the book's characters. The murders themselves, after all, are not the only source of cruft in the novel: at least as much is generated by characters' failed investigations. Even as good an officer as Martínez gets caught up in nonsense theories not worth either his or our attention, as when he wonders at length about a victim's discarded clothes: "[It was a]s if the killers had removed the victim's pants before tossing her in the bushes. Or as if they had brought her up there naked, with her pants in a bag, and later discarded the pants a few yards from the body. The truth is, none of it made sense."[116] The TV seer Florita Almada, meanwhile, attracts the attention of Santa Teresa's citizens with claims that she has had visions of the murders, but her rambling television addresses (always quoted at great length) provide even less insight, as they mostly comprise oddball dietary advice and mystic treacle like this: "The consumption of vegetable fiber, even though it doesn't provide us with usable energy-producing elements, is beneficial. When it isn't absorbed, the fiber causes the bolus, in its passage through the digestive tract, to retain its volume. And that causes pressure to be generated inside the intestine, which stimulates intestinal activity, assuring the easy passage of waste through the whole digestive tract. Diarrhea is hardly ever a good thing, but going to the bathroom once or twice a day brings serenity and balance, a kind of inner peace."[117] Even the lengthy retracings made late in this section by the American criminologist Albert Kessler end up going nowhere.[118] This also appears, at first, to be the case with Harry Magaña—arrived from Huntsville, Arizona to investigate the death of American Lucy Anne Sander—who follows his few leads in circles around Mexico for several pages without getting results. However, this apparent pointlessness comes to an end when he stumbles onto the last person to see Sander alive while the latter is attempting to dispose of a body, at which point he is surrounded by other men and likely killed.[119] His narrative suddenly appears to be more meaningful than Kessler's or Almada's, but it is promptly cut off before it can help us connect the plot together.

Without skimming over these scenes and undertaking the kind of plotting I have described, it is almost impossible to define and address the problems faced in Santa Teresa, which are so dire not because there is an all-powerful criminal conspiracy controlling life and death but because there does *not* seem to be one—or, rather, because there is a complex network of agents behind the crimes, which may include several moderately powerful (but not all-encompassing) criminal groups but are probably not exhausted by them. Some number of the killings may be deliberate serial murder-rapes perpetrated by one or more of Santa Teresa's several criminal organizations; others are likely just byproducts of the city's abundance of organized crime, whose success in the city is likely abetted by the socioeconomic changes globalization has brought; a number are probably localizable incidents, though encouraged by recent cultural changes in the city and overall police incompetence; and some are simply the violence that our species perpetrates on itself everywhere it settles.

This may not be a "solution," per se, but I believe it better accounts for the stories behind the narrative than any produced by the police, the protestors, or the book's critics. What the cruft in "The Part about the Crimes" ought to remind us, then, is that large-scale social phenomena are always composed of small-scale individual events, and that while we must consider large-scale causes when addressing large-scale problems, many of the constituent events defy obvious plotting in terms of those large-scale causes. In fact sometimes they defy explanation entirely, but their frequent mysteriousness cannot stop us from attempting to explain them, because sometimes they are less opaque than they may at first appear. To adequately respond to sociopolitical trends of this magnitude requires modes of cognition capable of addressing them at several different levels.

As may be implied by the convergence of characters from around the world on Santa Teresa in the novel's other sections—the European literary critics, the American journalist Oscar Fate, and Archimboldi—Santa Teresa's condition is increasingly characteristic of the contemporary world, less because it is especially violent than because it presents an enormous amount of information that resists straightforward processing. All these characters encounter a tangled mess in Santa Teresa out of which they need to extricate themselves: Fate must navigate himself away from the seemingly omnipresent gangsters with which his journalistic work has brought him into contact, while Archimboldi, existentially unmoored since his participation in World War II, has come hoping to unravel his nephew Haas's inextricably labyrinthine legal limbo. The totality of these messy conditions is well beyond their conscious understanding, which, like all of ours, is structured to comprehend smaller-scale narrative, but they must compress and rearrange what they find as best they can to survive. Perhaps this is best expressed by two of the literary critics, Jean-Claude Pelletier and Manuel Espinoza, whose long quest to locate the writer toward whose work they are inexplicably drawn is not dissimilar from the novels' other knotty mysteries. Upon realizing they will never quite find Archimboldi, the pair concludes, "The important thing is something else entirely. [. . .] That he's here [. . .] and we're here, and this is the closest we'll ever be to him."[120] "Close enough" is usually about as well as we can do. The struggle to plot the crimes might best be understood through the narrator of "The Part about the Crimes" himself—whom, Echevarría tells us, Bolaño imagined to be none other than his *Savage Detectives* alter ego, the futilely questing poet Arturo Belano.[121] He is not nearly so detached as critics describe him: as some of the quotes above show, he is by turns critical and bemused with the police efforts, yet he is aware he can do little but work from what they have discovered. His efforts do make a little progress beyond theirs, noting some clues they don't investigate, but he does not get very far.

As Roncal ambiguously tells Fate during a half-dreamed sequence in which they interview Haas in prison, "No one pays attention to these killings, but the secret of the world is hidden in them."[122] In one sense the "secret" could have something to do with violence or with economic conditions and misogyny during globalization, but it probably has as much to do with the first clause as the second—that is, with paying attention. That so many victims have died for such variegated causes renders those of us attending the crimes nearly incapable of focusing on any one without doing them injustice as a whole, and vice versa. When we ask who's killing the women of Santa Teresa, we also must ask how our brains are to plot such an enormous number of events at all.

6 The Epic and the Allegory

Meaning Too Much and Too Little

In the last chapter, we discussed James Wood's claim that mega-novels often become gratuitously overrun with arbitrary stories. Wood, however, does not stop there, proceeding to make a more serious attack on the very process through which mega-novels aspire to greater significance. Wood illustrates his complaint with this parody:

> If, say, a character is introduced in London, call him Toby Awknotuby (that is, "To be or not to be"—ha!) then we will be swiftly told that he has a twin in Delhi (called Boyt, which is an anagram of Toby, of course), who, like Toby, has the same very curious genital deformation, and that their mother belongs to a religious cult based, oddly enough, in the Orkney Islands, and that their father (who was born at the exact second that the bomb was dropped on Hiroshima) has been a Hell's Angel for the last thirteen years (but a very curious Hell's Angels group it is, devoted only to the fanatical study of late Wordsworth), and that Toby's mad left-wing aunt was curiously struck dumb when Mrs. Thatcher was elected prime minister in 1979 and has not spoken a word since. And all this, over many pages, before poor Toby Awknotuby has done a thing, or thought a thought![1]

This pastiche (which, we should agree, isn't far from what many mega-novelists have produced) is characterized by relentless but quirky mythologizing: the cataclysmic bombing of Hiroshima becomes an occasion for the origin of a literary family, the silencing of the Left during the 1980s is made supernaturally literal, and cultural touchstones from the postwar period are paralleled liberally and coincidentally to events in a fictional world. Wood implies, though, that such writing merely plays at myth. Myths, after all, require a coherent, integrated mythology in which to function, and this near-random collection of oddball events does not qualify. They may gesture at the idea of a larger worldview, but they do not create one. Summing up this critique in his dismissal of Thomas Pynchon, Wood claims, "his novels behave like allegories that refuse to allegorize. [. . .] [T]here are scenes that mean too much and scenes that mean too little."[2]

In some ways this is an argument not merely about mega-novels, but about the contemporary viability of figural narrative. In an era during which writers cannot take for granted what T. S. Eliot called a "framework of accepted and traditional ideas" to ground their cosmic artifices, any attempt to give a narrative figural significance threatens to be rendered silly.[3] If we agree that Toby Awknotuby's father's birth at the exact moment of the Hiroshima explosion is a strained conceit, how can we say any differently about the birth of Saleem Sinai in Salman Rushdie's *Midnight's Children* at the exact moment of Indian independence? If having Toby's aunt being struck mute upon Thatcher's election is a transparently overdetermined metaphor, why should Toru Okada's receipt of a blue mark on his cheek when afflicted with the psychic malady plaguing postwar Japan in Haruki Murakami's *The Wind-Up Bird Chronicle* be any less so? And if twinning the fates of the British and Indian nations through Toby and Boyt's shared genital deformation appears frivolous, isn't Don DeLillo's attempt to intertwine white and black America in *Underworld* via Nick Shay and Cotter Martin's mutual attachment to Bobby Thomson's home run ball similarly empty?

To address these questions, we will need to look at mega-novels' relationship to the two oldest and most venerated genres of figural narrative, the allegory and the epic. By doing so we may better understand how those forms create their semic structures and, consequently, determine to what extent mega-novels can make use of those structures. In fact this chapter will argue that allegory and epic essentially merge in the contemporary mega-novel, producing a volatile hybrid whose resulting abundance of both signification and cruft pressures to its greatest extent our ability to imagine ourselves with respect to the contemporary nation and world.

Allegoric/Epic Metanarratives and Paranoia

The definitions of allegory and epic have long overlapped.[4] They are both associated with the union of narrative and figuration: allegory is primarily distinguished from other figures by its emphasis on narrative, and, as Georg Lukács argued, the epic may be distinguished from other narrative forms because its hero "is, strictly speaking, never an individual" but a representative of the community.[5] Moreover these figural narratives tend to be grounded in an explicitly mythic system, which allows them to gesture toward the universal.[6] Deborah Madsen argues that in allegory "[n]arrative truth and absolute truth are conflated in the same quasi-transcendental source of legitimation that is invoked for both culture and society," while Lukács believes that epic asserts a "transcendental structure" that provides its readers with a metaphysical "home."[7] This capaciousness allows them to be drawn out to substantial scale, observed in epic as early as Aristotle and as true, though less obviously, in allegory.[8] Furthermore both epic and allegory access this figural-narrative fusion via rifts in temporality. As Mikhail Bakhtin notes, the epic, for all its pseudohistoricity, is really set in an "absolute past," while allegories, as Honig writes, tend to begin with a dreamy excursus into a timeless environment.[9] Upon entering this suspended temporal space, both tend to focus on generative, momentous conflict.[10] Using a temporal rift to depict figural conflict, of course, recalls Claude Lévi-Strauss's definition of myth as "both a sequence belonging to the past [. . .] and an everlasting pattern which can be detected in the present," which allows a narrative conflict from history to become relevant to the contemporary moment.[11]

If allegory and epic are to be distinguished, it is by the way readers are supposed to process their own personal relationships to the work's large-scale concepts. In epic readers are to understand the narrative as expressing their place in a nation—the "absolute past" to which Bakhtin refers is a "national epic past"—while in allegory readers are supposed to conceive the story as expressing the truths of a theophilosophic system, such as Christianity.[12] As a result the epic leans toward the exemplary rather than hermeneutic. When Philip Sidney praises Virgil's Aeneas, he claims not that the Trojan signifies Virtue but asks, "Who readeth Aeneas carrying old Anchises on his back, that wisheth not it were his fortune to perform so excellent an act?"[13] Allegory, on the other hand, in Angus Fletcher's straightforward definition, is text that "says one thing and means another," requiring the reader to interpret a deeper truth that is not literally stated.[14]

Regardless, though, in recent decades critical theory treated both genres as politically compromised. Since Jean-François Lyotard defined postmodernity as "incredulity toward metanarratives"—the latter defined as any all-encompassing "discourse of legitimation," among which Lyotard groups epic and allegory—scholarly consensus has joined his critique of the potential "totalitarian effect" of such "unitary and totalizing truth."[15] Consequently epic or allegorical elements in narrative are often accepted by contemporary critics only when they are construed as subverting the transcendent concepts traditionally associated with those genres. Famously Paul de Man construed allegory as dramatizing the gap between textual figure and meaning, rather than allowing access from one to the other, and a similar argument regarding the epic was suggested by Linda Hutcheon's elucidation of postmodern "historiographic metafiction," a genre within which "theoretical self-awareness of history and fiction as human constructs" is used to undermine the "narratives or systems that once allowed us to think we could unproblematically and universally define public agreement," rather than to exemplify them as epics do.[16]

This rejection of metanarratives, however, is theoretically problematic. As many critics have pointed out (I cite here Fredric Jameson), "the disappearance of master narratives has itself to be couched in narrative form."[17] That is, one cannot *not* have a metanarrative, because any overarching opposition to metanarratives itself creates a new metanarrative. Furthermore it is ethically questionable. As Eric L. Berlatsky argues, refusing all metanarrative erases the grounds on which groups against whom historical injustices have been committed can articulate that the injustice committed against them should be universally regarded as unjust or that its occurrence is historically true.[18] Moreover the argument that "totalization" is oppressively exclusionary seems to entail a contradiction: if one does *not* seek to encompass as much as possible, isn't one, by definition, excluding something?

Fundamentally this is a cognitive problem. How is a mind designed to process only the organism's immediate surroundings and kinship network supposed to understand its place within a globe of billions of people? Evolutionary psychologist Robin Dunbar has demonstrated that human neocortex size likely limits us to around 150 social relationships at a given time, which means that an accurate understanding of one's place even within a town as small as a few thousand people is beyond our capacities.[19] Jameson has called this the problem of adequate "cognitive mapping," the goal of which is "to enable a situational representation on the part of the individual subject to that vaster and properly unrepresentable totality which is the ensemble of society's structures as a whole."[20] He (predictably) proposes Marxism as the answer, but cognitive linguists like Mark Turner have argued for the role of figural narrative more generally, as the "[t]he projection of one story onto another [. . . is] a fundamental instrument of the mind," allowing us to convert complex global action into cognizable space, whether by spatializing a recession "taking away" jobs or a cosmic struggle treated as a dark night's journey.[21] But how can we determine which figural narratives are the right ones?

This conceptual tension is among the chief subjects engaged by allegory-epic mega-novels. Primarily they address it via a contemporary example of figural narrative, the conspiracy theory. On the one hand, the conspiracy theorist is an allegorist on an epic scale, explaining how events that appear to speak only to a local situation really refer to some historical metanarrative. As Richard Hofstadter writes in "The Paranoid Style in American Politics," conspiracy theorists "regard a 'vast' or 'gigantic' conspiracy as *the motive force* in historical events. History *is* a conspiracy, set in motion by demonic forces of almost transcendent power."[22] One would think, then, that literary critics opposed to totalizing metanarratives would be opposed to paranoid interpretation. Yet precisely the opposite is often the case. Consider, for instance, Thomas Pynchon's *Gravity's Rainbow*, in which many characters attribute much of what happens in Europe's immediate postwar moment to a conspiracy perpetuated by a shadowy military-industrial cabal dubbed "Them." For critics like Paul Maltby, this paranoia "is an appropriate response," because it is the only way to uncover the "*total system*" seeking to subject the world to its domination.[23] This apparent contradiction derives from the fact that paranoia is, as Eve Sedgwick noted, "*reflexive* and *mimetic*" as well as "a *strong theory*": if one wants to oppose all-encompassing systems, then one must adopt a paranoid interpretation capable of seeing such systems anywhere and everywhere they might instantiate themselves, which can quickly lead to the kind of cosmic dogmatism one is trying to critique.[24]

There are understandable neural bases for this kind of paranoia. Kevin Foster and Hanna Kokko have demonstrated that, given the limitations of our perceptual apparatuses, we have an inevitable cognitive bias toward spuriously linking unrelated stimuli to potential threats.[25] If rustling grass in our evolutionary past occasionally indicated a predator, then our species will retain long-term instinctive fear of all rustling noises, because the survival cost of having wrongly ignored such a noise was historically far greater than the cost of wrongly reacting to it. Our cognitive tendency toward generating patterns from our immediate environment is, moreover, frequently necessary for our mental health. A number of researchers have argued that human pattern-making tendencies are linked to the neurotransmitter dopamine, and for some mentally ill patients (e.g., schizophrenics), increased dopamine can engender more coherent perceptions of the world, even though it also increases receptivity to paranormal theories in others.[26] Along the same lines, paranoia makes the world easier to conceive by compressing innumerable particulars into several overarching forces. In an editorial praising paranoia, Salman Rushdie remarked that, "If the crimes of the past are only now being uncovered [. . .], how long will it take before we know about the crimes of the present?"; we can see in his comment the way that paranoia allows epistemological stability in the face of acknowledged ignorance.[27]

Similarly paranoia strengthens the self's sense of importance. Since attempts to realize the world in its totality will inevitably impress on the individual mind its own crippling insignificance, paranoia can rejuvenate it by allowing privileged access to a reality invisible to others. As Paul Ricoeur pointed out in describing the theoretical "hermeneutic of suspicion" (which Sedgwick identifies with critical paranoia), even writers like Marx, Nietzsche, and Freud, who "look upon the whole of consciousness primarily as 'false' consciousness," suspend their suspicion for one act of credulity, because "liberation is inseparable from a 'conscious insight' which victoriously counterattacks the mystification of false consciousness": in other words they believe nothing in culture is free from the corrupting force of ideology *except their own minds in theorizing that ideology*.[28] This specialness is especially pronounced for those paranoids who believe themselves at the center of the conspiracies they articulate: reflecting on *The Truman Show*, whose protagonist is the hero of a 24/7 reality show, Patrick O'Donnell notes that paranoia may be "the last refuge of identity."[29] Conceiving oneself as a combatant against an all-powerful Them in this manner makes one's life more meaningful.

However, paranoia also has serious drawbacks. Krummenacher and his colleagues show that, though the paranormally inclined and dopamine-elevated see more patterns, their pattern-detection is less accurate, because they tend to identify patterns out of stimuli that are gibberish.[30] Other empirical research has demonstrated that conspiracy theorists are especially vulnerable to confirmation bias, since they fill in informational gaps with whatever invented facts best suit the ideological patterns they have devised.[31] This is likely why Jameson refers to conspiracy as "a poor person's cognitive mapping."[32] The "conspiracy" to which the pejorative "conspiracy theory" refers, after all, isn't the one necessary to execute a plot, but the much vaster conspiracy *required to plant all the evidence suggesting there isn't one.* Holocaust deniers, for instance, are unbelievable not because the Allied forces couldn't have conspired to propagandize against Germany, but because they imaginatively summon an improbably efficient bureaucracy seamlessly generating millions of physical records and survivors' testimonies. Competing conspiracy theories can often prompt their partisans into games of paranoid one-upmanship, each new theory proposing ever more encompassing paranoid schemes, as Sedgwick implies is the case with Jameson's (to her, paranoid) Marxist critique of conspiracy theory.[33]

What is most important, paranoids' self-aggrandizement tends to isolate them, preventing either empathy or collective action. The fatalism of conspiracy theorists' paranoia has been found both to reduce their political activity and to cause them to otherwise make poor social decisions: for instance those who believe that AIDS is a government plot to exterminate African Americans are less likely to practice safe sex.[34] This is particularly so for total paranoia. As Jonathan Schell once commented, "The world of *undiscriminating cynicism*, where no one is trusted and nothing is believed, is in many ways a comfortable one. Every citizen enjoys the automatic right to a *sly, knowing, and superior attitude toward all authorities* but has no obligation to do anything about them."[35] Such a position renders the most ridiculous theories equally plausible to those deserving real attention, eliminating anyone's ability to do anything about them. For this reason, as Scott Sanders noted in an early essay on Pynchon, "a nation of paranoiacs would be a totalitarian's dream."[36]

This problem of establishing what constitutes an adequate cognitive mapping in the contemporary world, then, is among the mega-novel's major subjects, as its characters must manipulate and alter their figural narrative systems in search of a structure that can effectively conceive it. It is for that reason, then, that allegory and epic tend to merge in the mega-novel. Since allegory has traditionally relied on abstract ideologies like Christianity, then in an era when even nominal Christians often do not subscribe to many major tenets of the faith, allegory must find a different system on which to base its figuration. As Benedict Anderson has observed, the nation is the strongest such available system.[37] Similarly, while a classical epic might conceivably have spoken to all of a modestly sized city-state through one exemplary event from the absolute past, for larger modern nations, epics require the more elaborate figuration found in allegory to encompass the citizenry. In other words contemporary epics require allegory to achieve epic scale, while contemporary allegories require nationalism to provide a sufficiently solid conceptual structure. The resulting narratives, however, are unstable, because their tendency toward universal meaning is tempered by a suspicious recoiling toward particular event, and vice versa. As a result this process produces lengthy narratives in which any given element might, at any moment, be imbued with great significance, but also might be reduced to meaningless cruft.

How Is Everything Connected in *Underworld*?

The exemplary cases of how this process works involve the mantra Timothy Melley calls "the official slogan of postwar paranoia": "everything is connected."[38] As Brian McHale notes, the sentiment appears in many mega-novels, including *Gravity's Rainbow* and Umberto Eco's *Foucault's Pendulum*.[39] Its appeal likely derives from its simultaneously affirmative and terrifying connotations, suggesting both that the most humdrum elements of our lives might be tremendously important and that even these mundane things might be complicit in some pernicious scheme to which we are oblivious.

It is also, however, a basically meaningless statement. To claim that "everything is connected" is trivially true: semiotically Eco showed long ago that one can hop from any linguistic sign to any other given enough connections.[40] What it fails to address is *how closely* everything is connected. As the paranoia of, say, the American right wing ought to remind us, that two things can be "connected" in some way does not mean the connection is meaningful: for instance that President Obama once had a professional connection with the middle-aged academic Bill Ayers should not cause us to interpret Obama's politics as akin to the younger Ayers's violent antigovernment Marxism. "Everything is connected" can be a dangerous maxim, then, suggesting that those who speak it bear some special wisdom even though it conveys no real knowledge.

The phrase's contradictions might be explicated well via its appearances in Don DeLillo's *Underworld*. The first occurs in a conversation between waste management specialist Nick Shay and his colleagues Simeon "Big Sims" Biggs and Jesse Detwiler regarding a mysterious container ship nicknamed the Flying Liberian that has supposedly been traveling for years unable to dock. The men somberly theorize the ship could be the key to conspiracies involving anything from Mafia incinerator waste to a heroin shipment overseen by the CIA.[41] Aware, though, that they have no particular evidence for these speculations, Detwiler decides to justify their paranoia by saying, "You know why [we believe this]? Because it's easy to believe. We'd be stupid not to believe it. Knowing what we know."[42] The irony, of course, is that they construct these junk theories precisely because they *don't* know what, if anything, is going on, which Detwiler implicitly admits when he elaborates that "what we know" is merely that "everything's connected."[43] As with Nick's brother Matt's later use of the phrase, they simply don't want to seem naive.[44] As Wood remarks, though, "If what you start out from is what you do not know, this is an infinitely extendable mystical spectrum. One can always not know more."[45]

These speculations, though, are complicated by the men's parallel discussion of their profession's central concern, which is also the great recurring motif of allegory-epic mega-novels, namely garbage. Superficially, garbage is "connected" to "everything," since every aspect of human life generates it, but as Nick and Sims's discussion of the enormous amount of food waste produced by the restaurant industry shows, it is connected only in the weakest way, since garbage comprises largely the elements unimportant enough to each endeavor to dispense with.[46] However, Detwiler argues that this attitude has "everything backwards": instead of garbage being a by-product of civilization, he thinks, "garbage rose first, inciting people to build a civilization in response, in self-defense."[47] Waste is so voluminous, he points out, that it requires one to devise a holistic response to keep oneself from being overwhelmed by it, and such a response would necessarily generate a system of connectivity out of which society could be made. Detwiler suggests, then, that there might be something both socially valuable and aesthetically creative in finding new ways to connect trash to our lives, which is why he suggests we "[m]ake an architecture of waste. Design gorgeous buildings to recycle waste and invite people to collect their own garbage and bring it with them to the press rams and conveyors. Get to know your garbage"—a goal shared by characters like Klara Sax, who in an earlier scene makes an art installation out of junked World War II bombers.[48] Perhaps, then, composing junk theories out of the unverifiable rumors floating through the cultural atmosphere might be a valuable way to manage an otherwise incomprehensible geopolitical climate.

However, just because junk *can* be connected doesn't mean it *should* be. As Wood points out, most garbage comprises "objects of indifference, convenience, and hatred"—and, we might add, toxicity.[49] As we discussed in chapter 2, the scholar-protagonist of Eco's *Foucault's Pendulum* insists on gathering as much trivial data as possible for his index-card system, and to avoid boredom at his menial publishing job, he and his friend Jacopo Belbo use a computer program to randomly combine fragments from conspiracy-theory manuscripts into their own master allegory explaining all European history. This proves not to be difficult, because as Casaubon, notes, "Concepts are connected by analogy. There is no way to decide at once whether an analogy is good or bad, because to some degree everything is connected to everything else."[50] Though their results are amusing (e.g., "the specter haunting Europe" being the Illuminati), they are entirely arbitrary: as Casaubon's lover Lia points out, the most obvious interpretation of the puzzling medieval document that starts off their quest is that it is a shopping list.[51] Moreover such gratuitousness, no matter how entertaining, does not come without cost. The Plan ends up not being redemptive, but destructive, because the circle of conspiracy theorists from whom the scholars had taken these materials becomes convinced of its truth and convenes an ad hoc ritual at the Paris Conservatory of Arts and Crafts that ends up murdering Belbo.[52] As Lia earlier insists, "Your plan isn't poetic; it's grotesque."[53]

Are the efforts by *Underworld*'s characters to suggest that "everything is connected" similarly ill conceived? The answer is not clear. The ambiguity is most pronounced in the memorabilia collector Marvin Lundy, who believes in the "dot theory of reality, that all knowledge is available if you analyze the dots," which leads him to paranoid theories about Bobby Thomson's Shot Heard 'Round the World and the prophetic significance of Gorbachev's birthmark.[54] These theories are as ridiculous as anything in *Foucault's Pendulum*. Yet Nick's friend Brian Glassic feels "shamed" upon visiting Lundy, because these theories "exposed his own middling drift."[55] Glassic, like many of the characters, feels lost in the haze of conflicting paranoias characterizing the Cold War era and had indeed earlier tried to use the Thomson home run to locate himself in national history, claiming, "When JFK was shot, people went inside. We watched TV in dark rooms and talked on the phone with friends and relatives. We were all separate and alone. But when Thomson hit the homer, people rushed outside. People wanted to be together."[56] But he is not able to develop this thought much further, and from the unmoored perspective in which it leaves him, even Lundy's near-absurd belief in the significance of his detritus looks appealing.

Where is the boundary, then, between a poetic allegory of trash and a grotesque one? DeLillo's essay on the novel's creation, "The Power of History," suggests that, for him at least, his characters' theories lie on the poetic side. He valorizes the Thomson home run as "beautifully isolated in time—not subject to the debasing process of frantic repetition that exhausts a contemporary event before it has rounded into coherence."[57] When he claims that fictional re-creations of such moments are "all about reliving things," he implies that, if we were only able to connect up all the junk of the past again, we might finally understand our place in "the sweeping range of American landscape and experience."[58] His protagonist, however, is not so confident. Nick purchases from Lundy the home run ball, hoping it will lead him back to "the days when I was alive on the earth, rippling in the quick of my skin, heedless and real," but as time passes, he notes, "I tend to forget why I bought it," and it sits on his bookshelves in a tenuous gray area between icon and trash, "wedged between a slanted book and a straight-up book [. . .] a beautiful thing smudged green near the Spalding trademark and bronzed with nearly half a century of earth and sweat and chemical change."[59] As with many of Nick's meandering adventures through the book, it's not clear now what meaning it has.

So how do we interpret the ball? We could be cynical, with Catherine Morley, and call the ball's apotheosis a "political construction" that "works to aestheticise and erase international politics," like the crowd's racial tensions and the Soviet nuclear test occurring at the same time.[60] Certainly the historical significance Nick and Glassic attribute to it seems more impressionistic and idiosyncratic nostalgia than robust cultural theory. Yet it's hard to read DeLillo's description of the game's conclusion, with "[p]eople climbing the dugout roofs and the crowd shaking in its own noise"; Leo Durocher in "an ascetic rapture, a thing they do in mosques in Anatolia"; and Russ Hodges repetitively hollering, "*The Giants win the pennant!*" and be so steel-hearted.[61] The opening of *Underworld* might be the most spine-tingling chapter DeLillo has ever written—it feels wrong to call its occasion a scam. As David Cowart writes, "*Underworld*'s baseball [. . .] is at once McGuffin and grail, and the author presents it with considerable ambiguity."[62] To understand it would require a much more cogent understanding of how and why individuals imbue particular objects with larger meaning than I believe yet exists.

This conundrum is brought to its climax by the book's last use of "everything is connected," toward the conclusion, in which the batty Bronx nun Sister Edgar perceives the mystic apparition of a martyred Hispanic girl named Esmeralda on an overpass billboard, then dies and is absorbed into the nascent World Wide Web, where she becomes "open—exposed to every connection you can make," having in the process several visions: a nuclear explosion, J. Edgar Hoover, and the eyes of God.[63] They culminate in her realization that "[e]verything is connected in the end" and this final passage:

> And you can glance out the window for a moment, distracted by the sound of small kids playing a made-up game in a neighbor's yard, some kind of kickball maybe, and they speak in your voice, or piggyback races on the weedy lawn, and it's your voice you hear, essentially, under the glimmerglass sky, and you look at the things in the room, offscreen, unwebbed, the tissued grain of the deskwood alive in light, the thick live tenor of things, the argument of things to be seen and eaten, the apple core going sepia in the lunch tray, and the dense measures of experience in a random glance, the monk's candle reflected in the slope of the phone, hours marked in

> Roman numerals, and the glaze of the wax, and the curl of the braided wick, and the chipped rim of the mug that holds your yellow pencils, skewed all crazy, and the plied lives of the simplest surface, the slabbed butter melting on the crumbled bun, and the yellow of the yellow pencils, and you try to imagine the word on the screen becoming a thing in the world, taking all its meanings, its sense of serenities and contentments out into the streets somehow, its whisper of reconciliation, a word extending itself ever outward, the tone of agreement or treaty, the tone of repose, the sense of mollifying silence, the tone of hail and farewell, a word that carries the sunlit ardor of an object deep in drenching noon, the argument of binding touch, but it's only a sequence of pulses on a dullish screen and all it can do is make you pensive—a word that spreads a longing through the raw sprawl of the city and out across the dreaming bourns and orchards of the solitary hills.
>
> Peace.[64]

There is a certain breathless magic to the one-sentence paragraph, propelling us to the book's end with the feeling that we might have been given the key, finally, to understanding the novel's missing connections. Yet that sense of ecstasy is manufactured almost out of sheer syntax, because when we read it closely, it is obvious that nothing it lists is connected at all. Much of it, in fact, is literally trash. It is difficult to imagine that these words were meant to be read at any depth at all, but rather giddily raced past in hopes of communicating the *idea* of connectivity, rather than any specific connections. How Nick and the other characters relate to America, then, or how we might imagine such a relationship for ourselves, is left unresolved amid this final pile of cruft.

McHale once argued that the paranoid interpretation he associates with modernism ought to be scrapped in favor of "counter-paranoiac" reading, which he associated with Lia's approach to Casaubon and Belbo's project.[65] However, Lia is not really counterparanoid: she connects everything, too, just more plausibly than Casaubon does. This final page of *Underworld* is what counterparanoia would really look like, juxtaposing a bunch of objects without any apparent figural relationships. There has been some debate as to what degree *Underworld* is properly paranoid, "an extended demonstration of the hypothesis—at times even the faith—that everything is connected," or "post-paranoid," depicting a world in which people "don't have to believe, that what they don't know is the deep, secret, missing truth."[66] The answer to that question is probably that it is not so much either paranoid or postparanoid as it experiments across the spectrum of paranoia, examining the relationship between what James Wood refers to as the "centrifugal" tendency of theories like Lundy's and scattered "centripetal" text like the final page.[67] There are moments that follow each approach exclusively, and many others that vacillate back and forth between them, trying without success to find a place to settle.

What, then, is the role of cruft in the paranoia-laced allegory-epic mega-novel? It emerges on the extremes of both tendencies. As Wood notes, the paranoia of *Underworld*'s characters does not resemble the "private paranoia" of, say, Dostoevsky's Underground Man, which grows organically out of a specific psychological state and can be contrasted against what we are told of a real external world surrounding him. Instead it is a "political paranoia," targeted less at one subject's imagined conspiracy than vague musings shared more or less by many characters on the world at large.[68] The fact of the characters' paranoia might be important, but the specific form their paranoia takes is arbitrary. While private paranoias are inextricable from the narratives they spawn, most paranoid theories in *Underworld* (e.g., Lundy on Gorbachev's birthmark) might be substituted, moved, and sometimes even excised with no impact on the larger narrative. Such theories, moreover, are often adjacent to contrasting passages that lack much connectedness (e.g., the last paragraph), rendering them unassimilated and illegible within the novel's larger texture. In between these two poles of cruft, the novel presents a gray area of possible modes of connectedness with greater or lesser plausibility. Though Wood is right to note the incongruity in how mega-novelists' critics can never decide whether they are "great occultist[s]" or "visited hoaxer[s]," there is value in the cruft they produce.[69] By pressuring us from opposite directions, they call into question what would constitute an adequate figurative understanding of the world. Repelling us from a too-paranoid position, the narrative might push us toward a relatively counterparanoid attitude, but that perspective will likely render us incapable of managing other narrative elements and encourage us to develop a different form of paranoia. This sequence of feedback and calibration is the distinctive cognitive process provoked by the allegory-epic mega-novel.

World War II as the Contemporary Allegorical-Epic Event

This instability within the allegory-epic mega-novel probably derives from the unraveling of traditional figurative ideological systems over the past seventy-five years. This is probably why World War II often serves as the generative moment of epic conflict grounding them. Given how the war generated or upended so many national narratives, as well as significantly advancing internationalist sensibilities, it should not be surprising that it has substantively shaped ensuing epic narrative. Interestingly, in contrast to how World War I is often considered the defining event for modernism, World War II has never been associated as strongly with postmodernism, even though many of the great global postmodern novels, especially mega-novels, are responses to World War II.[70] If one were, for example, to describe a long, challenging novel in which a male protagonist—sympathetic in his way, but naive and unreliable in matters both perceptual and ethical—wanders across the strange landscape created in the war's wake, driven at any given moment by specific goals but unsure about what he ought to be doing in any larger sense, one might be discussing Günter Grass's *The Tin Drum* if that nation were Germany; but if it were Japan it could be Haruki Murakami's *The Wind-Up Bird Chronicle*; India, Salman Rushdie's *Midnight's Children*; the United States, not only *Underworld* but *Gravity's Rainbow* or William Gass's *The Tunnel*.

World War II and its legacy, however, have long defied straightforward artistic treatment. For World War I, as Samuel Hynes notes, there had been a unified "Myth of the War" about communal terror at modern military technology and the betrayal of innocent young men by doddering generals.[71] No such myth exists for World War II. While novelists who had witnessed the fighting often wished to resist any easy narrative of Good against Evil in characterizing the Allies and Axis, simply appropriating World War I's myth in the new postwar era would create an unpalatable equivalence between, say, the Nazis and their victims.[72] In attempting to write about the conflict, authors from different countries are faced with distinct difficulties: for writers in Axis countries, acknowledging their nations' role in the war at all has proved difficult; for those in Allied nations, admitting the human tragedy of Hiroshima, Nagasaki, Dresden, and Tokyo into the war's larger narrative has been problematic; and for writers in nations decolonized after the war, finding a balance between the lineages of Allied universalist humanism, with its attendant imperialist heritage, and self-determined local values, with their sectarian and regressive tendencies, has provided serious challenges.[73] This weakening of national narratives contributes significantly to difficulties in cognitive mapping. That is probably why Jameson mused hopefully that "third-world" literature might show a path out of this conundrum, because, he believed, it was always written "in the form of national allegory: *the story of the private individual destiny is always an allegory of the embattled situation of the public third-world culture and society.*"[74] This position was immediately critiqued as a dramatically inadequate simplification, of course, leaving the question of how to figure one's place in the contemporary world lacking any clear answer.[75]

This might be what makes paranoia-drenched postwar mega-novels so interesting. They tend to present their characters (and readers) with several potential mappings of a complicated international situation, ranging from rigid allegory to near-total disconnection. In some cases the national allegories turn out to be valuable to the characters' construction of a coherent sense of place, but in many cases they merely generate cruft. The characters' quest becomes how to distinguish modes of interpretation that are too paranoid to be cognitively tenable from those that are not paranoid enough, an exceedingly difficult task given how often apparently ridiculous theories end up being justified while apparently stable conceptions of communal identity easily disintegrate. The rest of the chapter will examine the different ways in which these books deploy and dismantle figuration, forcing us to develop more cogent ways of responding to the situations to which they are applied.

Catachresis and *The Wind-Up Bird Chronicle*

The first kind of allegorical cruft we will examine is the empty figure. Conventional rhetoric does not have a term for an apparent figure that does not actually figure anything, but the closest is probably catachresis. In contemporary use it refers to any figurative connection between two concepts "marked by the feature of illogicality, often close to absurdity, and generates far-fetched, strained associations," and empty figuration seems like a reasonable extension of this principle.[76] As Elżbieta Chrzanowska-Kluczewska notes, catachreses' "lack of definite reference and interpretation" has led them to be associated with "certain experiments in twentieth century modernist, but especially postmodernist, prose."[77] Yet there is clearly a point beyond which such disjunctions become more wasteful than illuminating. Mark Turner calls this the "invariance principle," the rule that, for the sake of our cognitive stability, "Conceptual projection [. . .] shall not result in an image-schematic clash in the target."[78] What makes catachreses especially difficult to manage, though, is that they usually cannot be identified immediately as catachrestic: in fact they often seem potentially intriguing until one has had time to play out their implications and determine how strained they are. That is frequently the case with their use in conspiracy theories, wherein signs are often attributed meanings that seem plausible at first but eventually break down into incoherence upon analysis. When they reach this stage, they become cruft.

Haruki Murakami's *The Wind-Up Bird Chronicle*, the author's response to criticism that his work had not engaged directly enough with the politics of postwar Japan, provides a case study in this phenomenon.[79] In some ways the book seems neatly allegorical. For example the narrator, the recently unemployed Toru Okada, has become estranged emotionally and literally from his wife, Kumiko, who has herself long felt an inner psychic split associated an abortion several years prior, contributing to the fact—observed by Toru upon receiving a serious of anonymous dirty phone calls—that the pair have not had sex in some time. Several supporting characters face similar psychological troubles, like the quasi-telepathic Creta Kano, a "mental prostitute" with a history of psychosexual dysfunction, as well as the psychic healer Nutmeg Akasaka and her son Cinnamon, the latter of whom has been mute ever since an enigmatic childhood dream involving a wind-up bird and two men burying something in his backyard. As the novel proceeds, these psychological holes are linked to World War II. Literal holes are often the figurative vehicle: Toru, for instance, receives a bequest from his late friend Mr. Honda by way of a Lieutenant Mamiya, who recounts how he has suffered from existential emptiness ever since being thrown down a dry well while stationed in Manchuria, prompting Toru to venture into the dry well across the alley behind his house. The personal and political are further linked when we discover the involvement of Kumiko's economist brother Noboru Wataya—who has just inherited the Diet seat held by his uncle Yoshitaka, the logistician in charge of Japanese imperial strategy during the war—in both Creta and his sister's sexual trauma, suggesting the hidden abusive tendencies in Japan's current political system.

The narrative, then, might be interpreted figurally as suggesting that World War II created a national psychic rift, with the cultural diseases expressed by prewar imperialism and postdefeat capitalism combining to impede the political and psychosexual functioning of its citizens. This sense of malfunction coalesces in the image of the wind-up bird itself, which shows up not only in Cinnamon's dream but in his grandfather's account of an episode from the war and in Toru's strolls through his neighborhood: as a paradoxical figure for both the world's orderly functioning and the artificial nature of that order, it tends to vanish when characters are stricken by the psychic rift. That the book climaxes with Noboru suffering a stroke in Nagasaki and Mamiya forging a new life with Creta as farmers in Hiroshima seems to resolve this allegory neatly, with the two cities destroyed by atomic bombs figuring the nation's rebirth.

Yet things are not quite so pat as this account suggests. Between the initial publication of the original edition's second and third books, in fact, Murakami's Japanese critics pointed out that many of the novel's apparent figures, rather than tying themselves up cleanly, were "hang[ing] aimlessly like threads in an unfinished tapestry."[80] Though by the end of the novel many of those apparently illegible figures are incorporated into the allegory—for instance Toru's anonymous caller is finally identified as a splintered element of Kumiko's psyche—others are catachrestic, presented *as if* they will eventually acquire clear figurative meaning without ever doing so. One example is the overture to Rossini's *The Thieving Magpie*, from which the novel's first book takes its name. The overture plays on the radio during the novel's first page, causing Toru to unconsciously whistle it several chapters later; its emblematic nature is apparently confirmed when it is hummed in the dream realm Toru visits while meditating in the well by a waiter walking toward a mysterious hotel room.[81] However, the opera itself does not seem to relate to the novel's allegory: even the two title birds have little in common, as one is an emblem of vulnerability and the other a mischievous trickster. For that matter Toru neither has nor particularly wants any personal associations with the piece. Late in the novel, he ponders, "If things ever settled down, I would have to go to the library and look it up in an encyclopedia of music. I might even buy a complete recording of the opera if it was available. Or maybe not. I might not care to know the answers to these questions by then."[82] As Jay Rubin writes, "The opera features prominently in the book not because its plot provides a key to the novel but precisely because it is just out of reach. [. . .] [F]or Toru *The Thieving Magpie* will always be something he hasn't quite understood. It is familiar, and yet its meaning eludes him."[83] Like Toru's missing-then-retrieved polka-dot necktie, or the bequest from Honda that turns out to be an empty box, it is connected to the allegory only very weakly.

These disjoint connections are intriguing because *Wind-Up Bird*'s characters otherwise adhere to the paranoid principle articulated by the Sheep Man in Murakami's earlier *Dance Dance Dance*, that "*[i]t's all connected.*"[84] Late in the novel, for example, Toru thinks:

> [Nutmeg and Cinnamon's] "clients" and I were joined by the mark on my cheek. Cinnamon's grandfather (Nutmeg's father) and I were also joined by the mark on my cheek. Cinnamon's grandfather and Lieutenant Mamiya were joined by the city of Hsin-ching. Lieutenant Mamiya and the clairvoyant Mr. Honda were joined by their special duties on the Manchurian-Mongolian border, and Kumiko and I had been introduced to Mr. Honda by Noboru Wataya's family. Lieutenant Mamiya and I were joined by our experiences in our respective wells—his in Mongolia, mine on the property where I was sitting now. Also on this property had once lived an army officer who had commanded troops in China. All of these were linked as in a circle, at the center of which stood prewar Manchuria, continental East Asia, and the short war of 1939 in Nomonhan.[85]

Yet many elements in the novel don't quite fit into this pattern. Finishing the above passage, Toru asks, "But why Kumiko and I should have been drawn into this historical chain of cause and effect I could not comprehend. All of these events had occurred long before Kumiko and I were born."[86] He is not the only one to feel that way, either, as his teenaged neighbor May Kasahara writes, upon dropping out of school to work in a wig factory, that her life seems as if "*one disconnected thing led to another disconnected thing, and that's how all kinds of stuff happened. [. . .] I don't have any idea what's happening to me.*"[87]

The characters are not satisfied with establishing that "Everything is connected," then, but ask "*How* is everything connected?" When we have put together what would otherwise seem like a plausible network of figurative connections, yet cannot fit into it many apparent figures, we should ask, as does Matthew Strecher, "whether these connections are real, imagined, or coincidental."[88] The elaborate connections Toru constructs may merely exist, after all, to cover up his own sense of emptiness and expendability. Early in the book, when discussing with Kumiko the mysticism of Malta Kano and Mr. Honda, he suggests that all such explanations are essentially arbitrary: "I mean, the world's full of things we can't explain, and somebody's got to fill that vacuum. Better to have somebody who isn't boring than somebody who is. Right?"[89] His allegorical narrative, intertwining his own malaise with that of millions of other Japanese, could well be elaborate nonsense. It may not bore him, but it might bore readers when they discover there's nothing behind it.

Amitrano, I think, articulates the best way to approach this problem when he notes in Murakami, as Wood does in DeLillo, a "tension between a centrifugal tendency towards the values of exactness and clarity [. . .] and the centripetal force that leads characters, events, themes so far from the center of narration as to become virtually invisible or disappear altogether."[90] Yet while Amitrano believes this serves largely to reflect the contemporary condition, I believe it serves an interesting cognitive effect, as well. A better way of putting it is that as we read, we come across any number of potential emblems, some of which might be meaningful and some of which are simply cruft, but *we don't know which is which until we have finished the book*. As a result we need to be prepared to read any figure as possibly having deep resonance but also as possibly being a waste of our attentional resources. As in *Underworld*, the opposing centrifugal and centripetal tendencies create a spectrum of meaningfulness among the novel's potential figures, requiring that we be primed to invest substantial attention in any one at any point, but also that we distribute it in such a way that we do not become too invested in something that ends up being meaningless.

For instance, at first we might interpret Toru and Kumiko's cat, who is named after Kumiko's brother Noboru, as figuring the same malignant forces the economist represents, especially when the cat vanishes at the novel's start and helps precipitate their psychic maladies. As the book proceeds, though, the connections between the human and feline Noborus grow weaker: the Okadas, after all, see their pet representing "something good that grew up between us."[91] Though the human Noboru's actions continue to figure larger societal ills and prolong Toru's anguish, the cat not only does not add further injury to the Okadas but suddenly reappears at the book's midpoint without resolving anything. This crashes the metaphor into the invariance principle. As if to admit the cat's limited figurative function from this point forward, Toru renames him "Mackerel."[92] To insist either that the cat reveals the novel's deeper figurative structure or that he subverts all such structures would be to miss the point: instead he possesses an important figurative resonance to Toru for some time, until he doesn't anymore. The abundance of such pseudo-emblems, whose relevance alters as our conception of the larger allegory changes, shows how difficult it is to maintain a coherent idea of our place in the world.

How we interpret the individual figures will also have an impact on how we interpret the larger figural narrative system about Japanese national identity of which they are part. Many of the book's characters, for instance, are mystified about their relationship to Japan, none more so than Mamiya. Being Japanese, for him, is not exactly determined by geography, because prior to the war, the land officially part of the Japanese empire waxed and waned with the state's imperial fortunes. While posted in Manchuria, he had felt that "[t]o protect my homeland, I too would fight and die. But it made no sense to me at all to sacrifice my one and only life for the sake of this desolate patch of soil."[93] Nor is his national identity exactly determined by shared ethnicity or culture, as the postwar shift in global power relations causes many of the nation's institutions and allegiances to be westernized, partly exemplified by how after being captured on the Soviet front, Mamiya attempts a realpolitik alliance with a Russian power broker that alienates him from his fellow Japanese prisoners of war.[94] When his last tie to Japan, kinship, dissolves upon his family's deaths in the nuclear strike on Hiroshima, Mamiya becomes incapable of relocating himself within Japan. His lack of nationality does not liberate but cripples him, and his inability to feel resonance with anything upon his return makes him think that "real life may have ended for me deep in that well in the desert of Outer Mongolia."[95] The catachrestic nature of his Japaneseness, then, should make us think through what would constitute a meaningful attitude toward the nation.

Similarly the novel's catachreses should make us wary about how we interpret the resolution of the novel's allegorical national crisis. At the novel's climax, Toru enters the dream world, locates the lost Kumiko in the hotel room, sees a TV news report about how a baseball-bat-wielding man resembling him has bludgeoned Noboru Wataya into critical condition, then takes a blood-stained bat from Kumiko and kills an invisible monster who challenges him, apparently prompting Noboru's real-world collapse.[96] As a subconscious figure, Toru seems to have received the bat—a complex symbol of both Japanese nationality and westernization—from Cinnamon's account of his grandfather's role in the war's late stages, which depicts a Japanese officer ordered to execute an escaped Chinese prisoner using the baseball bat that the escapee himself had used to kill his jailers.[97] When Kumiko gives the bat to him, then, it appears to complete a circle of connections to World War II. Yet the bat also has a literal existence that is almost total cruft. Near the novel's midpoint, Toru is followed by a guitarist who proceeds to attack him with a bat until Toru wrests it away and knocks him unconscious, subsequently keeping the bat and bringing it with him to the well.[98] Just before he enters the well for his climactic battle, though, the bat inexplicably disappears.[99] Any attempt we might have made to tie the literal bat into the figurative web is destroyed, as its existence is revealed to be entirely gratuitous. However, the figurative opaqueness of Toru's actual bat might prompt us to consider more closely, when attempting to find a meaning for it, the murders committed with the other bats. After all, the World War II execution is pointlessly brutal, the act of an imperial power too inflexible to acknowledge its impending defeat—not to mention totally ineffective, as the prisoner revives and has to be shot anyway. Is Toru's own ritual violence, then, merely an extension of the same cultural disease he attempts to eradicate? Or can it still serve its purgative function despite this association?

The uncertainty these questions leave may be why the novel's conclusion only partly resolves the myriad problems raised elsewhere in the book. On the one hand, a malevolent politician dies, Toru locates Kumiko and begins to resume written communication with her, and several minor characters experience happy endings. On the other hand, the fates of May Kasahara and the disappeared Malta Kano are left unresolved, and we do not know whether Toru and Kumiko's relationship will ever be fully restored: Kumiko is imprisoned after she removes her brother's life support and is not yet ready to speak to Toru in person.[100] Similarly it is not clear to what extent Noboru's death will actually cleanse Japan of its postwar malaise, or whether the psychic rift will persist. It is tempting to be clunkily Lacanian about such gaps, but the book's final words suggest that the problem is, fundamentally, a cognitive one. Pondering his situation as he takes the train home from visiting May, Toru tells us, "I closed my eyes and tried to sleep. But it was not until much later that I was able to get any real sleep. In a place far away from anyone or anywhere, I drifted off for a moment."[101] The novel's events have given Toru a stronger sense of local and national connections, but his continued inability to maintain a figural framework establishing his relationship to the rest of the world leaves him unable to sustain consistent focus. He remains "far away from anyone or anywhere" because his mind is still adrift, not quite able to process the many recalcitrant elements of his world.

The Elephantiasis of *Midnight's Children*

The narrator of Salman Rushdie's *Midnight's Children*, Saleem Sinai, has no such lack of conviction about his place within the nation. His introduction to the autobiographical chronicle about the first decades of Indian independence claims, after all, that "there are so many stories to tell, too many, such an excess of intertwined lives events miracles places rumors, so dense a commingling of the improbable and the mundane! I have been a swallower of lives; and to know me, just the one of me, you'll have to swallow the lot as well."[102] Being born at midnight on August 5, 1947—the exact moment of independence—means, he believes, that his "destinies [are] indissolubly chained to those of my country."[103] This is an ambitious claim, but it is not totally unfounded. For one, his heritage is a near microcosm of India's history: though he is raised by the well-off Sinai family, who comprise both western-educated professionals and Muslim traditionalists, he was born of a poor Hindu woman and a departing British officer, himself descended from the founder of Bombay. Furthermore Saleem's face is reminiscent of the Hindu god Ganesh, to whose scribal role he aspires.[104] Last, his moment of birth has given him telepathic abilities, allowing him to communicate with the thousand other supernaturally endowed children born during the first hour of independence, whom he dubs Midnight's Children. When Prime Minister Nehru addresses Saleem as "the newest bearer of that ancient face of India which is also eternally young," it seems quite plausible to suggest that his life might allegorically represent the entire history of India and its hope for the future.[105]

Early on, though, Saleem begins to worry about how to manage the scope of such a narrative. While recounting how his mother Amina's lover Nadir Khan fled the assassination of Mian Abdullah, Saleem tells us a brief story about Nadir's roommate, a painter whose works "had grown larger and larger as he tried to get the whole of life into his art," causing him to wail "I wanted to be a miniaturist and I've got elephantiasis instead!" Subsequently, and with no other explanation, the painter commits suicide.[106] Saleem likely means to communicate by this excursus anxieties regarding his own elephantiastic endeavor. Those worries become clearer a few chapters later, when he ruminates on whether the spectacular, but apparently coincidental, events that shape his life are motivated by chance or fate: "if everything is planned in advance, then we all have a meaning, and are spared the terror of knowing ourselves to be random, without a *why*; or else, of course, we might—as pessimists—give up right here and now, understanding the futility of thought decision action, since nothing we think makes any difference anyway; things will be as they will. Where, then, is optimism? In fate or in chaos?"[107] Believing everything is strongly connected, that is, may provide a sense of collectivity but does so at the price of emphasizing one's own insignificance to the enormous, predetermined pattern of fate. Yet Saleem cannot refuse fate, either, because its absence would render his actions insignificant for the opposite reasons, the lack of larger context to which to relate them. As Neil Ten Kortenaar writes, "what frightens Saleem is not excess or incongruity but rather the probable lack that excess can imply."[108] It is no coincidence, then, that Jameson's "national allegory" framework has been both enthusiastically applied and emphatically rejected by *Midnight's Children*'s critics: the book both prompts such a large-scale approach as necessary for conceptualizing an immense nation like India but also resists it as fatalist and potentially dogmatic.[109]

Consequently *Midnight's Children* is concerned less with showing that "everything is connected" than with the question "*how far* should everything be connected?" As the narrative proceeds, Saleem has increasing difficulty determining the lengths to which he should extend his allegory. For instance, when explaining why his ten-year-old self had sent a letter to Commander Sabarmati revealing the latter's wife Lila had been sleeping with the film producer Homi Catrack—leading in sequence to Lila and Homi's murder, the commander's imprisonment, and Saleem's filmmaker uncle Hanif committing suicide—Saleem assigns blame to fated narrative archetypes: "Radha and Krishna, and Rama and Sita, and Laila and Majnu; also (because we are not unaffected by the West) Romeo and Juliet, and Spencer Tracy and Katharine Hepburn. The world is full of love stories, and all lovers are in a sense the avatars of their predecessors. When Lila drover her Hindustan to an address off Colaba Causeway, she was Juliet coming out on to her balcony; when cream-scarfed, gold-shaded Homi sped off to meet her [. . .], he was Leander swimming the Hellespont toward Hero's burning candle."[110] None of these love stories, however, is a remotely adequate figure for the relationship of Lila and Homi, as none involves love triangles. The overextension of Saleem's figuration suggests his struggles with conceptualizing personal agency in a larger context, as at first he tells us, "As for my part in the business, I will not give it a name," using the power of fate to erase his culpability, but only a few pages later he uses it for precisely the opposite reason, declaring himself the commander's "puppet-master."[111] Neither is true—he has some, not total, responsibility—yet for someone who feels the importance of understanding his life as imbricated in the national future, but also acutely realizes his own smallness as only one citizen among hundreds of millions, that idea is difficult to articulate.

An even greater overextension occurs when Saleem notes, after his grandfather Aadam Aziz collapses on the road to Pakistan to mourn Hanif, that Nehru has fallen sick at around the same time. Recapping the past hundred pages, Saleem thinks:

> If I hadn't wanted to be a hero, Mr. Zagallo would never have pulled out my hair. If my hair had remained intact, Glandy Keith and Fat Perce wouldn't have taunted me; Masha Miovic wouldn't have goaded me into losing my finger. And from my finger flowed blood which was neither-Alpha-nor-Omega, and sent me into exile; and in exile I was filled with the lust for revenge which led to the murder of Homi Catrack; and if Homi hadn't died, perhaps my uncle would not have strolled off a roof into the sea-breezes; and then my grandfather would not have gone to Kashmir and been broken by the effort of climbing the Sankara Acharya hill. And my grandfather was the founder of my family, and my fate was linked by my birthday to that of the nation, and the father of the nation was Nehru. Nehru's death: can I avoid the conclusion that that, too, was all my fault?[112]

Despite its position at the end of several somewhat more plausible connections, the answer to the last question is obviously "no," especially since Nehru dies some months after Aadam anyway. The passage demonstrates in miniature Saleem's difficulties with circumscribing the Jamesian web of endless relations, as a plausible set of local connections gradually extends into a paranoid effusion of cruft too overdetermined to be coherently sustained.

The problem, however, is not simply an excess of figuration. Though Timothy Brennan argues that "Saleem is a culprit not because he fails to resist, or because he conspires for personal gain, but rather because he proliferates *metaphor*," the narrative's problems cannot be solved by simply rejecting Saleem's figurative impulses.[113] Granted, an overuse of figuration does cause real problems for Saleem, most visibly through his allegory's competition with (and similarity to) Indira Gandhi's totalitarian view that "*India is Indira and Indira is India*."[114] However, a Saleem who refused to understand his actions' figural place within the state would likely end up like *The Tin Drum*'s Oskar Matzerath, the lifelong Danzig resident who similarly narrates the twentieth-century history of his city in autobiographical terms.[115] Notably, Oskar refuses to adopt conscious Polish nationalism: he insists there is no connection between his antiauthority agitation, such as his literal refusal to grow up and his disruption of government gatherings with his drumming, and any political motivation, but that he is motivated purely by "private and what is more esthetic reasons."[116] His deliberate innocence does keep him from helping the Nazis, but it also makes his resistance to them narcissistic and destructive, prompting him toward theft, vandalism, and a near-sociopathic lack of empathy. Such negative consequences might illustrate why Roger Clark writes that *Midnight's Children*'s national mythos is not "a mere postmodern game. Rather, it derives from the great hope of a nation finding its way toward harmony and tolerance, and from the great fear of collapsing into chaos."[117] And figuration sometimes *does* provide real insight for Saleem. As Berlatsky writes, "Saleem's explicit references to metaphor imply that they have the potential to reveal reality, not obscure it," such as with "literalized metaphors" like Saleem's observation that the skin of India's businessmen grows whiter as the nation's economy integrates with western capitalism.[118]

The debate over whether Saleem's figuration is good or bad, then, misses the point. As an abstract concept, metaphor has neutral value: it can be extremely beneficial or quite dangerous, depending on how it is used. An extremely expansive figuration, like that between Midnight's Children and India itself, might be valuable through the way it imagines how native Indian abilities might guide the country toward an otherwise unimaginable independent identity and prosperous future. However, other similarly scaled allegories, like Saleem's account of Nehru's death, lead only into nonsense. Saleem addresses this problem near the novel's midpoint, upon receiving a form letter from Nehru: "'Your life, which will be, in a sense, the mirror of our own,' the Prime Minister wrote, obliging me scientifically to face the question: *In what sense?* How, in what terms, may the career of a single individual be said to impinge on the fate of the nation? I must answer in adverbs and hyphens: I was linked to history both literally and metaphorically, both actively and passively, in what our (admirably modern) scientists might term 'modes of connection' [. . .]: actively-literally, passively-metaphorically, actively-metaphorically and passively-literally, I was inextricably entwined with my world."[119] Saleem acknowledges shortly afterward, though, that "the Midnight's Children Conference [. . .] never became what I most wanted it to be; we never operated in the first, most significant of the 'modes of connection.' The 'active-literal' passed us by."[120] That the active-literal mode is the most difficult to achieve, in fact, suggests why Saleem's figuration is both necessary and dangerous. Since very few individuals in a nation of India's size can ever have a direct active-literal impact on the whole, conceptualizing and effecting change becomes feasible only if one reduces the nation to figurative concepts embodied in specific persons and events.

This leads to the basic paradox of modern democracy: giving voice to hundreds of millions of individuals creates a disorienting cacophony that no one can adequately attend, but restricting those voices to a small number of representatives inevitably concentrates power in a hierarchy. It is not for nothing that several of the novel's characters are desperate for the country to contain its exploding population, as with Dr. Narlikar's antifertility proselytizing and tetrapod venture, Indira and Sanjaya Gandhi's sterilization program, and Saleem's own vision of being "trample[d . . .], the numbers marching one two three, four hundred million five hundred six, reducing me to specks of voiceless dust."[121] Not only does population pose logistical and humanitarian problems, but it makes the nation impossible to coherently conceive. Even the allegorical representation of India's hundreds of millions via the hundreds of surviving Midnight's Children cannot evade this problem, because the reduced number still well exceeds Dunbar's 150-person limit for meaningful social relations. In blurring their voices upon describing them to us, Saleem admits that "my narrative could not cope with five hundred and eight-one fully-rounded personalities," which is probably why the telepathic meetings Saleem orchestrates for the group quickly dissolve into a "hundred squalling rows" over objectives, leadership, and personal agendas.[122]

Saleem's failure either to be a representative leader or to cognize a vast multiplicity of voices causes him to vacillate between unstable figural systems through the novel's latter stages. As Ten Kortenaar notes, Saleem sometimes gets turned around to the point where he "insists that national history is as often an allegory of his life as his life is an allegory of national history."[123] For instance consider his analysis of the 1965 Indo-Pakistani war. There is nothing inherently wrong with relating the war figurally to his family, as the trauma of their own displacement from India to Pakistan puts them in good position to experience the divisive and destructive nature of this conflict. However, bombarded with both the official Indian and Pakistani media's allegories of national invincibility, each so overextended as to totally revise reality—"Voice of Pakistan announced the destruction of more aircraft than India had ever possessed; in eight days, All-India Radio massacred the Pakistan Army down to, and considerably beyond, the last man"—Saleem is left no coherent space into which to project his own self, causing him to create another unsustainable allegory in response: "Let me state this quite unequivocally: it is my firm conviction that the hidden purpose of the Indo-Pakistani war of 1965 was nothing more nor less than the elimination of my benighted family from the face of the earth."[124] He is so unmoored that he believes this claim is a fully *objective* one, arguing that anyone who would "examine the bombing-pattern of that war with an analytical, unprejudiced eye" would agree.[125] This is transparently not true, of course, but devising a sounder theory under Saleem's cognitive conditions is not easy. Since not only has his own national allegiance been forced to waver between India and Pakistan over the course of the book, but the countries' own national narratives have grown alien and unacceptable to him, it is no wonder that his personal figuration becomes horribly distorted.

A brain injury caused by an explosion-propelled spittoon, however, causes Saleem to be "cleansed" of his "yearning for importance" at the war's end, turning him into a meditative Buddha figure with a supernatural sense of smell but no other acknowledgment of worldly or political matters.[126] Yet instead of leading him to enlightenment, this antifigural attitude prevents him from understanding the larger implications of his actions. When he is inducted into the Pakistani army prior to the 1971 Bangladesh Liberation War, he blithely follows his unit's orders to covertly kidnap Sheikh Mujib, leader of the independence movement, without any consciousness of what he is doing.[127] His inability to conceive himself as a Muslim Pakistani mindlessly hunting down a fellow Muslim Pakistani—or, for that matter, as a patriotic Indian further fragmenting an already fragmented subcontinent—allows him to be used for pernicious nationalist purposes.

Saleem understands this when narrating his tale years later, but by that point it is too late. Reflecting on a passing vagrant who brags that he can generate a fifteen-inch turd, Saleem tells us, "Once, when I was more energetic, I would have wanted to tell his life-story; the hour, and his possession of an umbrella, would have been all the connections I needed to begin the process of weaving him into my life, and I have no doubt that I'd have finished by proving his indispensability to anyone who wishes to understand my life and benighted times; but now I'm disconnected, unplugged, with only epitaphs left to write."[128] Though any figuration can be taken so far as to become nonsense, the flexibility to extend and contract figures, to consider different blends of concepts before deciding on one, is extremely valuable. By the novel's end, though, Saleem has exhausted this ability, his cognitive powers so decimated by three decades of attempting to manage the problem of his country's size that he lacks the focus to continue his efforts.

Given the wildly divergent evaluations of Saleem's narrative, the book's critics don't seem to have figured out how to manage that problem either. There is an odd contrast between the near unanimity in critical evaluation of *Midnight's Children* as an aesthetic success, culminating in its victories in the 1993 and 2008 "Booker of Bookers" competitions, and the substantial disagreement over what it actually succeeds in doing. In particular there is widespread disagreement over whether Saleem, in composing his epic, satisfies the subcontinent's "national longing for form."[129] John Su, for instance, believes that *Midnight's Children* succeeds only inasmuch as Saleem fails, claiming that the novel "rejects the heroic myth as the basis for an epic of India" and "locates in the unrepresentability of the future the possibility of unraveling deterministic national narratives and discovering political formations that are presently unimaginable."[130] However, despite this, Ten Kortenaar points out that the book "is most often read, inside and outside of India, as a triumphant celebration of the nation and as the first novel commensurate with India."[131] Perhaps Michael Gorra lays out this problem best, as he on the one hand celebrates how Rushdie presents a new "way to deal with politics on a large scale, rather than in terms of individual ethical dilemmas" but on the other worries that "the whole narrative of *Midnight's Children* remains so firmly under the thumb of [Rushdie's] self-regarding style that at times I find it hard to distinguish because the writer's fantasies on the one hand and the Widow's [Saleem's avatar for Indira Gandhi] on the other."[132] Just as Saleem is so overwhelmed by his nation's size that he cannot find his place within it, his readers are so overwhelmed by the range of possible figurations he presents that they cannot decide which are or are not adequate to the problems of mapping the contemporary world.

What the book does do is present acutely that predicament, in which the expanding networks that make up our society continue to outpace our ability to conceptualize them. Its cruft is emblematic of all the national figurations possible in the contemporary world, and how many of them quickly descend into absurdity. *Midnight's Children* requires us to consider how far we must allegorize any given event to make it comprehensible, but also where we must cease to allegorize so as not to make nonsense of its individual meaning. As the "two three, four hundred million five hundred six" souls that crush Saleem in its final pages increase to billions, that task only grows more difficult.

Us and Them in *Gravity's Rainbow*

If it were inevitable that this book's last chapter would be about allegory and epic, it may have been similarly inevitable that the chapter would end with *Gravity's Rainbow.* Though any of the preceding five chapters could've addressed Pynchon's masterpiece, it is a book that demands to be addressed terminally, and with a breadth of scale to which only the allegory and epic are appropriate. This is not merely because of its eschatological nature or its sizable cottage industry of commentaries, but because it has that rare property shared by only the greatest books: it turns us all into hypocrites. It does so by vacillating so rapidly between profound allegory and absurd conspiracy theory that it reveals how frighteningly inadequate are our cognitive apparatuses for distinguishing the two.

As with *The Wind-Up Bird Chronicle* and *Midnight's Children, Gravity's Rainbow*'s backdrop is the aftermath of World War II's demolition of preexisting national structures. It involves an epic quest, namely American lieutenant Tyrone Slothrop's journey through lawless postsurrender Germany ("the Zone") in search of a mysterious, apocalyptic rocket called the 00000, which is made up of a synthetic material ("Imipolex-G") to which he may have been sexually conditioned during infancy by a representative of an evil military-industrial cabal he dubs "Them." While fleeing Their pursuit, Slothrop becomes enmeshed in the Zone's numerous cultures and subcultures, as well as their attendant mythological systems, ranging from the Puritan eschatology of elect and preterite to Nordic tales of Tannhäuser to invented legends like that of "Plechazunga, the Pig-Hero who, sometime back in the 10th century, routed a Viking invasion."[133] In this way the novel figures the shifting borders and uncertain trajectory of the postwar global moment through Slothrop's own struggle to establish his identity. The narrator quips that "Slothrop [. . .] is as properly constituted a state as any other in the Zone these days," and the American later imagines that, "maybe for a little while all the fences are down, one road as good as another, the whole space of the Zone cleared, depolarized, and somewhere inside the waste of it a single set of coordinates from which to proceed, without elect, without preterite, without even nationality to fuck it up" might emerge.[134]

This allegorical sensibility, however, leads him toward extreme paranoia. Anticipating the narrator's famous claim that paranoia is "the leading edge of the discovery that *everything is connected*," Slothrop feels even before he enters the Zone that Their "plot against him has grown" even beyond the "monolithic, all-potent" one he'd imagined, turning into something that encompasses everyone he meets.[135] The gradual expansion of Slothrop's plotting of this conspiracy against him onto ever higher levels of organization is exemplified well by the passage in which he and Blodgett Waxwing infiltrate Shell's British headquarters to investigate the multinational's role in the creation of Imipolex-G, finding there "not [Minister of Supply] Mr. Duncan Sandys cowering before their righteousness [. . .]—but only a rather dull room, business machines arrayed around the walls calmly blinking, files of cards pierced frail as sugar faces." Subsequently he thinks:

> Duncan Sandys is only a name, a function in this, "How high does sit go?" is not even the right kind of question to be asking, because the organization charts have all been set up by Them, the titles and names filled in by Them, because
>
> Proverbs for Paranoids, 3: If they can get you asking the wrong questions, they don't have to worry about answers.
>
> Slothrop finds he has paused in front of the blue parts list that started all this. *How high does it go* . . . ahhhh. The treacherous question is not meant to apply to *people* at all, but to the *hardware!*[136]

Even hardware, Slothrop believes, might be conspiring against him. By entering the Zone, he seeks to investigate the very nature of connectedness itself, hoping to better understand the nature of a world that seems to be conspiring against him more and more each moment.

However, how to go about interpreting this vast network of connections has caused the novel's critics four decades' worth of headaches. One established tradition of Pynchonists interpret this omniconnectedness in a traditionally epic and allegorical manner, respectively exemplified by Thomas Moore's and Kathryn Hume's claims that *Gravity's Rainbow* generates, respectively, a "style of connectedness" based in Jungian archetypes or a syncretic "mythography" of Western culture.[137] The other major tradition, however, suggests that if there is value in the Zone's ontology, it is in how, as Leo Bersani puts it, it "resists analysis" by means of interpretation, such as those that allegory and epic presuppose.[138] Calling critics like Hume and Moore "good paranoid readers," for instance, McHale claims that while *Gravity's Rainbow* "engages our paranoid tendencies as readers," it "also solicits our participation at a higher, reflexive level of reading [. . . by] confronting us with irreducibly ambiguous, or, better, multiguous features."[139] Either the novel generates the postwar era's most rigorously structured figural narrative system, that is, or it is a quintessentially uninterpretable postmodern text. Even Deborah Madsen's book on Pynchon's allegories cannot decide whether *Gravity's Rainbow* figurations constitute "a construction or a cryptomorph."[140]

Yet this division reflects not so much two distinct interpretations as two starting points tending toward the same contradiction. On the one hand, those in the poststructuralist camp, like Peter Cooper, claim that the book "defies a 1 or 0 method of reading" yet often end up inscribing a rigid allegorical binary anyway by buying into the battle of Us versus Them, insisting there is "clear internal evidence of an evil and manipulative cabal."[141] Conversely those in the first camp often claim that paranoid reading is most valuable for how it promotes an unstructured subversiveness that "does not proceed rationally [. . .] but [. . .] appears to function, at least on one level, simply by violating the behavior They would predict."[142] This makes little more sense, because as Hofstadter wrote, "the paranoid mentality is far more coherent than the real world, since it leaves no room for mistakes, failures, or ambiguities. It is, if not wholly rational, at least intensely rationalistic."[143] Indeed generating schemes heroically pitting oneself in a cosmic battle against a demonized Other is characteristic not of those seeking to sympathize with a downtrodden preterite, Hofstadter points out, but "the megalomanic view of oneself as the Elect, wholly good, abominably persecuted."[144]

Regardless of the position with which we begin, that is, *Gravity's Rainbow* tends to twist it back against itself. I have written elsewhere about how this emerges in critical treatments of the novel's preterite-versus-elect pairing.[145] To address these issues in the novel as a whole, though, will require a bolder claim about how to approach the novel's paranoia, one that, though it has been gestured toward by a number of critics, has not been fully embraced: *"They" do not actually exist.*[146] This might seem a ridiculous assertion, as They are referred to by many characters throughout the narrative, but nevertheless They are only, as Slothrop puts it, "pasteboard images," and being able to acknowledge that while still navigating the book is probably the most serious challenge for *Gravity's Rainbow*'s readers.[147]

Few critics have actually been able to explain exactly what is meant by "Them." Most are forced to describe Them as did one of Pynchon's best early readers, Tony Tanner:

> What emerges from the book is a sense of a force and a system—something, someone, referred to simply as "the firm" or "They"—which is actively trying to bring everything to zero and beyond, trying to institute a world of nonbeing, an operative kingdom of death, covering the organic world with a world of paper and plastic and transforming all natural resources into destructive power and waste: the rocket and the debris around it. "They" are precisely nonspecific, unlocatable. There is always the possibility of a They behind the They, a plot behind the plot; the quest to identify "Them" sucks the would-be identifier into the possibility of an endless regression. But, whatever Their source and origin, They are dedicated to annihilation.[148]

I am reminded of Foucauldians discussing "power," wherein a critic's acknowledged inability to define a term does not limit the confidence with which it is wielded. This fuzziness, though, leads Tanner, and many other Pynchonists, into error. For example Tanner wrongly identifies Them with the Firm, even though the latter is used only to refer specifically to the British intelligence bureaucracy, while Them is used to refer not only to the Firm but to several other real or hypothesized power structures, including the German military bureaucracy.[149] The distinction is important, because while the Firm is up to all sorts of objectionable activities, their objectives are often directly opposed to those of their German counterparts and to other supposed branches of Them.

In other words, while there are clearly "conspiracies or plots here and there," in Hofstadter's words—for example Slothrop's uncle Lyle Bland definitely conspires with German scientist Laszlo Jamf to perform experiments on the infant Slothrop—and while those individual conspiracies are often "connected" via military-corporate entities like IG Farben, whether these connections can be mapped as a conspiracy of Them constituting "*the motive force* in historical events" is not nearly so clear.[150] Even in passages where it seems like "the existence of the opposing They-system and We-system is asserted" by the narrator himself, the evidence is not as straightforward as it might seem.[151] Consider the assault on Shell quoted above. As with most of the novel, the narrator does not speak directly here but uses a loose indirect discourse, melding his voice with the characters' thoughts.[152] The final paragraph confirms that the passage's characterization of Them comes primarily not from the narrator but from Slothrop's imagination, which is often barely reliable even for perceiving what's directly in front of him. In fact Slothrop explicitly refers to Them here not to exhibit any precise epiphany about Their true nature, but simply to admit he has no idea who or what They are.

The slipperiness with which Slothrop refers to "Them" increases when he enters the Zone. For instance, when he takes up with a bohemian Berlin collective led by Säure Bummer, he begins making wildly off-base political readings of objects he encounters, such as that a poster of Stalin is really of his ex-girlfriend and that the Reichstag is a defecating King Kong.[153] Looking at photos from recent Allied conferences, he thinks:

> Whoever it was, posing in the black cape at Yalta with the other leaders, conveyed beautifully the sense of Death's wings, rich, soft and black as the winter cape, prepared a nation of starers for the passing of Roosevelt, a being They assembled, a being They would dismantle. . . .
>
> Someone here is cleverly allowing for parallax, scaling, shadows all going the right way and lengthening with the day—but no, Säure can't be real, no more than these dark-clothed extras waiting in queues for some hypothetical tram, some two slices of sausage (sure, sure), the dozen half-naked kids racing in and out of this burned

> tenement so amazingly detailed—They sure must have the budget, all right. Look at this desolation, all built then hammered back into pieces, ranging body-size down to powder (please order by Gauge Number), as that well-remembered fragrance Noon in Berlin, essence of human decay, is puffed on the set by a hand, lying big as a flabby horse up some alley, pumping its giant atomizer. . . .[154]

Even the most paranoid critic ought to admit that reading the ruins of Berlin as a staged manipulation for Slothrop's benefit is dangerously narcissistic. It derives not from real knowledge about how "everything is connected" but from Slothrop's scrambled mental state. And in fact, if we look through the novel, nearly every mention of Them similarly derives more from the psychological needs of specific characters rather than any reliable narrative statement. That goes for the mentally broken German physicist Franz Pökler's suspicion that his superiors are replacing his daughter Ilse with lookalikes on her annual visit; Herero Oberst Enzian's methamphetamine-driven speculation that "this War was never political at all [; . . .] secretly, it was being dictated instead by the needs of technology," which is usually quoted without his subsequent rejection of this belief; and even Mexico's rationalization of his ineffective resistance to his superiors on the grounds that "[t]he Man has a branch office in each of our brains."[155]

Given their outspoken distaste for "binary thinking," why do so many of the novel's critics go along with this Us-versus-Them framework? A telling hint might come through Slothrop's worry that the manipulative, well-connected Bummer might be one of Them, a thought he rejects a moment later because he feels Bummer "can't possibly be on the Bad Guys' side. Whoever They are, Their game has been to extinguish, not remind."[156] That logic is quite flimsy—Hilary Bounce's reminders about Shell's political connections helped Slothrop theorize Them in the first place—so it ought to draw our attention to the phrase "the Bad Guys," a term that, like so much of Slothrop's consciousness, derives from cheap genre novels and Hollywood movies.[157] In such narratives, stereotypically, all persons, instead of possessing the complex mix of motivations common to real life and literary fiction, may be neatly divided into Good Guys working for society's best interests and Bad Guys working against it. This worldview is almost always condemned by literary critics as oversimplified, liable to encourage violent jingoism and decrease empathy. However, as this passage should make clear, it maps directly onto the Them-Us division assented to by most critics. Pynchonists believe that They exist, in other words, because amid the otherwise incomprehensible web of competing actions in the postwar Zone, they need to designate a set of Bad Guys to ground their understanding of the novel.

Given his situation, Slothrop may be forgiven for that desire. After all, he has just discovered his father and uncle have "sold [him] to IG Farben like a side of beef," learned from Stephen Dodson-Truck that he's being used by the British intelligence community, and gotten chased from Nordhausen by his own country's military under the command of Major Marvy.[158] His only real ally in the Zone has been the German Geli Tripping, lover of the Soviet officer Tcitcherine.[159] Since his sense of national and kinship allegiances have totally collapsed, it's understandable that he would merge the multiple agents exploiting him into one group and subsequently imagine himself at the center of their conspiracy. It is not until late in the novel, when Seaman Bodine tells him, "*Everything* is some kind of a plot, man," and Solange (really Franz's wife, Leni, in disguise) adds, "And yes but, the arrows are pointing in all different ways," that he is capable of realizing that "the Zone can sustain many other plots besides those polarized upon himself."[160] Elaborating on Solange/Leni's point, we might imagine the forces against Slothrop as several converging vectors, each characterized by opposed x-y components and a small but uniformly downward z component: the vectors themselves are quite distinct, but *as experienced at the point where they converge*, the x-y components cancel each other out and resolve into one strong downward force that acts *as if* it were a vector on its own. As critics, though, we cannot mistake this abstract resolution for the actual source vectors.

Yet in a novel as elaborate as *Gravity's Rainbow*, we will often need to simplify that which is complex. Refusing to allegorize entirely, indulging instead Fran Mason's view that "there may be no moral and that the events were 'just a bunch of stuff that happened'" leads to equally serious cognitive problems.[161] For instance, after leaving Bummer to head for Cuxhaven seeking a discharge, Slothrop witnesses this "great frontierless streaming":

> Volksdeutsch from across the Oder, moved out by the Poles and headed for the camp at Rostock, Poles fleeing the Lublin regime, others going back home, the eyes of both parties, when they do meet, hooded behind cheekbones, eyes much older than what's forced them into moving, Estonians, Letts, and Lithuanians trekking north again, all their wintry wool in dark bundles, shoes in tatters, songs too hard to sing, talk pointless, Sudetens and East Prussians shuttling between Berlin and the DP camps in Mecklenburg, Czechs and Slovaks, Croats and Serbs, Tosks and Ghegs, Macedonians, Magyars, Vlachs, Circassians, Spaniols, Bulgars stirred and streaming over the surface of the Imperial cauldron, colliding, shearing alongside for miles, sliding away, numb, indifferent to all momenta but the deepest, the instability too far below their itchy feet to give a shape to, white wrists and ankles incredibly wasted poking from their striped prison-camp pajamas, footsteps light as waterfowl's in this inland dust, caravans of Gypsies, axles or linchpins failing, horses dying, families leaving the vehicles beside the roads for others to come live in a night, a day, over the white hot Autobahns, trains full of their own hanging off the cars that lumber overhead, squeezing aside for army convoys when they come through, White Russians sour with pain on the way west, Kazakh ex-P/Ws marching east, Wehrmacht veterans from other parts of old Germany, foreigners to Prussia as any Gypsies, carrying their old packs [. . .][162]

I imagine most readers skim this passage. (You probably did just now.) Luc Herman and Steven Weisenburger write that it "gives one the feeling of being buried under a rubble of words naming things, concepts, techniques, and peoples; words with no clear reason for being tumbled together."[163] With the exception of a few vivid images, it is little more than a list of twenty-three Central and Eastern European ethnicities in stock images of displacement. That it is described so flatly in one sentence (which continues for a few more lines) seems to characterize it as Slothrop's pure perception, devoid of paranoid simplification or figuration. This descriptive approach does prevent Slothrop from committing his earlier paranoid absurdities, but it also keeps him from finding any meaningful patterns in this scene of displacement. When the narrator uses this list format elsewhere, in fact, it is primarily to describe waste products—for example, "rusted beer cans, rubbers yellow with preterite seed, Kleenex wadded to brain shapes hiding preterite snot, preterite tears, newspapers, broken glass, pieces of automobile"—about which he laments our inability to "make sense out of, to find the meanest sharp sliver of truth in so much replication, so much waste. . . ."[164]

This antiparanoid way of perceiving the landscape appears to be a backlash to the cognitive unsustainability of Slothrop's earlier paranoia. After several weeks in which his desire to discover the truth about the 00000 is overtaken by moment-to-moment survival on his assorted journeys with Bummer, he realizes that he's forgotten what he's doing in the Zone at all:

> Slothrop perceives that he is losing his mind. If there is something comforting—religious, if you want—about paranoia, there is still also anti-paranoia, where nothing is connected to anything, a condition not many of us can bear for long. Well right now Slothrop feels himself sliding onto the anti-paranoid part of his cycle, feels the whole city around him going back roofless, vulnerable, uncentered as he is, and only pasteboard images now of the Listening Enemy left between him and the west Sky.
>
> Either They have put him here for a reason, or he's just here. He isn't sure that he wouldn't, actually, rather have that *reason* . . . .[165]

Antiparanoia, in other words, is as mentally destructive as paranoia. Slothrop's perception that he is losing his mind is, in that sense, quite accurate.

Considered as an abstract dilemma, of course, paranoia and antiparanoia present something of a false choice. As Molly Hite has argued, "the contradictory of 'everything is connected' is '*not* everything is connected,' a proposition that leaves ample room for the possibility that some things are connected, and in innumerably different ways."[166] There are indeed options available for us on the continuum between paranoia and antiparanoia: it is quite possible to start moderately paranoid and become more or less so as the situation warrants. However, Slothrop faces not just an epistemological problem regarding his paranoia but a cognitive one: he must decide not only where to place himself on the paranoid continuum but also *how to determine where he is on that continuum at any given moment.* To discover in adulthood that one had been used in infancy as a test subject for a notorious psychological experiment might suggest that one has gone through life insufficiently paranoid, but to subsequently assume paranoid links regarding everything one sees will quickly lead to madness. Consequently Slothrop's level of paranoia vacillates wildly in response to feedback from his environment, and he is unable to find an approach that consistently works.

These fluctuations are what cause Slothrop's eventual disintegration, not any direct aggression by Them. When we are told midway through Slothrop's journey in the Zone that he "has begun to thin, to scatter," the proximate cause is explained in terms of Mondaugen's Law, that "[p]ersonal density [. . .] is directly proportional to temporal bandwith" or that "[t]he more you dwell in the past and in the future, the thicker your bandwidth, the more solid your persona. But the narrower your sense of Now, the more tenuous you are."[167] Fundamentally this principle is about attention: the longer one maintains focus, the more stable one is, but as attention span diminishes, "[i]t may get to where you're having trouble remembering what you were doing five minutes ago, or even—as Slothrop now—what you're doing *here*."[168] Paranoia, conversely, extends temporal bandwidth by locating one within a long-standing geopolitical framework. Many Pynchon critics valorize Slothrop's scattering as a victorious evasion of the System, but to my knowledge, none have sought to, like Slothrop, "spend whole days naked, ants crawling up his legs, butterflies lighting on his shoulders, watching the life on the mountain, getting to know shrikes and capercaillie, badgers and marmots."[169] Logistically there is nothing difficult about living this way: it is simply cognitively intolerable, a state of dissolution so total that one might as well have been hit by the ooooo.

The sense of national and spiritual identity provided by epic and allegory, of course, has long been a method of avoiding these problems. That is probably why "the one ghost-feather" of Slothrop's self that is last to dissolve is "America. Poor asshole, he can't let her go. She's whispered *love me* too often to him in his sleep, vamped insatiably his waking attention with come-hitherings, incredible promises."[170] While there are any number of potentially pathological things about nationalism, it is also the most powerful concept through which, as Anderson notes, "pasts are restored, fellowships are imagined, and futures dreamed."[171] Though Sascha Pöhlmann is not incorrect to claim that "the Zone as a textual device can be used as an exemplary space for postnationalism," he is also right to add that this is not necessarily a positive thing, because "[t]he Zone is born out of war, the migrants that traverse it are far from migrating by choice, and its openness is only the result of continent-wide destruction."[172] The only thing separating the "great frontierless streaming" from pure paratactic gibberish, after all, is its residual national divisions, which may also be all that makes it bearable for those traversing it.

Can one conceive an allegorical system adequate to these challenges that does not turn into an overdetermined paranoia? The "We-System" created by Slothrop's fellow functionaries in British intelligence, the Counter-Force, seeks to do so by creating a counterweight to Them. However, as Pynchon's source R. D. Laing once remarked, "The invention of Them creates Us, and We may require to invent Them to re-invent Ourselves."[173] In other words the Counter-Force does not rebel against a preexisting Them but allegorically constructs Them as its own raison d'être. This self-definition, though, dooms the Counter-Force to be "schizoid" and "double-minded," as Mexico reflects, though not for the reasons he thinks: since the Counter-Force constructs Their rationality as the enemy, its paranoid rebellion forces it into performing a stilted and hypocritically rational irrationality, as when Osbie Feel tells a fellow member of We, "*They're* the rational ones. We piss on Their rational arrangements," while belly dancing for no particular reason.[174] This tension is likely why the Counter-Force tries to stabilize its figural cosmos via the disintegrated Slothrop, whose recovery is one of its formative acts. However, as a spokesperson for the Counter-Force says decades later, "Opinion even at the start was divided. It was one of our fatal weaknesses. [. . .] Some called [Slothrop] a 'pretext.' Other felt he was a genuine, point-for-point microcosm."[175] They agree that he is to be considered figuratively but cannot decide what use to make of him, as epic hero or allegorical *figura*. The Counter-Force's inability to resolve its contradictions dooms it to incoherence.

A more successful approach may not exist, but if it does, it must be based in a method of figuration adequate to the book's complexities, able to consistently follow meaningful connections while ignoring those that descend into cruft. I am not sure there are general principles to be articulated regarding how to do that, so close in appearance are the meaningful and meaningless figural narratives characterizing the book's treatment of the postwar world. The role of criticism on *Gravity's Rainbow*, then, ought to be how to slowly and collectively explain how to determine which of the book's figurations are valuable for understanding our place in the contemporary world and which are not, as well as which of those moments that refuse figuration productively disassociate us from totalitarian allegory and which simply render themselves unreadable.

For instance how should we interpret the book's use of tarot? As with all fortune-telling, tarot is based in a highly figurative system that promises its subject access, via apparently unrelated signs, to a larger pattern. Also as with all fortune-telling, it is utter nonsense. As professional psychic Ian Rowland writes, tarot and other forms of "cold reading" are "the biggest, most enduring, and most popular scam of all time."[176] Consider, for example, the tarot drawn up for Major Weissmann, the mastermind behind the ooooo: his cards include the Tower, which we are told resonates phallicly with the Rocket's destructive portents; the Queen of Swords, which alludes to his queerness; and the King of Cups, which previews his future as a von-Braun-like sage in America.[177] This reading feels insightful, but as Rowland notes, "the actual significance each card is deemed to have is irrelevant. A serious book on interpreting tarot cards may tell you that 'The Tower' signifies change in existing relationships. However, the cold reader can attribute whatever significance she wants to any card [. . .]. All that matters is that it sounds convincing."[178] That Weissmann's spread is actually meaningless might be best seen in the card representing his future, the World. Though according to A. E. Waite's standard guide this card represents "the state of the soul in the consciousness of Divine Vision, reflected from the self-knowing spirit," Pynchonists generally interpret the World to mean precisely the opposite of that—"there is no escape, no transcendence"—because to associate the World's positive transcendence with Weissmann would be contrary to their view of him as the concatenation of western evil.[179] If the cards may simply be interpreted to reinforce whatever preconceived notions either narrator or reader holds, they tell us nothing. It would be simple enough, after all, to create a convincing reading about Weissmann from almost any tarot spread, or to reread these cards as describing characters with nothing in common with him.[180] As the passage acknowledges, tarot's allegories, like Slothrop's hallucinated Them, are "pasteboard."[181]

Yet we cannot entirely dismiss the tarot session as mere mumbo jumbo, because some cards do present intriguing lines of thought. For instance we are told that the card representing Weissmann himself—the industrious Page of Pentacles—is identical to that of his enslaved lover from his days as a colonial administrator, Enzian.[182] This is counterintuitive, at odds with a rigid Them-Us division, but there are real links between the two, dramatized in their parallel quests to understand the meaning of the Rocket. Furthermore, if we dismiss the tarot, should we do the same for references to the mythic-religious system from which much of it derives, kabbalah? As with many esoteric systems, much of kabbalah appears ridiculous to the uninitiated: when we read "Kabbalist spokesman Steve Edelman," high on Thorazine, tell us that "although the Rocket countdown appears to be serial, it actually conceals the Tree of Life, which must be apprehend all at once, together, in parallel," we probably ought to roll our eyes and skim ahead to the actual launch.[183] Yet having earlier heard Ensign Morituri's story about how German actress Margherita Erdmann, one of Slothrop's contacts in the Zone and among those connected to the 00000, had nearly sacrificed a small Jewish boy under the guise of "Shekhinah, queen, daughter, bride, and mother of God," we might take more seriously the relationship of mythic archetypes and human behavior.[184]

The problems with evaluating such figurative systems come to a head in the final scene, in which the Imipolex-G-coated 00000 (loaded with Weissmann's sex slave Gottfried) is fired from Germany on Easter 1945 and reappears in 1970s California. The rocket is launched parabolically upward until its fuel runs out, at which point its trajectory quickly decays, freezing the rocket at its highest point momentarily before it begins to fall. This arc is determined by real and unavoidable physical laws, which, inasmuch as they unite all action into a universal pattern, might justly be called allegorical. However, the narrator builds further allegories on top of these. He states, "This ascent will be betrayed to Gravity," echoing earlier, apocalyptic allegorizations of scattering and heat death as portending the species' collapse, and his subsequent declaration, "The victim, in bondage to falling, rises on a promise, a prophecy, of Escape," characterizes the rocket's propulsive force as a figure for humanity's attempts to surmount that collapse, with the moment of suspension in between ("The first star hangs between his feet") serving as something like enlightenment.[185] These additional figurations, though, are not so ineluctable as the physical equations. The feeling of transcendence is rooted at least as much in purely biological unease at the complex natural and synthetic forces working in concert on Gottfried's body. Similarly the destruction of one theater by one rocket does not necessarily portend the destruction of the whole world. On the other hand, when asked to imagine the planet from a heretofore unseen perspective, it is hard for us not to think about what beautiful or terrible knowledge might be newly gained. After all, the 00000's real-world rocket analogues are postwar America's two most sublime creations, the space shuttle and the ICBM ("a good Rocket to take us to the stars, an evil Rocket for the World's suicide"), bearing within them many of our postwar era's greatest hopes and fears about who we are and how we relate to the universe.[186]

In considering this final image, we should keep in mind that, despite the long line of Pynchon criticism that blames the destruction that the 00000's landing heralds on synthetic military-industrial control, the novel's two most common tropes for apocalypse—gravity and increased entropy—are entirely natural. It is not any rationalist analysis, but nature itself, that is the true source of death, in which none are elect and all are preterite, everything destined to be reduced eventually to undifferentiated particles. What exists otherwise are competing allegories that attempt to circumvent this principle. They are not all equally valid: some are so necessary to conceiving the world that we might as well call them true, while others are so contradictory, constricting, or destructive that we must call them false. Managing the spectrum between the two is the great challenge of human civilization, and as society becomes increasingly complicated, we need to become increasingly adept at filtering which of these allow us to orient our attention and which to dispatch.

Famously McHale claimed that the greatest difficulty in reading fiction like *Gravity's Rainbow* is its irresolvable ontological conflicts between different diegetic planes.[187] However, if *Gravity's Rainbow*'s reality were simply indeterminate, the book could be dismissed as incoherent. Instead the book presents us with a more difficult set of contradictions: not those within the semantics of a fictional storyworld, but those within our own modes of cognizing any world at all. Whether we perceive reality through the frames of religious or scientific epistemology, through universalist or relativist morality, through the Left or the Right, no matter how sound this apparatus appears when we are not reading the book, it will appear all too visibly inadequate when we do, its inconsistencies and holes dragged into the open and exposed. Though McHale has at times implied that postmodern fiction is "post-cognitive," this problem is very much a cognitive one, and no book raises it more profoundly than *Gravity's Rainbow*, the exemplary experiment in figural narrative systems, the subtlest distributor of cruft in our fiction, and the greatest of mega-novels.[188]

Conclusion

The Fate of the Mega-Novel

The past six chapters have analyzed how we process text in the mega-novel, ranging from its sentence-level lacunae up to its macro-scale figurations of nation and world. Given how utterly mega-novel text overwhelms our limited working memory and how often it dissolves its most important text into a large amount of cruft, I have argued that we must hone our ability to modulate attention to an extremely fine degree, filtering the latter so as to better perceive the former. Some passages should be processed closely and slowly, while others should be read more quickly; some are best read distantly, and others are best passed over entirely. Refining this procedure can be cognitively beneficial, I believe, because learning how to modulate attention in the mega-novel's controlled environment will allow us to apply this ability to the more unrestrained cascades of information we regularly encounter in our everyday lives.

Having made this argument in its particulars over the past several hundred pages, I would like now to articulate a few general conclusions. First, I would like to extrapolate some practical pedagogical implications. As N. Katherine Hayles suggests in her essay on hyper and deep attention, many university professors, afraid of boring their students, report a reluctance to assign novels of any substantial length, and since mega-novels have always clashed with what one of my graduate professors termed the Political Economy of Course Syllabi—approximated by Mark O'Connell's quip, "Why commit yourself to one gigantic classic when you can read a whole lot of small classics in the same period of time [. . .]?"—there is reason to worry that mega-novels may start to fall out of literature courses entirely.[1] While this trend is understandable, I think there is reason to push against it. As I pointed out in the introduction, literary education has long been principally concerned with the training of attention—a point we might remember, incidentally, when taking up our periodic defenses of the humanities—and while other literary genres have their own unusual relationships to that crucial element of cognition, the mega-novel uniquely pressures its nuances. As neuroscientist Michael Posner writes, "if the brain is plastic, it is as likely that any change [to attentional capacity] induced by the use of media could be changed back by a vacation in the woods with a long intense novel."[2] While I don't think he had *Gravity's Rainbow* in mind, the point still holds.

How to teach mega-novels so as to maximize this impact is a more complicated matter. Doubtless the problem admits a variety of solutions, whose success will vary based on the particular teacher, students, and mega-novel. However, I hope that this book has at least demonstrated that in the classroom setting, mega-novel difficulty should not simply be papered over. Instead it needs to be foregrounded and discussed, with the frustration and boredom it produces in students both acknowledged and validated. Those responses are not mere obstacles in the paths of students' understanding, but the most vital effect mega-novels produce. Those teachers who allow students to skip *Moby-Dick*'s whaling chapters, then, are half astute and half misguided: they understand how some of these chapters are a bit pointless but miss how important they are to shaping attention. When one's students complain of being bored with a mega-novel, one should not simply try to work around those passages or grouse about students' unwillingness to commit sufficient effort. One should take it, instead, as the starting point from which to examine students' cognitive processes and gradually alter them so that they can better attend the passages that warrant attention and read other passages with less investment.

Second, I'd like to address some theoretical points about mega-novels and literary criticism more broadly. One is the problem caused by the readers' guide approach, the view that everything in a mega-novel can be understood as deeply meaningful once one has corrected one's ignorance of its allusions and paid close attention to its text. Simply because a book contains an extremely complicated fictional world does not mean, necessarily, that puzzling out every detail of that world is worth anyone's time. I do not dispute the tremendous service done by the major mega-novel readers' guides in systematically articulating ways in which mega-novel text that many of us might otherwise have failed to give much notice to can be more closely attended. However, we must realize that many readers' difficulties in understanding mega-novels are at least as much caused by paying *too much attention in the wrong places*, to passages whose apparent connections never end up coming to fruition, and over whose surface mega-novel veterans have learned to skim.

Similarly the argument that mega-novels' outsized scope either exhibits or subverts an overweening and "totalizing" ambition that enlightened readers should reject is also misguided. This view has always been inherently self-contradictory: if one is going to imagine what it means to live in a heterogeneous, diffuse environment, one's fictional world needs the breadth and scope to match it. As Italo Calvino wrote of the literature of "multiplicity," "Overambitious projects may be objectionable in many fields, but not in literature. Literature remains alive only if we set ourselves immeasurable goals, far beyond all hope of achievement."[3] I will add that literature is largely exempt from the dangers of ambition because, by its fictionality, it can never assert the truth of any interpretive system, ethics, or epistemology. Its value comes through the range of thought it helps make possible, and mega-novels, by exploring the possibilities of imagination as widely as they can, do this as well as any other genre.

However, we can appreciate their scope only in a manner apposite to our minds' limited channel capacity. The perspective that we should read mega-novels with total disregard for order—inspired, for some readers, by Gilles Deleuze and Félix Guattari's concept of the rhizome, an approach to "multiplicity" in which "[t]here are no points or positions [. . .]. There are only lines," making it "open and connectable in all of its dimensions"—is also misconceived.[4] Given the unimaginably numerous stimuli we encounter in every waking moment of our lives, we have no choice but to simplify them into points, and once we have done so, we must hierarchize them by paying them different levels of attention based on their perceived importance. If you did not do this, you could not prioritize the words being spoken to you by a friend over those of a passer-by, or the book in your hands over the patch of air beside it; indeed you could not even distinguish your friend's words from environmental noise, nor the book from the surrounding atmosphere. Lines without points, after all, are not a multiplicity, but a mass of sameness.[5] In the best scenario you would end up like Funes the Memorious and merely incapable of thought; in the worst you would lose all capacity for higher consciousness. If Jesse Prinz is correct to claim that we are conscious of only that to which we have modulated our attention, in a basic way, consciousness *is* hierarchy: it is our knowledge of the stimuli that we have decided are worth paying attention to as opposed to our ignorance of those we have decided are not.[6] Our choice is not between constructing hierarchical versus nonhierarchical structures: it is between hierarchizing well and hierarchizing poorly, and as with all things, those who refuse to admit the nature of the choice will likely not choose well.

Yet if the poststructuralist conception of mind is not adequate to cognizing the information age, what model is? Hayles, examining this problem with respect to *Infinite Jest*, writes that "nothing less than a reconceptualization of subjectivity can offer a solution," because the novel's events show that "the idea of an autonomous liberal subject can be a recipe for disaster in a world densely interconnected with interlocking complex systems."[7] As chapter 2 demonstrated, however, the AA model Hayles recommends evacuates subjectivity of its critical faculties, rendering it vulnerable to exploitation. What is more interesting about her argument, though, is its relationship to her later concerns about students' limited attention spans, which verge, she believes, on ADHD.[8] ADHD is not primarily defined as an inherent incapacity for attention, but an inability to "self-regulate" attention—and "self-regulation," of course, has long been a term associated with the "autonomous liberal subject" whom poststructuralists like Hayles critique.[9] One always must be careful of transferring terminology across disciplines, but is it entirely off base to say that the poststructuralist subject, lover of rhizomes and *jouissance*, has ADHD? There is some research, after all, linking ADHD symptoms with the types of creativity poststructuralists prize, theorizing that an "inability to filter out information [. . .] makes these individuals constantly open to much more information, increasing the chances of them coming up with an original recombination of information."[10] Despite the obvious possible benefits of such a cognitive framework, however, I trust that the serious drawbacks that accompany this perpetual openness, primarily its susceptibility to distraction and incapacity for inhibition, are by this point clear.

Is there any other hypothetical construct for subjectivity better able to critically manage, filter, and modulate through information overload? And if not, can it be that after decades of theoretical assault within the academy, it turns out we actually need the autonomous liberal subject after all? So far as I can tell, no other model of subjectivity is capable of the attentional modulations required to make of the mind something more than a repository and replicator of memes. If it will mollify objections, let us say that to be an autonomous subject is not a given, that it is a status must be earned and developed gradually over time, and never really be fully achieved, only approached. It cannot, however, be curtly dismissed, least of all in the context of the mega-novel. While Borges might have once thought that only someone with Funes's capacities for memory could read a book like *Ulysses*, for the reasons I have articulated, the task is probably best undertaken not by an eidetic mind but one whose cognitive limitations make it necessary to isolate and prioritize the most important of the novel's many cross connections, rather than simply absorb them all at once, undifferentiated.[11]

I will end by illustrating this speculation with two quick stories that happened to bookend the initial composition of this work. In 2011, around the time I began, the IBM computer system Watson appeared on an episode of the quiz show *Jeopardy!*, handily defeating two of the series' most successful champions. I imagine this came as no shock to those conversant with recent developments in artificial intelligence, but I had not until then realized that computers not only could process encyclopedic text with incredible speed but also, for many practical intents and purposes, could demonstrate comprehension of it equal to that of any human. While subsequently wondering whether there would long be any function for the human mind in a world where computers seemed progressively capable of superseding its abilities, I consoled myself with the thought that Watson, for all his prodigious memory and even more astonishingly precise ability to search and filter it, would probably be baffled by *Finnegans Wake*. That said, if this observation is to help us conceptualize the continuing importance of human mind, we need to make sure Watson's confusion would not apply equally to most humans, too.

Two and a half years later, during in the summer of 2013, when I first drafted this conclusion (academic publication, sadly, can take a long time), former NSA contractor Edward J. Snowden leaked documents to several news outlets detailing some of the agency's elaborate surveillance programs, prominently including large-scale collections of metadata from some of the country's largest information companies, whose scale potentially extended into the yottabytes. Even though this event is now several years past, I do not think we have, culturally, quite understood its implications. The hubbub in the mainstream press about potential threats to privacy seems to me misplaced, at least if "privacy" is conceived as individuals' control over specific information they believe to be accessible only to them: so far as I can tell, there is no individual piece of information that such programs make available that could not have been accessible through one method or another previously. Besides, when one has the run of a database of such enormous size, one does not generally use it to look up for specific bits of data: the very quantity of information within it, after all, makes any individual datum nearly meaningless. Rather what one does is find novel ways to manipulate the data, representing it at three or four levels of compression, reordering it so that it provides answers to questions that otherwise could not even be asked. One uses it, in other words, to eliminate or subordinate the vast majority of its raw data while simultaneously synthesizing new information that even the individuals with whom it was originally associated are not likely to know.

What kinds of filtering, recoding, and sorting, then, will be done with the unthinkable amount of data our society will produce in the near future? What beneficial and pernicious effects might result? And what kinds of minds will we have to produce to adequately handle it?

Source Acknowledgments

Portions of the introduction and chapter 2 originally appeared as "Encyclopedic Novels and the Cruft of Fiction: *Infinite Jest*'s Endnotes" in *Studies in the Novel* 44.3 (Fall 2012): 304–324.

Portions of chapter 1 originally appeared as "Crossed-up Disciplinarity: What Norbert Wiener, Thomas Pynchon, and William Gaddis Got Wrong about Literature and Entropy" in *Contemporary Literature* 56.1 (Spring 2015): 23–55.

Notes

Introduction

1. Karl, *American Fictions*, 155.
2. LeClair, *Art of Excess*, vii, 1.
3. Juliet Lapidos, "Overrated," Slate.com, Washington Post Group, August 11, 2011, accessed September 29, 2011, http://www.slate.com/articles/arts/culturebox/2011/08/overrated.html.
4. Jonathan Franzen, "Mr. Difficult: William Gaddis and the Problem of Hard-to-Read Books," *New Yorker*, September 30, 2002, 111.
5. Mark O'Connell, "The Stockholm Syndrome Theory of Long Novels," *Millions*, May 16, 2011, accessed July 17, 2011, http://www.themillions.com/2011/05/the-stockholm-syndrome-theory-of-long-novels.html.
6. Federman, *Critifiction*, 66.
7. Marcus, "Why Experimental Fiction."
8. Gaddis, *J R*, 532. Throughout this book ellipses indicating omitted text in quoted matter are enclosed in brackets, and suspension points reproduced from the originals appear without brackets.
9. Barthes, "Introduction," 245, 249.
10. Barthes, "Reality Effect," 11.
11. Barthes, "Reality Effect," 12, 16.
12. Henry James, *Art of the Novel*, 84.
13. Henry James, *Art of the Novel*, 5.
14. Karl, *American Fictions*, 155.
15. Greif, "'Death of the Novel,'" 27.
16. James Wood, "Human, All Too Inhuman," review of *White Teeth* by Zadie Smith, *New Republic*, July 24, 2000, 42–43.
17. Moretti, *Modern Epic*, 5.
18. Raymond, *New Hacker's Dictionary*, 135.
19. *Wikipedia*, s.v. "Discussing Cruft," last modified October 11, 2010, accessed October 16, 2011, https://en.wikipedia.org/wiki/Wikipedia:Discussing_cruft.
20. *Wikipedia*, s.v. "Fancruft," last modified July 19, 2011, accessed October 16, 2011, https://en.wikipedia.org/wiki/Wikipedia:Fancruft.

21. Lubbock, *Craft of Fiction*, 41.
22. Steven Moore, *Novel*, 30.
23. Johnston, *Information Multiplicity*, 8.
24. Johnston, *Information Multiplicity*, 16.
25. LeClair, *Art of Excess*, 14–15.
26. Tabbi, *Postmodern Sublime*, 24.
27. Steven Moore, *William Gaddis*, 64.
28. Dames, *Physiology of the Novel*, 7.
29. Arata, "On Not Paying Attention," 200–201; Richards, *Practical Criticism*, 203, 240–42.
30. Hayles, "Hyper and Deep Attention," 187.
31. Gaddis, *J R*, 527.
32. William James, *Principles*, 403; Prinz, *Conscious Brain*, 89; Smithies, "Attention," 247.
33. Broadbent, *Perception and Communication*, 297; Allport, "Attention and Control," 203.
34. Hopfinger and Parks, "Involuntary Attention," 39–46.
35. Miller, "Magical Number Seven," 91. Since attention is closely related to memory, especially working memory, all my discussions of the former should be read as at least partly implicating the latter.
36. Broadbent, *Perception and Communication*, 34–35; Allport, "Attention and Control," 196.
37. Knudsen, "Midbrain," 132.
38. Posner, *Attention*, 18–22.
39. Posner, *Attention*, 78–88.
40. Knudsen, "Midbrain," 136.
41. Hopfinger and Parks, "Involuntary Attention," 47; Dehaene, *Reading*, 102.
42. See Savage et al., "Cognitive Processes"; Conners, "Attentional Control"; Smallwood, "Mind-Wandering."
43. Gaddy, van den Broek, and Sung, "Influence," 89.
44. Sanford and Emmott, *Mind, Brain, and Narrative*, 103–10.
45. Barthes, *Pleasure*, 11.
46. Rabinowitz, *Before Reading, 47-45.*
47. Rabinowitz, *Before Reading*, 51. The most famous attempt to give all elements of a text this kind of attention is, of course, Barthes's *S/Z*, which attempts to closely analyze every phrase of Balzac's "Sarrasine." David Richter's summary of *S/Z*'s reception should demonstrate Rabinowitz's point: "*S/Z* was simultaneously the masterpiece and the reductio ad absurdum of Barthes's holistic approach to fiction, because it made clear that any genu-

inely complete analysis of a fictional text would be so long and complex as to be nearly unreadable. It was widely admired but never imitated, even by Barthes himself" (*Critical Tradition*, 832).

48. Phillips, "Literary Neuroscience," 63.
49. Cheyne, Carriere, and Smilek, "Absent-Mindedness," 580.
50. Goldberg et al., "Boredom."
51. Fenichel, "Psychology of Boredom," 293.
52. Hägg, "Poetics of Boredom," 86.
53. Hogan, *Cognitive Science*, 9–11.
54. Hogan, *Cognitive Science*, 9.
55. Trilling, *Beyond*, 7.
56. See Fenske and Raymond, "Affective Influences"; Eastwood et al., "Unengaged Mind," 487–89; Weissman et al., "Neural Bases."
57. Spacks, *Boredom*, 261.
58. Ngai, *Ugly*, 262.
59. Spacks, *Boredom*, 1, 256.
60. Ngai, *Ugly*, 260, 262.
61. Goldsmith, *Uncreative Writing*, 24–27.
62. Gleick, *Information*, 402–3.
63. Wallace, *Pale King*, 84.
64. See Yoon, Sarial-Abi, and Gürhan-Canli, "Regulatory Focus."
65. Gleick, *Information*, 410.
66. James Wood, for instance, claims that DeLillo, Pynchon, and Wallace share with Flaubert the notion that "the novelist's job is to become, to impersonate what he describes, even when the subject itself is debased, vulgar, boring" (*How Fiction Works*, 33).
67. Eagleton, *How to Read a Poem*, 167.
68. Lev Grossman, "Whatever Happened to Hysterical Realism?," *Time*, July 11, 2012, accessed May 19, 2013, http://entertainment.time.com/2012/07/11/what-ever-happened-to-hysterical-realism/.
69. Pavel, *Fictional Worlds*, 94.
70. Moore et al., "Regular."
71. Barrett, Tugade, and Engle, "Differences," 563–64.
72. Wallace, *Pale King*, 438.
73. Clare, "Politics," 441; Hamilton, "Tedium," 169.
74. Wallace, *Pale King*, 27–28.
75. Goldsmith, *Uncreative Writing*, 158–74.
76. Herman and Vervaeck, "Narrative Interest."
77. Hirsch, *Validity*, 74.

78. Frow, *Genre*, 6–9.
79. See Zwaan, "Effect."
80. Sinding, "Framing Monsters," 474.
81. Mendelson, "Gravity's Encyclopedia," 161.
82. Weisenburger, *Fables*, 199–202.
83. Incidentally Robert Scholes's *The Fabulators*, one of the first monographs to conceptualize (what eventually came to be called) postmodern narrative, uses a chapter organization remarkably similar to my own, even though I developed it independently well before I was aware of Scholes's book. This corroborates, I think, Sinding's general point.
84. Derrida, "Law of Genre," 56.
85. Deleuze and Guattari, *Thousand Plateaus*, 3–25.
86. Sinding, "Framing Monsters," 472–73.
87. Borges, *Collected Fictions*, 137.
88. Steven Moore, *Novel*, 22. Ellen Spolsky has claimed that cognitive approaches to literature are actually not only compatible with, but the logical extension of, poststructuralist analysis. Spolsky's position, though, defines poststructuralism very broadly, essentially as including any approach in which categories are perceived as mutable ("Darwin and Derrida"). It is one thing to argue that categories are not given a priori, though, and quite another to believe that a critic's default position should be to dismantle all categories as rhetorical mystifications, which is frequently the poststructuralist stance. Bruno Latour has described the historical conflation of these two theoretical perspectives by noting, "Unwittingly, constructivism had become a synonym of its opposite number: deconstruction" (*Reassembling*, 92).
89. Northrop Frye, *Anatomy*, 303–14.
90. Kant, *Critique of Judgment*, 66.
91. Arthur Conan Doyle, *Complete Sherlock Holmes*, 692–98.
92. Catherine Emmott has examined the manipulation of attention in the whodunit. See Sanford and Emmott, *Mind, Brain, and Narrative*, 92–93.
93. The one quasi-exception is *Bouvard and Pécuchet*, which I address in chapter 2. However, while the novel in its extant form is of conventional length, it was projected to have an accompanying second volume that would have substantially increased its size—and this second volume, for reasons I explain in chapter 2, would have been laden with cruft.
94. See Bunce, Flens, and Neiles, "How Long."
95. Steven Moore, *William Gaddis*, 66.
96. Pavel, *Fictional Worlds*, 138.
97. Dimock, "Genres," 1386.

98. LeClair, *Art of Excess*, 30.
99. Herman and Vervaeck, "Narrative Interest," 126–27.
100. Northrop Frye, *Anatomy*, 313–14.
101. Joyce, *Ulysses*, 6.831. Contra Hugh Kenner's claim that Joyce cross-references everything "at least twice, in order to demonstrate that nothing is a flyspeck on the design, but an intended part" (*Stoic Comedians*, 63).

1. The Dictionary

1. The few cases of fictional dictionaries, such as Milorad Pavić's *Dictionary of the Khazars* or Flaubert's *Dictionary of Received Ideas*, tend to fit more in the category of encyclopedic novel, at least as I define the term in chapter 2.
2. Winchester, *Meaning*, 20–23.
3. Winchester, *Meaning*, 29.
4. The *Wake* has recently inspired Bill Cliett to compose a "lextionary" comprising definitions of eight hundred of Joyce's coinages, designed, like the first English dictionaries, to "jazz up your voca(l)bulary" (*"Finnegans Wake" Lextionary*).
5. Winchester, *Meaning*, 25–27.
6. Joyce, *Finnegans Wake*, 15.
7. Samuel Johnson, "Preface," 41, 28.
8. Wallace, *Consider*, 84–85.
9. George Steiner, "Crossed Lines," review of *J R* by William Gaddis, *New Yorker*, January 26, 1976, 106.
10. Steiner, "Crossed Lines," 106.
11. Wilson, *Axel's Castle*, 240.
12. Wilson, *Axel's Castle*, 239.
13. Shklovsky, *Theory of Prose*, 5–6.
14. Barthes, *S/Z*, 4–5; Barthes, *Pleasure*, 51–52. Barthes does not associate "writerly" text with difficult or experimental work but in fact states that "the writerly text is not a thing, we would have a hard time finding it in a bookstore"; instead we may only find it in "*ourselves writing*" (*S/Z*, 5). In other words the readerly and writerly are distinguished more by the reader's cognitive modes than the text itself. Similarly *The Pleasure of the Text* claims that "pleasure" and "bliss" should not be made "the source of absolute classifications" since "there is always a vacillation" between them (*Pleasure*, 4). This studied vagueness, characteristic of Barthes's later period, has not, however, stopped anyone from co-opting the terms for polemical purposes.
15. Tsur, *Toward a Cognitive Poetics*, 4.
16. Federman, *Critifiction*, 66, 70.
17. Sanford and Emmott, *Mind, Brain, and Narrative*, 25–27.

18. Sanford and Emmott, *Mind, Brain, and Narrative*, 99–100.
19. Sanford and Emmott, *Mind, Brain, and Narrative*, 112–14.
20. Borges, *Collected Fictions*, 115.
21. Borges, *Collected Fictions*, 114.
22. Borges, *Collected Fictions*, 115.
23. Borges, *Collected Fictions*, 14.
24. Hayles, *Posthuman*, 25–26, 247–49.
25. Shannon, "Mathematical," 10–11.
26. Li and Vitányi, *Introduction to Kolmogorov*, vii.
27. Shannon, "Mathematical," 10–11.
28. Wiener, *Human Use*, 21.
29. The otherwise astute Steven Weisenburger provides a case study. Discussing Gaddis's first novel, he claims, "Even in *The Recognitions*, though, Gaddis is well aware that cybernetic theorists had recently discovered a telling homology between the mathematical equation for computing entropy and the equation for calculating the information per message, that is, the message's susceptibility to *semiotic* entropy or 'noise'" (*Fables*, 212). There are four common misconceptions about entropy here: that it is inherently bad; that it can be conflated with the Second Law of Thermodynamics; that entropy has anything to say about semiotic meaning rather than textual structure, which Shannon explicitly separates; and that entropy is equivalent to noise, even though that concept refers not to improbable but to unintended text (Shannon, "Mathematical," 1, 2).
30. Hayles, *Posthuman*, 25.
31. Powers, *Gold-Bug Variations*, 330.
32. Eco, *Open Work*, 55, 119.
33. Gaddis, *J R*, 130–31.
34. Johnston, *Carnival*, 205; Johnston, *Information*, 126.
35. Wiener, Human Use, 17, 21, qtd. in Gaddis, *Rush*, 130.
36. LeClair, *Art of Excess*, 103; O'Donnell, "His Master's," para. 17; Tabbi, "Technology."
37. LeClair, *Art of Excess*, 88.
38. Steven Moore, *William Gaddis*, 65.
39. Gaddis, *Rush*, 130.
40. Gaddis, *J R*, 237–38.
41. Steven Moore, *William Gaddis*, 109.
42. Gaddis, *J R*, 116.
43. Jonathan Franzen, "Mr. Difficult: William Gaddis and the Problem of Hard-to-Read Books," *New Yorker*, September 30, 2002, 109.

44. George Steiner, "Crossed Lines," review of *J R* by William Gaddis, *New Yorker*, January 26, 1976, 109.
45. Steven Moore, *William Gaddis*, 109.
46. Orwell, "Politics," 156.
47. Orwell, "Politics," 170. In fact Gaddis may include a quick jab at Orwell's insistence on shorter Anglo-Saxon words in *The Recognitions*. In one party scene, "someone was engaged in writing a criticism of a work which contained forty-nine one-syllable words to seven of two syllables, thirty-one words of Anglo-Saxon origin to five of Latin and one-eighteenth of Greek. It was *honest*, this person said" (*Recognitions*, 619).
48. Orwell, "Politics," 164–65.
49. Orwell, "Politics," 170, 166.
50. Orwell, "Politics," 171.
51. Asimov, *Foundation*, 63–64; Orwell, "Politics," 166–67.
52. Gaddis, *J R*, 704.
53. Johnston, *Carnival*, 204.
54. Steven Moore, *William Gaddis*, 83–84.
55. Stein, *Making of Americans*, 306.
56. DeKoven, *Different Language*, 50.
57. Clement, "'Thing Not Beginning,'" 378.
58. Goldsmith, *Uncreative Writing*, 159.
59. Goldsmith, *Uncreative Writing*, 158–74.
60. Barth, *Friday*, 69.
61. Barth, *Friday*, 66.
62. Barth, *Friday*, 66–71.
63. Interestingly Goldsmith also invokes Pierre Menard (109–10), and characteristically he seems a bit disappointed that Borges didn't just retype *Don Quixote*. Goldsmith does point out that, even for a book as mechanical as *Day*, he had to make some original decisions regarding font, formatting, and other "literary properties that we're not able to see during our daily reading" of the newspaper (*Uncreative Writing*, 118). That said, these do not seem to produce particularly profound results to me.
64. Dubnick, *Structure*, 8–15.
65. Gass, "Introduction," in Stein, *Making of Americans*, ix.
66. Stein, *Lectures*, 166–67, 138.
67. Ngai, *Ugly*, 261, 266.
68. See Bean, "Repeating."
69. Meyer, *Irresistible Dictation*, 6.
70. Ruddick, *Reading*, 131.

71. Stephens, "'Reading at It,'" 139.
72. Stein, *Making of Americans*, 900.
73. Stein, *Making of Americans*, 443, 480.
74. Stein, *Making of Americans*, 903.
75. Stein, *Making of Americans*, 899.
76. Pound, qtd. in Ellmann, *James Joyce*, 584.
77. Joyce, *Finnegans Wake*, 15.29–16.3.
78. Margot Norris, *Decentered Universe*, 1.
79. See Rice, *Joyce*.
80. Epstein, *Guide*, 71.
81. McHugh, *Annotations*, 15.
82. Mahaffey, "Intentional Error," 246.
83. To my knowledge only James Connor has explicitly attempted to bridge these camps using information theory. However, he gets mixed up in his analysis of order and disorder. Connor claims that the *Wake* "belongs at the top of Shannon's bell curve, halfway between pure order and pure chaos, *constructed*, yet constructed in such a way that it packs a certain measure of improbability into every line" ("Radio," 826). That is a misreading of Shannon's graph. The midpoint of which he speaks is not between order and disorder, but between total probability that a binary digit reads "1" and total probability that it reads "0"—that is, the point at which either choice is equally likely, and thus where the text is maximally unpredictable and entropic.
84. Attridge, *Peculiar Language*, 205.
85. Conley, *Joyces Mistakes*, 59–80.
86. Derrida, "Two Words for Joyce," 145.
87. Shannon, "Redundancy," 250–54. Indeed Shannon's explicitly cites *Finnegans Wake* as a work with low redundancy, as the book "enlarges the vocabulary and is alleged to achieve a compression of semantic content" ("Mathematical," 15).
88. Loepp and Wootters, *Protecting Information*, 128–45.
89. Letzler, "Redundancy."
90. Bennett, "Logical Depth," 227–30. Intriguingly Bennett also invokes Borges's Pierre Menard, in his case to demonstrate the difference in time between how long it would take to independently generate such a work as *Quixote* (Menard has time only to finish a few chapters) and the lesser amount of time it would take to simply copy it ("Logical Depth," 231). Note how the latter aligns with Goldsmith's poetics.
91. Greetham, "Begin," 21.
92. Dehaene, *Reading*, 12.

93. Joyce, *Finnegans Wake*, 23.3–23.4.
94. That the sounds are similar seems important. While I don't think anyone would favor "lacy" over "easy" on the grounds that *l* is only seven letters from *e* while *s* is sixteen away from *c*, something about phonetic structure makes the close relation of the voiced and unvoiced alveolar fricatives represented by *c* and *s* significant.
95. Joyce, *Finnegans Wake*, 23.2.
96. Joyce, *Finnegans Wake*, 23.1.
97. Eco, *Aesthetics*, 97; Attridge, *Peculiar Language*, 205.
98. Empson, *Seven Types of Ambiguity*, 131–32.
99. Joyce, *Finnegans Wake*, 16.10–16.19.
100. Moretti, *Way*, 194.
101. Joyce, *Finnegans Wake*, 23.16.
102. Joyce, *Ulysses*, 9.228–9.229.
103. Borg, "Neologizing," 162.

2. The Encyclopedia

1. I focus on the use of specialized information so as to keep the "encyclopedic novel" from overlapping with the "epic novel," which I treat in chapter 6. Critical treatments frequently merge the two. For instance Northrop Frye identifies the epic as the subset of the encyclopedic in his modal theory (*Anatomy*, 315–26). Mendelson makes a greater effort to separate the encyclopedia and epic, but he still claims, "Encyclopedic narrative evolves out of epic, and often uses epic structure as its organizing skeleton" ("Gravity's Encyclopedia," 162), which is why Franco Moretti, though acknowledging that he and Mendelson are discussing a similar canon, thinks these books are better referred to as "modern epics" (*Epic*, 4). Paul Saint-Amour has worked hardest to separate the two, claiming that epics suffer from a self-assured "coherentism," while an encyclopedic work "understand[s] itself as disproportionate, transitory, and full of the wrong amounts of the wrong things" (*Tense Future*, 188–89). As my arguments in chapters 2 and 6 should make clear, I believe epics are less coherent, and encyclopedias more so, than Saint-Amour argues, and that the chief difference involves the focus on data transmission versus a focus on national narrative.
2. Mendelson, "Gravity's Encyclopedia," 162; Northrop Frye, *Anatomy*, 55.
3. LeClair, *Art of Excess*, 1, 17.
4. Kenner, *Stoic Comedians*, 35.
5. Burn, "Collapse," 51, 59. Burn only explicitly refers here to the work of William Gaddis but implicitly extends his view toward the encyclopedic novel generally.

6. Strecker, "Narrative," 296; Herman and van Ewijk, "Gravity's Encyclopedia Revisited," 167.
7. Deleuze and Guattari, *Thousand Plateaus*, 3–25.
8. Cohn, *Distinction*, 1.
9. See Iser, *Act*, 163–79; Pavel, *Fictional Worlds*, 43–72; Sanford and Emmott, *Mind, Brain, and Narrative*, 45–52.
10. Marsh, Meade, and Roediger, "Learning," 525–35.
11. Zunshine, *Why We Read*, 47–54.
12. Green and Brock, "Role," 708–12.
13. Foucault, *Order*, xv; Quian Quiroga, *Borges*, 198.
14. Quian Quiroga, *Borges*, 198.
15. Mendelson, "Gravity's Encyclopedia," 164; Vincent, "Trying-Out," 124.
16. Melville, *Moby-Dick*, 136.
17. Melville, *Moby-Dick*, 138–41. Charles Olson attempts to extricate Ishmael on that point by noting the distinction between baleen whales and toothed whales before asserting, "Melville was satisfied with the biggest of the toothed whales, the sperm" ("Call Me," 22–23). This exemplifies, I think, the slipperiness with which critics arguing the classical encyclopedic position make their case.
18. Greenberg, "Cetology," 2; Duquette, "Speculative Figuring," 42.
19. Melville, *Moby-Dick*, 141.
20. Jennifer Doyle, *Sex Objects*, 2. Though the cetological chapters were once argued as necessary to inform readers about key terms central to the plot later (Vincent, "Trying-Out," 122–25), these plotless expository chapters are clearly written by choice rather than dramatic necessity. For instance in chapter 72, "The Monkey-Rope," Ishmael has no difficulty introducing and defining his central whaling term during the action (Melville, *Moby-Dick*, 319–22).
21. Milder, "*Moby-Dick*," 37.
22. Hilary Clark, "Encyclopedic," 99.
23. Yeo, *Encyclopaedic Visions*, 4, 6–9.
24. Yeo, *Encyclopaedic Visions*, 16.
25. Reagle, *Good Faith*, 20–24.
26. Accuracy per se has become less of a problem for Wikipedia (Reagle, *Good Faith*, 137–68), but accuracy is merely necessary, not sufficient, for a good encyclopedia. For instance as of this writing, Wikipedia's article on the ongoing Boko Haram insurgency quickly devolves from a disciplined overview of a key world event into an accurate but sprawling account of paratactic occurrences, hindering comprehension of the subject for a casual reader ("Boko Haram Insurgency," *Wikipedia*, Wikimedia Foundation, March 6, 2016, web, accessed March 8, 2016).

27. John Considine, "Casaubon, Isaac (1559–1614)," *Oxford Dictionary of National Biography* (2010): 1, *Biography Reference Center*, web, accessed December 11, 2011.
28. George Eliot, *Middlemarch*, 47–48.
29. George Eliot, *Middlemarch*, 243–45, 314.
30. Eco, *Foucault's Pendulum*, 215–16.
31. Pynchon, *Gravity's Rainbow*, 279.
32. Eco, *Foucault's Pendulum*, 217.
33. Musil, *Man*, 502–3.
34. Rasula, "Textual Indigence," para. 23.
35. Melville, *Moby-Dick*, 7, 3.
36. Flaubert, *Bouvard and Pécuchet*, xx.
37. Flaubert, *Bouvard and Pécuchet*, 228.
38. Moretti, *Modern Epic*, 72, 95.
39. Bersani, *Culture*, 130.
40. Kenner, *Stoic Comedians*, 4; Codebó, *Narrating*, 103; Swigger, "Fictional Encyclopedism," 356.
41. Flaubert, *Bouvard and Pécuchet*, 105.
42. Flaubert, *Bouvard and Pécuchet*, 4, 11.
43. Flaubert, *Bouvard and Pécuchet*, 10–11.
44. Flaubert, *Bouvard and Pécuchet*, 14.
45. Flaubert, *Bouvard and Pécuchet*, 23.
46. Flaubert, *Bouvard and Pécuchet*, 27, 29.
47. Flaubert, *Bouvard and Pécuchet*, 30, 31, 26.
48. Flaubert, *Bouvard and Pécuchet*, 51.
49. Kovács, "Bureaucratization," 32; Koren and Kauffman, "Impossible Conclusion," 211.
50. Trilling, *Opposing*, 166.
51. Trilling, *Opposing*, 167.
52. Calvino, *Six Memos*, 114.
53. Swigger, "Fictional Encyclopedism," 357.
54. Some critics (e.g., Donato, "'Mere Labyrinth of Letters'") have suggested that Flaubert's inability to finish the book before his death speaks to the indefinite and consequently nonsensical nature of all knowledge, but this misses the point—the first volume is essentially finished, and the second is designed to be so arbitrary that Flaubert could've completed it swiftly.
55. Trilling, *Opposing*, 180.
56. Flaubert, *Bouvard and Pécuchet*, 293.
57. Flaubert, *Bouvard and Pécuchet*, 292.
58. Grafton, *Footnote*, 15.

59. Grafton, *Footnote*, 6.
60. Kenner, *Stoic Comedians*, 40; Benstock, "Footnotes," 204.
61. Genette, *Paratexts*, 319–43; Maloney, "Footnotes in Fiction."
62. Fishburn, "Footnote," 287–88.
63. Hayles and Gannon, "Mood Swings," 117.
64. Danielewski, *House*, 107–52.
65. Danielewski, *House*, 109.
66. Martone, *Blue Guide*, 39–40.
67. Chanen, "Surfing," 171–72.
68. Vollman, *Europe Central*, 753. Vollmann does admit that *Europe Central* is less "rigorously grounded in historical fact" than his *Seven Dreams* series of historical novels (*Europe Central*, 753). I do think that the points I make, however, hold for those books too, especially for the notes. Vollmann writes in his prefatory statement to each volume, "The reader is encouraged to use the Chronology and Glossary only as needed [. . .]. As for the Source Notes, they may be ignored or skimmed" (*Argall*, n. pag). See Caserio, "Historical Fiction," for an approach to these books that demonstrates the limitations of their historicity.
69. Vollman, *Europe Central*, 753.
70. Christensen, "Shostakovich," 97–100.
71. Vollman, *Europe Central*, 774–77.
72. Vollman, *Europe Central*, 646.
73. Bolaño, *Nazi Literature*, 205–27.
74. Cioffi, "Anguish," 162.
75. Wallace, *Infinite Jest*, 516, 1036, 251, 1000.
76. Wallace, *Infinite Jest*, 53.
77. Wallace, *Infinite Jest*, 984.
78. Boswell, *Understanding*, 120.
79. Even Jeffrey Karnicky, who claims that the filmography's entries reveal the work's "asignifying stasis," really claims that they *represent* that stasis via how the films' characters are made catatonically passive by the spectacles they watch (*Contemporary*, 91–123), rather than the descriptions being pointless in themselves.
80. Wallace, *Infinite Jest*, 990, 992.
81. Wallace, *Infinite Jest*, 989–90.
82. Wallace, *Infinite Jest*, 64.
83. Wallace, *Infinite Jest*, 987.
84. See Wallace, *Supposedly*, 21–81.
85. Burn, *Reader's Guide*, 21.
86. Wallace, *Infinite Jest*, 992–93, 27–31.

87. Wallace, *Infinite Jest*, 993.
88. Wallace, *Infinite Jest*, 991, 157–69, 491–503, 990–91.
89. Wallace, *Infinite Jest*, 16, 941, 944–45, 971.
90. Wallace, *Infinite Jest*, 687–89, 689, 703–6, 711–14.
91. Wallace, *Infinite Jest*, 1004–22.
92. Wallace, *Infinite Jest*, 1055–62, 994, 995, 1031, 1055.
93. Wallace, *Infinite Jest*, 313, 1022.
94. Wallace, *Infinite Jest*, 1048.
95. Wallace, *Infinite Jest*, 1002.
96. Hayles, "Illusion," 693.
97. Wallace, *Infinite Jest*, 270.
98. Wallace, *Infinite Jest*, 68–78, 128–35, 144–51.
99. Wallace, *Infinite Jest*, 706, 1053.
100. Wallace, "Deciderization," xxi.
101. Wallace, "Deciderization," xxii.
102. Tresco, "Impervious," 120–21.
103. Wallace, "Deciderization," xx.

3. Life-Writing

1. Sterne, *Tristram Shandy*, 266.
2. Woolf, *Essays* 4, 160.
3. Gubar, "'Blank Page,'" 299.
4. DuPlessis, "For the Etruscans," 279.
5. Cixous, "Laugh of the Medusa," 876.
6. Rodker, Review of *Interim*, 40.
7. Randall Swingler, "The Fog of War," review of *The Golden Notebook*, by Doris Lessing, *Times Literary Supplement*, April 27, 1962, 280.
8. Altieri, "Aspect-Seeing," 78.
9. William James, *Principles*, 224, 239.
10. Sinclair, "Novels," 444.
11. Wilson, *Axel's Castle*, 203.
12. Bowling, "What Is the Stream," 345.
13. William James, *Principles*, 284, 287.
14. William James, *Principles*, 286.
15. William James, *Principles*, 402. Current thought on the relation of attention to consciousness, however, is not at a consensus. There exist contemporary proponents of James's view, like Declan Smithies, who believes that "there is consciousness without attention, but there is no attention without consciousness" ("Attention," 247). However, theorists from Bernard Baars (*Theater*, 99) to Jesse Prinz (*Conscious Brain*, 89) see attention as engen-

dering consciousness in the first place, rather than constricting it subsequently. Antonio Damasio splits the difference, believing that low-level orienting attention is a precondition for consciousness, while higher-level executive attention is an aftereffect of it (*Feeling*, 18). Still, in all these theories consciousness is conceived as a holistic subjective experience and attention a constricting force.

16. Watzel, "Attention," 150.
17. Damasio, *Feeling*, 11, 16.
18. Baars, *In the Theater*, 44. Though Baars attempts to reconcile this idea with a stream (125–26), the metaphors clearly diverge. A stream progresses steadily and equally forward, while a spotlight can wander back and forth willy-nilly.
19. Dennett, *Consciousness*, 253, 356.
20. William James, *Principles*, 247, 285. Moreover the "one undivided state of consciousness" that his stream suggests (276) is inconsistent with his later work. In *The Varieties of Religious Experience*, he writes, "our normal waking consciousness, rational consciousness as we call it, is but one special type of consciousness, whilst all about it, parted from it by the filmiest of screens, there lie potential forms of consciousness entirely different. [. . .] How to regard them is the question,—for they are so discontinuous with ordinary consciousness" (388).
21. Edelman and Tononi, *Universe*, 151–52.
22. Shklovsky, *Theory*, 6.
23. Certeau, *Practice*, xi.
24. Baars, *Theater*, 18–21, 179–82.
25. Lefebvre, *Critique*, 132; Certeau, *Practice*, 96.
26. Proust, *Swann's Way*, 62–64.
27. Joyce, *Ulysses*, 6.121–6.128.
28. Woolf, *Mrs. Dalloway*, 80–81.
29. Dorrit Cohn's *Transparent Minds*, though it never defines the stream-of-consciousness technique, comes to a similar conclusion about the balance between representing the mind in "psycho-narration" and "quoted interior monologue" (the latter of which she claims is more favored by modernists following Joyce). She writes, "Compared to psycho-narration, what the quoted monologue gains in directness it loses in—depth? mystery? complexity?," while psycho-narration "has the opposite disadvantages: what it gains in depth it loses in directness" (98).
30. Matthews, "Diary," 288.
31. Nussbaum, "Toward Conceptualizing," 137.
32. Lejeune, *Diary*, 182.

33. Seidensticker, "Autobiography," 48.
34. Rosenwald, *Emerson*, 17.
35. Rosenwald, *Emerson*, 17.
36. Rosenwald, *Emerson*, 25.
37. Lejeune, *Diary*, 31.
38. Raoul, *French Fictional Journal*, vii.
39. Raoul, *French Fictional Journal*, 5.
40. Lejeune, *Diary*, 207.
41. Greene, *Doris Lessing*, 94–96.
42. Robert Taubman, "Free Women," review of *The Golden Notebook* by Doris Lessing, *Winger's Landfall* by Stuart Lauder, and *Europe* by Richard Stern, *New Statesman*, April 20, 1962, 569.
43. Lessing, *Golden Notebook*, xii.
44. Lessing, *Golden Notebook*, xvii, xix.
45. Lessing, *Golden Notebook*, 316.
46. Lessing, *Golden Notebook*, 226–38, 316.
47. Lessing, *Golden Notebook*, 351, 352.
48. Lessing, *Golden Notebook*, 320.
49. Lessing, *Golden Notebook*, 321–22, 346–48, 352.
50. Lessing, *Golden Notebook*, 448.
51. Lessing, *Golden Notebook*, 448–55.
52. Martinson, *In the Presence*, 135.
53. Lessing, *Golden Notebook*, 590.
54. Lessing, *Golden Notebook*, 448.
55. Hite, "Doris," 20.
56. Lessing, *Golden Notebook*, 325, 448.
57. Lessing, *Golden Notebook*, 352.
58. Lessing, *Golden Notebook*, 316.
59. Lessing, *Golden Notebook*, 318, 332.
60. Lessing, *Golden Notebook*, 448.
61. Lessing, *Golden Notebook*, 324–25, 328, 335.
62. Lessing, *Golden Notebook*, 325.
63. DuPlessis, "For the Etruscans," 279.
64. Joanne Frye, *Living Stories*, 170.
65. Lessing, *Golden Notebook*, 325.
66. Lessing, *Golden Notebook*, 448.
67. Lessing, *Golden Notebook*, 325.
68. Lessing, *Golden Notebook*, 326.
69. Lessing, *Golden Notebook*, 448.
70. Lessing, *Golden Notebook*, 416.

71. Lessing, *Golden Notebook*, 417.
72. Lessing, *Golden Notebook*, 421.
73. Lessing, *Golden Notebook*, 516–17.
74. Lessing, *Golden Notebook*, 517.
75. Lessing, *Golden Notebook*, 619–22.
76. Lessing, *Golden Notebook*, 239.
77. Lessing, *Golden Notebook*, 427, 501–3.
78. Rubenstein, *Novelistic Vision*, 106.
79. Beth Boehm smartly points out that critical disapproval of *Free Women* tends to be ex post facto, after it has been revealed to be Anna's novella rather than impartial narration. In polls of her students, she finds they tend to prefer the *Free Women* sections—which are, after all, quite well-composed on their own merits ("Reeducating," 93). As we will see later, there is a lot that *Free Women* does well that the notebooks don't.
80. Lessing, *Golden Notebook*, 580.
81. Draine, "Nostalgia," 33; Lessing, *Golden Notebook*, xv.
82. Lessing, *Golden Notebook*, xii.
83. Lessing, *Golden Notebook*, 635.
84. Lessing, *Golden Notebook*, xix.
85. Lessing, *Golden Notebook*, 323.
86. Lessing, *Golden Notebook*, 3.
87. DuPlessis, *Writing*, 102.
88. Lessing, *Golden Notebook*, 5.
89. Radford, *Dorothy Richardson*, 2.
90. Richardson famously rejected the term "stream of consciousness," suggesting that she preferred to think of consciousness as a "fountain" (qtd. in Kumar, *Bergson*, 46). This provides yet another metaphor to list beside the ones listed earlier in the chapter.
91. Kumar, *Bergson*, 63.
92. Melvin Friedman, *Stream*, 179.
93. Mansfield, "Dragonflies," 310; Woolf, *Essays*, 2:12.
94. Richardson, *Pilgrimage*, 2:64–65.
95. Frank Norris, *McTeague*, 18, 38.
96. Mepham, "Dorothy Richardson's 'Unreadability,'" 454.
97. Randall, *Modernism*, 88.
98. This is why writers like George Thomson, author of *A Reader's Guide to Dorothy Richardson's Pilgrimage*, can (astonishingly) argue—echoing Steven Moore on William Gaddis—that this two-thousand-page novel is "exactingly selective" (*Guide*, 6). Richardson seemed to think so, too. In a let-

ter to E. B. C. Jones about the ninth installment, *Oberland*, in which Miriam vacations for two weeks at a Swiss alp, Richardson wrote: "It is due partly to the need to condense that grows with each vol. & partly to M's becoming more out-turned really living [. . .]. Each episode could have filled a single volume in the old manner—but I should have been in my grave before M's fortnight was at an end" (qtd. in Felber, *Gender*, 16). That is, Richardson found it exceedingly difficult to constrain a book involving little more than a few incidents of pretty sunrises and exuberant tobogganing to one hundred pages and would have been inclined to seven hundred or so. For comparison that is roughly the length of Thomas Mann's *The Magic Mountain*, which covers a full seven years of his protagonist's visit to a mountain resort.

99. Sinclair, "Novels," 446.
100. Sinclair, "Novels," 445.
101. Richardson, *Pilgrimage*, 1:140–41.
102. Pease, *Modernism*, 79.
103. Pease, *Modernism*, 81.
104. Richardson, "About Punctuation," 415.
105. Richardson, *Pilgrimage*, 2:92.
106. Richardson, *Pilgrimage*, 2:163.
107. Richardson, *Pilgrimage*, 2:233.
108. Richardson, *Pilgrimage*, 1:457–58.
109. Richardson, *Pilgrimage*, 1:458–60.
110. Richardson, *Pilgrimage*, 3:133.
111. Richardson, *Pilgrimage*, 3:207–13.
112. Richardson, *Pilgrimage*, 4:363. Some, like Kara Watts, react to this passage by claiming, "The resultant reading strategy proposed by *Pilgrimage* [. . .] involves an amassing of life itself that confounds neat interpretation" ("Miriam's Waste Paper Basket," 60). As this chapter makes clear, though, such amassed details are not necessarily an obvious good.
113. Richardson, *Pilgrimage*, 4:424.
114. Felber, *Gender*, 110–12.
115. Richardson, *Pilgrimage*, 4:658.
116. Richardson, *Pilgrimage*, 4:170, 1:262; Fish, *Artifacts*, 233.
117. Richardson, *Pilgrimage*, 4:506.
118. Richardson, *Pilgrimage*, 4:450–51, 4:508.
119. Richardson, *Pilgrimage*, 3:357.
120. Richardson, *Pilgrimage*, 4:29.
121. Stevens, *Collected Poetry and Prose*, 224.

4. The Menippean Satire

1. For a capacious application of the term to mega-novels generally, see Weisenburger, *Fables*, 199–256. Elaine Safer's *The Contemporary American Comic Epic* does not use the phrase "Menippean satire" explicitly but covers similar territory.
2. White, *Subtreasury*, xvii.
3. Gaddis, *Recognitions*, 568–69.
4. Salemi, "Art as Expiation," 50.
5. Rod Martin, *Psychology of Humor*, 6–7.
6. Tsur, *Toward a Cognitive Poetics*, 11–12.
7. Bergson, *Laughter*, 29.
8. Bergson, *Laughter*, 34.
9. Bergson, *Laughter*, 32.
10. Green, *Fire the Bastards*, 17.
11. Griffin, *Satire*, 24; Dryden, "Discourse," lxxiv.
12. Rosenheim, *Swift*, 31. There have been several criticisms that this formulation is too limiting (see Griffin, *Satire*, 29–30), but I see no way for the genre to be articulated at all without it. As Rosenheim notes, both the *fiction* and *historic particulars* are vital: if one attacks historical particulars without writing a manifest fiction, one has composed not satire but polemic (17–18), and if one writes a manifest fiction without attacking historical particulars, one has written fantasy (29–30).
13. Tsur, *Toward a Cognitive Poetics*, 24.
14. John Martin, *Beyond Belief*, 126.
15. Vonnegut, *Mother Night*, v.
16. Bogel, *Difference*, 23.
17. Bogel, *Difference*, 42.
18. Norman Podhoretz, "Uncle Sam and the Phantom," review of *The Public Burning* by Robert Coover, *Saturday Review* September 17, 1977, 34; Estes, "American Folk Laughter," 255; LeClair, *Art of Excess*, 111.
19. Podhoretz, "Uncle Sam," 27.
20. Salemi, "Art as Expiation," 50.
21. Bruce Friedman, "Foreword," ix.
22. Weisenburger, *Fables*, 26.
23. Weisenburger, *Fables*, 198. Alastair Fowler further points out that this apparently subversive postmodern approach to satire actually "proves the rule [about the genre's normative stability]: it is addressed to true believers who already share the satirist's views" (*Kinds*, 66–67).
24. Dryden, "Discourse," xcvi.

25. Fowler, *Kinds*, 64.
26. Northrop Frye, *Anatomy*, 309–12.
27. Bakhtin, *Problems of Dostoevsky's Poetics*, 108, 114, 119.
28. Weinbrot, *Menippean Satire*, 6.
29. Bakhtin, *Problems of Dostoevsky's Poetics*, 108; Bakhtin, *Rabelais*, 11–12.
30. Bakhtin, *Rabelais*, 308.
31. Barth, *Sot-Weed*, 389–92.
32. Griffin, *Satire*, 69, 89, 109.
33. Barth, *Sot-Weed*, 245–50.
34. Kenner, *Stoic Comedians*, 54–55.
35. Bergson, *Laughter*, 39.
36. Cook, "Sot-Weed," 26–27.
37. Barth, *Sot-Weed*, 441.
38. Barth, *Sot-Weed*, 442.
39. Barth, *Sot-Weed*, 441–47.
40. Charles Harris, *Passionate Virtuosity*, 62.
41. Gass, "I've Got a Little List," 38.
42. Barth, *Sot-Weed*, 384–85, 496, 563–64.
43. Barth, *Sot-Weed*, 108–13.
44. Barth, *Sot-Weed*, 77–93, 271–73, 405–23.
45. Barth, *Sot-Weed*, 443.
46. Barth, *Sot-Weed*, 10.
47. Puetz, "John Barth's *The Sot-Weed Factor*," 455.
48. Barth, *Sot-Weed*, 213.
49. Joseph, *John Barth*, 29–30.
50. Morrell, *John Barth*, 47.
51. Barth, *Sot-Weed*, 410, 414, 421.
52. Schulz, *Black Humor*, 17; Morrell, *John Barth*, 55.
53. Walkiewicz, *John Barth*, 53–57.
54. Barth, *Sot-Weed*, 72, 264, 301, 599.
55. Barth, *Sot-Weed*, 266, 434–36.
56. Barth, *Sot-Weed*, 536.
57. Pearce, "Circus"; Estes, "American Folk Laughter"; Coover, *Public Burning*, 447–56.
58. That said, he does not reveal that history is necessarily subject to "the arbitrary nature of fictional systems" (McCaffery, *Metafictional Muse*, 88). Many critics are fond of invoking Uncle Sam's insistence that, "Hell, *all* courtroom testimony about the past is ipso facto and teetotaciously a baldface lie" (*Public Burning*, 86) and *Time*'s later claim that "objectivity

is an impossible illusion [. . .] *only* through the frankly biased and distorting lens of art is any real grasp of the facts—not to mention Ultimate Truth—even remotely possible" (*Public Burning*, 320). But both of these pronouncements are uttered by characters seeking to pervert truth to destructive ends. As Frank L. Cioffi notes, "Many critics have noted that the novel is about how the factual is essentially a fictional construct. [. . .] But I wonder to what extent this novel is also about how some fictions are better orderings of an AW [actual world] than others" ("Coover's (Im)Possible," 37).

59. Coover, *Public Burning*, 282–88.
60. Robert Towers, "Nixon's Seventh Crisis," review of *The Public Burning* by Robert Coover, *New York Review of Books*, September 29, 1977, accessed July 20, 2012, http://www.nybooks.com/articles/1977/09/29/nixons-seventh-crisis/.
61. LeClair, *Art of Excess*, 114.
62. Towers, "Nixon's Seventh Crisis."
63. Coover, *Public Burning*, 8.
64. Richard Anderson, *Robert Coover*, 124; Ramage, "Myth," 55.
65. Walsh, "Narrative Inscription," 345.
66. Coover, *Public Burning*, 320, 190.
67. Coover, *Public Burning*, 190.
68. Viereck, "Clown," 77.
69. Coover, *Public Burning*, 409.
70. Hite, "'Parody,'" 87.
71. Coover, *Public Burning*, 355, 356.
72. Coover, *Public Burning*, 423–24.
73. Coover, *Public Burning*, 458–61.
74. Coover, *Public Burning*, 425–27.
75. Coover, *Public Burning*, 454–55.
76. Coover, *Public Burning*, 450.
77. Maltby, *Dissident*, 102.
78. Coover, *Public Burning*, 429–46.
79. Coover, *Public Burning*, 482.
80. Coover, *Public Burning*, 483.
81. Coover, *Public Burning*, 484.
82. Coover, *Public Burning*, 485–94, 516–17.
83. Pughe, *Comic Sense*, 67, 81.
84. Coover, *Public Burning*, 534.
85. Coover, *Public Burning*, 533.
86. Steven Moore, *William Gaddis*, 41.

87. The exact totals are a bit arbitrary, as so many extremely minor characters' horrific outcomes are mentioned only in passing and some more important characters' activities are merely implied (e.g., Otto's likely death of his mysterious disease under Dr. Fell's treatment, the likely statutory rape of Giono by Big Anna, etc.). There are several that I double- or triple-count, for that matter (e.g., Esme attempts suicide, is institutionalized, then dies of an arcane illness).
88. Safer, *Contemporary American Comic Epic*, 112; Christopher Knight, *Hints*, 24–46; Steven Moore, *William Gaddis*, 15; Weisenburger, *Fables*, 216.
89. Johnston, *Carnival*, 152.
90. Comnes, *Ethics*, 81.
91. Johnston, *Carnival*, 7.
92. Tanner, *City of Words*, 394.
93. Moretti, *Modern Epic*, 72.
94. Thielemans, "Energy," 105.
95. Flaubert, *Bouvard and Pécuchet*, 21.
96. This is most apparent in the passages dealing with Mr. Pivner's devotion to his evening radio and Dale Carnegie's *How to Win Friends and Influence People* (285–93, 498–501). Compared to his sympathetic treatment of Wyatt and the Reverend Gwyon's attachments to weird religious doctrines, Gaddis describes no compelling attraction that Pivner might find either to the radio or to Carnegie's book. The narrator generally invites readers to join him in feeling culturally superior to Pivner, which—despite claims by those like Weisenburger of the book's radicalness—is the most conservative form of satire. Its highbrow complacency, as Peter Wolfe has noted, expresses an uncomfortably high disdain for anyone without Gaddis's prep-school-through-Harvard education and aesthetic tastes (*Vision*, 55–57).
97. Gaddis, *Recognitions*, 65.
98. Gaddis, *Recognitions*, 63.
99. Gaddis, *Recognitions*, 67.
100. Comnes, *Ethics*, 70.
101. Gaddis, *Recognitions*, 286, 309, 505.
102. Gaddis, *Recognitions*, 514–20.
103. Gaddis, *Recognitions*, 574.
104. Gaddis, *Recognitions*, 578, 585, 593.
105. Gaddis, *Recognitions*, 637.
106. Gaddis, *Recognitions*, 643.
107. Gaddis, *Recognitions*, 616–17, 602–3, 591–92, 620–21.
108. Auden, "Musée," 3–4.
109. Gaddis, *Recognitions*, 757–63.

110. Gaddis, *Recognitions*, 942, 956.

5. Episodic Narrative

1. Myers, "Reader's Manifesto," 108.
2. Forster, *Aspects*, 42.
3. James Wood, "Human, All Too Inhuman," 41.
4. James Wood, "Human, All Too Inhuman," 41.
5. James Wood, *Broken Estate*, 204.
6. Genette, *Narrative*, 30; Barthes, "Introduction," 245.
7. Moretti, "Serious Century," 369–70.
8. Fludernik, *Towards a "Natural" Narratology*, 29.
9. McHale, "Weak Narrativity," 165.
10. See Alber and Heinze, *Unnatural Narratives*.
11. Pynchon, *Mason & Dixon*, 552.
12. Pynchon, *Mason & Dixon*, 573.
13. These four possibilities are reminiscent of those facing Oedipa Maas in *The Crying of Lot 49* (i.e., that the Trystero exist, that she is hallucinating the Trystero, that there is a conspiracy to make her believe there is a Trystero, and that she is hallucinating a conspiracy to make her believe there is a Trystero) (140–41). In my view the way those choices self-negate is a failing of that book.
14. Eco, *Open Work*, 116–18.
15. Abbott, "How Do We Read," 104.
16. Abbott, "How Do We Read," 106.
17. Damasio, *Feeling*, 171.
18. Damasio, *Feeling*, 178, 174, 168.
19. Dennett, *Consciousness*, 113, 218–20.
20. Borges, *Collected Fictions*, 123–28.
21. Duyfhuizen, "Reading," 140.
22. Aristotle, *Poetics*, 51b.
23. Bakhtin, *Dialogic Imagination*, 84.
24. Ardila, "Introduction," 3–5.
25. Guillén, *Literature as System*, 84; Wellek and Warren, *Theory of Literature*, 215.
26. Brooks, *Reading*, 38.
27. Clements and Gibaldi, *Anatomy*, 5–6. For this chapter's purposes, I use a restricted definition of the genre. There is even less consensus on the frame-tale's definition than the picaresque's, which sometimes causes the cornice-novella structure to merge with more general and messier concepts of "framing." As William Nelles observes, even ordinary dialogue cannot be

rigorously distinguished structurally from framed narrative under this broad definition (*Frameworks*, 123–25). I am not counting as frame-tales those simply making use of common tropes of *mise en abyme* (see Caws, *Reading Frames*) and document transmission (see Duyfhuizen, *Narratives of Transmission*), nor those involving extra- or paratextual material (see Berlatsky, "Lost," 166).

28. Clements and Gibaldi, *Anatomy*, 42–49.
29. Brooks, *Reading*, 61.
30. Wicks, *Picaresque*, 55.
31. Irwin, "What's in a Frame," 36–39; Gittes, *Framing*, 14.
32. See Clerc, *Mason & Dixon and Pynchon*, 89–91; McHale, "Mason & Dixon in the Zone," 49–50.
33. Reed, *Exemplary History*, 71–92.
34. Pynchon, *Mason & Dixon*, 349.
35. Pynchon, *Mason & Dixon*, 410–35, 485, 656–57.
36. Pynchon, *Mason & Dixon*, 345.
37. Rodriguez, "*Mason & Dixon* and Historiographic Metafiction," 75.
38. Pynchon, *Mason & Dixon*, 542; see Thomas, *Pynchon*, 37–38.
39. Seed, "Mapping," 96.
40. Kolbuszewska, *Poetics of Chronotope*, 205.
41. Pynchon, *Mason & Dixon*, 630.
42. Pynchon, *Mason & Dixon*, 478–79.
43. Pynchon, *Mason & Dixon*, 479.
44. Pynchon, *Mason & Dixon*, 253.
45. Cohen, "*Mason & Dixon* and the Ampersand," 280.
46. Pöhlmann, *Pynchon's Postnational Imagination*, 231, 232.
47. Pynchon, *Mason & Dixon*, 304, 571.
48. Pynchon, *Mason & Dixon*, 97.
49. Prince, "Disnarrated," 2.
50. Pynchon, *Mason & Dixon*, 644, 666–69.
51. I am using Todorov's definition of the fantastic, which defines a state in which we do not know whether to plot an event as marvelous (i.e., legitimately supernatural) or merely uncanny (i.e., a natural illusion) (*Fantastic*, 25). See also de Bourcier for a discussion of the compatibility of pre- and post-Enlightenment concepts in the novel (*Pynchon and Relativity*, 185–86).
52. Pynchon, *Mason & Dixon*, 739–41, 772.
53. Pynchon, *Mason & Dixon*, 547.
54. Pynchon, *Mason & Dixon*, 371–81.
55. Pynchon, *Mason & Dixon*, 612–13.

56. Pynchon, *Mason & Dixon*, 152–53.
57. Pynchon, *Mason & Dixon*, 701.
58. Pynchon, *Mason & Dixon*, 706–13.
59. Brooks, *Reading*, 23–29.
60. Burgelin, *Georges Perec*, 173–74.
61. Perec, *Life*, 649–53. If one counts the preamble and epilogue, there are 101, a number as symmetrical as Shahrazad's (Burgelin, *Georges Perec*, 174). For a more extensive look at the connections between the *Thousand and One Nights* and *Life a User's Manual*, see Joly, *Connaissement*, 304–13, 1102–11).
62. Perec, *Life*, xviii.
63. Perec, *Life*, xvii–xviii.
64. Perec, *Life*, 152–55, 205–9.
65. Perec, *Life*, 15–18.
66. Schwartz, *Georges Perec*, 95.
67. Perec, *Life*, 369–71; Kim, *Imaginaire*, 59–64.
68. Qtd. in Bellos, *Georges Perec*, 647.
69. Bartlebooth's name has three sources, and while the first two are intrepid questers—the grail-seeking knight Parsifal and Valery Larbaud's gentleman traveler A. O. Barnabooth—the third is one of the exemplary useless men of literature, Herman Melville's Bartleby the Scrivener (Burgelin, *Georges Perec*, 188).
70. Perec, *Life*, 133, 134.
71. Schwartz, *Georges Perec*, 87.
72. Perec, *Species of Spaces*, 33–35.
73. Paul Harris, "Invention of Forms," 56; Motte, *Poetics of Experiment*, 68–83.
74. Perec, *Life*, 16–18; Perec, *Cahiers*, 4.
75. Perec, *Life*, 525, 15.
76. Perec, *Life*, 148–51, 525–27, 12–14.
77. Josipovici, "Georges Perec's Homage," 191.
78. Perec, *Life*, 156–73.
79. Perec, *Life*, 94–109.
80. Perec, *Life*, 6, 565.
81. Alison James, *Constraining Chance*, 68–69.
82. Perec, *Life*, 366–67.
83. Perec, *Life*, 46–47, 550–60.
84. Perec, *Life*, 116–20, 173–75, 359–67, 393–95, 518–19.
85. Perec, *Life*, 327–29.
86. Magné, "Georges Perec on the Index," 88.
87. Perec, *Life*, 593.
88. Perec, *Life*, 31, 458, 576.

89. Perec, *Life*, 413–15, 200, 495–500; see also Ribaupierre, *Le roman*.
90. Perec, *Life*, 199–200.
91. Perec, *Life*, 336.
92. Calvino, *Six Memos*, 124.
93. Bellos, Georges Perec, 632–35.
94. Monteser, *Picaresque*, 118.
95. Cercas, qtd. in Medina, "Arts of Homelessness," 551–52.
96. Andrews, *Roberto Bolaño's Fiction*, 94–116.
97. Daniel Zalewski, "Vagabonds," *New Yorker*, March 26, 2007, 88.
98. Bolaño, *2666*, 632–33.
99. Bolaño, *2666*, 353.
100. Bolaño, *2666*, 417–19.
101. Bolaño, *2666*, 361–72.
102. Three of the thirteen, furthermore, include features that put the official conclusion into question. For two cases, those of Mónica Posadas (Bolaño, *2666*, 460–62) and Aurora Ibánez Medel (*2666*, 573–74), there are inconsistencies in the confessions provided by the arrested killers. For the third, the case of Esther Perea Peña (*2666*, 625–26), questions are raised within the police department about the plausibility of the official reconstruction.
103. Bolaño, *2666*, 895.
104. Andrews, *Roberto Bolaño's Fiction*, 205–29.
105. Deckard, "Peripheral Realism," 354.
106. Farred, "Impossible Closing," 694.
107. Bolaño, *2666*, 392–93.
108. Bolaño, *2666*, 607.
109. Bolaño, *2666*, 563, 552–53.
110. Bolaño, *2666*, 563.
111. Bolaño, *2666*, 540.
112. Franco, *Cruel Modernity*, 244.
113. Bolaño, *2666*, 470–71.
114. Poe, "Mystery of Marie Roget," 752.
115. "Distant reading" is, of course, Franco Moretti's coinage (*Distant*, 48–49).
116. Bolaño, *2666*, 595.
117. Bolaño, *2666*, 457.
118. Bolaño, *2666*, 605–6.
119. Bolaño, *2666*, 438–49.
120. Bolaño, *2666*, 158–59.
121. Bolaño, *2666*, 898.
122. Bolaño, *2666*, 348.

6. The Epic and the Allegory

1. James Wood, "Human, All Too Inhuman," 41.
2. James Wood, *Broken Estate*, 200–202.
3. T. S. Eliot, "William Blake," 279.
4. This is partly because the epic, going back to the Greeks, has traditionally been considered a formal mode or genre (e.g., Aristotle, *Poetics*, 49b), while allegory often instead suggests a mode of interpretation independent from textual form (Treip, *Allegorical Poetics*, 4). Allegorical interpretation of epics, in fact, pre-dates the writing of narratives explicitly intended as allegories (Treip, *Allegorical Poetics*, 55).
5. Gary Johnson, *Vitality*, 6; Lukács, *Theory of the Novel*, 66.
6. Honig, *Dark Conceit*, 21; Frederick Turner, *Epic*, 212.
7. Madsen, *Postmodernist Allegories*, 3; Lukács, *Theory of the Novel*, 40–41.
8. Aristotle, *Poetics*, 59b; Fletcher, *Allegory*, 367.
9. Bakhtin, *Dialogic Imagination*, 15; Honig, *Dark Conceit*, 68–81.
10. Fletcher, *Allegory*, 157; Frederick Turner, *Epic*, 117.
11. Lévi-Strauss, "Structural Study of Myth," 430.
12. Bakhtin, *Dialogic Imagination*, 13; Honig, *Dark Conceit*, 25.
13. Sidney, "Apology," 145.
14. Fletcher, *Allegory*, 2.
15. Lyotard, *Postmodern Condition*, xxiii–xxiv, 27–29, 12–13.
16. de Man, *Blindness and Insight*, 187–208; Hutcheon, *Poetics of Postmodernism*, 5, 7.
17. Jameson, *Postmodernism*, xi.
18. Berlatsky, *Real*, 26–34.
19. Dunbar, *Grooming*, 63, 69.
20. Jameson, *Postmodernism*, 51.
21. Mark Turner, *Literary Mind*, 5, 35, 44.
22. Hofstadter, "Paranoid Style," 29.
23. Maltby, *Dissident Postmodernists*, 150.
24. Sedgwick, *Touching Feeling*, 130–36. Patrick O'Donnell claims that paranoia does not actually form grand narratives, but is "a form of accommodation for the loss of those grand narratives" (*Latent*, 16), probably believing, as Peter Knight does, that paranoia does not assert truth but is "an ironic stance toward knowledge and the possibility of truth" (*Conspiracy Culture*, 2). This is perhaps true of paranoia conceived as prophylactic, reflexive cynicism for insulating the subject against the public sphere (which, of course, has its own problems). However, there are many paranoid theories intended seriously to generate knowledge.
25. Foster and Kokko, "Evolution of Superstition."

26. Krummenacher et al., "Dopamine," 1670, 1676.
27. Rushdie, *Step across This Line*, 319.
28. Ricoeur, *Freud and Philosophy*, 33, 34–35.
29. O'Donnell, *Latent*, 9.
30. Krummenacher et al., "Dopamine," 1675–76.
31. Swami and Coles, "Truth," 562.
32. Jameson, "Cognitive Mapping," 356.
33. Sedgwick, *Touching Feeling*, 125.
34. Swami and Coles, "Truth," 561, 563.
35. Schell, qtd. in Coale, *Paradigms*, 1.
36. Sanders, "Pynchon's Paranoid History," 158.
37. Benedict Anderson, *Imagined Communities*, 1–4.
38. Melley, "Paranoid Modernity."
39. McHale, *Constructing Postmodernism*, 87–88.
40. Eco, *Aesthetics*, 67.
41. DeLillo, *Underworld*, 289.
42. DeLillo, *Underworld*, 289.
43. DeLillo, *Underworld*, 289.
44. DeLillo, *Underworld*, 465.
45. James Wood, *Broken Estate*, 219.
46. DeLillo, *Underworld*, 283–84.
47. DeLillo, *Underworld*, 287.
48. DeLillo, *Underworld*, 286, 68–71.
49. James Wood, *Broken Estate*, 215.
50. Eco, *Foucault's Pendulum*, 602.
51. Eco, *Foucault's Pendulum*, 521.
52. Eco, *Foucault's Pendulum*, 565–81.
53. Eco, *Foucault's Pendulum*, 525.
54. DeLillo, *Underworld*, 175.
55. DeLillo, *Underworld*, 177.
56. DeLillo, *Underworld*, 94.
57. DeLillo, "The Power of History," *New York Times Magazine*, September 7, 1997, 61.
58. DeLillo, "Power of History," 63, 60.
59. DeLillo, *Underworld*, 810, 809.
60. Morley, *Quest for Epic*, 145.
61. DeLillo, *Underworld*, 43–44.
62. Cowart, *Don DeLillo*, 198.
63. DeLillo, *Underworld*, 824–26.

64. DeLillo, *Underworld*, 827.
65. McHale, *Constructing Postmodernism*, 186–87.
66. Peter Knight, *Conspiracy Culture*, 239; Michael Wood, "Post-paranoid," review of *Underworld*, by Don DeLillo, *London Review of Books*, February 5, 1998, 3–5.
67. James Wood, *Broken Estate*, 213.
68. James Wood, *Broken Estate*, 215.
69. James Wood, *Broken Estate*, 200.
70. Hynes, *War Imagined*, 433.
71. Hynes, *War Imagined*, x, 449.
72. Homberger, "United States," 174–79.
73. Guest, "Japan," 216; Rau, "War," 207–8; Brennan, *Salman Rushdie*, 85–100.
74. Jameson, "Third-World Literature," 69.
75. See Ahmad, "Jameson's Rhetoric."
76. Chrzanowska-Kluczewska, "Catachresis," 41. Adapting its meaning this way would actually be an example of the classical catachresis, which Quintilian defined as a term that "adapts, to whatever has no proper term, the term which is nearest" (*Institutes of Oratory*, 8:34).
77. Chrzanowska-Kluczewska, "Catachresis," 49.
78. Mark Turner, *Literary Mind*, 108.
79. Suter, *Japanization*, 52.
80. Amitrano, *Japanese Novel*, 32.
81. Murakami, *Wind-Up Bird*, 5, 60, 243.
82. Murakami, *Wind-Up Bird*, 554.
83. Rubin, *Haruki Murakami*, 218.
84. Murakami, *Dance Dance Dance*, 124.
85. Murakami, *Wind-Up Bird*, 497–98.
86. Murakami, *Wind-Up Bird*, 498.
87. Murakami, *Wind-Up Bird*, 461–62.
88. Strecher, *Dances with Sheep*, 167.
89. Murakami, *Wind-Up Bird*, 48.
90. Amitrano, *New Japanese Novel*, 34.
91. Murakami, *Wind-Up Bird*, 603.
92. Murakami, *Wind-Up Bird*, 378.
93. Murakami, *Wind-Up Bird*, 146.
94. Murakami, *Wind-Up Bird*, 538–47.
95. Murakami, *Wind-Up Bird*, 170.
96. Murakami, *Wind-Up Bird*, 574–87.
97. Murakami, *Wind-Up Bird*, 517–20.
98. Murakami, *Wind-Up Bird*, 335–36.

99. Murakami, *Wind-Up Bird*, 549.
100. Murakami, *Wind-Up Bird*, 601–5.
101. Murakami, *Wind-Up Bird*, 607.
102. Rushdie, *Midnight's Children*, 4.
103. Rushdie, *Midnight's Children*, 3.
104. Rushdie, *Midnight's Children*, 170, 176.
105. Rushdie, *Midnight's Children*, 139.
106. Rushdie, *Midnight's Children*, 49.
107. Rushdie, *Midnight's Children*, 86.
108. Ten Kortenaar, *Self, Nation, Text*, 93.
109. Kane, "Migrant Intellectual," 95; Mossman, "National Narrative," 66–67.
110. Rushdie, *Midnight's Children*, 297.
111. Rushdie, *Midnight's Children*, 297, 300.
112. Rushdie, *Midnight's Children*, 319.
113. Brennan, *Salman Rushdie and the Third World*, 98.
114. Rushdie, *Midnight's Children*, 483.
115. Rushdie has cited *The Tin Drum* as a model for *Midnight's Children* (*Imaginary*, 277).
116. Grass, *Danzig*, 93.
117. Roger Clark, *Stranger Gods*, 62.
118. Berlatsky, *Real*, 121; Rushdie, *Midnight's Children*, 204.
119. Rushdie, *Midnight's Children*, 272–73.
120. Rushdie, *Midnight's Children*, 273.
121. Rushdie, *Midnight's Children*, 200–202, 492–97, 533.
122. Rushdie, *Midnight's Children*, 262, 292.
123. Ten Kortenaar, *Self, Nation, Text*, 31.
124. Rushdie, *Midnight's Children*, 388, 386.
125. Rushdie, *Midnight's Children*, 386.
126. Rushdie, *Midnight's Children*, 403.
127. Rushdie, *Midnight's Children*, 409.
128. Rushdie, *Midnight's Children*, 527.
129. Rushdie, *Midnight's Children*, 344.
130. Su, "Epic of Failure," 548, 562.
131. Ten Kortenaar, *Self, Nation, Text*, 12.
132. Gorra, *After Empire*, 147, 145.
133. Pynchon, *Gravity's Rainbow*, 577.
134. Pynchon, *Gravity's Rainbow*, 295, 566.
135. Pynchon, *Gravity's Rainbow*, 717, 240.
136. Pynchon, *Gravity's Rainbow*, 254–55.
137. Thomas Moore, *Style of Connectedness*; Hume, Pynchon's *Mythography*.

138. Bersani, *Culture of Redemption*, 194.
139. McHale, *Constructing Postmodernism*, 112–13.
140. Madsen, *Postmodernist Allegories*, 111.
141. Cooper, *Signs and Symptoms*, 212, 161.
142. Siegel, *Pynchon*, 19.
143. Hofstadter, "Paranoid Style," 36.
144. Hofstadter, "Paranoid Style," 38.
145. Letzler, "Character of Preterition."
146. Molly Hite, for example, has argued against the critical view of Them as an all-powerful conspiracy, modeling her analyses roughly on Russell's Paradox and Gödel's Incompleteness Theorem (*Ideas*, 123–24) and finally claiming "that there is no real They in the final analysis" (*Ideas*, 144). However, she does not foreground this in her larger treatment of the book, and consequently it hasn't had much impact.
147. Pynchon, *Gravity's Rainbow*, 441.
148. Tanner, "Gravity's Rainbow," 73.
149. Thomas Moore, *Style of Connectedness*, 92; Pynchon, *Gravity's Rainbow*, 406–28.
150. Hofstadter, "Paranoid Style," 29; Pynchon, *Gravity's Rainbow*, 85–86, 288–91.
151. Kolbuszewska, *Poetics of Chronotope*, 125.
152. Hägg, *Narratologies*, 93–121.
153. Pynchon, *Gravity's Rainbow*, 374.
154. Pynchon, *Gravity's Rainbow*, 380.
155. Pynchon, *Gravity's Rainbow*, 424–25, 529–30, 727.
156. Pynchon, *Gravity's Rainbow*, 445.
157. Pynchon, *Gravity's Rainbow*, 243–47.
158. Pynchon, *Gravity's Rainbow*, 291, 214–21, 313–19.
159. Pynchon, *Gravity's Rainbow*, 334–36.
160. Pynchon, *Gravity's Rainbow*, 613, 614.
161. Mason, "'Just a Bunch of Stuff,'" 169.
162. Pynchon, *Gravity's Rainbow*, 558–59.
163. Herman and Weisenburger, *"Gravity's Rainbow," Domination*, 141.
164. Pynchon, *Gravity's Rainbow*, 638, 601.
165. Pynchon, *Gravity's Rainbow*, 441.
166. Hite, *Ideas*, 17.
167. Pynchon, *Gravity's Rainbow*, 517.
168. Pynchon, *Gravity's Rainbow*, 517.
169. Bersani, *Culture of Redemption*, 195; Pynchon, *Gravity's Rainbow*, 635.

170. Pynchon, *Gravity's Rainbow*, 635.
171. Benedict Anderson, *Imagined Communities*, 154.
172. Pöhlmann, *Pynchon's Postnational Imagination*, 286, 292.
173. Laing, *Politics of Experience*, 60–61.
174. Pynchon, *Gravity's Rainbow*, 727, 651.
175. Pynchon, *Gravity's Rainbow*, 753.
176. Rowland, *Full Facts Book of Cold Reading*, 9.
177. Pynchon, *Gravity's Rainbow*, 760–64.
178. Rowland, *Full Facts Book of Cold Reading*, 75. Exemplarily, T. S. Eliot, who famously uses tarot as a key element of *The Waste Land*, admits, "I am not familiar with the exact constitution of the Tarot pack of cards, from which I have obviously departed to suit my own convenience." His association of the Three of Staves with the Fisher King, for example, is made "quite arbitrarily" (*Complete Poems* 51).
179. Waite, *Pictorial Key to the Tarot*, 156; Tatham, "Tarot," 587.
180. Were we to select Lizzy Bennet, for instance, we would interpret the Tower as Wickham's seduction of Lydia, the Queen of Swords as the obstinate Mrs. Bennet, the King of Cups as Lizzy's desired marriage to Mr. Darcy, and so on.
181. Pynchon, *Gravity's Rainbow*, 763.
182. Pynchon, *Gravity's Rainbow*, 763.
183. Pynchon, *Gravity's Rainbow*, 768.
184. Pynchon, *Gravity's Rainbow*, 486.
185. Pynchon, *Gravity's Rainbow*, 774–75.
186. Pynchon, *Gravity's Rainbow*, 741.
187. McHale, *Postmodernist Fiction*, 10.
188. McHale, *Postmodernist Fiction*, 10.

Conclusion

1. Hayles, "Hyper," 188; Mark O'Connell, "The Stockholm Syndrome Theory of Long Novels," *Millions*, May 16, 2011, accessed July 17, 2011, http://www.themillions.com/2011/05/the-stockholm-syndrome-theory-of-long-novels.html.
2. Posner, *Attention*, 139.
3. Calvino, *Six Memos*, 112.
4. Deleuze and Guattari, *Thousand Plateaus*, 8, 12.
5. This is why Deleuze and Guattari's work, antirhizomically, always foregrounds a small number of key phrases, like "lines of flight" and "body without organs," so that others may focus on and export them.

6. Prinz, *Conscious Brain*, 89.
7. Hayles, "Illusion of Autonomy," 693, 696.
8. Hayles, "Hyper," 195.
9. Barkley, "Behavioral Inhibition."
10. Healey and Rucklidge, "Investigation," 422.
11. Borges, qtd. in Quian Quiroga, *Borges and Memory*, 12–14.

Bibliography

Abbott, H. Porter. "How Do We Read What Isn't There to Be Read? Shadow Stories and Permanent Gaps." In *The Oxford Handbook of Cognitive Literary Studies*, edited by Lisa Zunshine, 104–19. New York: Oxford University Press, 2015.

Ahmad, Aijaz. "Jameson's Rhetoric of Otherness and the 'National Allegory.'" *Social Text* 17 (1987): 3–25.

Alber, Jan, and Rüdiger Heinze, eds. *Unnatural Narratives—Unnatural Narratology*. Boston: de Gruyter, 2011. Lingua and Litterae 9.

Allport, Alan. "Attention and Control: Have We Been Asking the Wrong Questions? A Critical Review of Twenty-Five Years." In *Attention and Performance XIV: Synergies in Experimental Psychology, Artificial Intelligence, and Cognitive Neuroscience*, edited by David E. Meyer and Sylvan Kornblum, 183–218. Cambridge MA: MIT Press, 1993.

Altieri, Charles. "Aspect-Seeing and Stevens' Ideal of Ordinary Experience." *Wallace Stevens Journal* 36.1 (2012): 78–93.

Amitrano, Giorgio. *The New Japanese Novel: Popular Culture and Literary Tradition in the Work of Murakami Haruki and Yoshimoto Banana*. Kyoto: Italian Institute of Culture, 1996. Italian School of East Asian Studies Occasional Papers 7.

Anderson, Benedict. *Imagined Communities: Reflections on the Origin and Spread of Nationalism*. Revised ed. New York: Verso, 1991.

Anderson, Richard. *Robert Coover*. Boston: Twayne, 1981. Twayne's United States Authors 546.

Andrews, Chris. *Roberto Bolaño's Fiction: An Expanding Universe*. New York: Columbia University Press, 2014.

Arata, Stephen. "On Not Paying Attention." *Victorian Studies* 46.2 (2004): 193–205.

Ardila, J. A. G. "Introduction: Transnational Picaresque." *Philological Quarterly* 89.1 (2010): 1–11.

Aristotle. *Poetics*. Translated by Malcolm Heath. New York: Penguin, 1996.

Asimov, Isaac. *The Foundation Trilogy*. New York: Avon, 1974. First published 1951.

Attridge, Derek. *Peculiar Language: Literature as Difference from the Renaissance to James Joyce*. Ithaca NY: Cornell University Press, 1988.

Auden, W. H. "Musée des Beaux Arts." In *Collected Poems*, edited by Edward Mendelson, 179. New York: Modern Library, 2007.

Baars, Bernard J. *In the Theater of Consciousness: The Workspace of the Mind*. New York: Oxford University Press, 1997.

Bakhtin, M. M. *The Dialogic Imagination: Four Essays*. Translated by Caryl Emerson and Michael Holquist. Austin: University of Texas Press, 1981. University of Texas Press Slavic Series 1.

———. *The Problems of Dostoevsky's Poetics*. Translated by Caryl Emerson. Minneapolis: University of Minnesota Press, 1984. Theory and History of Literature 8.

———. *Rabelais and His World*. Translated by Helene Iswolsky. Cambridge MA: MIT Press, 1968.

Barkley, Russell. "Behavioral Inhibition, Sustained Attention, and Executive Functions: Constructing a Unifying Theory of ADHD." *Psychological Bulletin* 121.1 (1997): 65–94.

Barrett, Lisa Feldman, Michele M. Tugade, and Randall W. Engle. "Individual Differences in Working Memory Capacity and Dual-Process Theories of the Mind." *Psychological Bulletin* 130.4 (2004): 553–73.

Barth, John. *The Friday Book*. New York: G. P. Putnam's Sons, 1984.

———. *The Sot-Weed Factor*. New York: Anchor, 1987. First published 1960.

Barthes, Roland. "Introduction to the Structural Analysis of Narrative." Translated by Lionel Dusit. *New Literary History* 6.2 (Winter 1975): 237–72. On Narrative and Narratives.

———. *The Pleasure of the Text*. Translated by Richard Miller. New York: Farrar, Strauss, & Giroux, 1975.

———. "The Reality Effect." Translated by R. Carter. In *French Literary Theory Today*, edited by Tzvetan Todorov, 11–17. New York: Cambridge University Press, 1982.

———. *S/Z*. Translated by Richard Miller. New York: Farrar, Strauss, & Giroux, 1974.

Bean, H. R. "Repeating Gertrude Stein: Language, Performativity, and Hypermediated Theater." *Text and Performance Quarterly* 27.3 (2007): 168–93.

Bellos, David. *Georges Perec: A Life in Words*. New York: HarperCollins, 1993.

Bennett, Charles H. "Logical Depth and Physical Complexity." In *The Universal Turing Machine: A Half-Century Survey*, edited by Rolf Herken, 227–57. New York: Oxford University Press, 1988.

Benstock, Shari. "At the Margins of Discourse: Footnotes in the Fictional Text." PMLA 98.2 (1983): 204–25.

Bergson, Henri. *Laughter: An Essay on the Meaning of the Comic*. Translated by Cloudesley Brereton and Fred Rothwell. New York: Macmillan, 1928.

Berlatsky, Eric L. "Lost in the Gutter: Within and between Frames in Narrative and Narrative Theory." *Narrative* 17.2 (2009): 162–87.

———. *The Real, the True, and the Told: Postmodern Historical Narrative and the Ethics of Representation*. Columbus: Ohio State University Press, 2011.

Bersani, Leo. *The Culture of Redemption*. Cambridge MA: Harvard University Press, 1990.

Boehm, Beth A. "Reeducating Readers: Creating New Expectations for *The Golden Notebook*." *Narrative* 5.1 (1997): 88–98.

Bogel, Fredric V. *The Difference Satire Makes*. Ithaca NY: Cornell University Press, 2001.

Bolaño, Roberto. *Nazi Literature in the Americas*. Translated by Chris Andrews. New York: New Directions, 2008. First published 1996.

———. *The Savage Detectives*. Translated by Natasha Wimmer. New York: Picador, 2007.

———. *2666*. Translated by Natasha Wimmer. New York: Picador, 2008.

Borg, Ruben. "Neologizing in *Finnegans Wake*: Beyond a Typology of the Wakean Portmanteau." *Poetics Today* 28.1 (Spring 2007): 143–64.

Borges, Jorge Luis. *Collected Fictions*. Translated by Andrew Hurley. New York: Penguin, 1998.

Boswell, Marshall. *Understanding David Foster Wallace*. Columbia: University of South Carolina Press, 2003.

Bowling, Lawrence Edward. "What Is the Stream of Consciousness Technique?" *PMLA* 65.4 (1950): 333–45.

Brennan, Timothy. *Salman Rushdie and the Third World*. London: Macmillan, 1989.

Broadbent, D. E. *Perception and Communication*. New York: Oxford University Press, 1987. First published 1958.

Brooks, Peter. *Reading for the Plot: Design and Intention in Narrative*. Cambridge MA: Harvard University Press, 1992. First published 1984.

Bunce, Diane M., Elizabeth Flens, and Kelly Y. Neiles. "How Long Can Students Pay Attention in Class? A Study of Student Attention Decline Using Clickers." *Journal of Chemical Education* 87.12 (2010): 1438–43.

Burgelin, Claude. *Georges Perec*. Paris: Éditions de Seuil, 1988.

Burn, Stephen. "The Collapse of Everything: William Gaddis and the Encyclopedic Novel." In *Paper Empire: William Gaddis and the World System*, edited by Joseph Tabbi, 46–62. Tuscaloosa: University of Alabama Press, 2007.

———. *David Foster Wallace's "Infinite Jest": A Reader's Guide*. New York: Continuum, 2003.

Calvino, Italo. *Six Memos for the Next Millennium*. New York: Vintage, 1993. First published 1988.

Caserio, Robert L. "James, Cather, Vollmann, and the Distinction of Historical Fiction." *symplokē* 12.1–2 (2004): 106–29.

Caws, Mary Ann. *Reading Frames in Modernist Fiction*. Princeton NJ: Princeton University Press, 1985.

Certeau, Michel de. *The Practice of Everyday Life*. Translated by Steven F. Rendall. Berkeley: University of California Press, 1984.

Chanen, Brian W. "Surfing the Text: The Digital Environment in Mark Z. Danielewski's *House of Leaves*." *European Journal of English Studies* 11.2 (2007): 163–76.

Cheyne, James Allan, Jonathan S. A. Carriere, and Daniel Smilek. "Absent-Mindedness: Lapses of Conscious Awareness and Everyday Cognitive Failures." *Consciousness and Cognition* 15 (2006): 578–92.

Christensen, Peter G. "Shostakovich in Love: William T. Vollmann's *Europe Central*." *Journal of the Midwest Modern Language Association* 40.1 (2007): 97–108.

Chrzanowska-Kluczewska, Elżbieta. "Catachresis: A Metaphor or a Figure in Its Own Right?" In *Beyond Cognitive Metaphor Theory: Perspectives on Literary Metaphor*, edited by Monica Fludernik, 36–57. New York: Routledge, 2011.

Cioffi, Frank L. "'An Anguish Become Thing': Narrative as Performance in David Foster Wallace's *Infinite Jest*." *Narrative* 8.2 (2000): 161–81.

———. "Coover's (Im)Possible Worlds in *The Public Burning*." *Critique: Studies in Contemporary Fiction* 42.1 (Fall 2000): 26–39.

Cixous, Hélène. "The Laugh of the Medusa." Translated by Keith Cohen and Paula Cohen. *Signs* 1.4 (1976): 875–93.

Clare, Ralph. "The Politics of Boredom and the Boredom of Politics in David Foster Wallace's *The Pale King*." *Studies in the Novel* 44.4 (2012): 428–46.

Clark, Hilary A. "Encyclopedic Discourse." *SubStance* 21.1 (1992): 95–110.

Clark, Roger Y. *Stranger Gods: Salman Rushdie's Other Worlds*. Montreal: McGill-Queen's University Press, 2001.

Clement, Tanya E. "'A Thing Not Beginning and Not Ending': Using Digital Tools to Distant-Read Gertrude Stein's *The Making of Americans*." *Literary and Linguistic Computing* 23.2 (2008): 361–81.

Clements, Robert J., and Joseph Gibaldi. *Anatomy of the Novella: The European Tale Collection from Boccaccio and Chaucer to Cervantes*. New York: New York University Press, 1977.

Clerc, Charles. *Mason & Dixon and Pynchon*. Lanham MD: University Press of America, 2000.

Cliett, Bill Cole. *A "Finnegans Wake" Lextionary: Let James Joyce Jazz Up Your Voca(l)bulary*. Seattle: CreateSpace, 2011.

Coale, Samuel Chase. *Paradigms of Paranoia: The Culture of Conspiracy in Contemporary American Fiction*. Tuscaloosa: University of Alabama Press, 2005.

Codebó, Marco. *Narrating from the Archive: Novels, Records, and Bureaucrats in the Modern Age*. Cranbury NJ: Associated University Presses, 2010.

Cohen, Samuel. "*Mason & Dixon* and the Ampersand." *Twentieth-Century Literature* 48.3 (2002): 264–91.

Cohn, Dorrit. *The Distinction of Fiction*. Baltimore: Johns Hopkins University Press, 1999.

———. *Transparent Minds: Narrative Modes for Presenting Consciousness in Fiction*. Princeton NJ: Princeton University Press, 1978.

Comnes, Gregory. *The Ethics of Indeterminacy in the Novels of William Gaddis*. Gainesville: University Press of Florida, 1994.

Conley, Tim. *Joyces Mistakes: Problems of Intention, Irony, and Interpretation*. Toronto: University of Toronto Press, 2003.

Conners, Frances A. "Attentional Control and the Simple View of Reading." *Reading and Writing* 22 (2009): 591–613.

Connor, James A. "Radio Free Joyce: 'Wake' Language and the Experience of Radio." *James Joyce Quarterly* 30.4–31.1 (Summer/Fall 1993): 825–43.

Cook, Ebenezer. "The Sot-Weed Factor; or, A Voyage to Maryland." In *Early Maryland Poetry*, edited by Bernard C. Steiner, 11–32. Baltimore: John Murphy, 1900. First published 1708.

Cooper, Peter. *Signs and Symptoms: Thomas Pynchon and the Contemporary World*. Berkeley: University of California Press, 1983.

Coover, Robert. *The Public Burning*. New York: Grove, 1998. First published 1978.

Cowart, David. *Don DeLillo: The Physics of Language*. Revised ed. Athens: University of Georgia Press, 2002.

Damasio, Antonio. *The Feeling of What Happens: Body and Emotion in the Making of Consciousness*. New York: Harcourt, 1999.

Dames, Nicholas. *The Physiology of the Novel: Reading, Neural Science, and the Form of Victorian Fiction*. New York: Oxford University Press, 2007.

Danielewski, Mark Z. *House of Leaves*: The Remastered, Full-Color Edition. New York: Pantheon, 2000.

de Bourcier, Simon. *Pynchon and Relativity: Narrative Time in Thomas Pynchon's Later Novels*. New York: Continuum, 2012.

Deckard, Sharae. "Peripheral Realism, Millennial Capitalism, and Roberto Bolaño's *2666*." *Modern Language Quarterly* 73.3 (2012): 351–72.

Dehaene, Stanislas. *Reading in the Brain: The Science and Evolution of a Human Invention*. New York: Penguin, 2009.

DeKoven, Marianne. *A Different Language: Gertrude Stein's Experimental Writing*. Madison: University of Wisconsin Press, 1983.

———. *Underworld*. New York: Scribner, 1997.

Deleuze, Gilles, and Félix Guattari. *A Thousand Plateaus: Capitalism and Schizophrenia*. Translated by Brian Massumi. Minneapolis: University of Minnesota Press, 1987.

de Man, Paul. *Blindness and Insight: Essays in the Rhetoric of Contemporary Criticism*. 2nd ed. Minneapolis: University of Minnesota Press, 1983. First published 1971.

Dennett, Daniel C. *Consciousness Explained*. Boston: Back Bay, 1991.

Derrida, Jacques. "The Law of Genre." Translated by Avital Ronell. *Critical Inquiry* 7.1 (1980): 55–81.

———. "Two Words for Joyce." In *Post-structuralist Joyce: Essays from the French*. Edited by Derek Attridge and Daniel Ferrer. New York: Cambridge University Press, 1984.

Dimock, Wai Chee. "Introduction: Genres as Fields of Knowledge." *PMLA* 122.5 (2007): 1377–88.

Donato, E. "'A Mere Labyrinth of Letters': Flaubert and the Quest for Fiction; A Montage." *MLN* 89.6 (1974): 885–910.

Doyle, Arthur Conan. *The Complete Sherlock Holmes*. Garden City NY: Doubleday, 1930.

Doyle, Jennifer. *Sex Objects: Art and Dialectics of Desire*. Minneapolis: University of Minnesota Press, 2006.

Draine, Betsy. "Nostalgia and Irony: The Postmodern Order of *The Golden Notebook*." *Modern Fiction Studies* 26.1 (1980): 31–48.

Dryden, John. "Discourse concerning the Original and Progress of Satire." In *The Satyrs of Decimus Junius Juvenalis and of Aulius Persius Flaccus*, iii–cxi. 3rd ed. London: J. Tonson, 1726. First published 1693.

Dubnick, Randa. *The Structure of Obscurity: Gertrude Stein, Language, and Cubism*. Urbana: University of Illinois Press, 1984.

Dumesnil, René. "Bouvard et Pécuchet sont-ils les imbeciles?" *En marge de Flaubert*, 31–58. Paris: Librarie de France, 1928.

Dunbar, Robin. *Grooming, Gossip, and the Evolution of Language*. Cambridge MA: Harvard University Press, 1996.

DuPlessis, Rachel Blau. "For the Etruscans." In *The New Feminist Criticism*, edited by Elaine Showalter, 271–91. New York: Pantheon, 1985.

———. *Writing beyond the Ending: Narrative Strategies of Twentieth-Century Woman Writers*. Bloomington: Indiana University Press, 1985.

Duquette, Elizabeth. "Speculative Cetology: Figuring Philosophy in *Moby-Dick*." ESQ: *A Journal of the American Renaissance* 47.1 (2001): 33–57.

Duyfhuizen, Bernard. *Narratives of Transmission*. Rutherford NJ: Fairleigh Dickinson University Press, 1992.

———. "Reading at the 'Crease of Credulity.'" In *Pynchon and "Mason & Dixon,"* edited by Brooke Horvath and Irving Mallin, 132–42. Cranbury NJ: Associated University Presses, 2000.

Eagleton, Terry. *How to Read a Poem*. Malden MA: Blackwell, 2007.

Eastwood, John D., et al. "The Unengaged Mind: Defining Boredom in Terms of Attention." *Perspectives on Psychological Science* 7 (2012): 482–95.

Eco, Umberto. *The Aesthetics of Chaosmos: The Middle Ages of James Joyce*. Translated by Ellen Esrock. Cambridge MA: Harvard University Press, 1989. First published 1982.

———. *Foucault's Pendulum*. Translated by William Weaver. New York: Harcourt, 1989.

———. *The Open Work*. Translated by Anna Cancogni. Cambridge MA: Harvard University Press, 1989.

Edelman, Gerald, and Giulio Tononi. *A Universe of Consciousness: How Matter Becomes Imagination*. New York: Basic Books, 2000.

Eliot, George. *Middlemarch*. Edited by Gregory Maertz. Peterborough, Ontario: Broadview, 2004.

Eliot, T. S. *Complete Poems and Plays 1909–1950*. New York: Harcourt, Brace & World, 1952.

———. "William Blake." In *Selected Essays of T. S. Eliot*, 275–80. New York: Harcourt, Brace, 1950.

Ellmann, Richard. *James Joyce*. New and revised ed. New York: Oxford University Press, 1982.

Empson, William. *Seven Types of Ambiguity*. New York: New Directions, 1947. First published 1930.

Epstein, Edmund Lloyd. *A Guide through "Finnegans Wake."* Gainesville: University Press of Florida, 2009.

Estes, David C. "American Folk Laughter in Robert Coover's 'The Public Burning.'" *Contemporary Literature* 28.2 (Fall 1987): 239–56.

Farred, Grant. "The Impossible Closing: Death, Neoliberalism, and the Postcolonial in Bolaño's *2666*." *Modern Fiction Studies* 56.4 (2010): 689–708.

Federman, Raymond. *Critifiction: Postmodern Essays*. Albany: State University of New York Press, 1993.

Felber, Lynette. *Gender and Genre in Novels without End: The British* Roman-Fleuve. Gainesville: University Press of Florida, 1995.

Fenichel, Otto. "On the Psychology of Boredom." *Collected Papers*. Vol. 1. New York: Norton, 1953.
Fenske, Mark J., and Jane E. Raymond. "Affective Influences of Selective Attention." *Current Directions in Psychological Science* 15.6 (2006): 312–16.
Fish, Stanley E. *Self-Consuming Artifacts: The Experience of Seventeenth-Century Literature*. Berkeley: University of California Press, 1972.
Fishburn, Evelyn. "A Footnote to Borges Studies: A Study of the Footnotes." In *Renscrituras: Texto y Teoría*, edited by Luz Rodríguez-Carranza and Marilene Nagle, 285–302. New York: Rodopi, 2004. Estudios Culturales 33.
Flaubert, Gustave. *Bouvard and Pécuchet*. Translated by Mark Polizzotti. Champaign IL: Dalkey Archive, 2005. First published 1881.
Fletcher, Angus. *Allegory: The Theory of a Symbolic Mode*. Revised ed. Princeton NJ: Princeton University Press, 2012.
Fludernik, Monika. *Towards a "Natural" Narratology*. London: Routledge, 1996.
Foucault, Michel. *The Order of Things: An Archaeology of the Human Sciences*. New York: Vintage, 1973.
Forster, E. M. *Aspects of the Novel*. New York: Harcourt, 1957. First published 1927.
Foster, Kevin R., and Hanna Kokko. "The Evolution of Superstition and Superstitious-Like Behavior." *Proceedings of the Royal Society B* (2009): n.p. Web. Accessed April 1, 2016.
Fowler, Alastair. *Kinds of Literature: An Introduction to the Theory of Genres and Modes*. Cambridge MA: Harvard University Press, 1982.
Franco, Jean. *Cruel Modernity*. Durham NC: Duke University Press, 2013.
Friedman, Bruce Jay. "Foreword." In *Black Humor*, edited by Bruce Jay Friedman, vii–xi. New York: Bantam, 1965.
Friedman, Melvin. *Stream of Consciousness: A Study in Literary Method*. New Haven CT: Yale University Press, 1955.
Frow, John. *Genre*. New York: Routledge, 2006. New Critical Idiom.
Frye, Joanne. *Living Stories, Telling Lives: Women and the Novel in Contemporary Experience*. Ann Arbor: University of Michigan Press, 1986.
Frye, Northrop. *Anatomy of Criticism*. Princeton NJ: Princeton University Press, 2000. First published 1957.
Gaddis, William. *J R*. New York: Penguin, 1993. First published 1975.
———. *The Recognitions*. New York: Penguin, 1993. First published 1955.
———. *The Rush for Second Place*. Edited by Joseph Tabbi. New York: Penguin, 2002.
Gaddy, Michelle L., Paul van den Broek, and Yung-Chi Sung. "The Influence of Text Cues on the Allocation of Attention during Reading." In *Text Representation: Linguistic and Psycholinguistic Processes*, edited by Ted

Sanders, Joost Schilperoord, and Wilbert Spooren. Amsterdam: John Benjamins, 2001. Human Cognitive Processing 8.
Gass, William H. "I've Got a Little List." *Salmagundi*, nos. 109–10 (1996): 20–38.
Genette, Gérard. *Narrative Discourse*. Translated by Jane E. Lewin. Ithaca NY: Cornell University Press, 1980.
———. *Paratexts: Thresholds of Interpretation*. Translated by Jane E. Lewin. New York: Cambridge University Press, 1997.
Gittes, Katharine S. *Framing the "Canterbury Tales": Chaucer and the Medieval Frame Narrative Tradition*. Westport CT: Greenwood, 1991. Contributions to the Study of World Literature 41.
Gleick, James. *The Information: A History, a Theory, a Flood*. New York: Pantheon, 2011.
Goldberg, Yael K., et al. "Boredom: An Emotional Experience Distinct from Apathy, Anhedonia, or Depression." *Journal of Social and Clinical Psychology* 30.6 (2011): 647–66.
Goldsmith, Kenneth. *Uncreative Writing: Managing Language in the Digital Age*. New York: Columbia University Press, 2011.
Gorra, Michael. *After Empire: Scott, Naipaul, Rushdie*. Chicago: University of Chicago Press, 1997.
Grafton, Anthony. *The Footnote: A Curious History*. Cambridge MA: Harvard University Press, 1997.
Grass, Günter. *The Danzig Trilogy: "The Tin Drum," "Cat and Mouse," "Dog Days."* Translated by Ralph Mannheim. New York: MJF Books, 1987.
Green, Jack. *Fire the Bastards*. Edited by Steven Moore. Normal IL: Dalkey, 1992. First published 1962.
Green, Melanie C., and Timothy C. Brock. "The Role of Transportation in the Persuasiveness of Public Narratives." *Journal of Personality and Social Psychology* 79.5 (2000): 701–21.
Greenberg, Robert. "Cetology: Center of Multiplicity and Discord in *Moby-Dick*." *ESQ: A Journal of the American Renaissance* 27.1 (1981): 1–13.
Greene, Gayle. *Doris Lessing: The Poetics of Change*. Ann Arbor: University of Michigan Press, 1996.
Greetham, David. "Begin Again . . . Stop!" Introduction to *Finnegans Wake* by James Joyce, edited by Danis Rose and John O'Hanlon, 17–28. Cornwall: Houyhnhnm, 2010.
Greif, Mark. "'The Death of the Novel' and Its Afterlives: Toward a History of the 'Big, Ambitious Novel.'" *boundary2* 36.2 (2009): 11–30.
Griffin, Dustin. *Satire: A Critical Reintroduction*. Lexington: University of Kentucky Press, 1994.

Gubar, Susan. "'The Blank Page' and Issues of Female Creativity." In *The New Feminist Criticism*, edited by Elaine Showalter, 292–313. New York: Pantheon, 1985.

Guest, Harry. "Japan: A Perspective." In *The Second World War in Fiction*, edited by Holger Klein, John Flower, and Eric Homberger, 206–18. London: Macmillan, 1984.

Guillén, Claudio. *Literature as System: Essays Toward the Theory of Literary History*. Princeton NJ: Princeton University Press, 1971.

Hägg, Samuli. *Narratologies of "Gravity's Rainbow."* Joensuu, Finland: University of Joensuu Press, 2005. Publications in the Humanities 37.

———. "Pynchon's Poetics of Boredom: Cognitive and Textual Aspects of Novelistic Dreariness." In *Narrative, Interrupted: The Plotless, the Disturbing and the Trivial in Literature*, edited by Markku Lehtimäki, Laura Karttunen, and Maria Mäkelä, 75–90. Boston: de Gruyter, 2012.

Hamilton, Robert C. "'Constant Bliss in Every Atom': Tedium and Transcendence in David Foster Wallace's *The Pale King*." *Arizona Quarterly* 70.4 (2014): 169–90.

Harris, Charles B. *Passionate Virtuosity: The Fiction of John Barth*. Urbana: University of Illinois Press, 1983.

Harris, Paul A. "Invention of Forms: Perec's *Life a User's Manual* and a Virtual Sense of the Real." *SubStance* 23.2 (1994): 56–85.

Hayles, N. Katherine. *How We Became Posthuman: Virtual Bodies in Cybernetics, Literature, and Informatics*. Chicago: University of Chicago Press, 1999.

———. "Hyper and Deep Attention: The Generational Divide in Cognitive Modes." *Profession* 19 (2007): 187–99.

———. "The Illusion of Autonomy and the Fact of Recursivity: Virtual Ecologies, Entertainment, and *Infinite Jest*." *New Literary History* 30.3 (1999): 675–97.

Hayles, N. Katherine, and Todd Gannon. "Mood Swings: The Aesthetics of Ambient Emergence." In *The Mourning After: Attending the Wake of Postmodernism*, edited by Neil Brooks and Josh Toth, 99–142. New York: Rodopi, 2007. Postmodern Studies 40.

Healey, Dione, and Julia Rucklidge. "An Investigation into the Relationship among ADHD Symptomathology, Creativity, and Neuropsychological Functioning in Children." *Child Psychology* 12 (2006): 421–38.

Hemmingson, Michael. "William T. Vollmann's End Matter (Appendices, Glossaries, and Effluvia): Are They Necessary?" William T. Vollmann: Methodologies and Morals. MLA Annual Convention. J. W. Marriott, Los Angeles. January 8, 2011. Address.

Herman, Luc, and Petrus van Ewijk. "Gravity's Encyclopedia Revisited: The Illusion of a Totalizing System in *Gravity's Rainbow*." *English Studies* 90.2 (2009): 167–79.

Herman, Luc, and Bart Vervaeck. "Narrative Interest as Cultural Negotiation." *Narrative* 17.1 (2009): 111–29.

Herman, Luc, and Steven Weisenburger. *"Gravity's Rainbow," Domination, and Freedom*. Athens: University of Georgia Press, 2013.

Hirsch, E. D., Jr. *Validity in Interpretation*. New Haven CT: Yale University Press, 1967.

Hite, Molly. "Doris Lessing's *The Golden Notebook* and *The Four-Gated City*: Ideology, Coherence, and Possibility." *Twentieth-Century Literature* 34.1 (1988): 16–29.

———. *Ideas of Order in the Novels of Thomas Pynchon*. Columbus: Ohio State University Press, 1983.

———. "'A Parody of Martyrdom': The Rosenbergs, Cold War Theology, and Robert Coover's *The Public Burning*." NOVEL: *A Forum on Fiction* 27.1 (Autumn 1993): 85–101.

Hofstadter, Richard. "The Paranoid Style in American Politics." In *The Paranoid Style in American Politics and Other Essays*, 3–40. Cambridge MA: Harvard University Press, 1996. First published 1964.

Hogan, Patrick Colm. *Cognitive Science, Literature, and the Arts: A Guide for Humanists*. New York: Routledge, 2003.

Homberger, Eric. "United States." In *The Second World War in Fiction*, edited by Holger Klein, John Flower, and Eric Homberger, 173–205 London: Macmillan, 1984.

Honig, Edwin. *Dark Conceit: The Making of Allegory*. New York: Oxford University Press, 1966. First published 1959.

Hopfinger, Joseph B., and Emily L. Parks. "Involuntary Attention." In *The Neuroscience of Attention: Attentional Control and Selection*, edited by George R. Mangun, 30–53. New York: Oxford University Press, 2011.

Hume, Kathryn. *Pynchon's Mythography: An Approach to "Gravity's Rainbow."* Carbondale: South Illinois University Press, 1987.

Hutcheon, Linda. *A Poetics of Postmodernism: History, Theory, Fiction*. New York: Routledge, 1988.

Hynes, Samuel. *A War Imagined: The First World War in English Culture*. London: Bodley Head, 1990.

Irwin, Bonnie D. "What's in a Frame? The Medieval Textualization of Traditional Storytelling." *Oral Tradition* 10.1 (1995): 27–53.

Iser, Wolfgang. *The Act of Reading: A Theory of Aesthetic Response*. Baltimore: Johns Hopkins University Press, 1980.

James, Alison. *Constraining Chance: Georges Perec and the Oulipo*. Evanston IL: Northwestern University Press, 2009.

James, Henry. *The Art of the Novel: Critical Prefaces*. Edited by R. P. Blackmur. Chicago: University of Chicago Press, 2011.

James, William. *The Principles of Psychology*. Vol. 1. New York: Henry Holt, 1890.

———. *The Varieties of Religious Experience: A Study in Human Nature*. New York: Longman, Green, 1917. First published 1902.

Jameson, Fredric. "Cognitive Mapping." In *Marxism and the Interpretation of Culture*, edited by Cary Nelson and Lawrence Grossberg, 347–57. Urbana: University of Illinois Press, 1988.

———. *Postmodernism; or, The Cultural Logic of Late Capitalism*. Durham NC: Duke University Press, 1991.

———. "Third-World Literature in the Era of Multinational Capitalism." *Social Text* 15 (1986): 65–88.

Johnson, Gary. *The Vitality of Allegory: Figural Narrative in Modern and Contemporary Fiction*. Columbus: Ohio State University Press, 2012.

Johnson, Samuel. "Preface to *A Dictionary of the English Language*." *Samuel Johnson's Dictionary: Selections from the 1755 Work That Defined the English Language*, edited by Jack Lynch, 25–42. New York: Walker, 2004.

Johnston, John. *Carnival of Repetition: Gaddis' "The Recognitions" and Postmodern Theory*. Philadelphia: University of Pennsylvania Press, 1990.

———. *Information Multiplicity: American Fiction in the Age of Media Saturation*. Baltimore: Johns Hopkins University Press, 1998.

Joly, Jean-Luc. *Connaissement du monde: Multiplicité, exhuastivité, totalité dans l'oeuvre de Georges Perec*. Lille: Atelier national de reproduction des theses, 2004.

Joseph, Gerhard. *John Barth*. Minneapolis: University of Minnesota Press, 1970. Pamphlets on American Writers 91.

Josipovici, Gabriel. "Georges Perec's Homage to Joyce (and Tradition)." *Yearbook in English Studies* 15 (1985): 179–200.

Joyce, James. *Finnegans Wake*. New York: Penguin, 1999. First published 1939.

———. *Ulysses*. Edited by Hans Walter Gabler. New York: Random House, 1984.

Kane, Jean M. "The Migrant Intellectual and the Body of History: Salman Rushdie's 'Midnight's Children.'" *Contemporary Literature* 37.1 (1996): 94–118.

Kant, Immanuel. *Critique of Judgment*. Translated by Werner S. Pluhar. Indianapolis: Hackett, 1987.

Karl, Frederick R. *American Fictions 1980–2000: Whose America Is It Anyway?* Bloomington IN: Xlibris, 2001.

Karnicky, Jeffrey. *Contemporary Fiction and the Ethics of Modern Culture*. New York: Palgrave Macmillan, 2007.
Kenner, Hugh. *The Stoic Comedians: Flaubert, Joyce, and Beckett*. Berkeley: University of California Press, 1961.
Khapertian, Theodore. *A Hand to Turn the Time: The Menippean Satires of Thomas Pynchon*. Rutherford NJ: Fairleigh Dickinson University Press, 1990.
Kim, Myoung-Sook. *Imaginaire et espaces urbains: Georges Perec, Patrick Modiano et Kim Sung-ok*. Paris: L'Hartmattan, 2009.
Klapp, Orrin E. *Overload and Boredom: Essays on the Quality of Life in the Information Society*. New York: Greenwood, 1986. Contributions in Sociology 57.
Knight, Christopher J. *Hints and Guesses: William Gaddis's Fiction of Longing*. Madison: University of Wisconsin Press, 1997.
Knight, Peter. *Conspiracy Culture: From the Kennedy Assassination to "The X Files."* New York: Routledge, 2000.
Knudsen, Eric I. "Midbrain and Forebrain Systems for Bottom-Up Control of Spatial Attention." In *The Neuroscience of Attention: Attentional Control and Selection*, edited by George R. Mangun, 131–50. New York: Oxford University Press, 2011.
Kolbuszewska, Zofia. *The Poetics of Chronotope in the Novels of Thomas Pynchon*. Lublin, Poland: Learned Society of the Catholic University of Lublin Press, 2000.
Koren, Roselynne, and Judith Kauffmann. "The Impossible Conclusion: Irony in Gustave Flaubert's *Bouvard et Pécuchet*." In *The Uses of Adversity: Failure and Accommodation in Reader-Response*, edited by Ellen Spolsky, 197–214. Bucknell PA: Associated University Presses, 1990.
Kovács, Katherine S. "The Bureaucratization of Knowledge and Sex in Flaubert and Vargas Llosa." *Comparative Literature Studies* 21.1 (1984): 30–51.
Krummenacher, Peter, et al. "Dopamine, Paranormal Belief, and the Detection of Meaningful Stimuli." *Journal of Cognitive Neuroscience* 22.8 (2010): 1670–81.
Kumar, Shiv. *Bergson and the Stream of Consciousness Novel*. Westport CT: Greenwood, 1962.
Laing, R. D. *The Politics of Experience and the Birds of Paradise*. New York: Penguin, 1984. First published 1967.
Latour, Bruno. *Reassembling the Social: An Introduction to Actor-Network Theory*. New York: Oxford University Press, 2005.
LeClair, Tom. *The Art of Excess: Mastery in Contemporary American Fiction*. Urbana: University of Illinois Press, 1989.
Lefebvre, Henri. *Critique of Everyday Life*. Vol. 1. Translated by John Moore. New York: Verso, 2008.

Lejeune, Philippe. *On Diary*. Translated by Katherine Durnin. Edited by Jeremy D. Popkin and Julie Rak. Cambridge MA: Harvard University Press, 2009.

Lessing, Doris. *The Golden Notebook*. New York: HarperPerennial, 1999. First published 1962.

Letzler, David. "The Character of Preterition: An Apology for Pointsman." In *Thomas Pynchon and the (De)vices of (Post)modernity*, edited by Zofia Kolbuszewska, 334–49. Lublin, Poland: John Paul II Catholic University Press, 2013.

———. "Redundancy, Modernism, and Readers' Expectations: An Experiment in Joyce Prediction." *Hypermedia Joyce Studies* 11.1 (2014): n.p. Web. Accessed September 9, 2014.

Lévi-Strauss, Claude. "The Structural Study of Myth." *Journal of American Folklore* 68.270 (1955): 428–44.

Li, Ming, and P. M. B. Vitányi. *An Introduction to Kolmogorov Complexity and Its Applications*. 3rd ed. New York: Springer, 2008.

Loepp, Susan, and William K. Wootters. *Protecting Information: From Classical Error Correction to Quantum Cryptography*. New York: Cambridge University Press, 2006.

Lubbock, Percy. *The Craft of Fiction*. New York: Viking, 1957. First published 1921.

Lukács, Georg. *The Theory of the Novel: A Historico-philosophical Essay on the Forms of Great Epic Literature*. Translated by Anna Bostock. Cambridge MA: MIT Press, 1971.

Lyotard, Jean-François. *The Postmodern Condition: A Report on Knowledge*. Translated by Geoff Bennington and Brian Massumi. Minneapolis: University of Minnesota Press, 1984. Theory and the History of Literature 10.

Madsen, Deborah. *The Postmodernist Allegories of Thomas Pynchon*. London: Leicester University Press, 1991.

Magné, Bernard. "Georges Perec on the Index." *Yale French Studies* 105 (2004): 72–88.

Mahaffey, Vicki. "Intentional Error: The Paradox of Editing Joyce's *Ulysses*." In *James Joyce's "Ulysses,"* edited by Derek Attridge, 231–55. New York: Oxford University Press, 2004.

Maltby, Paul. *Dissident Postmodernists: Barthelme, Coover, Pynchon*. Philadelphia: University of Pennsylvania Press, 1991.

Maloney, Edward. "Footnotes in Fiction: A Rhetorical Approach." PhD diss., Ohio State University, 2005.

Mansfield, Katherine. "Dragonflies." Review of *Interim* by Dorothy Richardson. In *The Gender of Modernism*, edited by Bonnie Kime Scott, 310. Bloomington: Indiana University Press, 1990.

Marcus, Ben. "Why Experimental Fiction Threatens to Destroy Publishing, Jonathan Franzen, and Life as We Know It: A Correction." *Harper's*, October 2005, 39–52.
Marsh, Elizabeth J., Michelle L. Meade, and Henry L. Roediger III. "Learning Facts from Fiction." *Journal of Memory and Language* 49 (2003): 519–36.
Mason, Fran. "'Just a Bunch of Stuff That Happened': Narratives of Resistance in *Gravity's Rainbow*." *Pynchon Notes* 42–43 (1998): 167–80.
Martin, John. *Beyond Belief: The Real Life of Daniel Defoe*. Pembroke, UK: Accent, 2006.
Martin, Rod A. *The Psychology of Humor: An Integrative Approach*. New York: Elsevier, 2007.
Martinson, Deborah. *In the Presence of Absence: The Self in Diaries and Fiction*. Columbus: Ohio State University Press, 2003.
Martone, Michael. *The Blue Guide to Indiana*. Tallahassee FL: FC2, 2001.
Matthews, William. "The Diary: A Neglected Genre." *Sewanee Review* 85.2 (1977): 286–300.
McCaffery, Larry. *The Metafictional Muse: The Works of Robert Coover, Donald Barthelme, and William H. Gass*. Pittsburgh: University of Pittsburgh Press, 1982.
McHale, Brian. *Constructing Postmodernism*. New York: Routledge, 1992.
———. "Mason & Dixon in the Zone; or, A Brief Poetics of Pynchon-Space." In *Pynchon and "Mason & Dixon,"* edited by Brooke Horvath and Irving Mallin, 43–62. Cranbury NJ: Associated University Presses, 2000.
———. *Postmodernist Fiction*. New York: Routledge, 1987.
———. "Weak Narrativity: The Case of Avant-Garde Narrative Poetry." *Narrative* 9.2 (2001): 161–67.
McHugh, Roland. *Annotations to "Finnegans Wake."* 3rd ed. Baltimore: Johns Hopkins University Press, 2006.
Medina, Albert. "Arts of Homelessness: Roberto Bolaño or the Commodification of Exile." *Novel* 42.3 (2009): 547–54.
Melley, Timothy. "Paranoid Modernity and the Diagnostics of Cultural Theory." *Electronic Book Review*, May 5, 2008, n.p. Web. Accessed March 23, 2013.
Melville, Herman. *Moby-Dick; or, The Whale*. Evanston IL: Northwestern University Press, 1988. First published 1851.
Mendelson, Edward. "Gravity's Encyclopedia." In *Mindful Pleasures: Essays on Thomas Pynchon*, edited by George Levine and David Leverenz, 161–94. Boston: Little, Brown, 1976.
Mepham, John. "Dorothy Richardson's 'Unreadability': Graphic Style and Narrative Strategy in a Modernist Novel." *English Literature in Transition: 1880–1920* 43.4 (2000): 442–64.

Meyer, Stephen. *Irresistible Dictation: Gertrude Stein and the Correlations of Writing and Science*. Palo Alto CA: Stanford University Press, 2001.

Milder, Robert M. "*Moby-Dick*: The Rationale of Narrative Form." In *Approaches to Teaching Melville's "Moby-Dick,"* edited by Martin Bickman, 35–49. New York: MLA, 1985.

Miller, George A. "The Magical Number Seven, Plus or Minus Two: Some Limits on Our Capacity for Processing Information." *Psychological Review* 63.2 (1956): 81–97.

Monteser, Frederick. *The Picaresque Element in Western Literature*. Tuscaloosa: University of Alabama Press, 1975.

Moore, Adam, Thomas Gruber, Jennifer Derose, and Thomas Malinowski. "Regular, Brief Mindfulness Meditation Practice Improves Electrophysiological Markers of Attentional Control." *Frontiers in Human Neuroscience* 6 (2012): 1–15.

Moore, Steven. "Annotations from *A Reader's Guide to William Gaddis' 'The Recognitions.'*" *The Gaddis Annotations*. 2005. http://www.williamgaddis.org/. Accessed April 2, 2012.

———. *The Novel: An Alternative History*. Vol. 1: *Beginnings to 1600*. New York: Continuum, 2010.

———. *William Gaddis*. Boston: Twayne, 1989. Twayne's United States Authors 546.

Moore, Thomas. *The Style of Connectedness: "Gravity's Rainbow" and Thomas Pynchon*. Columbia: University of Missouri Press, 1987.

Moretti, Franco. *Distant Reading*. New York: Verso, 2013.

———. *Modern Epic: The World-System from Goethe to García Márquez*. Translated by Quinton Hoare. New York: Verso, 1996. First published 1994.

———. "Serious Century." In *The Novel*, edited by Franco Moretti. Vol. 1: *History, Geography, and Culture*, 364–400. Princeton NJ: Princeton University Press, 2007.

———. *The Way of the World: The* Bildungsroman *in European Culture*. New York: Verso, 1987.

Morley, Catherine. *The Quest for Epic in Contemporary American Fiction: John Updike, Philip Roth and Don DeLillo*. New York: Routledge, 2009.

Morrell, David. *John Barth: An Introduction*. University Park PA: Penn State University Press, 1976.

Mossman, Mark. "Salman Rushdie's *Midnight's Children*: National Narrative as a Liminal Voice." *Midwest Quarterly* 41.1 (1999): 66–78.

Motte, Warren F. *The Poetics of Experiment: A Study of the Work of Georges Perec*. Lexington KY: French Forum, 1984.

Murakami, Haruki. *Dance Dance Dance*. Translated by Alfred Birnbaum. New York: Vintage, 1994. First published 1988.

———. *The Wind-Up Bird Chronicle*. Translated by Jay Rubin. New York: Vintage, 1997. First published 1995.

Musil, Robert. *The Man without Qualities*. Translated by Sophie Wilkins. New York: Vintage, 1995.

Myers, B. R. "A Reader's Manifesto: An Attack on the Growing Pretentiousness of American Literary Prose." *Atlantic Monthly* 288.1 (2001): 104–22.

Nelles, William. *Frameworks: Narrative Levels and Embedded Narrative*. New York: Peter Lang, 1997. American University Studies, General Literature 33.

Ngai, Sianne. *Ugly Feelings*. Cambridge MA: Harvard University Press, 2005.

Norris, Frank. *McTeague: A Story of San Francisco*. New York: Signet, 1964. First published 1899.

Norris, Margot. *The Decentered Universe: A Structuralist Analysis*. Baltimore: Johns Hopkins University Press, 1976.

Nussbaum, Felicity. "Toward Conceptualizing Diary." In *Studies in Autobiography*, edited by James Olney, 128–40. New York: Oxford University Press, 1988.

O'Donnell, Patrick J. "His Master's Voice: On William Gaddis's *J R*." *Postmodern Culture* 1.2 (1991): n. pag. Web. Accessed April 2, 2012.

———. *Latent Destinies: Cultural Paranoia and Contemporary U.S. Narrative*. Durham NC: Duke University Press, 2000.

Olson, Charles. *Call Me Ishmael*. New York: Reynal & Hitchock, 1947.

Orwell, George. "Politics and the English Language." In *A Collection of Essays*, 156–71. New York: Harvest, 1970. First published in 1946.

Pavel, Thomas G. *Fictional Worlds*. Cambridge MA: Harvard University Press, 1986.

Pearce, Richard. "The Circus, the Clown, and Coover's *Public Burning*." In *The Scope of the Fantastic: Culture, Biography, Themes, Children's Literature*, edited by Robert A. Collins and Howard D. Pearce, 129–36. Westport CT: Greenwood, 1985. Contributions to the Study of Science Fiction and Fantasy 11.

Pease, Allison. *Modernism, Feminism, and the Culture of Boredom*. New York: Cambridge University Press, 2012.

Perec, Georges. *Cahiers des charges de "La Vie mode d'emploi."* Edited by Hans Hartje, Bernard Magné, and Jacques Neefs. Paris: Zulma, 1993.

———. *Life a User's Manual*. Translated by David Bellos. Boston: Verba Mundi, 1987.

———. *Species of Spaces and Other Pieces*. Translated by John Sturrock. New York: Penguin, 1997.

Phillips, Natalie. "Literary Neuroscience and History of Mind: An Interdisciplinary fMRI Study of Attention and Jane Austen." In *The Oxford Handbook of Cognitive Literary Studies*, edited by Lisa Zunshine, 55–81. New York: Oxford University Press, 2015.

Poe, Edgar Allan. "The Mystery of Marie Roget." In *The Collected Works of Edgar Allan Poe*, edited by Thomas Ollive Mabbot. Vol. 3: *Tales and Sketches*, 715–88. Cambridge MA: Harvard University Press, 1978.

Pöhlmann, Sascha. *Pynchon's Postnational Imagination*. Heidelberg: Universitätsverlag Winter, 2010. American Studies 188.

Posner, Michael. *Attention in a Social World*. New York: Oxford University Press, 2012. Series in Social and Cognitive Neuroscience.

Powers, Richard. *The Gold-Bug Variations*. New York: HarperCollins, 1991.

Prince, Gerald. "The Disnarrated." *Style* 22.1 (1988): 1–8.

Prinz, Jesse J. *The Conscious Brain: How Attention Engenders Experience*. New York: Oxford University Press, 2012.

Proust, Marcel. *Swann's Way*. Translated by C. K. Moncrieff, Terence Kilmartin, and D. J. Enright. New York: Modern Library, 2003.

Puetz, Manfred. "John Barth's *The Sot-Weed Factor*: The Pitfalls of Mythopoesis." *Twentieth-Century Literature* 22.4 (1976): 454–66.

Pughe, Thomas. *Comic Sense: Reading Robert Coover, Stanley Elkin, Philip Roth*. Basel: Birkhäuser Verlag, 1994.

Pynchon, Thomas. *The Crying of Lot 49*. New York: Perennial, 1999. First published 1966.

———. *Gravity's Rainbow*. New York: Penguin, 2006. First published 1973.

———. *Mason & Dixon*. New York: Henry Holt, 1997.

Quian Quiroga, Rodrigo. *Borges and Memory: Encounters with the Human Brain*. Translated by Juan Pablo Fernández. Cambridge MA: MIT Press, 2012.

Quintilian. *Institutes of Oratory*. Edited by Lee Honeycutt. Translated by John Selby Watson. Iowa State University, 2006. Web. Accessed March 24, 2013.

Rabelais, François. *Gargantua and Pantagruel*. Translated by M. A. Screech. New York: Penguin, 2006.

Rabinowitz, Peter J. *Before Reading: Narrative Conventions and the Politics of Interpretation*. Ithaca NY: Cornell University Press, 1987.

Radford, Jean. *Dorothy Richardson*. Bloomington: Indiana University Press, 1991.

Ramage, John. "Myth and Monomyth in Coover's *The Public Burning*." *Critique* 23.3 (1982): 52–68.

Randall, Bryony. *Modernism, Daily Time, and the Everyday Life*. New York: Cambridge University Press, 2007.

Raoul, Valerie. *The French Fictional Journal: Fictional Narcissism / Narcissistic Fiction*. Toronto: University of Toronto Press, 1980.

Rasula, Jed. "Textual Indigence in the Archive." *Postmodern Culture* 9.3 (1999): n.p. Web. Accessed March 7, 2011.

Rau, Petra. "The War in Contemporary Fiction." In *The Cambridge Companion to the Literature of World War II*, edited by Marina Mackay, 207–19. New York: Cambridge University Press, 2009.

Raymond, Eric S. *The New Hacker's Dictionary*. 4th ed. Cambridge MA: MIT Press, 1996.

Reagle, Joseph. *Good Faith Collaboration: The Culture of Wikipedia*. Cambridge MA: MIT Press, 2010. History and the Foundations of Information Science 2.

Reed, Walter L. *An Exemplary History of the Novel: The Quixotic versus the Picaresque*. Chicago: University of Chicago Press, 1981.

Ribaupierre, Claude de. *Le roman généalogique: Claude Simon et Georges Perec*. Bruxelles: Presses de l'Académie royale des Beaux-Arts, 1999.

Rice, Thomas Jackson. *Joyce, Chaos, and Complexity*. Urbana: University of Illinois Press, 1997.

Richards, I. A. *Practical Criticism: A Study of Literary Judgment*. London: Routledge, 1929.

Richardson, Dorothy. "About Punctuation." In *The Gender of Modernism*, edited by Bonnie Kime Scott, 415–17. Bloomington: Indiana University Press, 1990.

———. *Pilgrimage*. 4 vols. Milton Keynes: Virago, 1979. First published 1967.

Richter, David, ed. *The Critical Tradition: Classic Texts and Contemporary Trends*. 3rd ed. Boston: Bedford / St. Martin's, 2007.

Ricoeur, Paul. *Freud and Philosophy: An Essay on Interpretation*. Translated by Denis Savage. New Haven CT: Yale University Press, 1970.

Rodker, John. Review of *Interim*, by Dorothy Richardson. *Little Review* 6.5 (1919): 40–41.

Rodriguez, Francis Collado. "*Mason & Dixon*, Historiographic Metafiction and the Unstable Reconciliation of Opposites." In *American Postmodernity: Essays on the Recent Fiction of Thomas Pynchon*, edited by Ian D. Copestake, 71–81. New York: Peter Lang, 2003.

Rosenheim, Edward W., Jr. *Swift and the Satirist's Art*. Chicago: University of Chicago Press, 1963.

Rosenwald, Lawrence. *Emerson and the Art of Diary*. New York: Oxford University Press, 1988.

Rowland, Ian. *The Full Facts Book of Cold Reading*. 4th ed. London: Ian Rowland, 2008.

Rubenstein, Roberta. *The Novelistic Vision of Doris Lessing: Breaking the Forms of Consciousness*. Urbana: University of Illinois Press, 1979.

Rubin, Jay. *Haruki Murakami and the Music of Words*. New York: Random House, 2002.

Ruddick, Lisa. *Reading Gertrude Stein*. Ithaca NY: Cornell University Press, 1990.

Rushdie, Salman. *Imaginary Homelands: Essays and Criticism 1981–1991*. London: Granta, 1992.

———. *Midnight's Children*. New York: Random House, 2006. First published 1981.

———. *Step across This Line: Nonfiction 1992–2002*. New York: Random House, 2003.

Safer, Elaine. *The Contemporary American Comic Epic*. Detroit: Wayne State University Press, 1988.

Saint-Amour, Paul. *Tense Future: Modernism, Encyclopedic Form, Total War*. New York: Oxford University Press, 2015.

Salemi, Joseph S. "Art as Expiation in *The Recognitions*." *In Recognition of William Gaddis*, edited by John Kuehl and Steven Moore, 46–57. Syracuse NY: Syracuse University Press, 1984. First published 1977.

Sanders, Scott. "Pynchon's Paranoid History." In *Mindful Pleasures: Essays on Thomas Pynchon*, edited by George Levine and David Leverenz, 139–60. Boston: Little, Brown, 1976.

Sanford, Anthony J., and Catherine Emmott. *Mind, Brain, and Narrative*. Cambridge, UK: Cambridge University Press, 2012.

Savage, John, et al. "Cognitive Processes in Children's Reading and Attention: The Role of Working Memory, Divided Attention, and Response Inhibition." *British Journal of Psychology* 97 (2006): 365–85.

Scholes, Robert. *The Fabulators*. New York: Oxford University Press, 1967.

Schulz, Max F. *Black Humor Fiction of the Sixties: A Pluralistic Definition of Man and His World*. Athens: Ohio University Press, 1973.

Schwartz, Paul. *Georges Perec: Traces of His Passage*. Birmingham AL: Summa, 1988.

Sedgwick, Eve Kosofsky. *Touching Feeling: Affect, Pedagogy, Performativity*. Durham NC: Duke University Press, 2003.

Seed, David. "Mapping the Course of Empire in the New World." In *Pynchon and "Mason & Dixon,"* edited by Brooke Horvath and Irving Mallin, 84–99. Cranbury NJ: Associated University Presses, 2000.

Seidensticker, Edwin. "Autobiography." *Biography* 22.1 (1999): 46–56.

Shannon, Claude E. "The Mathematical Theory of Communication." *Bell Labs*. Alcatel-Lucent Technologies. https://www.alcatel-lucent.com. First published 1948. Accessed June 5, 2011.

———. "The Redundancy of English." In *Cybernetics: The Macy Conferences 1946–1953*. Vol. 1: *Transactions*, edited by Claus Pias, 248–72. Zürich: Diaphanes, 2003. First published 1950.

Shklovsky, Viktor. *Theory of Prose*. Translated by Benjamin Shur. Champaign IL: Dalkey, 1990.

Sidney, Philip. "An Apology for Poetry." In *The Critical Tradition*, edited by David H. Richter, 135–59. Boston: Bedford / St. Martin's, 2007. First published 1595.

Siegel, Mark Richard. *Pynchon: Creative Paranoia in "Gravity's Rainbow."* Port Washington NY: Kennikat, 1978.

Sinclair, May. "The Novels of Dorothy Richardson." Review of *Honeycomb*, by Dorothy Richardson. In *The Gender of Modernism*, edited by Bonnie Kime Scott, 442–47. Bloomington: Indiana University Press, 1990.

Sinding, Michael. "Framing Monsters: Multiple and Mixed Genres, Cognitive Category Theory, and *Gravity's Rainbow*." *Poetics Today* 31.3 (2010): 465–505.

Slepon, Raphael. *Finnegans Wake Extensible Elucidation Treasury*. Raphael Slepdon, June 21, 2013. Web. Accessed July 7, 2013.

Smallwood, Jonathan. "Mind-Wandering While Reading: Attentional Decoupling, Mindless Reading and the Cascade Model of Inattention." *Language and Linguistics Compass* 5.2 (2011): 63–77.

Smithies, Declan. "Attention Is Rational-Access Consciousness." In *Attention: Philosophical and Psychological Essays*, edited by Christopher Moles, Declane Smithies, and Wayne Wu, 247–73. New York: Oxford University Press, 2011.

Spacks, Patricia Meyer. *Boredom: The Literary History of a State of Mind*. Chicago: University of Chicago Press, 1995.

Spolsky, Ellen. "Darwin and Derrida: Cognitive Theory as a Species of Poststructuralism." In *Introduction to Cognitive Cultural Studies*, edited by Lisa Zunshine, 292–310. Baltimore: Johns Hopkins University Press, 2010.

Stein, Gertrude. *Lectures in America*. Boston: Beacon, 1957. First published 1935.

———. *The Making of Americans: Being a History of a Family's Progress*. Champaign IL: Dalkey, 1995. First published 1925.

Steiner, George. *On Difficulty and Other Essays*. New York: Oxford University Press, 1978.

Stephens, Paul. "'Reading at It': Gertrude Stein, Information Overload, and the Makings of Americanitis." *Twentieth-Century Literature* 59.1 (2013): 126–56.

Sterne, Laurence. *The Life and Opinions of Tristram Shandy, Gentleman*. Edited by Robert Folkenflik. New York: Modern Library, 2004. First published 1759–67.

Stevens, Wallace. *Collected Poetry and Prose*. Edited by Frank Kermode and Joan Richardson. New York: Library of American, 1997.

Strecher, Matthew Carl. *Dances with Sheep: The Quest for Identity in the Fiction of Murakami Haruki*. Ann Arbor: University of Michigan Press, 2002. Series in Japanese Studies 37.

Strecker, Trey. "Narrative Ecology and Encyclopedic Narrative." In *Avant-Post: The Avant-Garde under Post Conditions*, edited by Louis Armand, 281–98. Prague: Litteraria Pragensia, 2006.

Su, John. "Epic of Failure: Disappointment as Utopian Fantasy in *Midnight's Children*." *Twentieth-Century Literature* 41.4 (Winter 2001): 545–68.

Suter, Rebecca. *The Japanization of Modernity: Haruki Murakami between Japan and the United States*. Cambridge MA: Harvard University Press, 2011.

Sutherland, Donald. *Gertrude Stein: A Biography of Her Work*. New Haven CT: Yale University Press, 1951.

Swami, Viren, and Rebecca Coles. "The Truth Is Out There." *Psychologist* 23.7 (2010): 560–63.

Swigger, Ronald T. "Fictional Encylopedism and the Cognitive Value of Literature." *Comparative Literature Studies* 12.4 (1975): 351–66.

Tabbi, Joseph. *The Postmodern Sublime: Technology and American Writing from Mailer to Cyberpunk*. Ithaca NY: Cornell University Press, 1995.

———. "The Technology of Quotation: William Gaddis's J R and Contemporary Media." *Mosaic* 28.4 (1995): 143–64.

Tadié, Benoît. "The Room of Infinite Possibilities: Joyce, Flaubert, and the Historical Imagination." *Études Anglaises* 58.2 (2005): 131–40.

Tanner, Tony. *City of Words: American Fiction 1950–1970*. New York: Harper & Row, 1971.

———. "Gravity's Rainbow: An Experience in Modern Reading." In *Thomas Pynchon's "Gravity's Rainbow,"* edited by Harold Bloom, 69–83. New York: Chelsea House, 1986.

Tatham, Campbell. "Tarot and *Gravity's Rainbow*." *Modern Fiction Studies* 32.4 (1986): 581–90.

Ten Kortenaar, Neil. *Self, Nation, Text in Salman Rushdie's "Midnight's Children."* Montreal: McGill-Queen's University Press, 2004.

Thielemans, Johan. "The Energy of an Absence: Perfection as Useful Fiction in the Novels of Gaddis and Sorrentino." In *Critical Angles: European Views on American Literature*, edited by Marc Chénetier, 105–24. Carbondale: Southern Illinois University Press, 1986.

Thomas, Samuel. *Pynchon and the Political*. New York: Routledge, 2007.

Thomson, George H. *A Reader's Guide to Dorothy Richardson's "Pilgrimage."* Greensboro, NC: ELT, 1996.

Todorov, Tzvetan. *The Fantastic: A Structural Approach to a Literary Genre*. Translated by Richard Howard. Cleveland: Case Western University Press, 1973.

Treip, Mindele Anne. *Allegorical Poetics and the Epic: The Renaissance Tradition to "Paradise Lost."* Lexington: University Press of Kentucky, 1994. Studies in the English Renaissance.

Tresco, Matt. "Impervious to U.S. Parsing: Encyclopedism, Autism, and *Infinite Jest*." In *Consider David Foster Wallace: Critical Essays*, edited by David Hering, 113–22. Los Angeles: Sideshow, 2010.

Trilling, Lionel. *Beyond Culture*. New York: Harcourt, Brace, & Jovanovich, 1965.

———. *The Opposing Self: Nine Essays in Criticism*. New York: Harcourt & Brace, 1955.

Tsur, Reuven. *Toward a Cognitive Poetics*. 2nd ed. Sussex, UK: Sussex Academic Press, 2008.

Turner, Frederick. *Epic: Form, Content, History*. New Brunswick NJ: Transaction, 2012.

Turner, Mark. *The Literary Mind: The Origins of Thought and Language*. New York: Oxford University Press, 1996.

Viereck, Elisabeth. "The Clown Knew It All Along: The Medium Was the Message." *Delta* 28 (1989): 63–81.

Vincent, Howard. *The Trying-Out of Moby-Dick*. Carbondale: Southern Illinois University Press, 1965. First published 1949.

Vollmann, William T. *Argall*. New York: Viking, 2001.

———. *Europe Central*. New York: Viking, 2005.

Vonnegut, Kurt. *Mother Night*. New York: Delta, 1996. First published 1961.

Waite, Arthur Edward. *The Pictorial Key to the Tarot*. Stamford CT: U.S. Games Systems, 1971. First published 1910.

Walkiewicz, E. P. *John Barth*. Boston: Twayne, 1986. Twayne United States Authors Series 505.

Wallace, David Foster. *Consider the Lobster*. New York: Little, Brown, 2005.

———. "Deciderization 2007—a Special Report." Introduction to *Best American Essays 2007*, edited by Wallace, i–xv. Boston: Houghton Mifflin, 2007.

———. *Infinite Jest*. New York: Little, Brown, 1996.

———. *The Pale King*. New York: Little, Brown, 2011.

———. *A Supposedly Fun Thing I'll Never Do Again*. New York: Little, Brown, 1997.

Walsh, Richard. "Narrative Inscription: History and the Reader in Robert Coover's *The Public Burning*." *Studies in the Novel* 25.3 (1993): 332–46.

Watts, Kara. "Miriam's Waste Paper Basket: Reading Economies in *Pilgrimage*." *Pilgrimages: A Journal of Dorothy Richardson Studies* 6 (2013–14): 46–62.

Watzl, Sebastian. "Attention as Structuring of the Stream of Consciousness." In *Attention: Philosophical and Psychological Essays*, edited by Christopher

Moles, Declane Smithies, and Wayne Wu, 145–73. New York: Oxford University Press, 2011.

Weinbrot, Howard. *Menippean Satire Reconsidered: From Antiquity to the Eighteenth Century*. Baltimore: Johns Hopkins University Press, 2005.

Weisenburger, Steven C. *Fables of Subversion: Satire and the American Novel, 1930–1980*. Athens: University of Georgia Press, 1995.

Weissman, D. H., et al. "The Neural Bases of Momentary Lapses in Attention." *Nature Neuroscience* 7 (2006): 971–78.

Wellek, René, and Austin Warren. *Theory of Literature*. 3rd ed. New York: Harvest, 1976. First published 1948.

White, E. B., ed. *A Subtreasury of American Humor*. New York: Modern Library, 1948.

Wicks, Ulrich. *Picaresque Narrative, Picaresque Fictions: A Theory and Research Guide*. Westport CT: Greenwood, 1989.

Wiener, Norbert. *The Human Use of Human Beings: Cybernetics and Society*. Revised ed. Cambridge MA: Da Capo, 1989. First published 1954.

Wilson, Edmund. *Axel's Castle: A Study in the Imaginative Literature of 1870–1930*. New York: Collier, 1991. First published 1931.

Winchester, Simon. *The Meaning of Everything: The Story of the Oxford English Dictionary*. New York: Oxford University Press, 2003.

Wolfe, Peter. A Vision of His Own: The Mind and Art of William Gaddis. Teaneck NJ: Fairleigh Dickinson University Press, 1996.

Wood, James. *The Broken Estate: Essays on Literature and Belief*. London: Jonathan Cape, 1999.

———. *How Fiction Works*. New York: Farrar, Strauss, & Giroux, 2008.

Woolf, Virginia. *The Essays of Virginia Woolf*. Edited by Andrew McNeillie and Stuart N. Clarke. 6 vols. New York: Harcourt Brace Jovanovich, 1986–2010.

———. *Mrs. Dalloway*. New York: Harcourt, 1981. First published 1925.

Yeo, Richard. *Encyclopaedic Visions: Scientific Dictionaries and Enlightenment Culture*. New York: Cambridge University Press, 2001.

Yoon, Yeosun, Gülen Sarial-Abi, and Zeynep Gürhan-Canli. "Effect of Regulatory Focus on Selective Information Processing." *Journal of Consumer Research* 39 (2012): 93–110.

Zunshine, Lisa. *Why We Read Fiction: Theory of Mind and the Novel*. Columbus: Ohio State University Press, 2006. Theory and Interpretation of Narrative.

Zwaan, Rolf A. "Effect of Genre Expectations on Text Comprehension." *Journal of Experimental Psychology* 20.4 (1994): 920–33.

Index

IN THE FRONTIERS OF NARRATIVE SERIES:

Unnatural Narrative: Impossible Worlds in Fiction and Drama
by Jan Alber

Useful Fictions: Evolution, Anxiety, and the Origins of Literature
by Michael Austin

Stories and Minds: Cognitive Approaches to Literary Narrative
edited by Lars Bernaerts, Dirk De Geest, Luc Herman, and Bart Vervaeck

Telling Children's Stories: Narrative Theory and Children's Literature
edited by Mike Cadden

Strange Narrators in Contemporary Fiction: Explorations in Readers' Engagement with Characters
Marco Caracciolo

Refiguring Minds in Narrative Media
by David Ciccoricco

Coincidence and Counterfactuality: Plotting Time and Space in Narrative Fiction
by Hilary P. Dannenberg

The Emergence of Mind: Representations of Consciousness in Narrative Discourse in English
edited by David Herman

Story Logic: Problems and Possibilities of Narrative
by David Herman

Handbook of Narrative Analysis
by Luc Herman and Bart Vervaeck

Affective Narratology: The Emotional Structure of Stories
by Patrick Colm Hogan

Imagining Kashmir: Emplotment and Colonialism
by Patrick Colm Hogan

Spaces of the Mind: Narrative and Community in the American West
by Elaine A. Jahner

The Storyworld Accord: Econarratology and Postcolonial Narratives
by Erin James

Talk Fiction: Literature and the Talk Explosion
by Irene Kacandes

Ethos and Narrative Interpretation: The Negotiation of Values in Fiction
by Liesbeth Korthals Altes

Contemporary Comics Storytelling
by Karin Kukkonen

The Cruft of Fiction: Mega-Novels and the Science of Paying Attention
by David Letzler

The Imagined Moment: Time, Narrative, and Computation
by Inderjeet Mani

Storying Domestic Violence: Constructions and Stereotypes of Abuse in the Discourse of General Practitioners
by Jarmila Mildorf

New Narratives: Stories and Storytelling in the Digital Age
edited by Ruth Page and Bronwen Thomas

Fictional Minds
by Alan Palmer

Writing at the Limit: The Novel in the New Media Ecology
by Daniel Punday

Narrative Beginnings: Theories and Practices
edited by Brian Richardson

Opening Acts: Narrative Beginnings in Twentieth-Century Feminist Fiction
by Catherine Romagnolo

Narrative across Media: The Languages of Storytelling
edited by Marie-Laure Ryan

Storyworlds across Media: Toward a Media-Conscious Narratology
edited by Marie-Laure Ryan and Jan-Noël Thon

Fictional Dialogue: Speech and Conversation in the Modern and Postmodern Novel
by Bronwen Thomas

Transmedial Narratology and Contemporary Media Culture
by Jan-Noël Thon

www.ingramcontent.com/pod-product-compliance
Lightning Source LLC
Chambersburg PA
CBHW021942130226
39667CB00016B/343/J
* 9 7 8 0 8 0 3 2 9 9 6 2 7 *